THE PLEASURE OF HIS COMPANY

THE PLEASURE OF HIS COMPANY

MALE TOGETHERNESS IN FOUND PHOTOGRAPHS

VINTAGE PHOTOGRAPHS FROM THE COLLECTION OF JOHN IBSON

JOHN IBSON

RIT PRESS
ROCHESTER, NEW YORK

Published and distributed by:
RIT Press
90 Lomb Memorial Drive
Rochester, New York 14623
https://press.rit.edu

Printed in the United States of America

ISBN 978-1-956313-40-6 (softcover)
ISBN 978-1-956313-56-7 (hardcover)
ISBN 978-1-956313-41-3 (electronic)

Library of Congress Control Number: 2026936969

We gather on the traditional territory of the Onöndowa'ga:' or "the people of the Great Hill." In English, they are known as Seneca people, "the keeper of the western door." They are one of the six nations that make up the sovereign Haudenosaunee Confederacy.

We honor the land on which RIT was built and recognize the unique relationship that the Indigenous stewards have with this land. That relationship is the core of their traditions, cultures, and histories. We recognize the history of genocide, colonization, and assimilation of Indigenous people that took place on this land. Mindful of these histories, we work towards understanding, acknowledging, and ultimately reconciliation.

Cover: Real photo postcard, AZO stamp box, ca. 1910.
Image background expanded with Adobe Firefly.
See page 29 for original image.
Designed by Marnie Soom

For Steve

You are the rose of my heart.
You are the love of my life.
—“Rose of My Heart,” Hugh Moffatt (ca. 1984)

CONTENTS

INTRODUCTION

FINDING PHOTOGRAPHS

As a gay man, I have a particular attraction to male imagery. And that attraction was the initial inspiration for what now is a notably large collection of everyday photographs of American males together in various settings—all of these "found photographs" of persons unknown to me. As someone who's taught and written about American masculinity, though, I've come to the conclusion that American culture has, for more than a century, made way too much of an issue of sexual orientation, to the detriment of virtually all American males, regardless of the direction of their sexual yearnings. So what? Addressing *that* question is a central purpose of this introduction.

Because so much has been made of sexual orientation throughout my lifetime, my experience as "the other" has surely influenced much of what I've written and taught during a professional career half a century long. What drew me to collect the sort of photographs displayed in this book in the first place? What has collecting them actually meant to me, and how might the personal significance of the collection have changed since I began gathering these images? Alongside every author's dream of a large audience, for whom is the upcoming glimpse of my collection mostly meant?

We don't study, teach, or write in a vacuum. As long as one doesn't cook the books, and as long as teachers and authors don't try to deny or hide their beliefs, values, or feelings, I believe that the quality of both teaching and writing is enhanced by an open acknowledgment of an instructor's or an author's personal stake in what is taught or written about. I wasn't taught this way: In my own undergraduate and grad school experience during the 1960s and early 1970s, historians and social scientists were not to be confused with artists; with some of my teachers, it even seemed that there was danger in caring too much about what one researched, taught, or wrote. That harsh lesson somehow never stuck with me.

In commenting on my Brandeis doctoral dissertation about Irish Americans, my dissertation's director, Morton Keller, observed that mine was definitely a *felt* piece of work. Accurate it surely was, but I was never quite sure whether Professor Keller's assessment carried with it some praise or was simply an expression of resignation. Some academics continue to be suspicious of caring "too much" with regard to whatever one teaches or writes about, rarely acknowledging their own motives for choosing a particular topic to study, fearful that they might be seen as having lost the objectivity or distance they've been trained to value. If one's own passionate interest in a topic is unacknowledged or absent, though, the likelihood of arousing much interest in one's students or readers seems slim to me.

Let me be as clear as possible about what I am, and am not, endorsing. I'm reminded here of Daniel Patrick Moynihan's astute observation that while one is "entitled to his own opinions, he is not entitled to his own facts." A scholar's feelings must not be confused with, or presented as, facts—hence my warning above about not cooking the books. Certain aspects of recent American political history are cruel reminders of what happens when feelings alone—apart from facts, regardless of facts, masquerading as facts—run the show. I'm delighted to acknowledge—to celebrate, really—how much the photographs in this book have meant to me and how much my own queer identity has undoubtedly had to do with my choice of subject matter to collect and later write about. Nonetheless, in books and classrooms alike, my ultimate task has been to uncover the past as honestly and as meaningfully as possible; my identity as a historian is central to what I've done.

■ ■ ■

Collecting and photography have been longstanding interests of mine, but they didn't become joined until I was of middle age. In childhood I collected stamps; among its other virtues, that hobby was a particularly instructive way for a kid to learn about colonialism. Attracted to politics since Republican presidential candidate Thomas Dewey's mustache appealed to me when I was four—much to my Democratic parents' dismay—I collected campaign literature and buttons in the 1950s and 1960s, but not beyond. Collecting of any sort disappeared for a while, but my partner (now, my husband) Steve Harrison and I began collecting California landscape paintings in the 1990s, and we still do that. As for photography, the first camera of my own that I remember was a Brownie Hawkeye, popular throughout the 1950s. I haven't been without my own camera since, to which shelves of photo albums, from all those years before cell phones, will attest. Today my phone overflows with photos.

A blending of collecting and photography, my collection of vintage photographs of American males together began in 1994. In a Maine antique shop Steve and I visited that summer, I was attracted to a few tintypes and cabinet cards, struck by the apparent comfort with which the male subjects in these photos had posed together more than a century earlier. I knew very little then of photography's history, didn't even know that I was holding images called "tintypes" and "cabinet cards." Although I distinctly recall deciding on the spot that old photographs of males together would make an appealing collection, I hadn't the vaguest idea that day in Maine what I was embarking upon: the other antique shops, the military memorabilia sales at gun shows, the photography shows, the swap meets (or flea markets), and the countless eBay auctions that awaited me. I had no idea in 1994 how much fun I would have collecting. I didn't realize then how much I'd learn as the collecting became research, as I went from simply acquiring images I fancied to trying to place images in context, to discerning how common was a particular pose at a particular time and what the frequency or infrequency of certain poses might signify. I came to view everyday photographs of people as performances by the photographs' subjects, interpreting images of two or more persons together as a distinctive kind of sign of the relationship between and among the subjects. Seeking a comprehensive portrait of American males, I wanted to study and acquire not only photos that might seem to display affection, but I also looked for and collected ones that seemed to show when and where physical affection between males was comparatively rare. As I began to think of vernacular photos as cultural evidence, then, I realized that I had to at least observe, if not always acquire, many more images than if I were simply searching for photos I liked. I acquired a lot, building a major, perhaps even singular, collection of American male imagery. And in archives across the country, online and in person, as well as in daily offerings on eBay, I observed a lot more.

I'd eventually collect more than 10,000 photographs—daguerreotypes from before the Civil War to snapshots from the 1950s. I've taken tremendous pleasure in discovering and acquiring these images, in their instructiveness in my classrooms, in papers I delivered at academic conferences, and in their value as focal points in books that I've written. Chatting with Steve that day in Maine about the images I purchased was just the first of what would be countless conversations we'd have about the collection in the years to come. As with so much else in our life together, Steve's interest, encouragement, candor, and good sense regarding my collecting has been invaluable. It's utterly appropriate that he was literally by my side when the collecting adventure began.

Collecting vintage everyday photos of any subject seemed uncommon, at least to me, in the mid-1990s. People with various interests had probably been collecting found (or vernacular) photos for many years, but the internet made such imagery much more readily available and more widely displayed, with collecting greatly facilitated—indeed, transformed.[1] Additionally, it was around this same time that vernacular photographs began to be recognized by galleries and museums as a form of artistic expression. An exhibition titled "Snapshots: The Photography of Everyday Life, 1888 to the Present" was held at the San Francisco Museum of Modern Art in 1998, for instance, and nine years later the National Gallery of Art had an exhibition titled "The Art of the American Snapshot, 1888–1978." Having by then established scholarly credentials in the field, I was honored to be one of those invited to address the conference that was held in connection with the National Gallery exhibition.

Before the late 1990s appearance of eBay, that enormous flea market and antique shop in cyberspace, old photos in an antique shop, if indeed a shop carried such items at all, were often relegated to a box sarcastically labeled "Instant Relatives." And before eBay dominated the vintage photography market, there once were auctions-by-phone of historical photos, complete with catalogs of images mailed before the auction to bidders from previous sales. Some of these catalogs, expensively produced, were themselves worth collecting; others were homemade. In addition to these auctions and the occasional antique shop, swap meets were a good source of vintage photos when I began collecting. There was a different large swap meet on each of three weekends a month in Southern California during the 1990s and early 2000s, and, typically, at least a half a dozen or so vendors could be counted on to have a fresh supply of found photos, with a few sellers even specializing in vintage photography. Notably, while I was hardly the first to collect vernacular images of males together, there were no books devoted to such images, or even to found photographs in general, until after my collecting was well under way.[2]

This book, like the collection it surveys, examines the history of emotions. We don't always realize that emotions even *have* a history—that joy, anger, jealousy, sadness, and love have existed in different ways and to different degrees in different times and places. In studying this emotional history, as in the study of history in general, we can also learn about ourselves today—our pain, our pleasure, and our potential.

The photos I've collected often display intimacy, tenderness, and affection—not necessarily sexual yearning, even though sexual attraction was surely a component of some of the imagery. We know that men's "romantic friendships"—some of them sexual, some not—were once common in the United States, at least until the early twentieth century, when the notion of oriented sexuality entered American culture and made *any* closeness between males scorned and suspect as never before.[3] In my judgment, there are very few photos in this book (or in my entire collection) that unambiguously portray sexual chemistry: an image of two men passionately embracing while kissing on the mouth, for instance, or photos known to have come from a queer gathering. But I haven't avoided collecting more explicitly sexual imagery—vernacular photos of men having oral or anal sex, for example. In my experience, such images, especially those from the 1950s and earlier, are virtually impossible to find, outside of archives.[4] It nonetheless seems likely that most other American collectors of found photos of males together were, and still are, also gay men. These collectors are, perhaps, mainly gay men of my generation and older, males who were at least into their twenties before the Stonewall Rebellion of 1969—men, that is, who had been raised in an intensely homophobic America, a place in which depictions of male affection were noteworthy, objects of either scorn or envy. Value attaches to that which is thought to be rare: If seldom seen in everyday life, affectionate males in photographs might come to be valued, worthy of collection. Conversations with other collectors and with sellers of vintage photography suggest the soundness of my notion of who collects photos similar to those I've acquired.

Individual photos in those boxes of "Instant Relatives" rarely sold for more than a dollar, but prices for vintage imagery considered unusual rose dramatically as the popularity of collecting increased during the 1990s. As noted above, perception of rarity drives up prices. Such was the stigma attached to intimacy between males that unselfconscious public displays of male closeness were uncommon in American everyday life late in the twentieth century.

Not surprisingly, then, photographs thought to portray male intimacy from any period of time carried a connotation of taboo and came to be among the more highly priced found photographs. An eBay auction of one "gay interest" photograph might eventually fetch hundreds of dollars, particularly if the males were shirtless or were handsome by conventional standards and if there were kissing, bed-sharing, handholding, or lap-sitting.

It seems relevant that while *Picturing Men*, my first book on this topic, was reviewed in several academic journals and in a few mainstream newspapers, it was the gay press that reviewed the book most extensively. (In 2002, most major American cities still had their own hard-copy newspapers and magazines primarily for gay and lesbian readers. And there also were publications with a national focus, such as *The Advocate*, *Out*, and the *Gay and Lesbian Review*). Interestingly, marketers at *Picturing Men*'s hardcover publisher, Smithsonian Institution Press, were hesitant to have the book named what I originally wanted for it, *Picturing Men Together*; they were fearful that the title alone sounded "too gay" and might diminish wider sales. Once the gay press embraced the book, however, and after it was extensively promoted by a gay and lesbian book club, the people in marketing were quite happy to promote gay sales. The only book signings they scheduled for me were in gay bookstores.

It takes a dominant culture to have made such a powerful taboo of physical affection between males that we *necessarily* see queerness in most of the photos in *Picturing Men* or here, in *The Pleasure of His Company*. Ours, of course, has been precisely such a culture, at least during the lifetime of every American alive today. What many of these photographs *do* often show clearly is affection, mirth, and comfort between and among males. And they suggest, as well, that unselfconscious affection was once more common, as captured in photographs, than it would be later on. Especially for those of us, gay and straight, who lived through the intense homohatred of post–World War II America, uneasiness and male affection were partnered.[5] With photos like many in this book, one might feel a certain longing, a kinship, a historical rootedness—finding "Instant Relatives," to borrow that wording once used on signs in antique shops. In the United States during the 1950s, the very idea that gayness actually had an American history was still only on the horizon.

Homophobia, I believe, has emotionally deprived most American males. The fear has not only stigmatized people who actually yearn sexually for those of their own sex, but, especially with males, has also made suspect any sort of expression of affection. A discomfort with affection is what prompts the pathetic, obligatory cry of "no homo" with which so many young American males, even today, will follow an expression of affection for another guy. Homophobia's more direct targets—we actual "homos," those who do yearn for sexual involvement with other males—have experienced a particular sort of emotional deprivation. Consequently, queer males might feel a particular attraction to and kinship with some of the photos in this book, might therefore be the more likely seekers of the imagery that vendors and collectors often call "male affection." Better late than never, but I wish I'd seen photos like many of these when I was much younger, had thus realized that simple affection and tenderness between males actually had an American history, was once not at all taboo, but instead commonplace. To this day, that news could do with wider circulation. The readers of this book, then, I hope for the most? Young males, and not just the gay ones.

The history of male sexual involvements and the history of the political struggles in our society over queer rights have been increasingly recognized. But this recognition—an awareness that American queerness actually has a history—began only forty years or so ago, with the first publications from gay history's pioneers, Jonathan Ned Katz and John D'Emilio.[6] Male affection, romance, and tenderness that don't include sexual activity, though, remain much less written about and understood than is male sexual involvement. Our understanding of American males' capacity for same-sex emotional attachments, and the extent to which such attachments occur, is far from thorough.

Thin, too, is our understanding of the relationship—potential and actual— between sex and affection in the everyday experiences of contemporary American males. Recent works by two sociologists, Jane Ward and Tony Silva, examine sexual activity between men who identify as straight. Ward never considers whether emotional attachments, even if repressed and unacknowledged, might ever be part of the sexual activity she studied: mostly coerced contacts in fraternity rituals. To Ward, the sex tells the entire story. And, incredible as this sounds, according to her, this particular sex between men serves to reinforce the heterosexual identity of those who control the encounters. Silva has studied sex with more parity between the participants. His work recognizes that tender emotions sometimes accompany the sexual activity; revealingly, though, the men involved still endeavor to keep the sex and the feelings a secret.[7]

Psychologist Niobe Way is the singular scholar who has elaborately demonstrated that young American boys are fully capable of profound emotional attachments to each other, with or without sex. Way has maintained that homophobia and American individualism do not take their typical toll—pervasive loneliness—until these males approach adulthood and then face what she revealingly calls a "crisis of connection."[8]

History's essential lesson—a warning to some, a reassurance to others—is that most aspects of human encounters are neither inevitable nor everlasting, but rather are the product of a particular cultural moment. As with my previous scholarship, and much of my teaching, I mean for *The Pleasure of His Company* to convey—to literally portray— that lesson regarding males together.

■■■

Books presenting found photos of males together emerged relatively recently—with the appearance of Russell Bush's *Affectionate Men: A Photographic History of a Century of Male Couples, 1850–1950*, in 1998; David Deitcher's *Dear Friends: American Photographs of Men Together, 1840–1918*, in 2001; and my *Picturing Men: A Century of Male Relationships in Everyday American Photography*, in 2002.[9] Though all three authors are themselves collectors, these three books differ markedly in purpose, scope, and approach to historical imagery. They complement rather than compete, each contributing to a refreshed recognition of an important genre of American photography: males in each other's company.

Having yearned to be the first author to refresh that recognition, I thought I was scooped by Bush's book, and then, so close to the upcoming publication of *Picturing Men*, I felt one-upped by Deitcher's handsomely produced volume. The naivete of my chagrin strikes me still. In the absence of plagiarism, no book duplicates another, and a topic of any importance deserves many volumes to cover it adequately. Bush, the first in print, dealt only with photos of male couples that he deemed affectionate, and Deitcher emphasized what the photos displayed in his book meant to him as a gay male living long after the subjects of the photos had lived.

Picturing Men, on the other hand, sought to use everyday photographs as a means of better understanding the shifting history of various sorts of male relationships in our society, relationships that might have had a romantic or sexual dimension and those that contained no such component. I tried in particular to describe and account for how male relationships of many types had changed over the century that my book covered, stressing the ways that photographs may have reflected and reinforced certain cultural assumptions about American masculinity and male togetherness. I interpreted the photographs in *Picturing Men*, then, as cultural documents, and I described the act of having a photograph taken with someone else as a cultural performance, mirroring and shaping certain cultural assumptions about males in each other's company.

Mine wasn't an approach to everyone's liking. Communications scholar Michele White, in assessing *Picturing Men*, declared that by "suggesting he has the knowledge and authority to read images correctly, Ibson resists the pleasures of queering images [labeled 'gay interest'] on eBay."[10] On the contrary, as I've noted, it was as a gay male of the late twentieth century that I was drawn to collecting these images in the first place. On first sight I did derive pleasure from seeing something homoerotic in a good many of them. But having acquired them and eventually having seen countless other photographs of males together, then in trying to use images as a way of better understanding the periods in which they were produced, I set the "queering" aside as anachronistic. Surely some of the men in the photos I collected were sexually drawn to other males, I maintained, but simply their display of affection in a photograph was no proof of that. Nowhere in *Picturing Men* or elsewhere, though, did I use—and I hope I've never implied—as wooden a notion as "correctly," White's wording in describing my interpretations. Instead, I stand with anthropologist Clifford Geertz in his assertion that those who seek certainty (or correctness) in cultural interpretation are expecting the impossible. "What gets better," Geertz wrote, "is the precision with which we vex each other."[11]

Other books featuring historical photos of males together followed Bush's, Deitcher's, and mine, often concentrating on photos of servicemen. Notable among these are Evan Bachner's two handsome volumes, *At Ease: Navy Men of World War II* and *Men of WWII: Fighting Men at Ease*.[12] By no means everyday photographs, the evocative images in *At Ease* are all from the National Archives, the work of the Naval Aviation Photographic Unit that was led during World War II by eminent American photographer Edward Steichen. Work produced by the Naval Unit is also present in Bachner's *Men of World War II*, but that book also features photos from the National Archives that are part of Army, Army Air Force, and Marine collections. These images in *Men of World War II* lack the polish of the work Steichen inspired for the Navy and, consequently, have more of an everyday, vernacular feel.[13]

Simply because so many men have served, military service has indeed produced abundant imagery of men together, especially during wartime and other periods when a military draft was in effect. Photographs of servicemen comprise an important segment of both *Picturing Men* and *The Pleasure of His Company*, but segments only. Military settings abound in my collection of more than 10,000 photos and comprise about a quarter of the 385 images in this book, but adult civilian life and boyhood deserve considerable attention. In my collection and my scholarship, my goal has been a more comprehensive portrait of American males and masculinity than would result from photos confined to servicemen or just to males thought to have been sexually involved.

Sebastien Lifshitz's 2014 work, *The Invisibles: Vintage Portraits of Love and Pride*, features plenty of early twentieth-century civilians, females as well as males, and isn't confined to American subjects.[14] Additionally, *The Invisibles* is meant to be a queer book: guided by his own sense of things, based on the nature of the posing and the subjects' attire or lack of attire, Lifshitz declares that the queerness of the photographs in his book is either "apparent," "highly probable," or "'played at.'"[15] In *Picturing Men*, I warned against the assignment—or the denial—of queerness in vintage photographs, lest one read history backward, using possibly inappropriate contemporary attitudes about same-sex closeness in evaluating historical imagery. I chose instead to examine what I believe photos from different periods are better able to reveal: cultural shifts in the encouraged physical intimacy between males, shifts that assuredly have taken place. That warning of mine notwithstanding, I don't find Lifshitz's declaration of his book's unambiguous queerness to be incautious. Such are the images in the book that it does not seem particularly problematic for the dust jacket of *The Invisibles* to announce that the "volume is a charming collection of vintage photographs of gay couples from 1900 to 1960."[16]

A more recent book of photos of male couples declared to be "men in love," Hugh Nini and Neal Treadwell's *Loving: A Photographic History of Men in Love, 1850s–1950s*, is much larger in size and presents larger conceptual issues than *The Invisibles*. In an odd coincidence, Nini and Treadwell's collection of around 2,800 images of male couples began, as had my more diverse collection, with a discovery in an antique shop. And Nini and Treadwell decided that such were their own powers of perception that they could just know, simply from looking at a photograph, whether its two subjects were likely to have been in love with each other. If they "believe that it's at least 50% likely that we're looking at two men who are romantically involved," a photo is deemed suitable for their collection.[17] Even though they are aware that cultural notions regarding acceptable forms of male-to-male expression of affection have varied over time and space, Nini and Treadwell seem undaunted in trusting their ability to recognize love, regardless of where or when lovers were photographed. If not infallible, their gaydar is allegedly pretty powerful.

While there is some thematic logic as to how the hundreds of hugely appealing photographs are arranged in *Loving*, there is no attention to either chronology or geography. Additionally—and crucially—Nini and Treadwell seem utterly untroubled by, perhaps even unaware of, the nearly total whiteness of the couples whose images they have gathered.[18] The arrogance—or, if you prefer, the naivete—of their selection standards aside, *Loving* is a beautifully produced work of formidable size, and its marketing has been as carefully designed as its layout. What bothers me about *Loving* clearly hasn't troubled its many enthusiastic readers one bit; those readers would probably see my objections as merely a professor's quibbles. And really, what author wouldn't relish receiving the quality and quantity of Amazon reviews that *Loving* has attracted?[19] For all its appeal, though, *Loving* is not something it declares itself to be: a work of history. An observation of mine in reviewing another work also pertains directly to *Loving*: "If it seeks to be a history and not merely a meditation on present-day concerns, any work addressing sexual involvements in the past must carefully consider whether today's sexual attitudes, practices, and meanings were equally relevant, or even existent, in earlier times. And if a work studies visual representation, it should assess what an image might have meant to its original creators, subjects, and observers, perhaps something quite different from what the same image would mean today."[20] My criteria for evaluating a work that calls itself historical are, then, directly at odds with the criteria that *Loving*'s authors used in deciding whether to add a photo to their collection. But there's still no denying their book's considerable charm.

Not only have several books recently examined found photographs of males together, but such imagery abounds on the Internet as well. Most numerous are the thousands of photos offered daily for bids on eBay, typically designated as "gay" if there appears to be the slightest amount of closeness between the male subjects, a culturally revealing designation that makes Nini and Treadwell's criteria seem guarded. Websites, Flickr pages, Facebook groups, and Instagram postings are devoted to images of male affection, among them those on the website *Bosom Buddies: A Photo History of Male Affection.*[21]

Other works of mine—two books and an article—have offered interpretations of found photographs of men together.[22] *The Pleasure of His Company*, however, is not a work of elaborate interpretation but is essentially one of presentation—a heretofore unpublished look at my collection. This book emphasizes the theme in its title: males who seem to be enjoying being with each other. It's in my previous work that there is more compelling photographic evidence of the distancing between males than the twentieth century brought. There are 385 photos in this book, only around 5 percent of the entire collection, but some of my favorites nonetheless, and a good representation of the collection's range in format, setting, subject, and era. Photos become my "favorites" because of poses, attire, the image's clarity, humor, poignance, paradigmatic quality, and, yes, possible queerness. Missing in this book are other favorites of mine that have been previously published: the 142 that appeared in *Picturing Men*, the 29 from *The Mourning After*, and 22 more that were in an article about "the transformation of boyhood in 1950s America."

▮▮▮

Chronology and context matter in *The Pleasure of His Company.* The first four chapters feature, respectively, couples, groups, military men, and males performing masculinity. Then there are five separate sections within the final chapter. That fifth chapter deals with what I see as some "special occasions" for American males from the dawn of photography to the middle years of the twentieth century: boyhood, sport, work, membership in certain organizations, and being at a beach. Each chapter's images are arranged chronologically, with as much exactitude as I could muster. I've noted the format, size, inscriptions, and whatever else I might know about a photo in the Index to Photographs section at the end of the book.

Together with the images already published in other works of mine, *The Pleasure of His Company* captures well the feel and scope of what I've gathered during roughly thirty years of collecting. Seeing the entire collection—housed in dozens of albums, in the drawers of a cabinet built especially for the purpose, and framed on tabletops and the walls of our home—takes a while, as one might imagine. To select those most appropriate for this book, I looked at every photo in the collection, no small undertaking. Although I'd often looked at certain sections over the years, I hadn't reviewed the entire collection since it was much smaller, some two decades ago when I was writing *Picturing Men*. Seeing it in its entirety, as it is now, was sometimes like a visit with old friends, and I, of course, hope readers will appreciate seeing this portion that I've gathered. The photos in this book should be a source of much more than nostalgia; I believe there is hope for the future in these pages. American men can be much better off than they are today.

As nearly five decades of students have heard me say, I believe that devising a title for a book or an essay should be done with great care. If a work has coherence, it should have an overriding theme, message, query, or point. An apt title should visit that centrality and capture it somehow, succinctly telling readers what's in store for them. I believe that taking profound pleasure in one another's company has been at the very heart of the American male experience, and that vernacular photographs capture the pleasure in a distinctive way, whether in a photographer's studio, in a dorm room or a boarding house, away together at summer camp or aboard a ship, or in the living room of their own home. Ever since the notion of sexual orientation and the stigmatizing of homosexuality entered American culture at the turn of the twentieth century, homophobia has sometimes distorted or destroyed the pleasure of male association, making some of the photos in this book, especially the older images, a visit to a lost world.

American masculinity receives considerable criticism nowadays, much of it deserved. But differences among American males are underappreciated. Toxicity is not universal, nor is it uniform, and its causes are poorly understood. The misplacing, if not the total loss, of the world that this book seeks to recapture is, I believe, an important element in some of the gross and tragic behavior of some American males today, behavior directed at women and at other males as well. Contented, well-adjusted persons don't behave like that.

Do we really need another book full of photographs of American men posing together? Obviously, I hope we do, and I hope that there's more than immodesty in my assertion that there hasn't yet been a book of male imagery quite like this one, in the range of its poses, settings, and concerns, and in the lenses I've used to view the photographs. Are there collections similar to mine, perhaps still-larger ones? I simply don't know; perhaps this book's publication will bring attention to even better gatherings of images.

In visiting what I've described as a lost world of American males, this book tries to do what historical works commonly seek to accomplish: to show that current human conventions aren't inevitable, that things could and have been different, sometimes radically so. We're in the midst of a particularly bleak period of American and world history. To know that things *can* be different, *will* someday be different, can be a source of solace, hope, and reassurance. Even in good times, there's never enough of that. ∎

1 Roc Morin comments interestingly on "The People Who Collect Strangers' Memories," *The Atlantic* (September 26, 2016), https://www.theatlantic.com/technology/archive/2016/09/snapshot-collectors/501614/.

2 On found photographs in general, see James Nocito, *Found Lives: A Collection of Found Photographs* (Layton, UT: Gibbs Smith Publisher, 1998); Douglas R. Nickel, *Snapshots: The Photography of Everyday Life, 1888 to the Present* (San Francisco: San Francisco Museum of Modern Art, 1998); Thomas Waither, *Other Pictures: Anonymous Photographs from the Collection of Thomas Waither* (Santa Fe, NM: Twin Palms Publishers, 2000); Robert Flynn Johnson, *Anonymous: Enigmatic Images from Unknown Photographers* (New York: Thames and Hudson, 2004); and, especially, Sarah Greenough and Diane Waggoner, *The Art of the American Snapshot, 1888–1978* (Washington, DC: National Gallery of Art, 2007).

3 As have many other scholars, I address the phenomenon of male "romantic friendships" in John Ibson, *Picturing Men: A Century of Male Relationships in Everyday American Photography* (Washington, DC: Smithsonian Institution Press, 2002; Chicago: University of Chicago Press, 2006), 128–29.

4 For an analysis of "porn archives" and a valuable listing of places that house this material, see Tim Dean, Steven Ruszczycky, and David Squires, *Porn Archives* (Durham, NC: Duke University Press, 2014).

5 I examine some causes and consequences of postwar homophobia in John Ibson, *The Mourning After: Loss and Longing among Midcentury American Men* (Chicago: University of Chicago Press, 2018).

6 Foundational works are Jonathan Ned Katz, *Gay American History: Lesbians and Gay Men in the U.S.A.* (New York: Avon Books, 1978); and John D'Emilio, *Sexual Politics, Sexual Communities: The*

Making of a Homosexual Minority in the United States, 1940–1970 (Chicago: University of Chicago Press, 1983).

7 See Jane Ward, *Not Gay: Sex between Straight White Men* (New York: NYU Press, 2015); Tony Silva, *Still Straight: Sexual Flexibility among White Men in Rural America* (New York: NYU Press, 2021). Also see Ritch C. Savin-Williams, *Mostly Straight: Sexual Fluidity among Men* (Cambridge, MA: Harvard University Press, 2017).

8 Niobe Way, *Deep Secrets: Boys' Friendships and the Crisis of Connection* (Cambridge, MA: Harvard University Press, 2013). Belgian director Lukas Dhont's 2023 film *Close* is a singularly sensitive examination of adolescent male romance and its possibly tragic consequences. Interestingly, Dhont was influenced by Way's scholarship. Mark Greene, "'Close': The Oscar-nominated Movie That Names the Threat to Our Sons' Lives," *Ms. Magazine*, https://msmagazine.com/2023/02/08/close-lukas-dhont-masculinity/.

9 Russell Bush, *Affectionate Men: A Photographic History of a Century of Male Couples, 1850–1950* (New York: St. Martin's Press, 1998); David Deitcher, *Dear Friends: American Photographs of Men Together* (New York: Harry N. Abrams, 2001); Ibson, *Picturing Men.* There had been one book published slightly before Bush's whose subtitle—*One Hundred & Fifty Years of Gay Life in Pictures*—suggested that it might belong with the three works just mentioned. James Gardiner's *Who's a Pretty Boy Then?*, however, contains few vernacular photographs and is instead an eclectic collection of photos from newspaper articles, drawings, and professional portraits (London: Serpent's Tail, 1998).

10 Michele White, "My Queer eBay: 'Gay Interest' Photographs and the Visual Culture of Buying," in Ken Hillis and Michael Petit, eds., *Everyday eBay: Culture, Collecting, and Desire* (New York: Routledge, 2006), Chapter 16, 245–65, 254.

11 Clifford Geertz, *The Interpretation of Cultures* (New York: Basic Books, 2017), 3rd ed., 32.

12 Evan Bachner, *At Ease: Navy Men of World War II* (New York: Henry N. Abrams, 2004); *Men of World War II: Fighting Men at Ease* (New York: Henry N. Abrams, 2007).

13 An appealing collection of vernacular photographs of sailors that includes images from well before the Second World War is Kevin Bentley, *Sailor: Vintage Photos of a Masculine Icon* (San Francisco: Council Oak Books, 2000). Imagery from snapshots, professional photographs, and advertisements appears in Dian Hansen, *My Buddy: World War II Laid Bare* (Cologne, Germany: Taschen, 2018). Additional vernacular imagery of servicemen from both the First and Second World Wars and from the armed forces of both the United States and Germany is featured in Michael Stokes, *My Naked Soldier: Nudity in the Armed Forces, WWI–WWII* (Los Angeles, Sebastian Publishing, 2020).

14 Sebastien Lifshitz, *The Invisibles: Vintage Portraits of Love and Pride* (New York: Rizzoli, 2014).

15 Lifshitz, *Invisibles.*

16 In reality, there are several photos of groups and a few images of lone individuals in the book; it is, however, mostly of couples. A much more ambitious and problematic undertaking is Pierre Borhan's *Man to Man: A History of Gay Photography* (New York: The Vendome Press, 2007).

17 Hugh Nini and Neal Treadwell, *Loving: A Photographic History of Men in Love, 1850s–1950s* (Milan: 5 Continents Editions, 2020), 16. For more of the same, see Nini and Treadwell, *Loving II: More Photographic History of Men in Love 1850s–1950s* (5 Continents, 2025).

18 I discuss the underrepresentation of males of color in found photographs in *Picturing Men*, 43, 146, 148, 212; and in Ibson, *Mourning After*, 4–5. See also "John Ibson: Picturing African American Men with Men," outhistory, https://outhistory.org/exhibits/show/john-ibson/image-collection and https://outhistory.org/exhibits/show/john-ibson/picturing-african-american-men

19 https://www.amazon.com/Loving-Photographic-History-Love-1850s-1950s/dp/8874399286.

20 John Ibson, review of Pierre Borhan, *Man to Man: A History of Gay Photography* (New York: The Vendome Press, 2007), *Archivaria: The Journal of the Association of Canadian Archivists*, 68 (Fall 2009): 324–27, 326.

21 See, for example, https://www.artofmanliness.com/articles/bosom-buddies-a-photo-history-of-male-affection/.

22 *Picturing Men* and *The Mourning After* are the books. See also John Ibson, "Picturing Boys: Found Photographs and the Transformation of Boyhood in 1950s America," *Thymos: Journal of Boyhood Studies* 1 (Spring 2007): 1, 68–83.

CHAPTER 1

ALL THESE FRIENDS AND LOVERS

MALE COUPLES IN FOUND PHOTOGRAPHS

As soon as modern photography's 1839 invention (by Louis Daguerre in France), pairs of American males began having their photographic images taken by early practitioners of the new type of portraiture. In found photographs, the exact nature of the relationships these pairs of males shared is usually impossible to discern today with anything beyond guesswork. But a display of physical affection of some sort—initially arms around each other and, later on, heads on shoulders, lap-sitting, and holding each other's hands—was commonplace. We do know that a fondness between two American males that was deep enough to deserve the name "romantic friendship" was also quite common in the nineteenth century—until, that is, late in the century, when the cultural notion emerged that a person's sexuality was oriented, as if a point on a compass in one direction or another, based entirely on the sex of one's sexual partner. As the twentieth century progressed, intimate feelings and behavior between males became newly suspect, as perhaps an indication of an "orientation" considered perverse. For a time, however, as these images attest, unselfconscious male closeness was encouraged, often preserved in a photograph.

There was indeed a common practice for American male twosomes throughout the nineteenth century and the early years of the twentieth: visiting a photographer's studio to have their portrait taken together—surely sometimes as a treasured token of their relationship. Sometimes the men would don costumes and act out humorous scenes. The commonality of this portrait-taking, of which there are several examples in chapters 1 through 4 (and countless more in my collection), is powerful evidence of male bonding, just as the virtual disappearance of the practice suggests either a fraying of the bonds or at least a shift to other forms of involvement. Going to the photographer together was mostly gone by the 1930s, but it returned among servicemen during World War II, only to largely disappear at that war's end. Twentieth-century males still posed together, of course, sometimes in photo booths and often in snapshots, but it was the disappearance of males' going to the portrait studio that led me to call the visit to the photographer a "lost ritual" in *Picturing Men.*[23]

Chapter 1's Image 25 is a favorite of mine because, like Images 5 and 17, it represents how common a liquor bottle or a beer mug had become as a symbol of masculinity in nineteenth-century images; but I also like Image 25 simply because it's such an early snapshot, a photograph, that is, that didn't require a visit to a photographer. When George Eastman introduced snapshot photography, with his invention of roll film, in 1888 and for a few years thereafter, printed images had to be round, like the camera's lens.

Perhaps, at times because of the privacy it afforded, the photo booth became a popular place for twentieth-century men to continue to have their portraits taken, and chapters 1 and 3 have several appealing examples of such imagery. Chapter 1's Images 44 and 45, though, are quite special, I think, their attractive frames possibly an indication of how much the photos meant to at least one of the subjects.

I have plenty of photographs in my collection, some in this chapter, of two or more males sharing a bed, but no others have as appealing an inscription as does chapter 1's Image 63, of Herman and Olaf in 1905, "prior to getting up one morning." And the sheer joyousness captured in Chapter 1's Images 73, 91, 100, 105, and 106 seem to perfectly capture the theme of mutual pleasure that gave this book its title.

During the early years of the twentieth century, mail began to be delivered to rural homes as well as urban residences in the United States, and this wider circulation of mail gave postcards an unprecedented popularity. Especially popular were photographic postcards, featuring either a snapshot or a photo taken in some sort of a studio, from fancy ones downtown to makeshift affairs set up at a county fair or amusement park. These studio portraits typically employed a backdrop, meant to be either serious, silly, dramatic, or romantic—from simulated railroad cars to garden gates, with a photo's subjects sometimes standing in a make-believe barroom or sitting atop a paper moon in its crescent phase. Studios often provided costumes so that a photo's subjects could present themselves, for example, as cowboys or convicts. I have collected 715 so-called real photo postcards, and examples are present in each chapter of this book.[24]

Cards that were actually mailed sometimes contained interesting, revealing messages, while some messages remain intriguingly mysterious. Image 38, for instance, mailed from Des Moines in 1912 from Edgor E. to his sister Nellie, is a snapshot of two young men posing close with their arms around each other. "This," Edgor explained without elaboration, "is my wife Dr Joe Winnett." A very popular studio prop for postcard photos was the crescent moon, on which might sit a single subject or a group as large as five. Frequently, a man and a woman would pose together on a moon, but also, two males would often pose together, or, less often in my observations, two females would. Images 33 and 34 are examples of two men on a moon, the former a rather bizarre photo, the latter a possibly romantic one. My collection includes thirty-one photos of males together on a moon.

Whether the decision to pose together on a moon was meant to imply romantic involvement is usually unclear. Similar is the ambiguous symbolism of certain long, firm, cylindrical objects that appear with notable frequency in photos of males together: Cigars were ubiquitous, especially around the turn of the century, as were rifles and liquor bottles, and, less often, pipes and cigarettes. Three snapshots—Images 94, 95, and 96—show two males touching cigarettes, possibly to symbolize a kiss. Another object that some might see as phallic, an umbrella, shows up in four of the photos—Images 57, 58, 59, and 60. Interestingly, in their visual catalog of males they think were surely lovers, Nini and Treadwell declare that males posing beneath an umbrella had become "a signal that two men were romantically involved," and, remarkably, they maintain that they have "about fifty 'umbrella couples' now."[25] The extraordinary length of one man's pipe in Image 35 does invite a Freudian interpretation, yet one is reminded of Freud's own reported (yet much-disputed) admonition to Jung that "sometimes a cigar is just a cigar." While every man who once posed beneath an umbrella with a male companion might not have been romantically involved with that partner, their pose undeniably signaled a closeness with which twentieth-century American culture would make many a male uncomfortable.

This book is about much more than males in couples, with or without umbrellas or cigars. The male couple closely posed together was nonetheless a common subject from photography's earliest days, and the frequency of that coupling and posing is of considerable cultural significance. ▮

23 *Picturing Men*, Chapter 2, "The Lost Ritual: American Men Together in Studio Portraits," 9–49.

24 Hal Morgan and Andreas Brown instructively examine the variety and popularity of the real photo postcard (RPPC) in *Prairie Fires and Paper Moons: The American Photographic Postcard* (Boston: David R. Godine, Publisher, 1981).

25 Nini and Treadwell, *Loving*, 19. I have not seen, let alone acquired, nearly that many photos of male couples that included umbrellas.

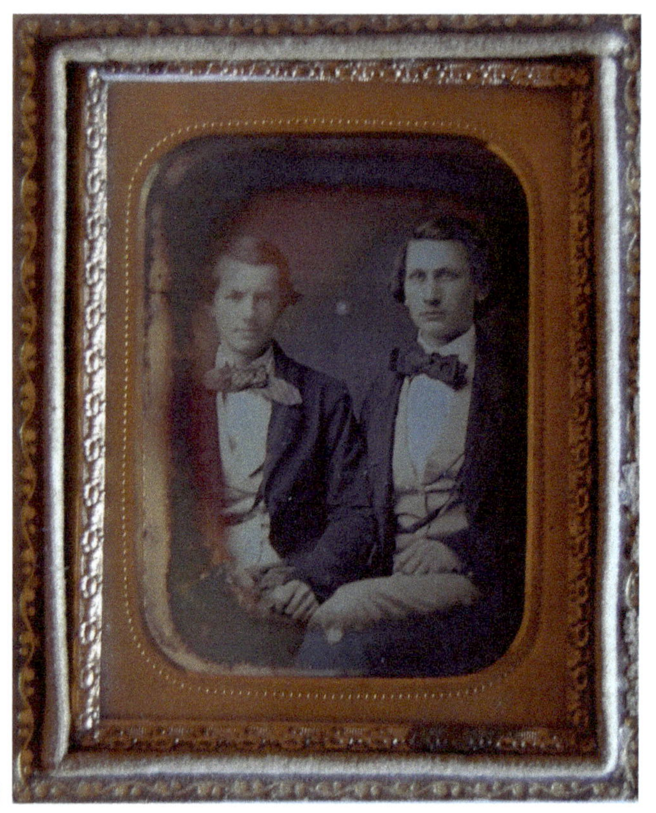

1

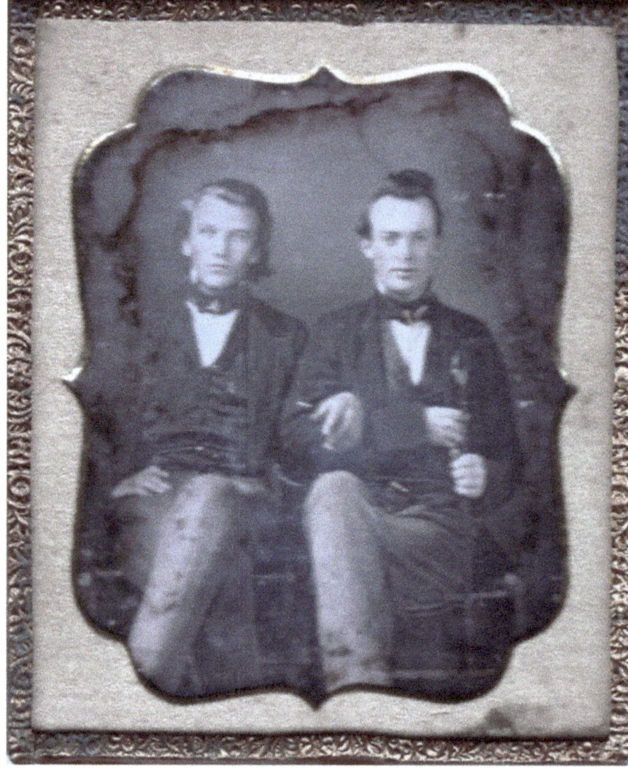

2

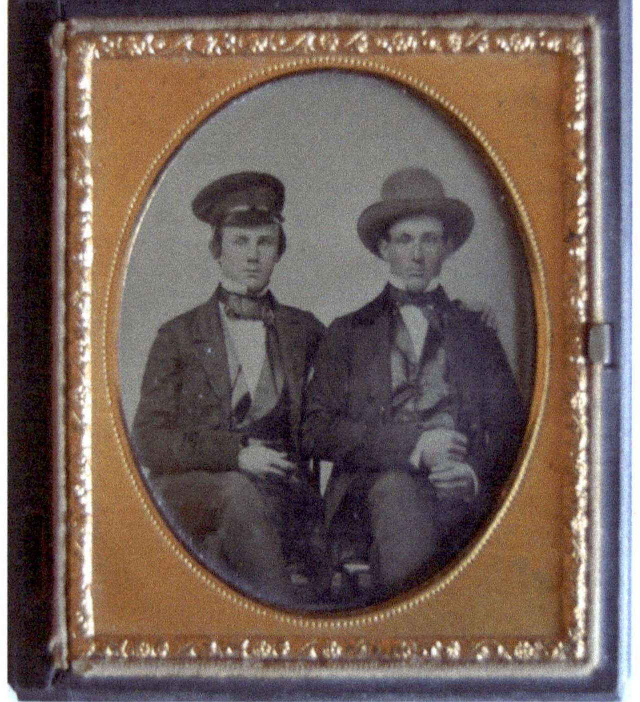

3

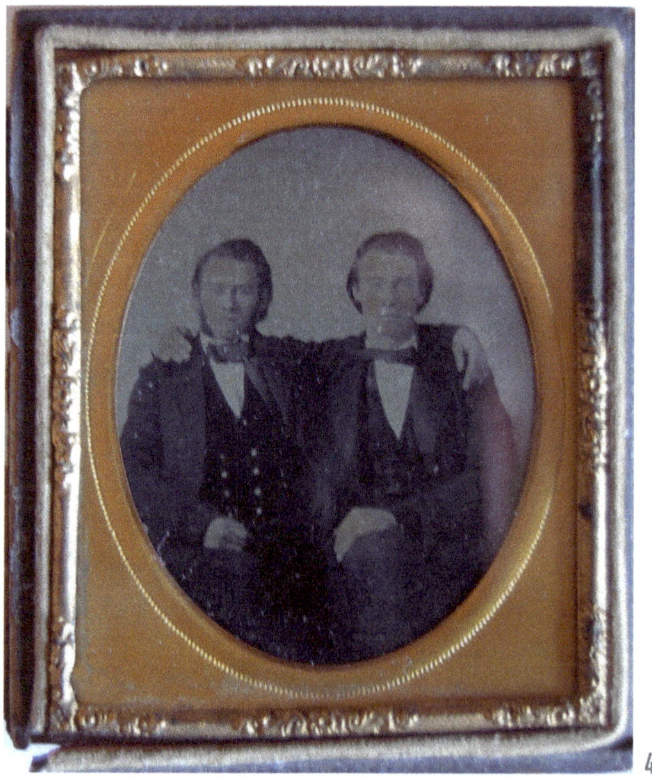

4

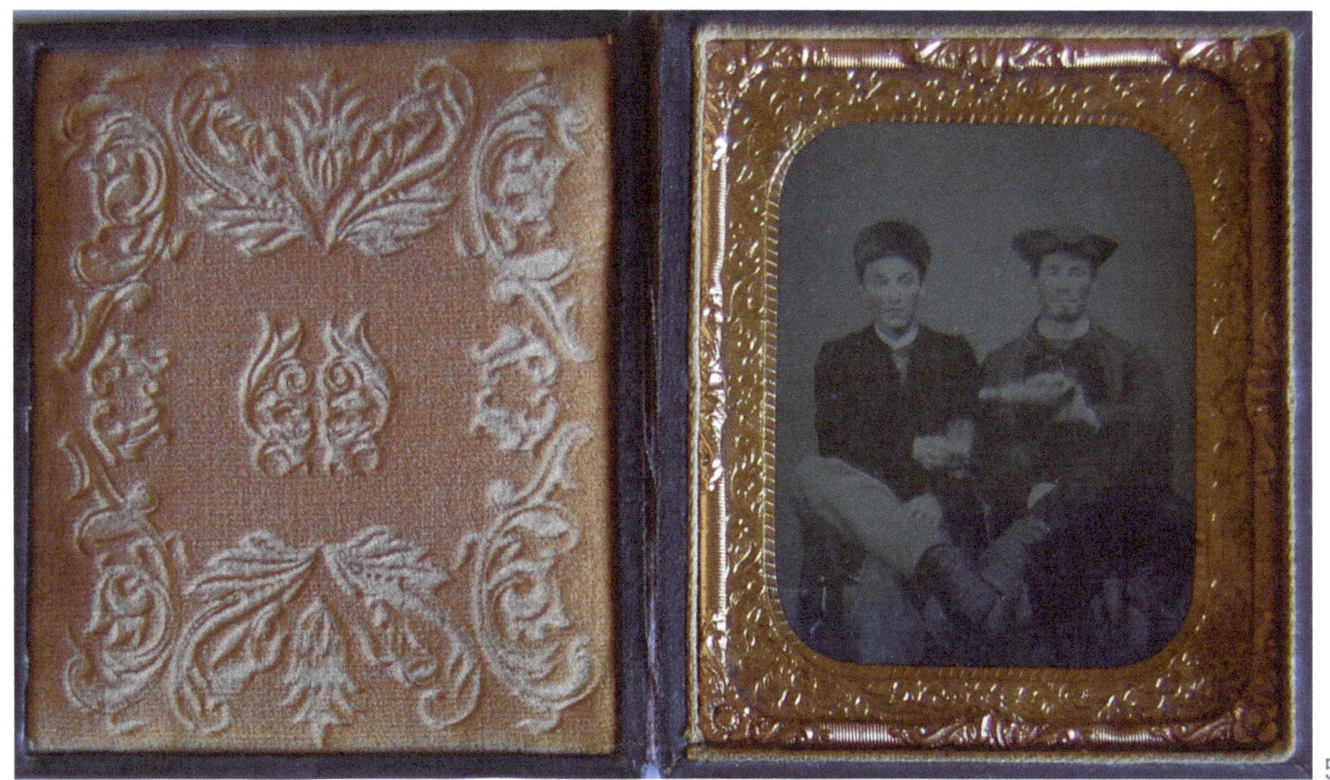
5

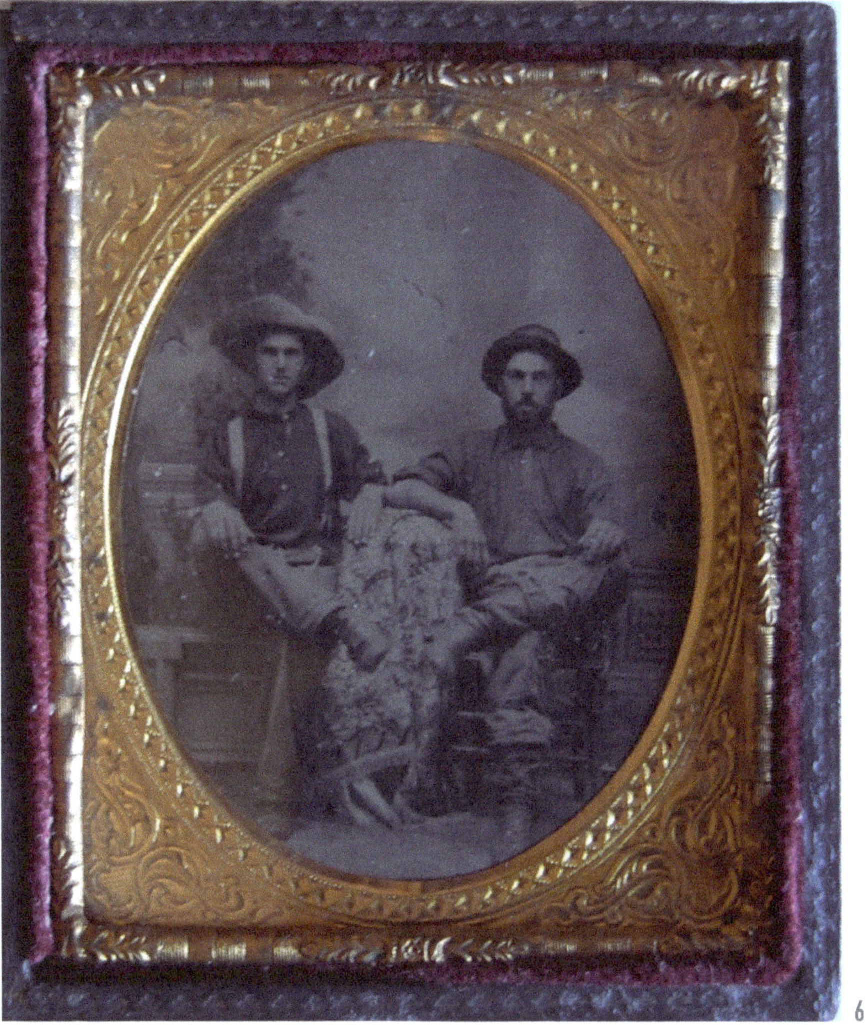
6

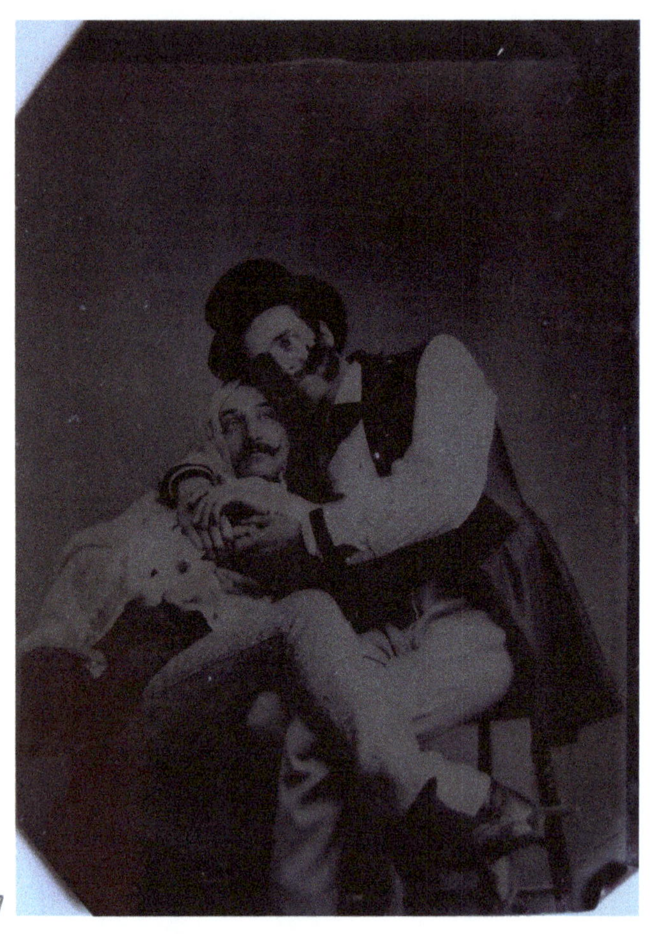
7

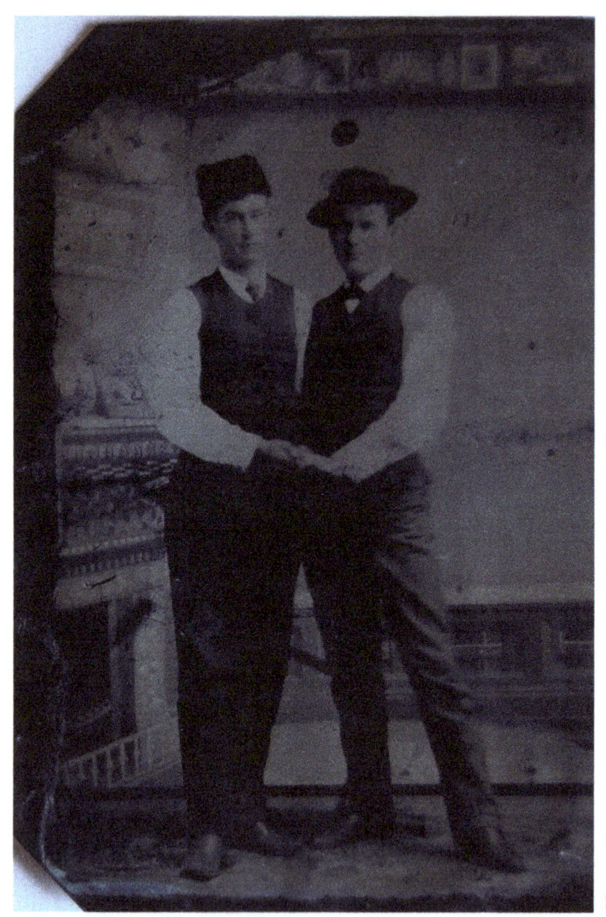
8

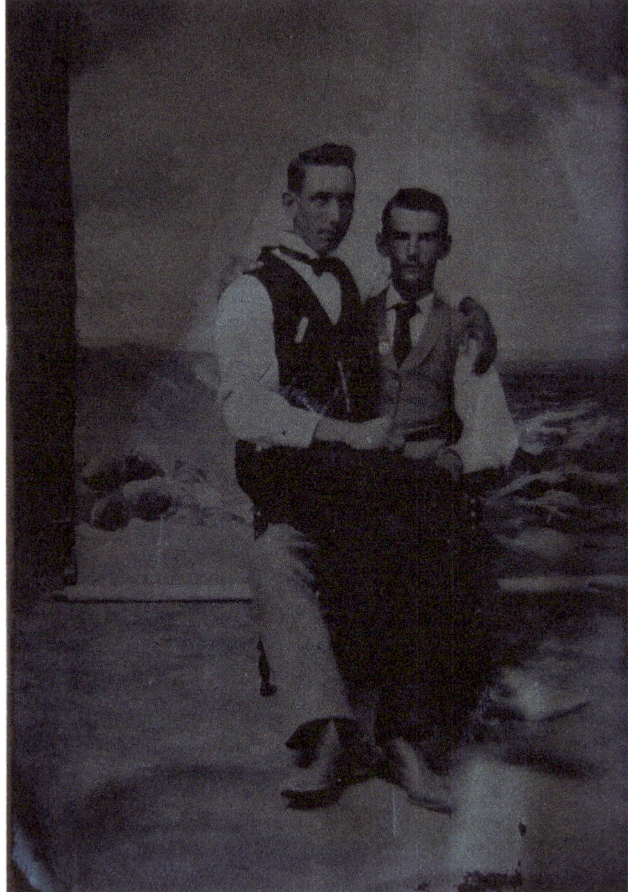
9

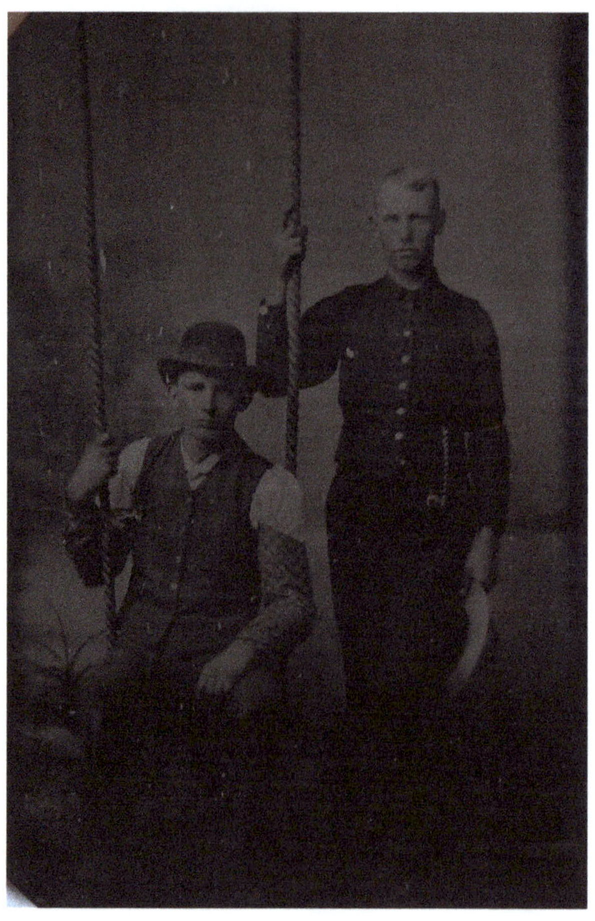
10

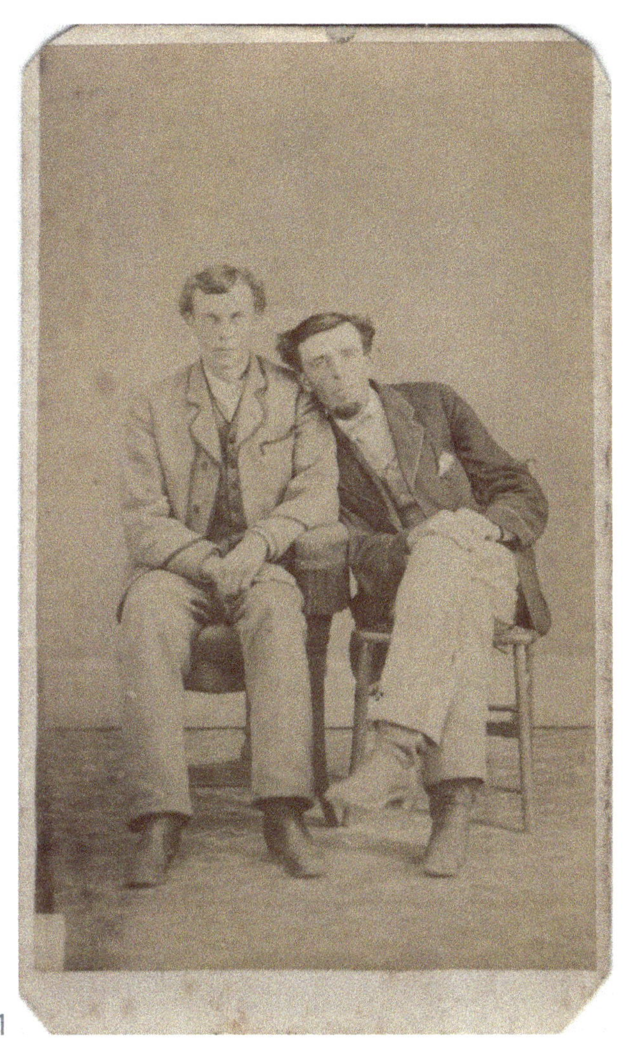
11

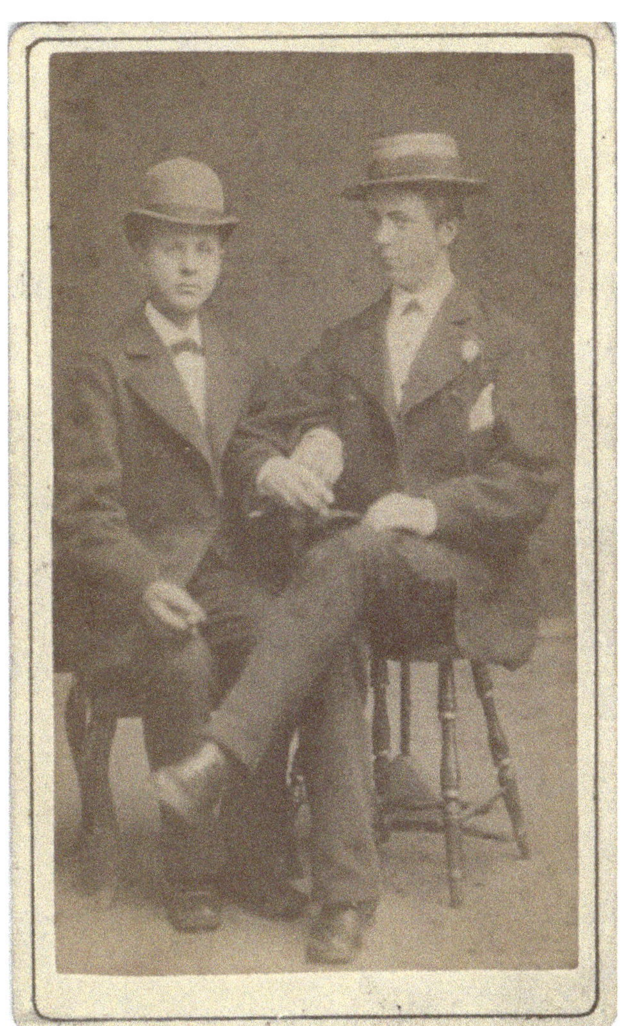
12

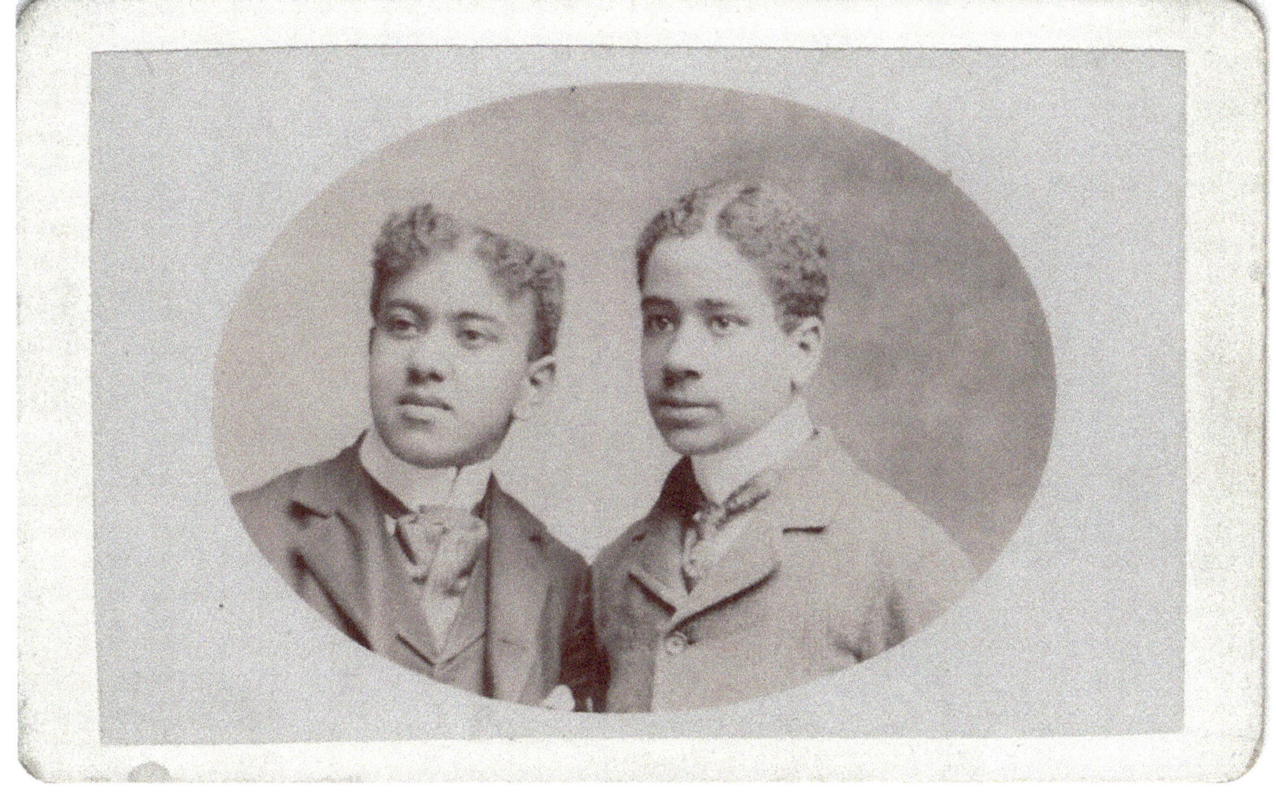
13

Ritter Bros.
FRIEST.
MASSILLON, OHIO.
14

H. H. Peterson, Jr.,
Hyrum,
Utah.
15

DE SMET,
COOLEDGE,
S. DAKOTA.
16

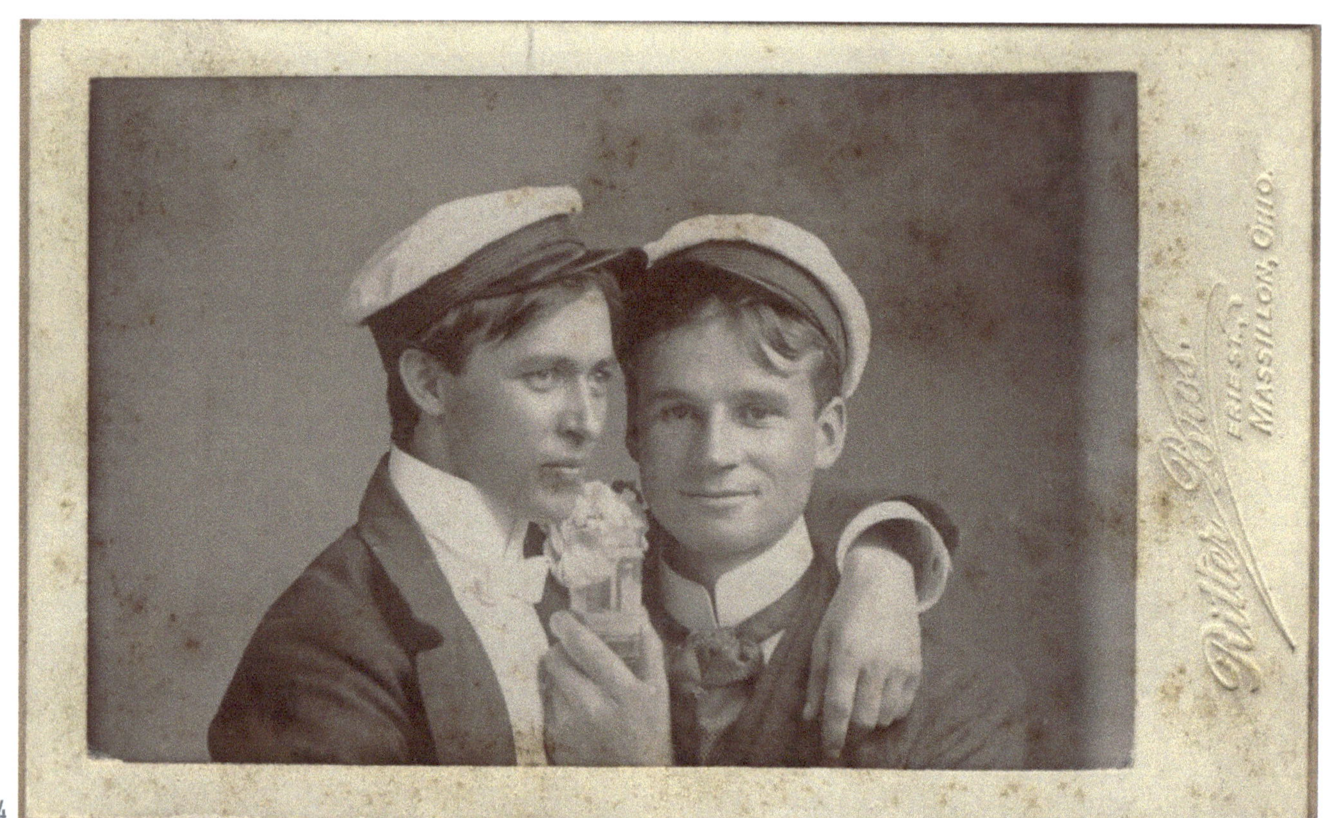

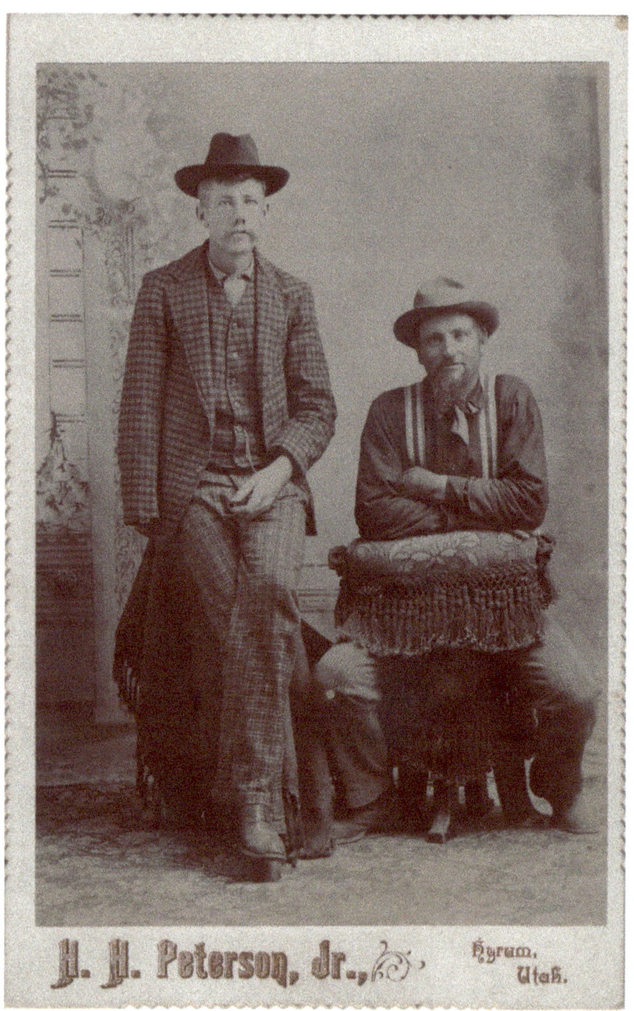

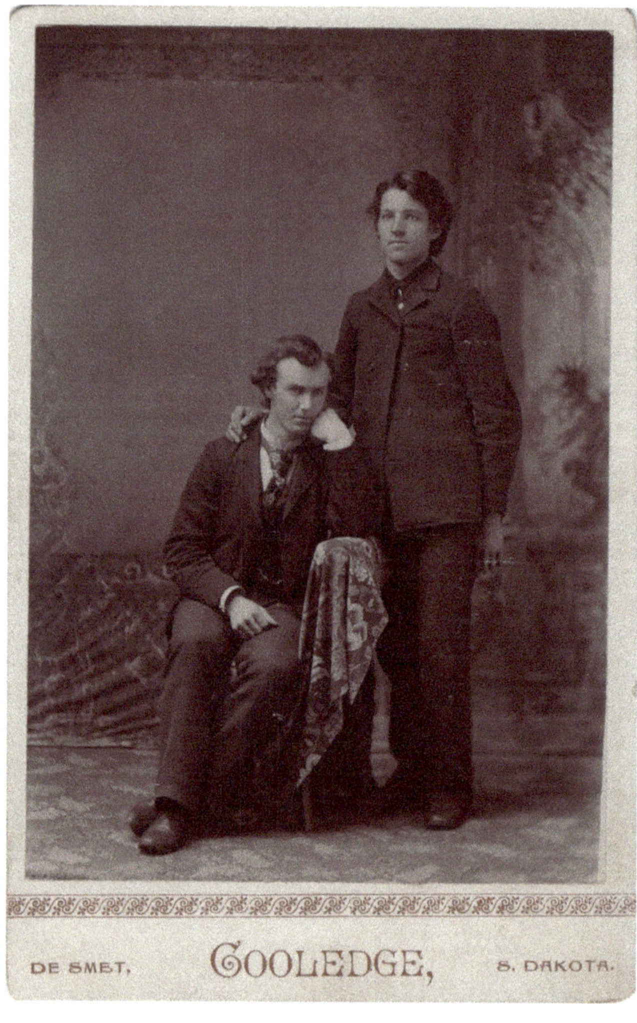

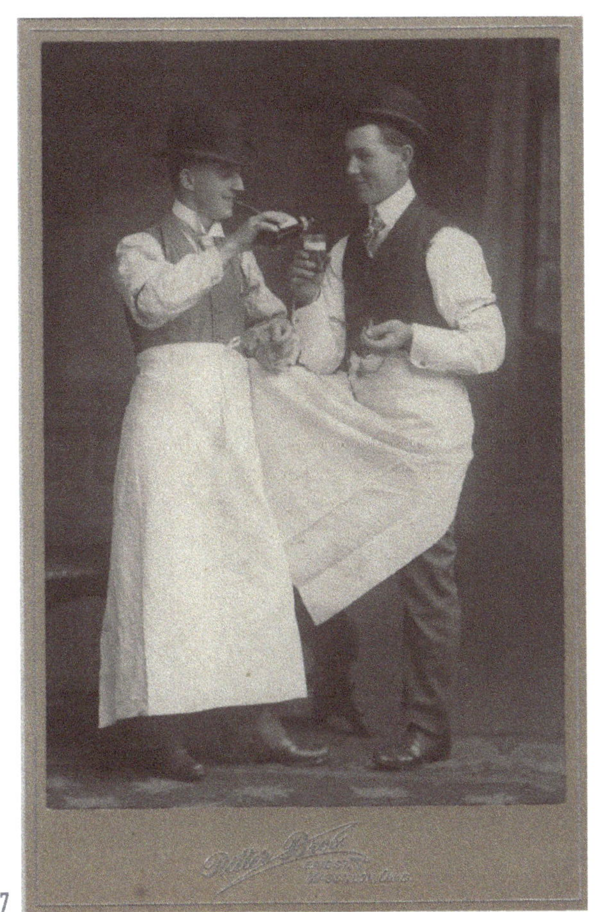
17

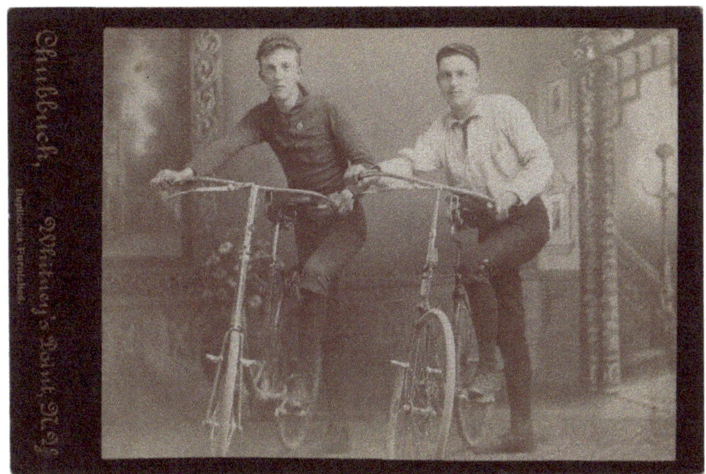
18

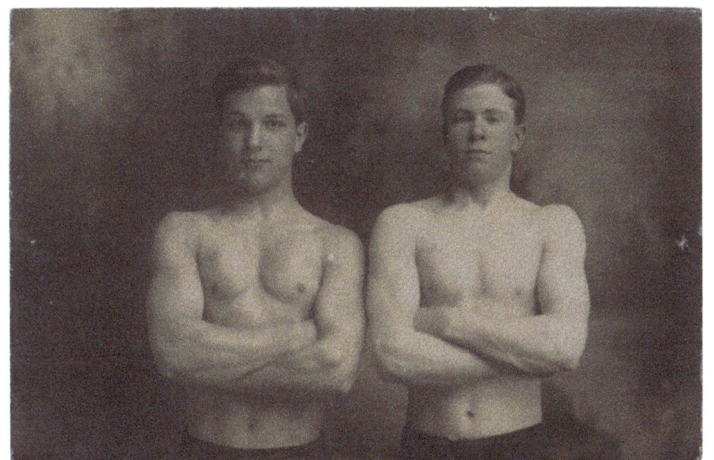
20

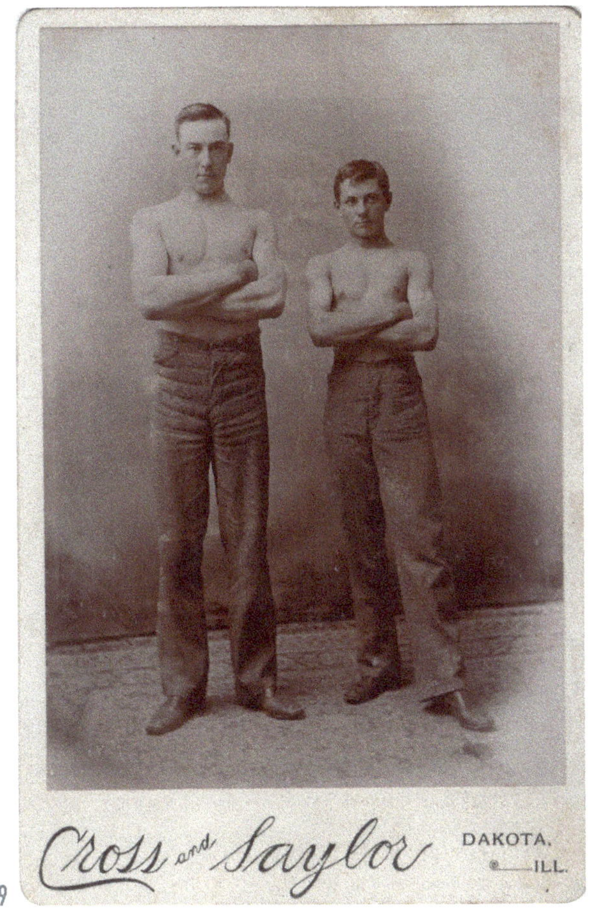

19

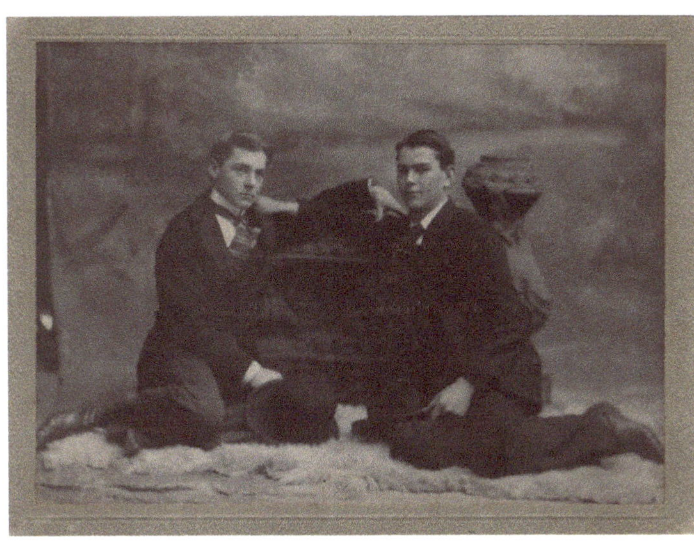
21

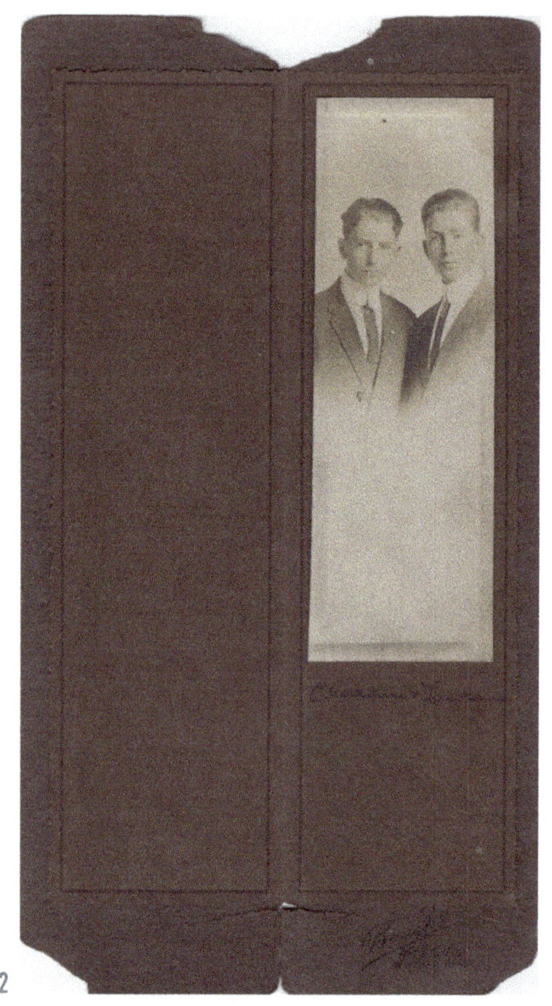

22

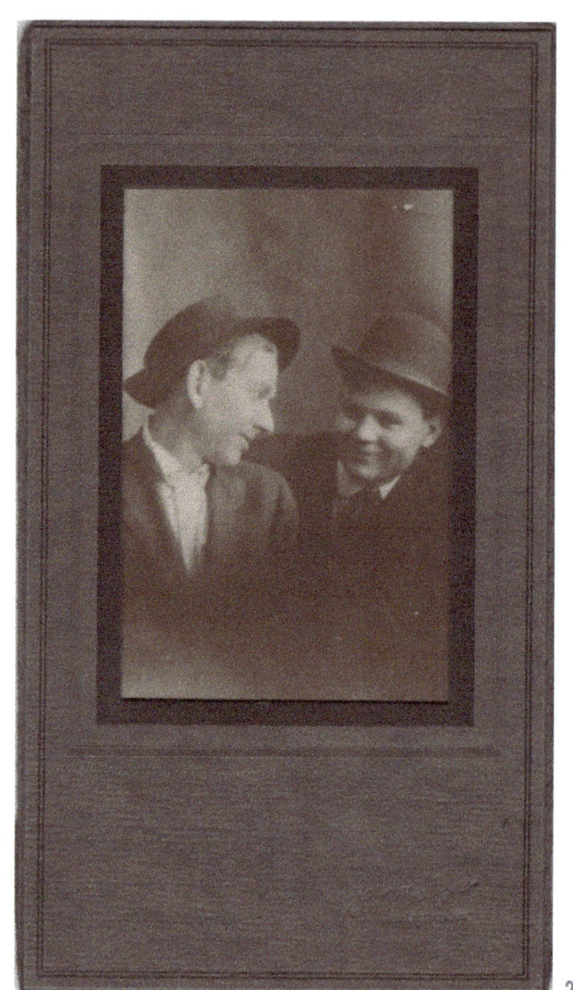

23

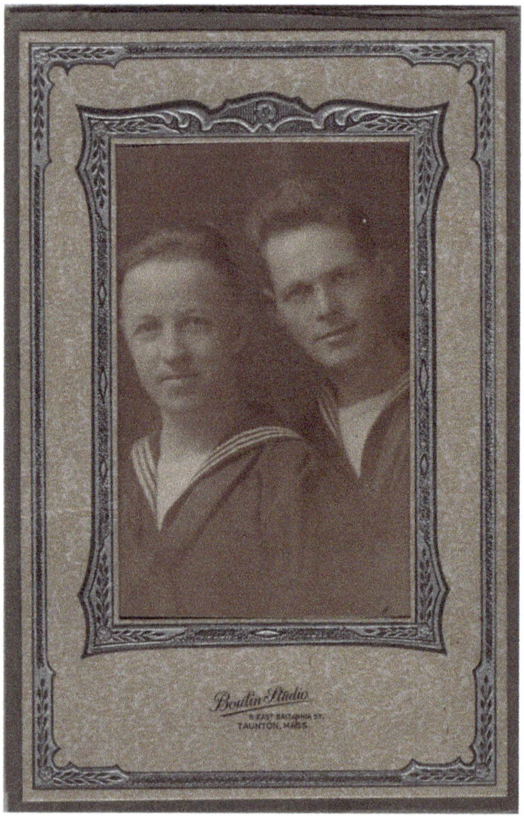

24

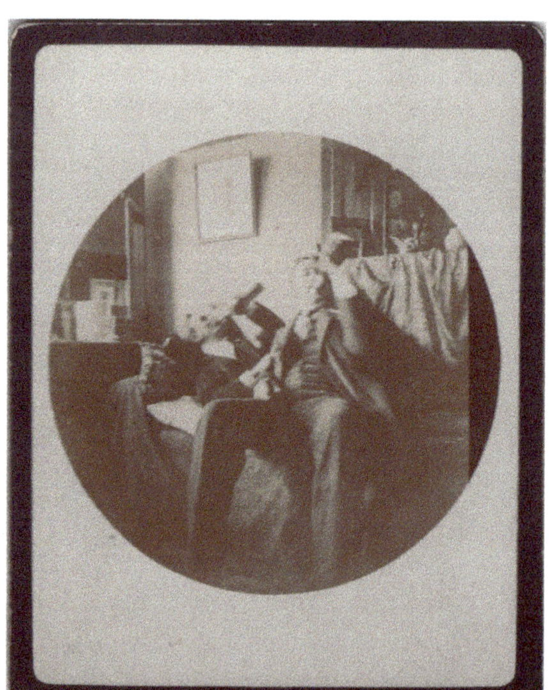

25

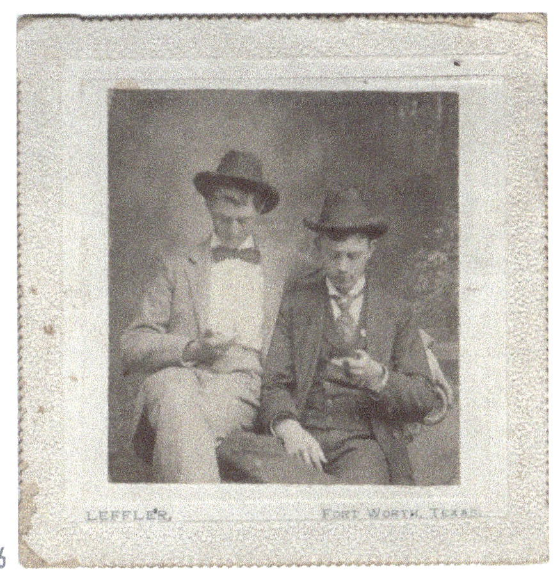

26

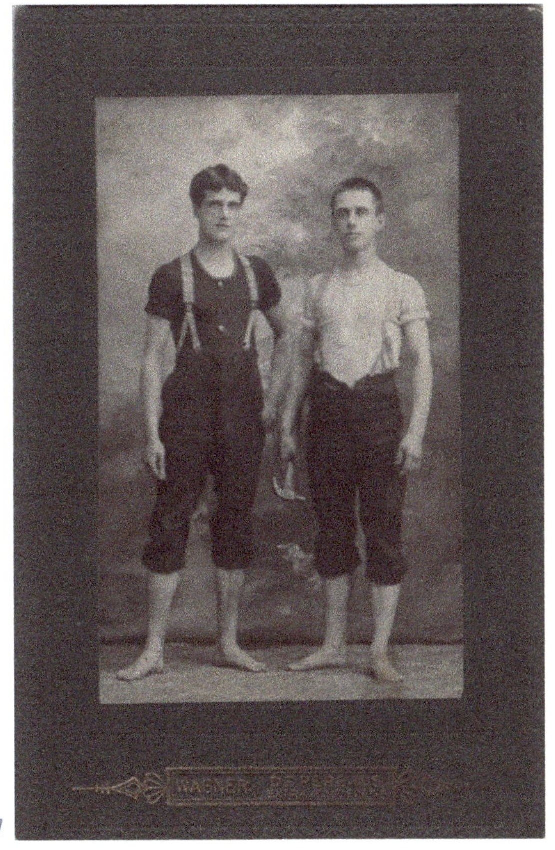
27

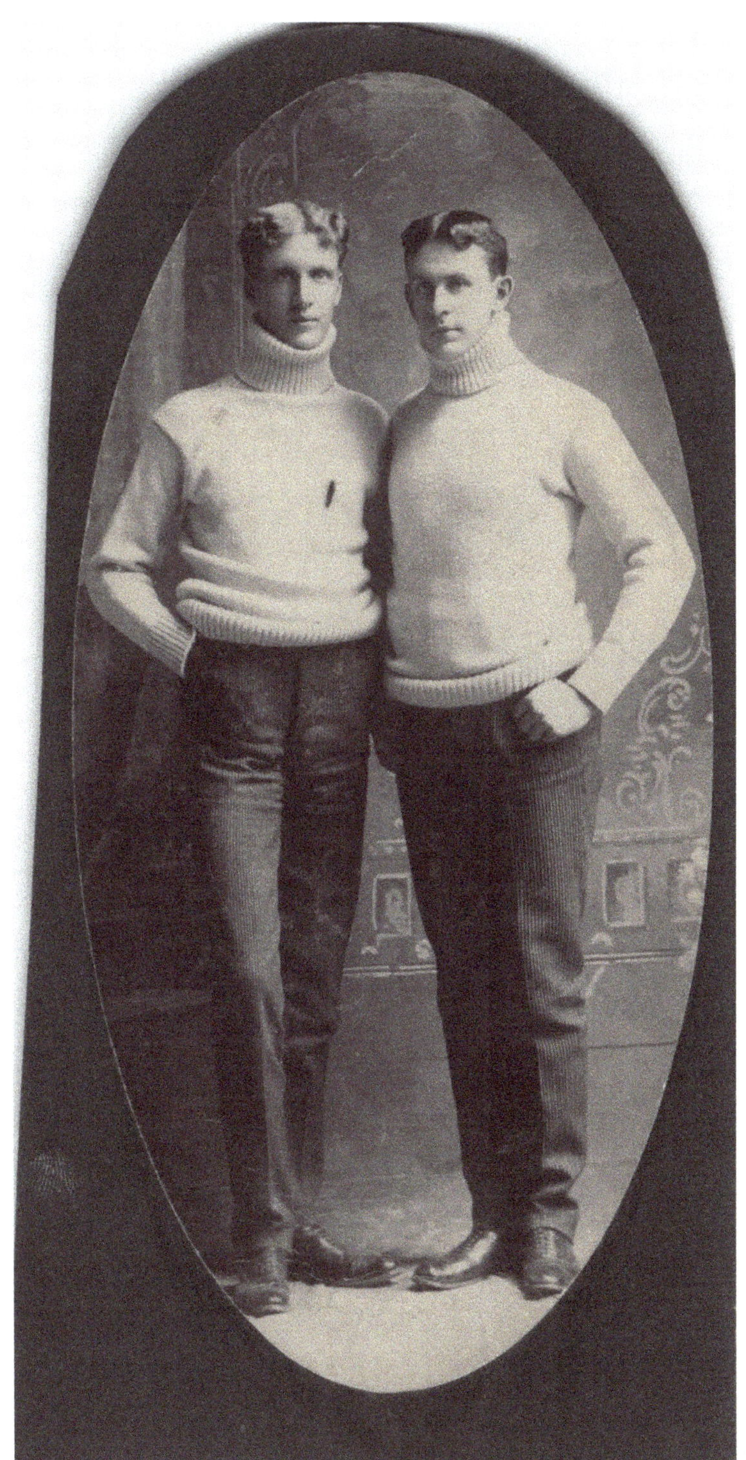
28

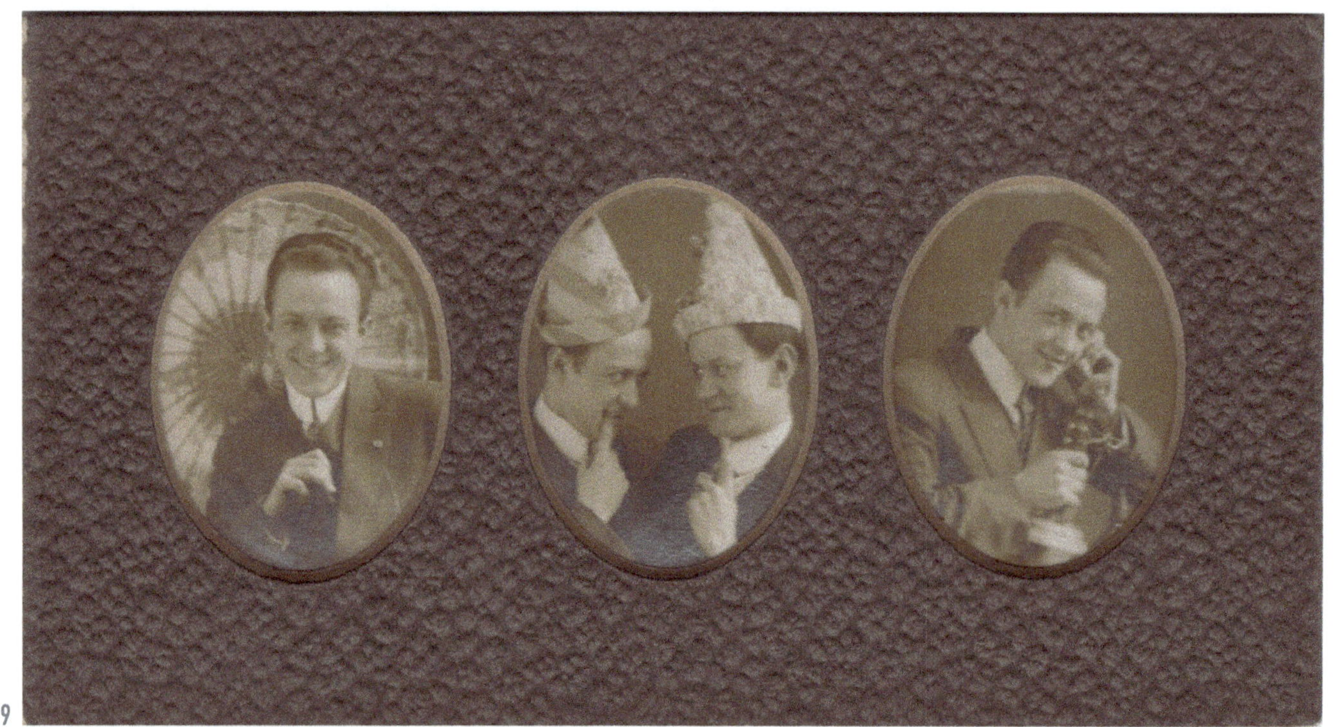

29

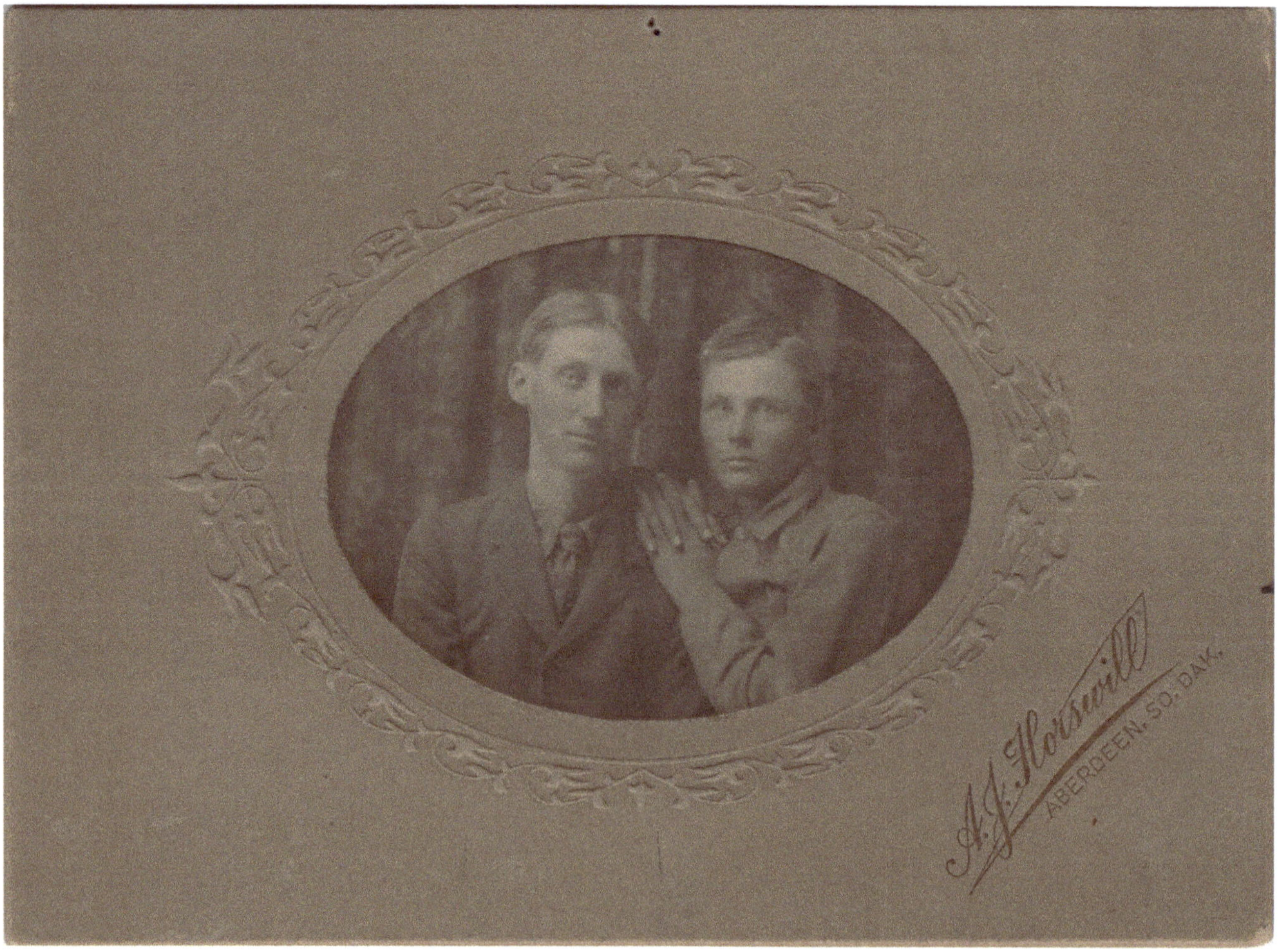

A. J. Horswill
ABERDEEN, SO. DAK.

30

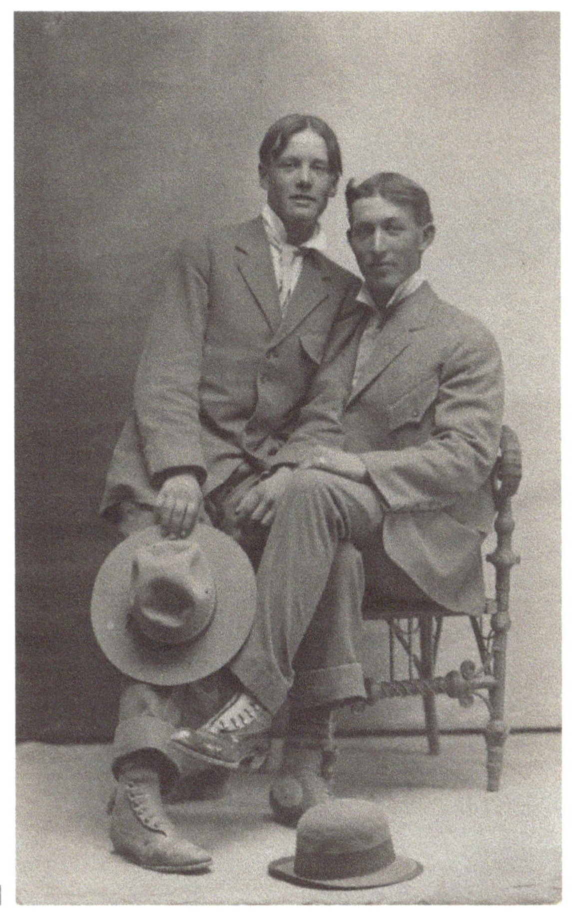
31

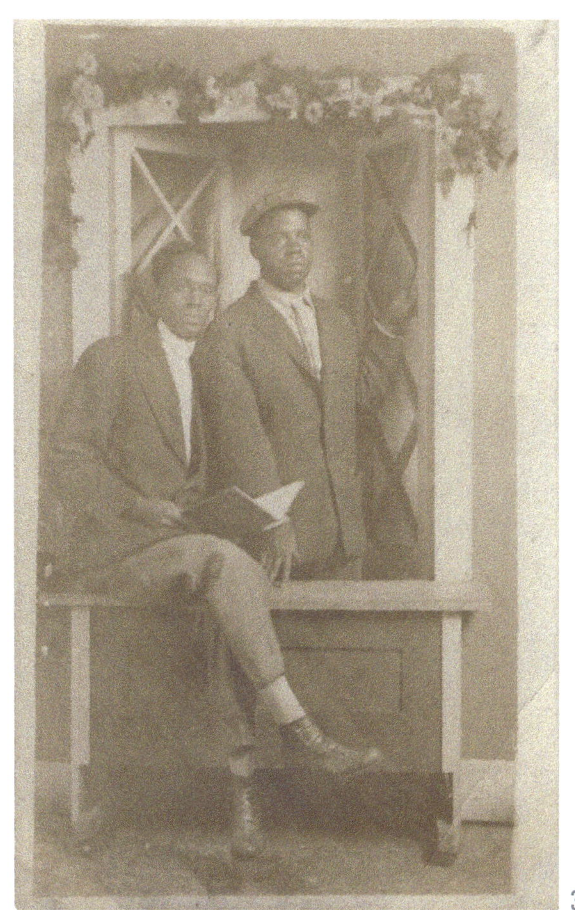
32

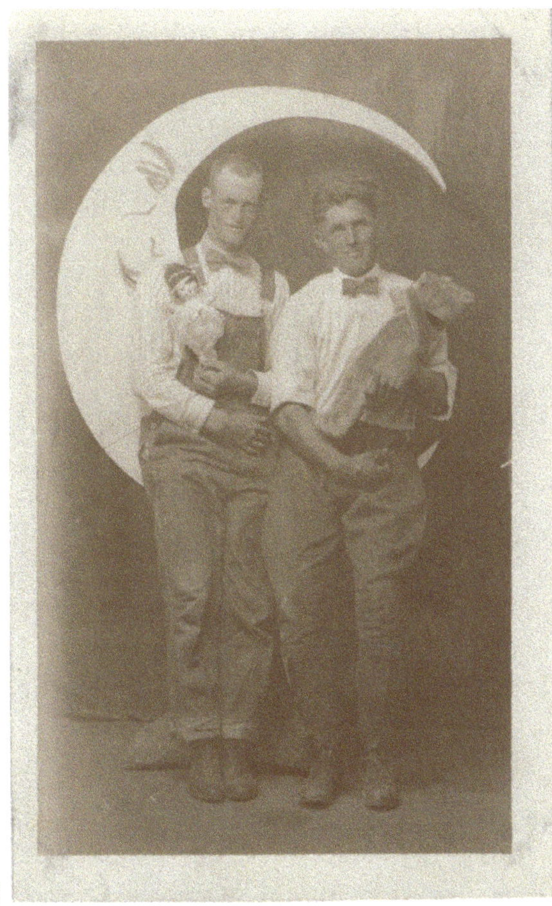
33

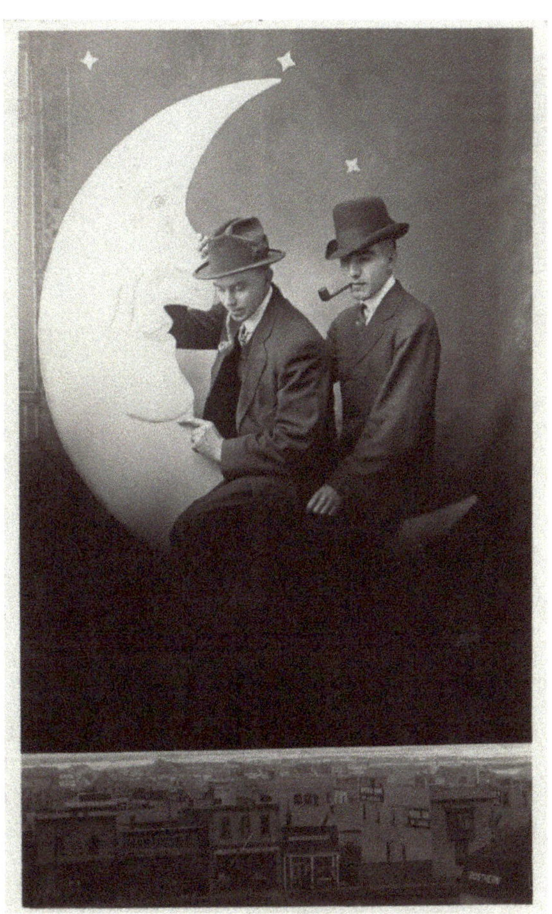
34

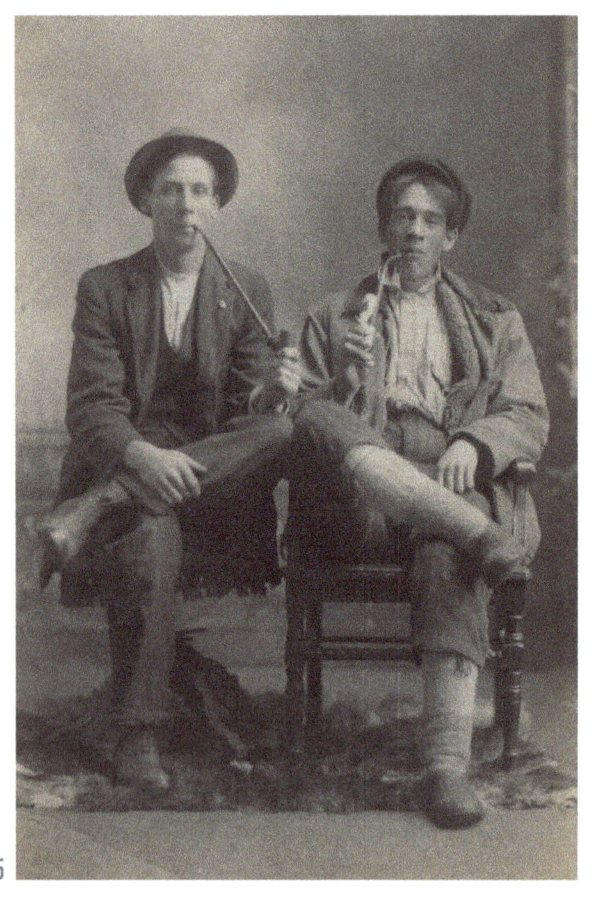
35

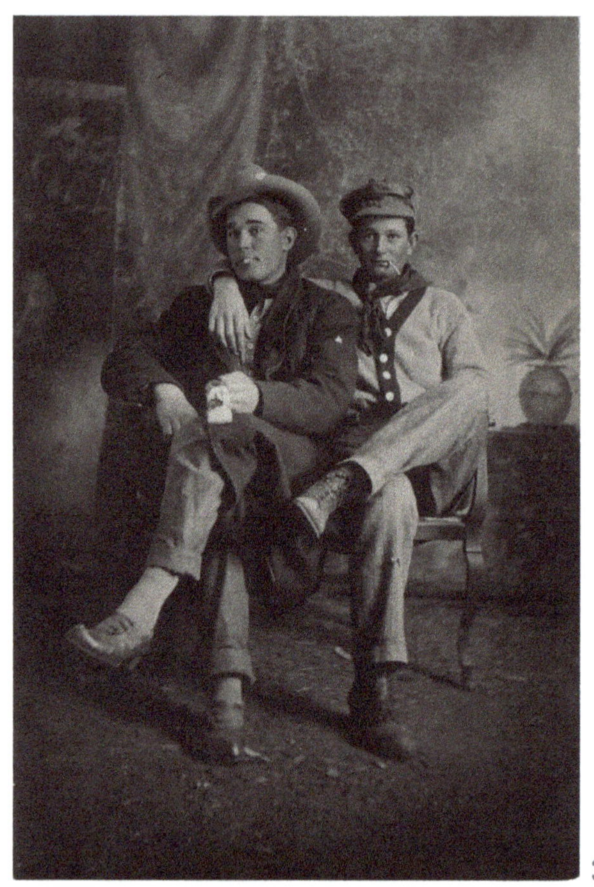
36

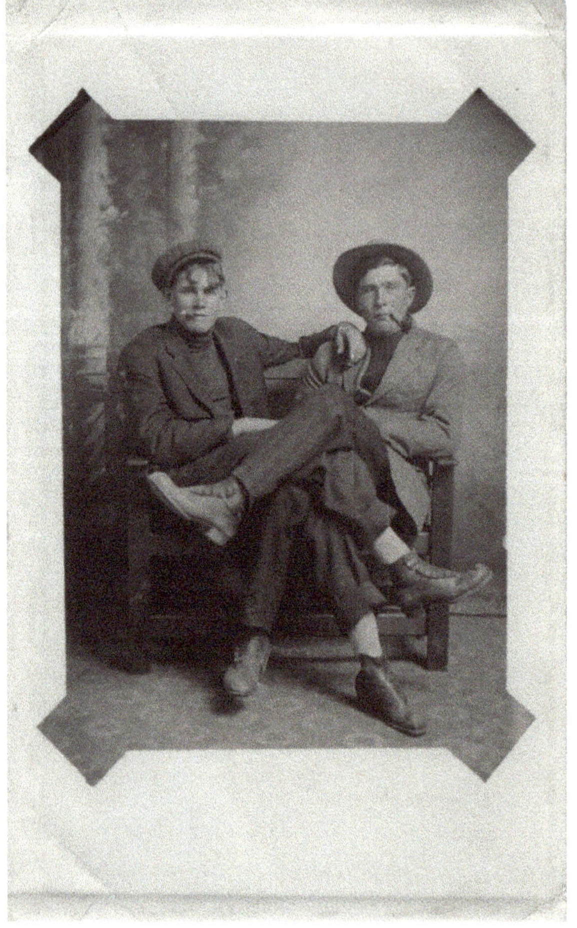
37

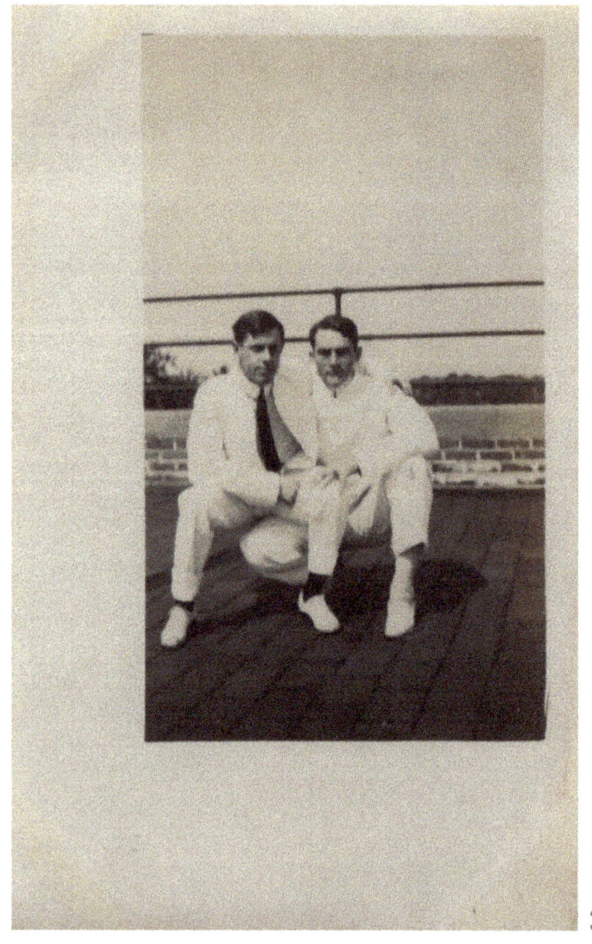
38

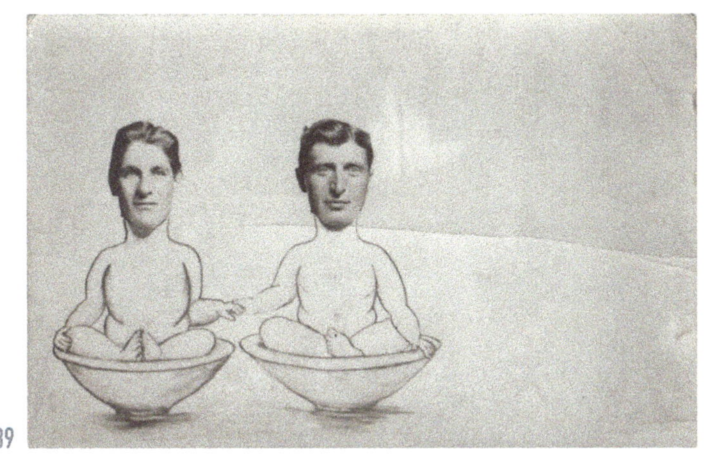

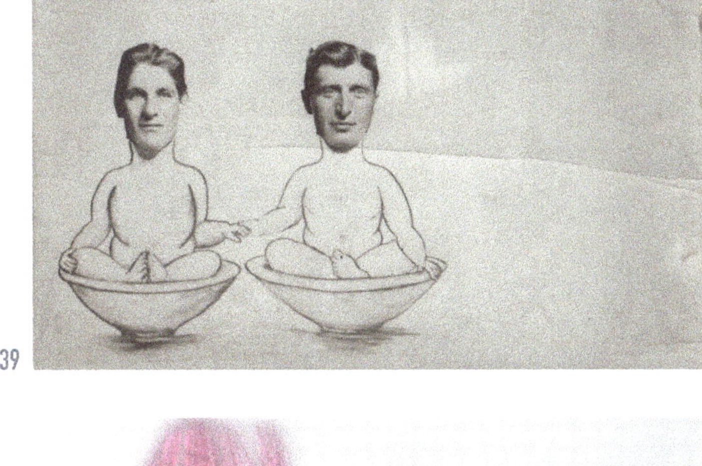

39

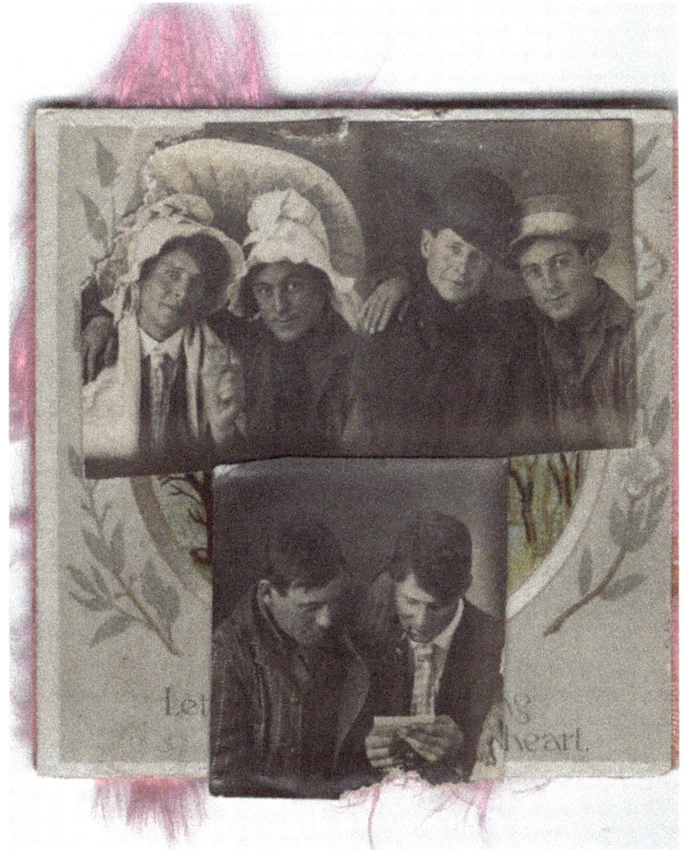

41

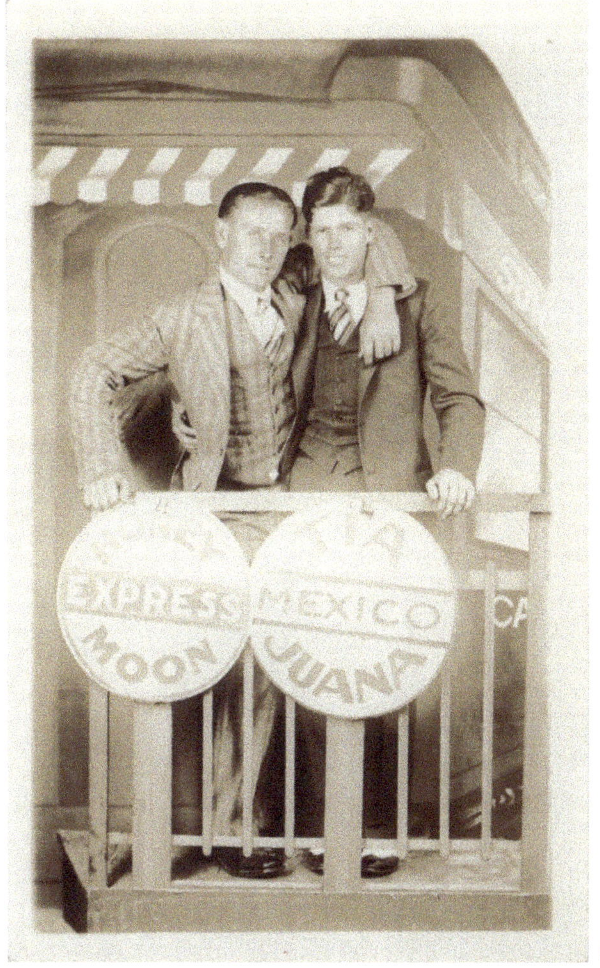

40

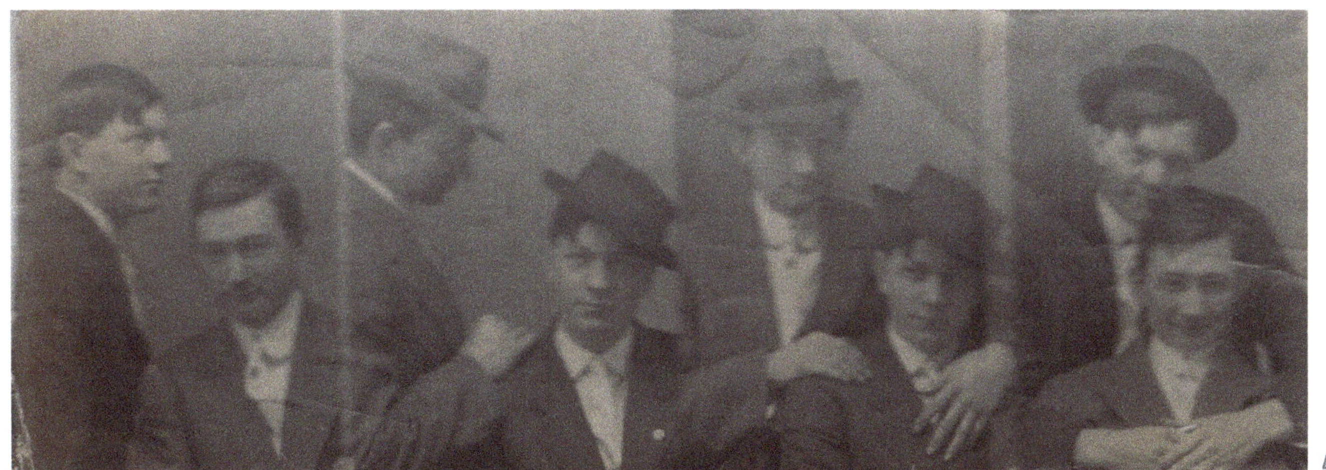

42

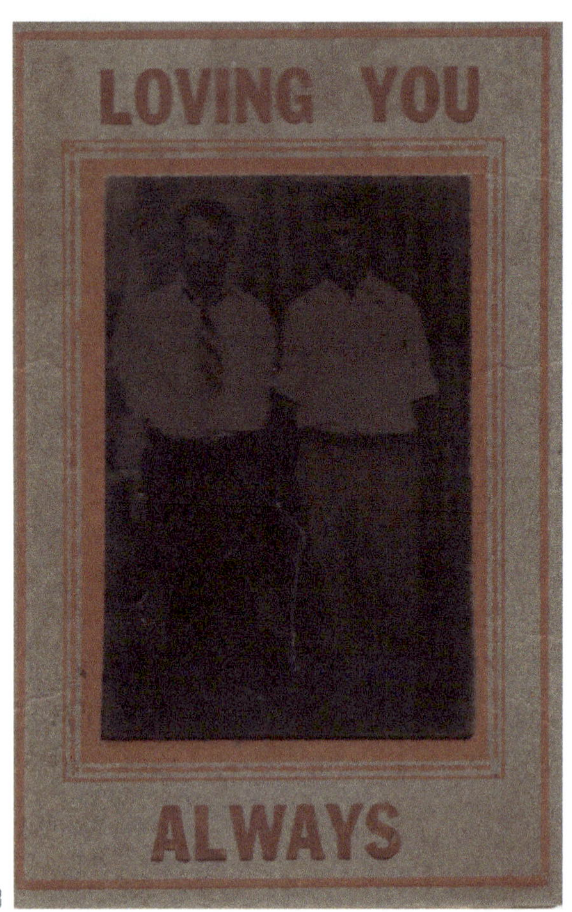

43

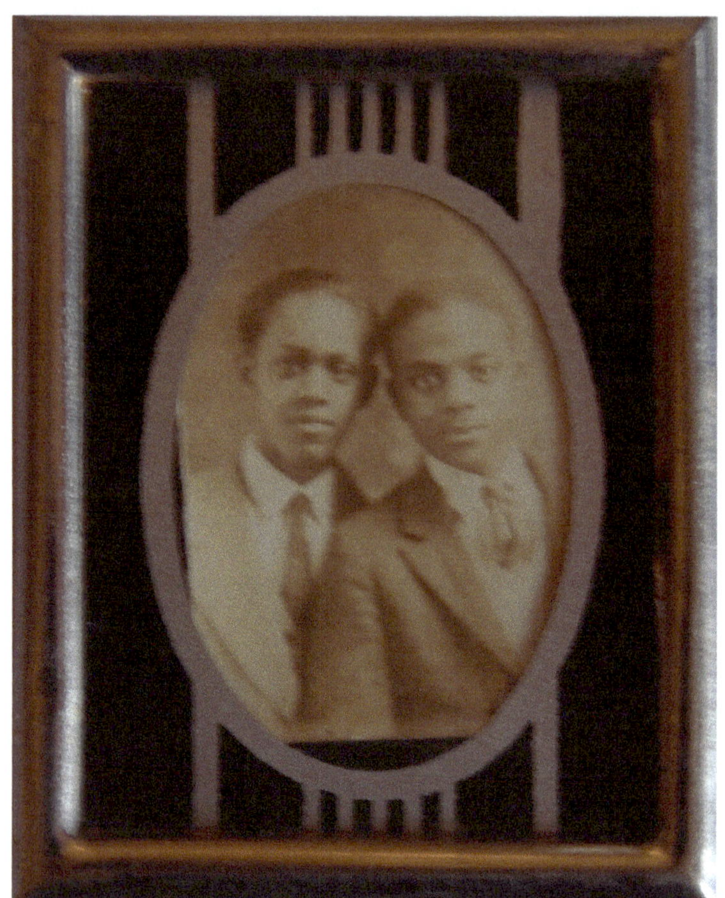

44

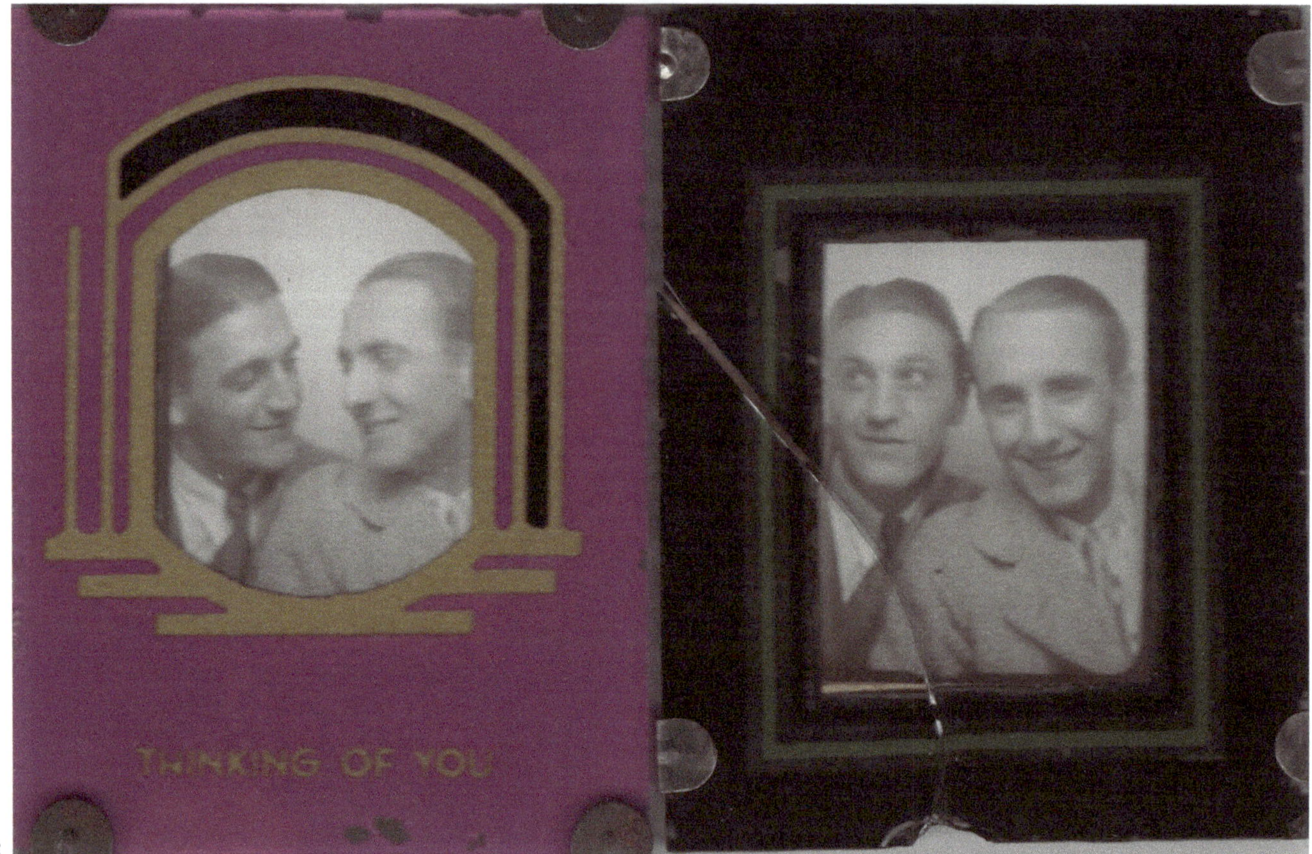

45

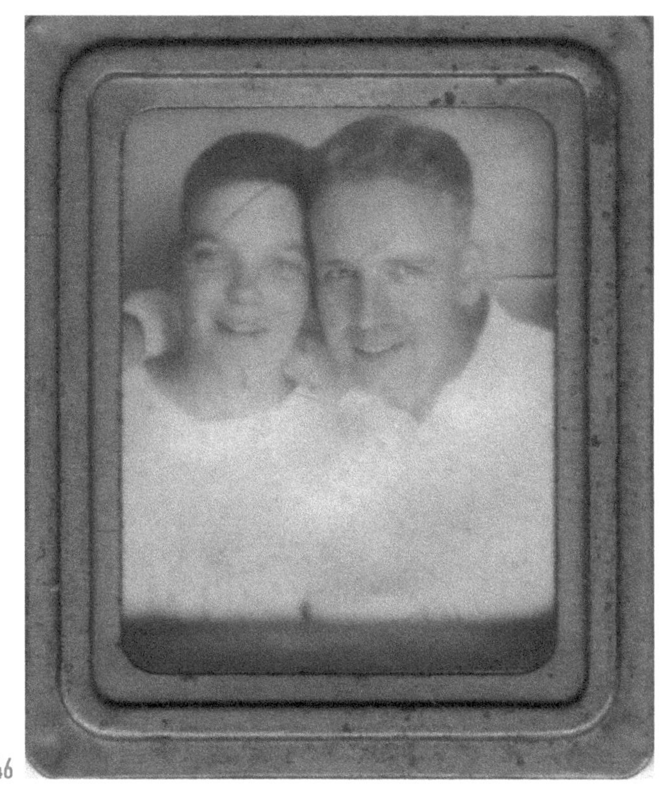
46

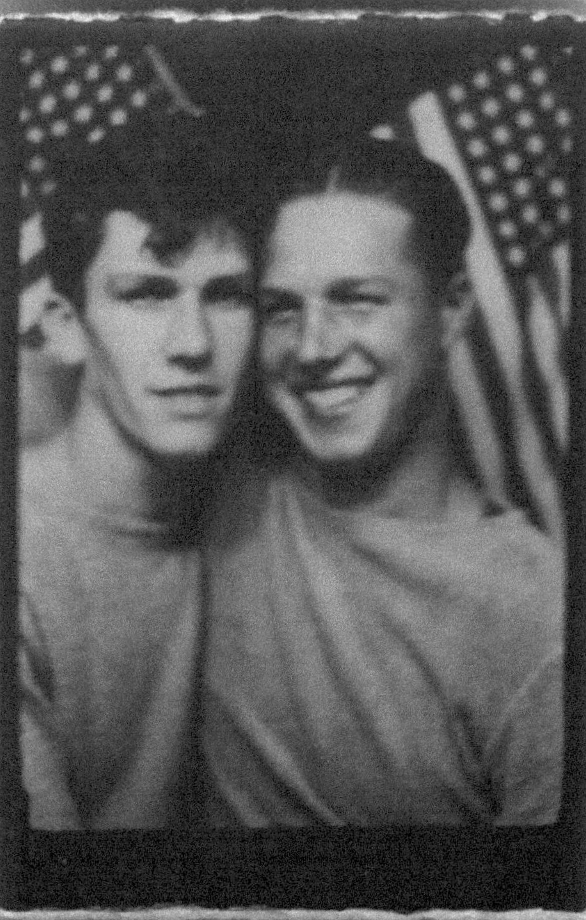

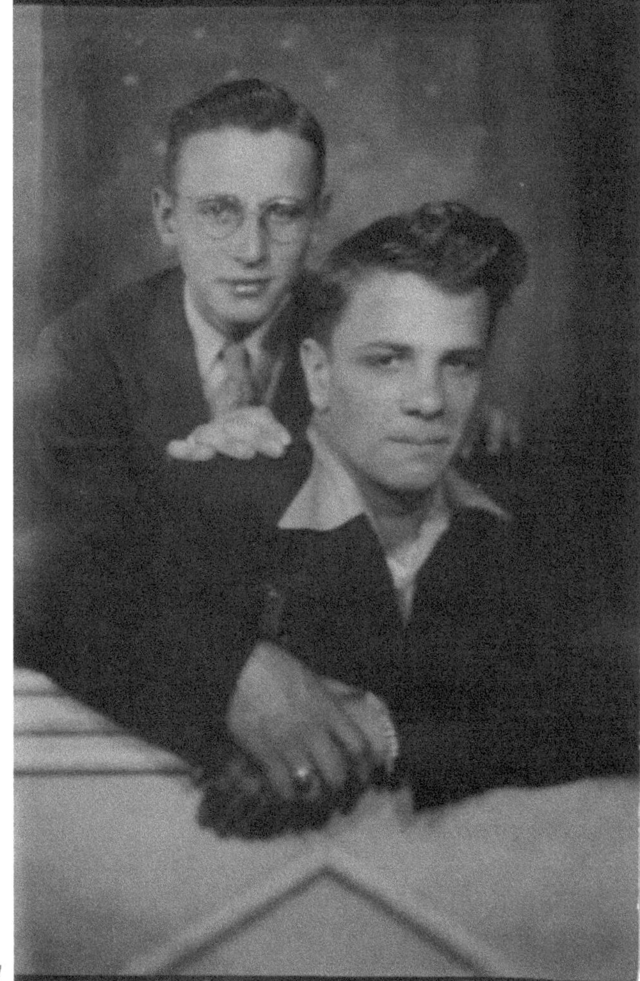
47

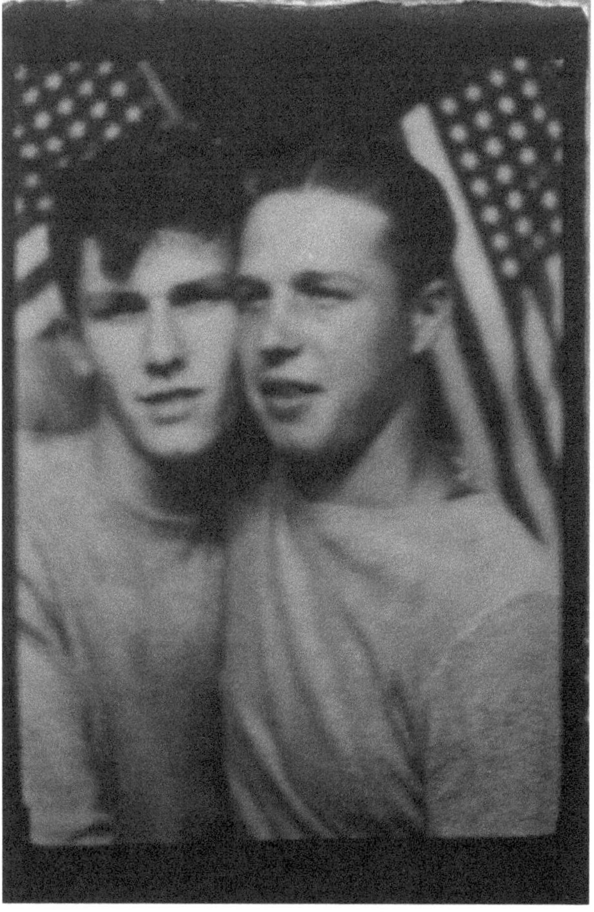
48

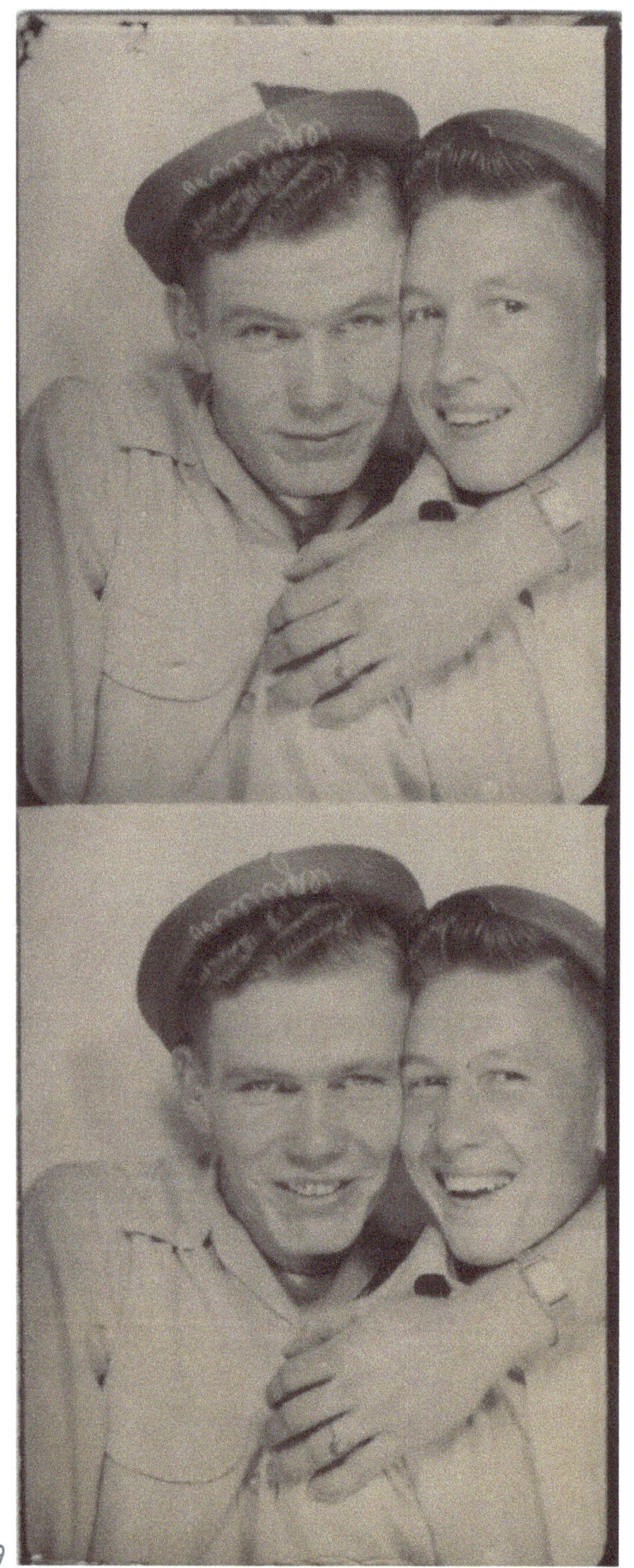

49

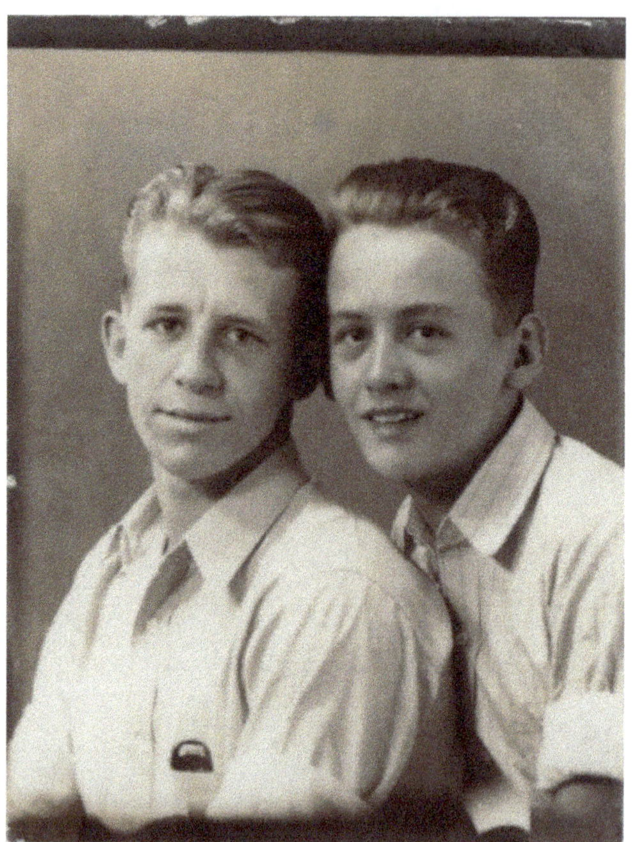

50

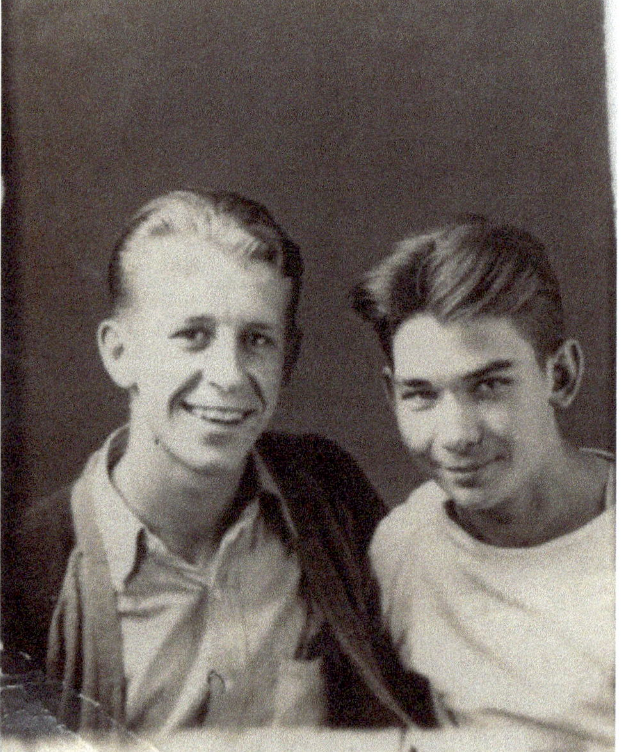

51

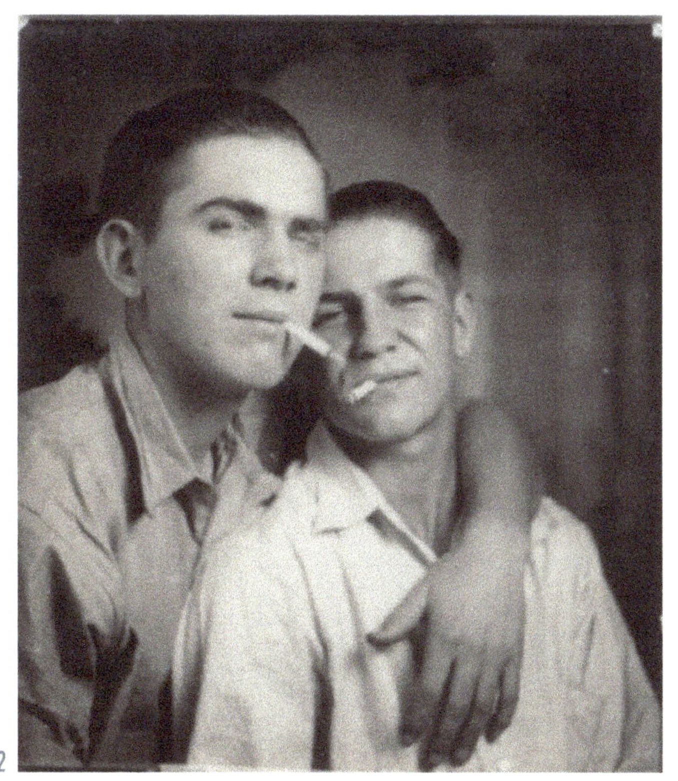

52

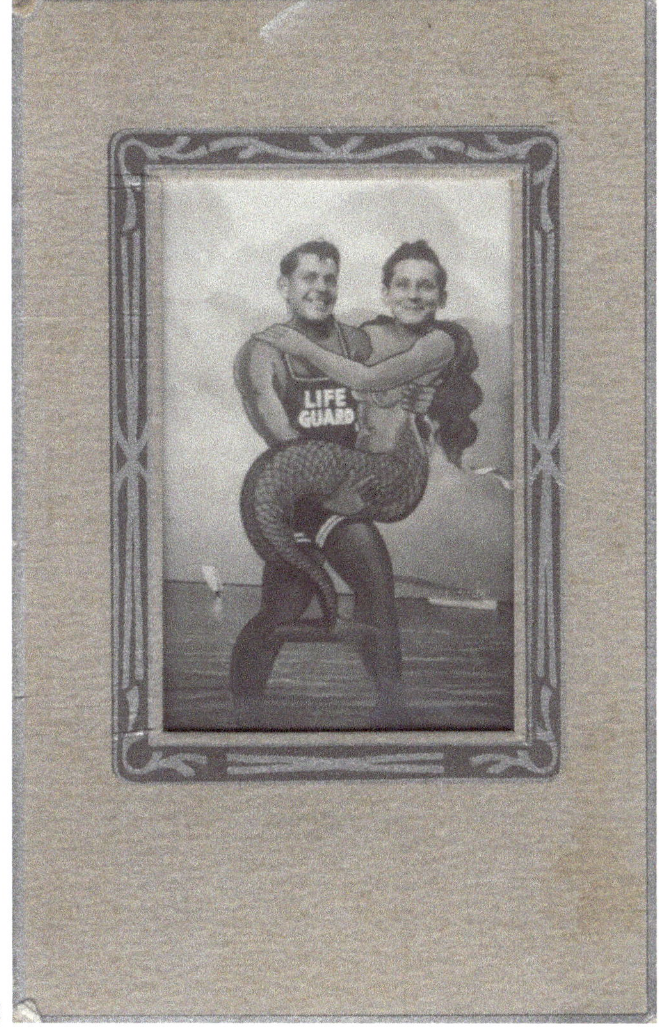

53

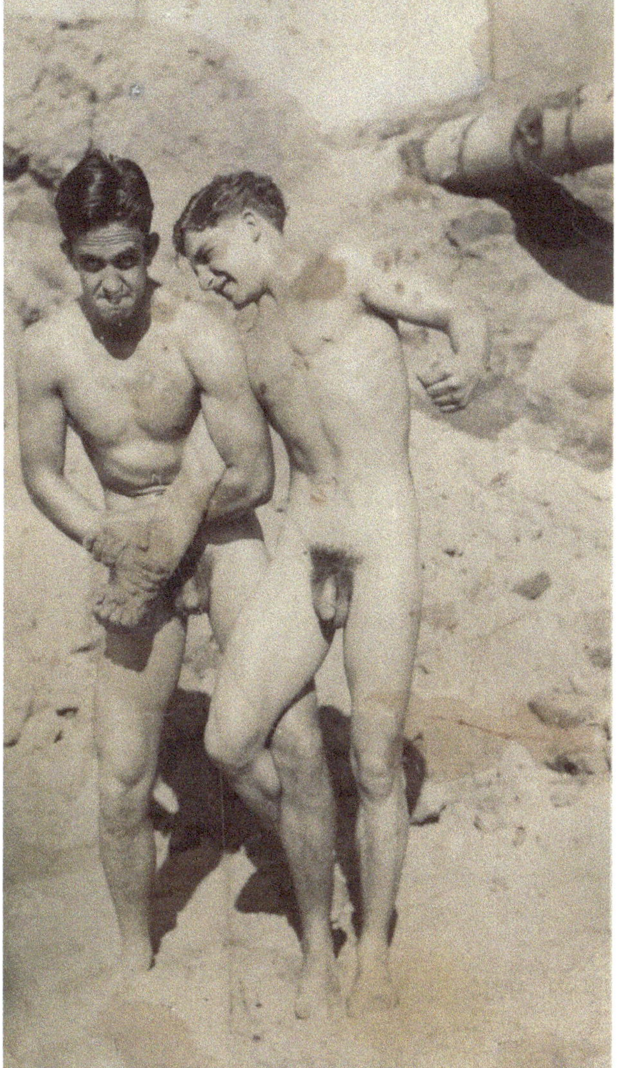

54

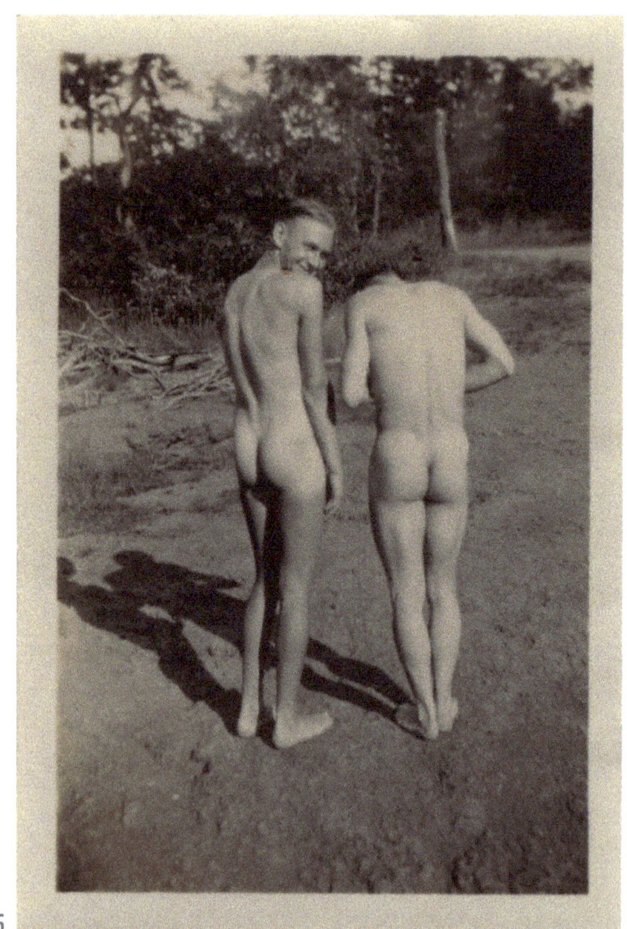

55

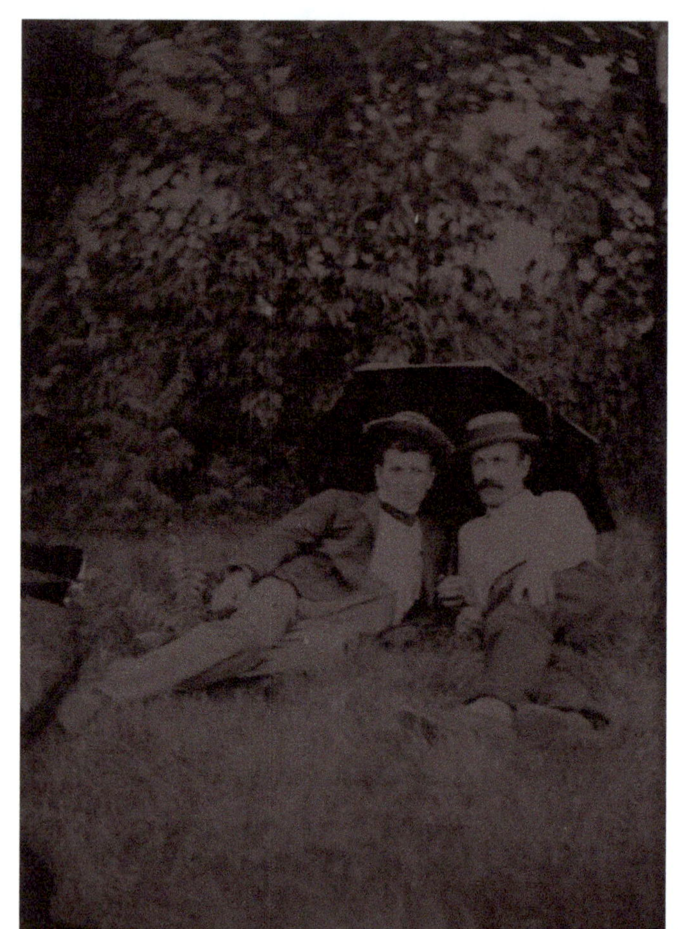

57

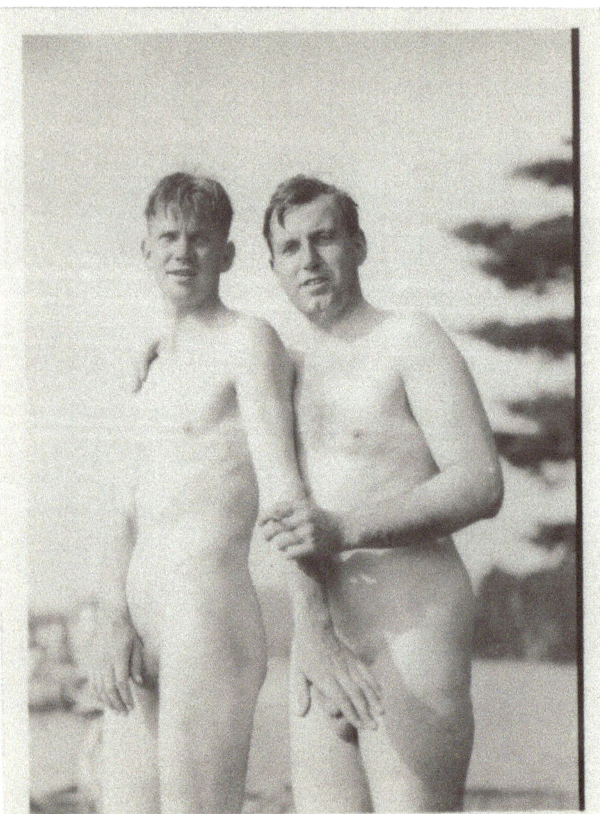

56

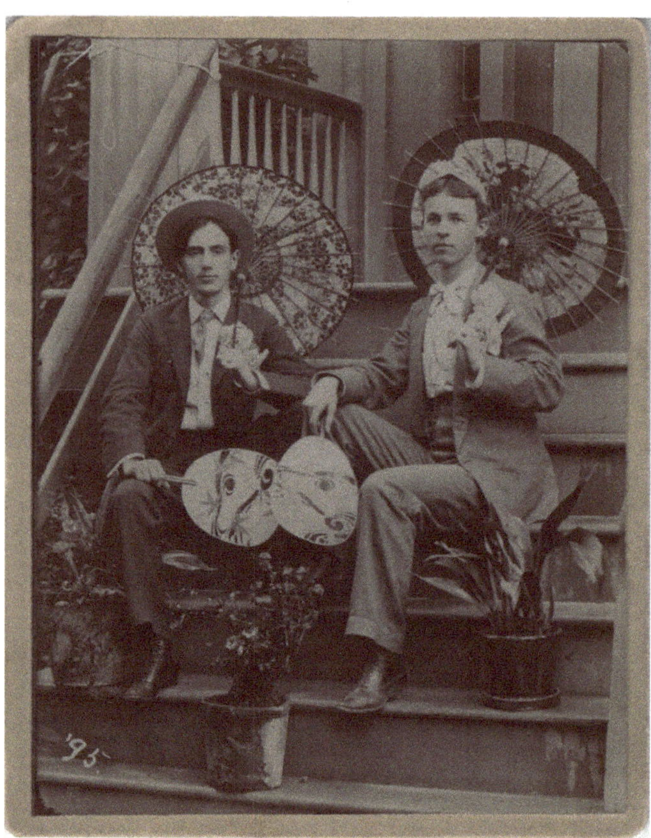

58

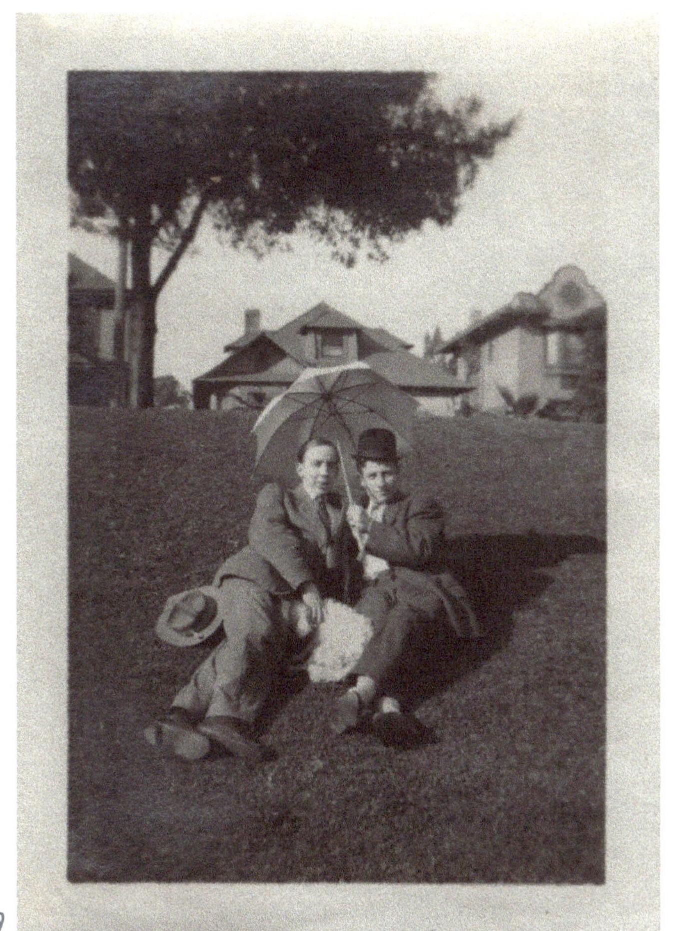
59

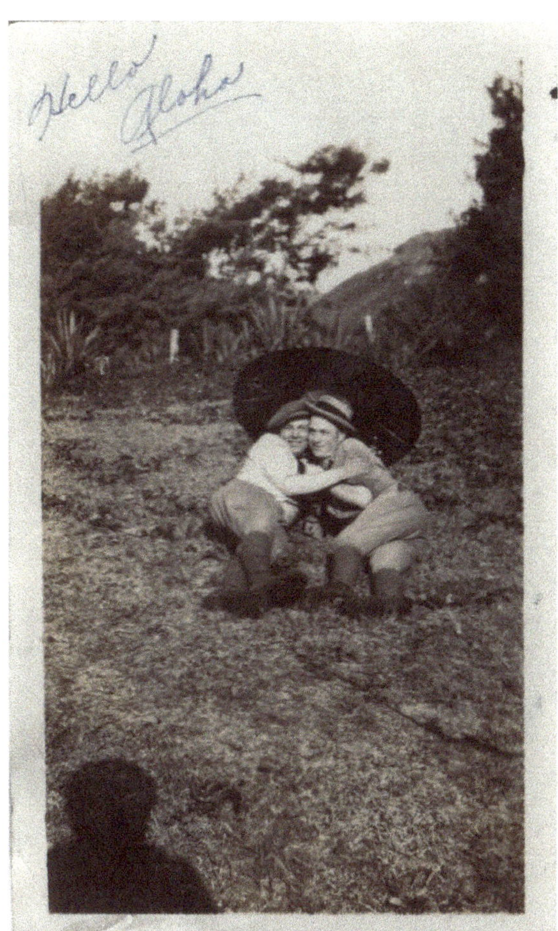

60

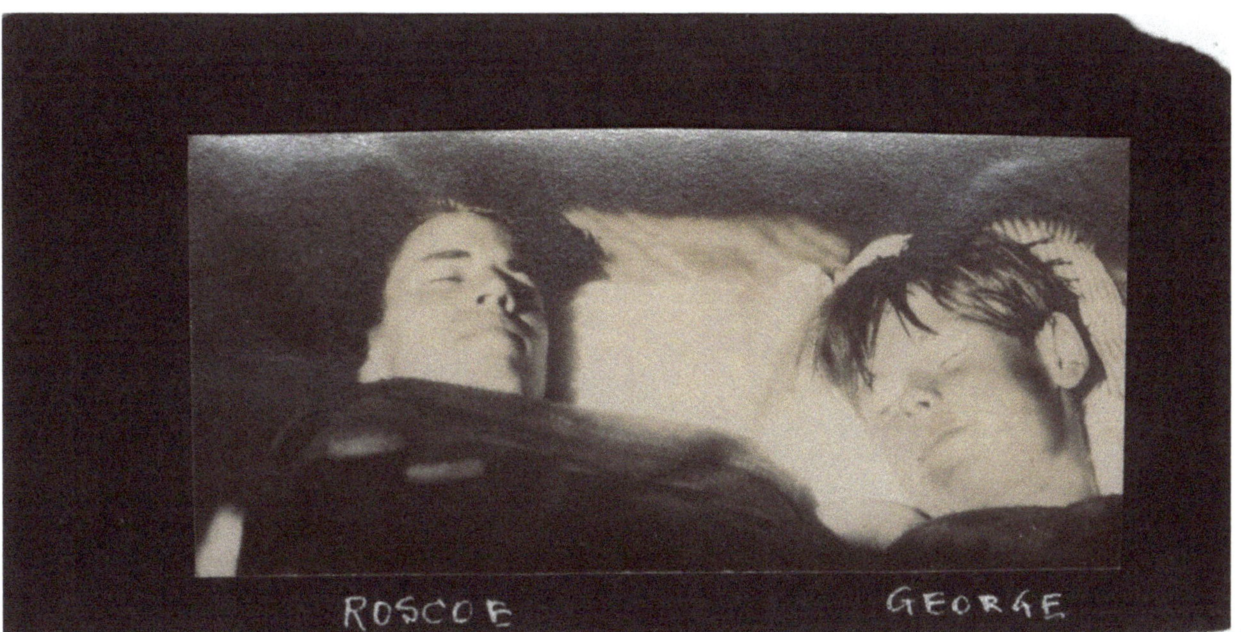

61

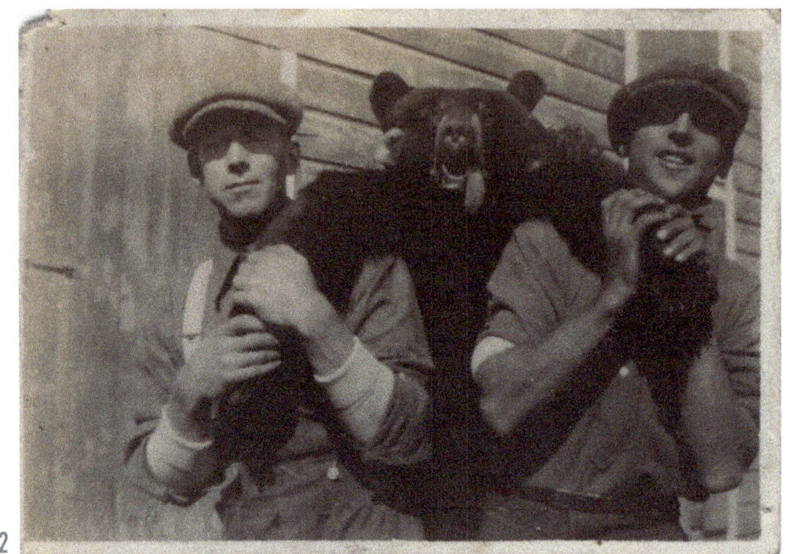
62

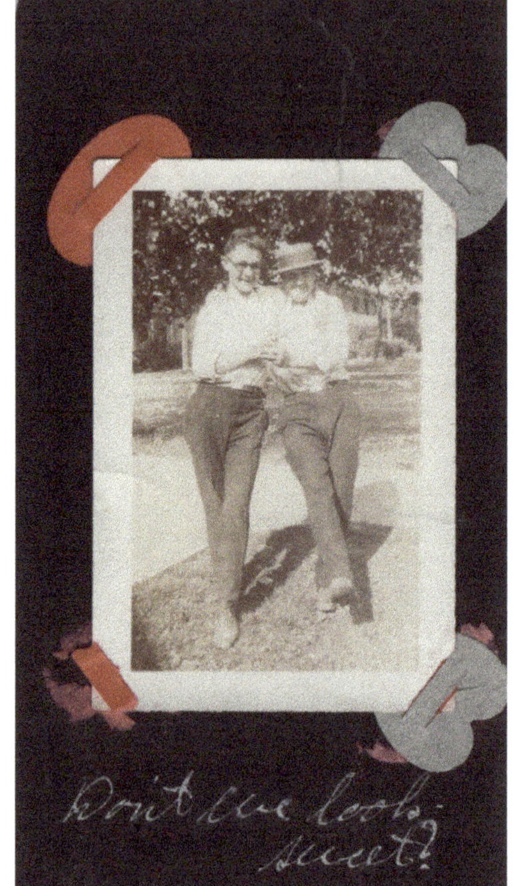

65

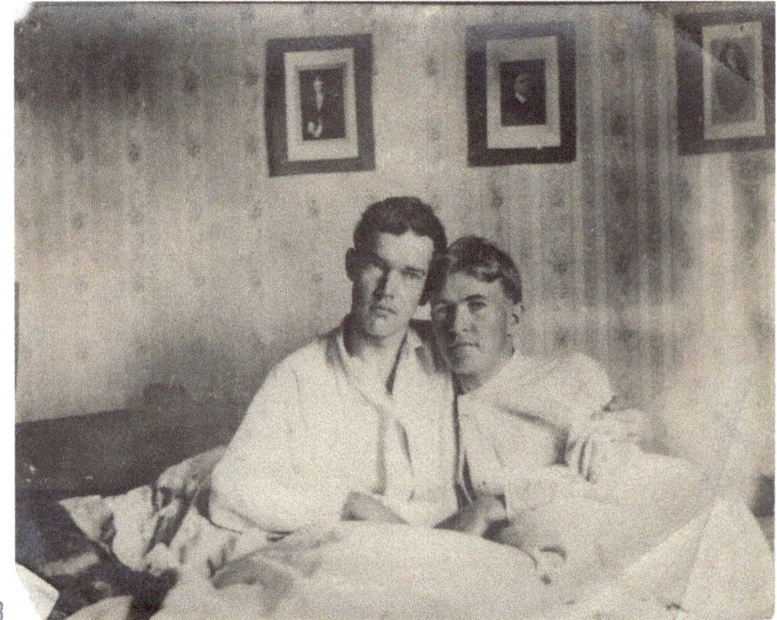
63

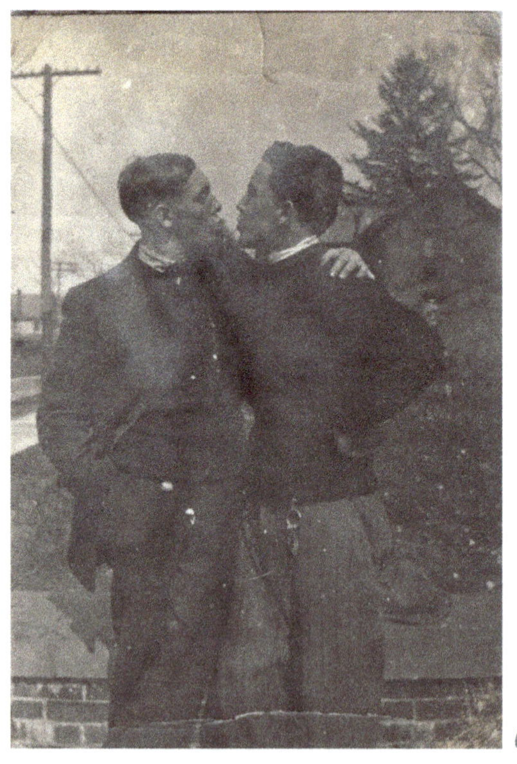
66

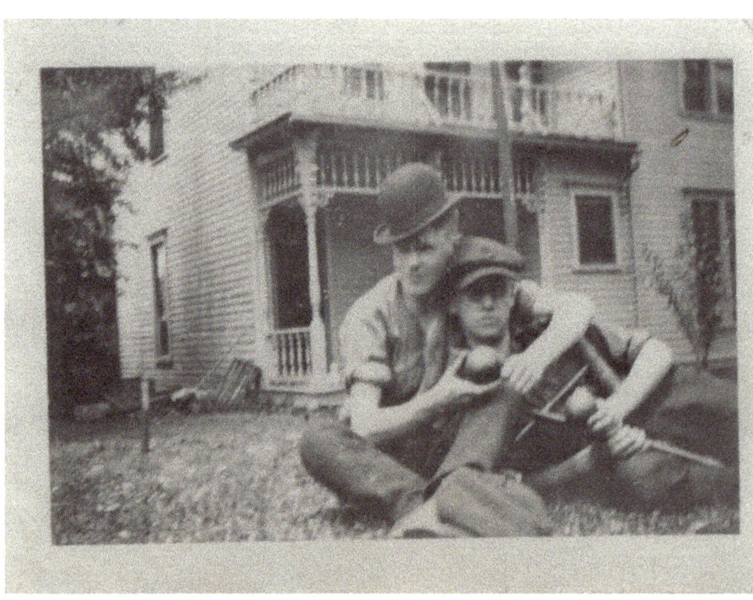
64

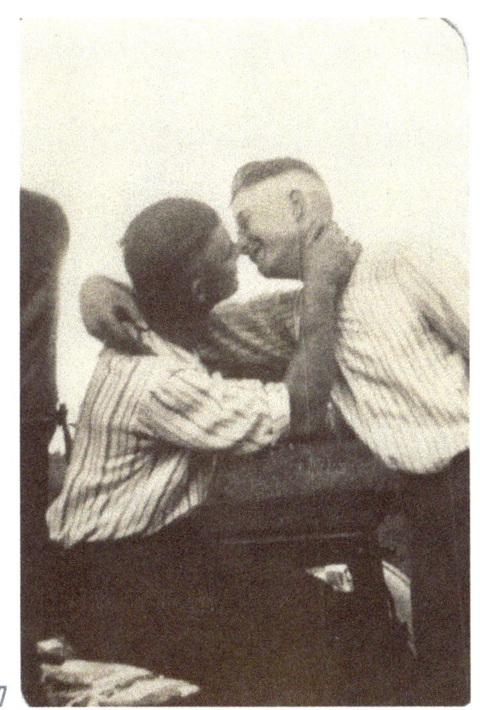
67

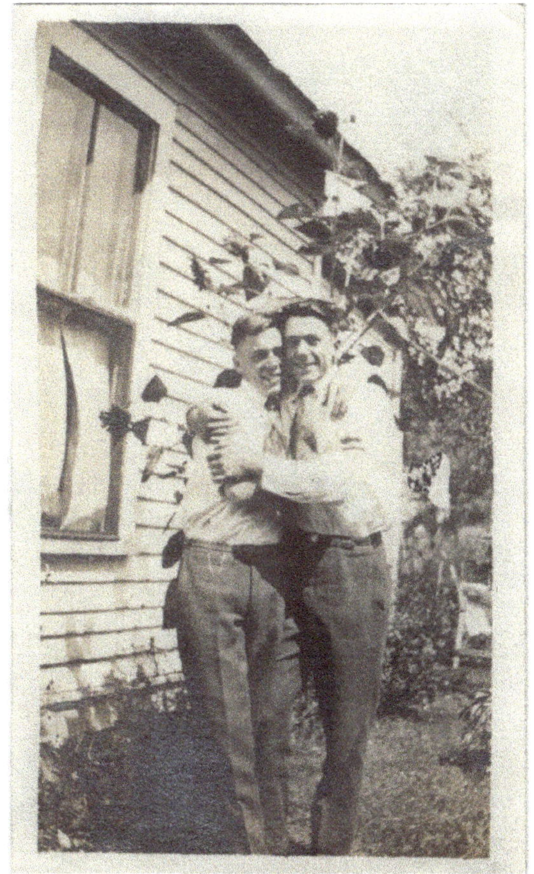
68

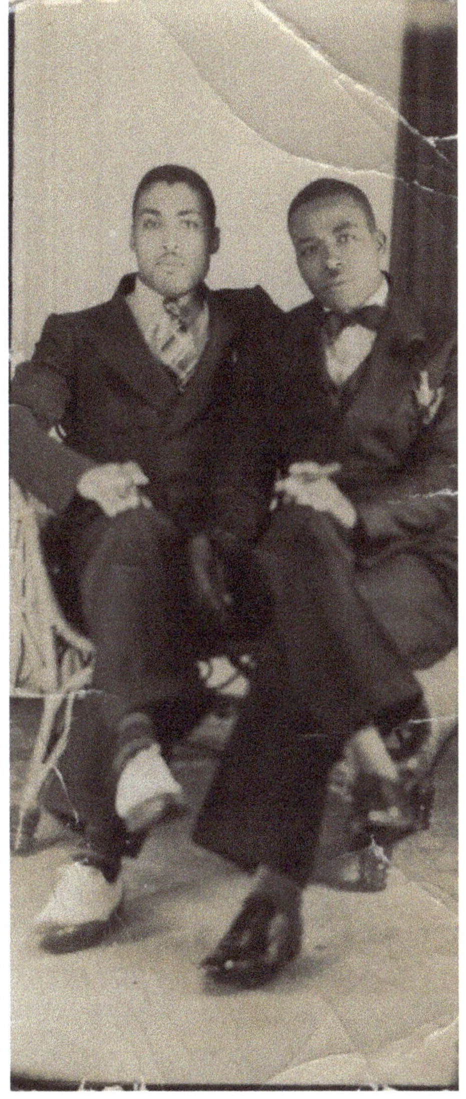
69

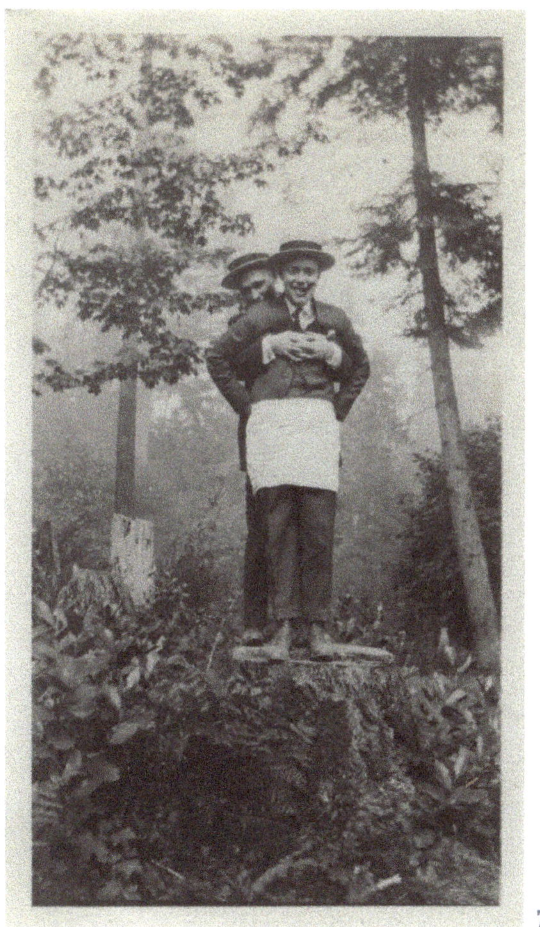
70

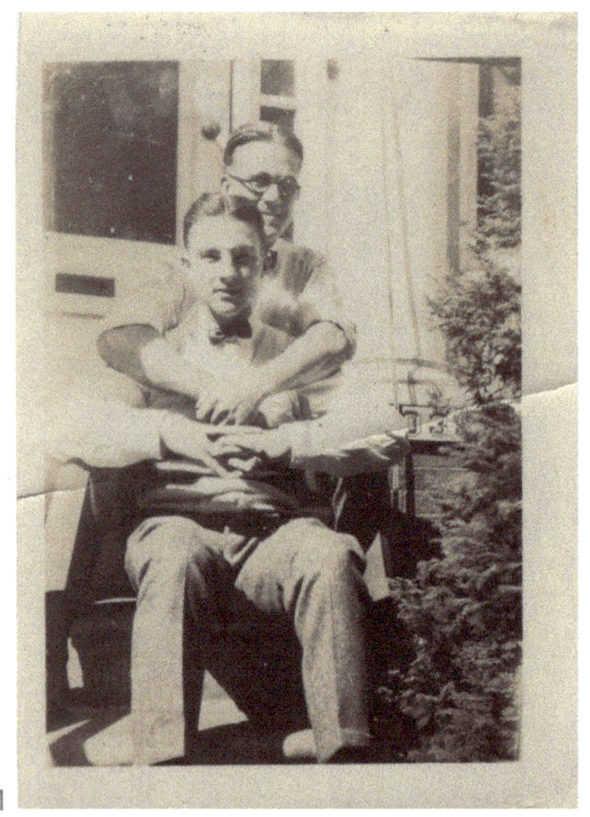

71

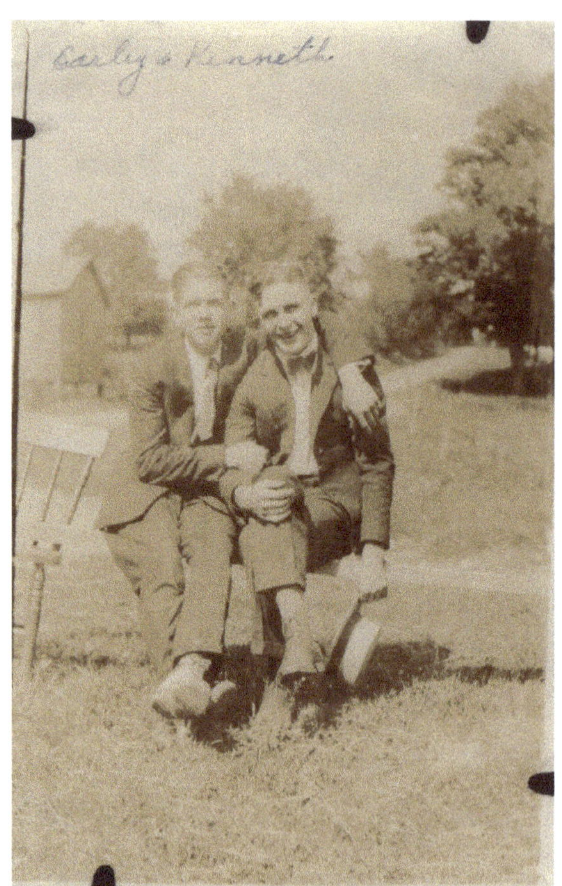

72

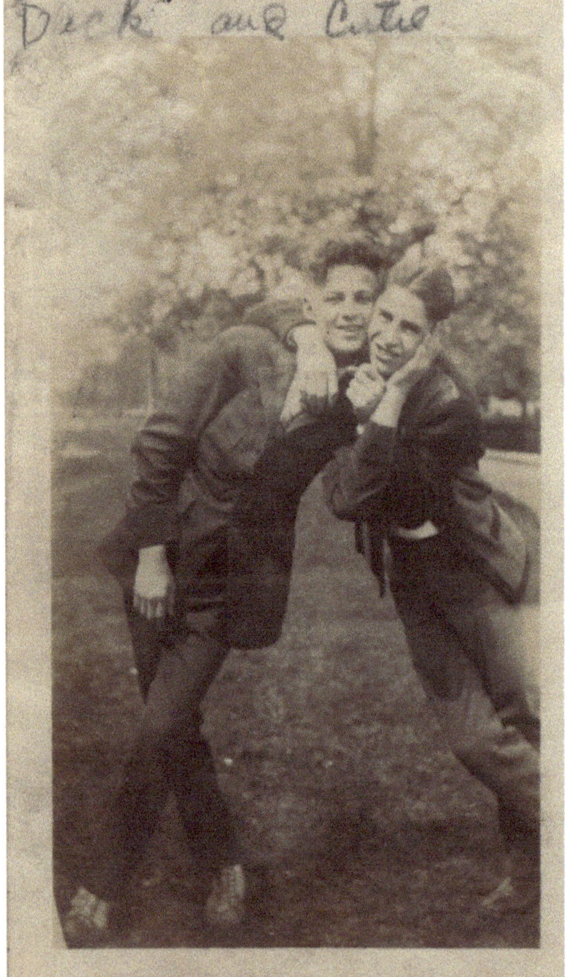

73

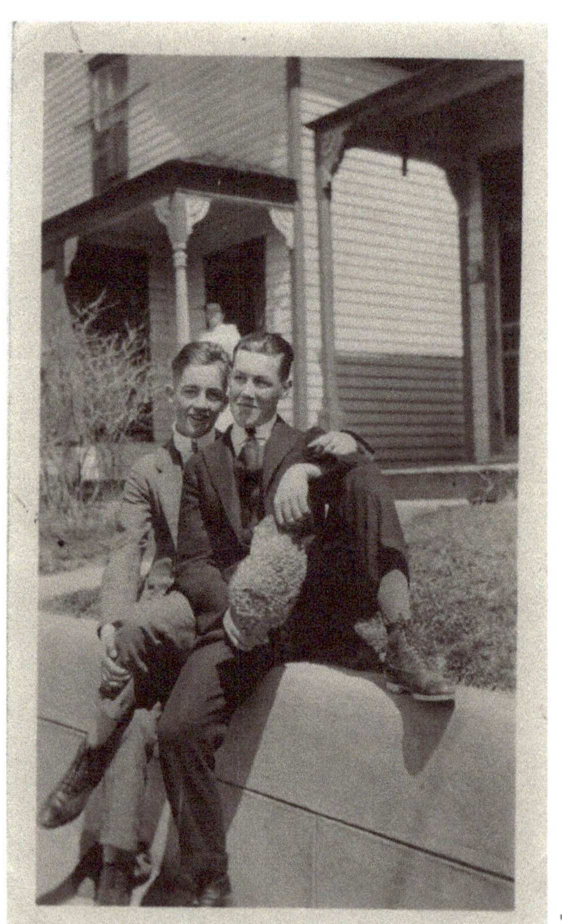

74

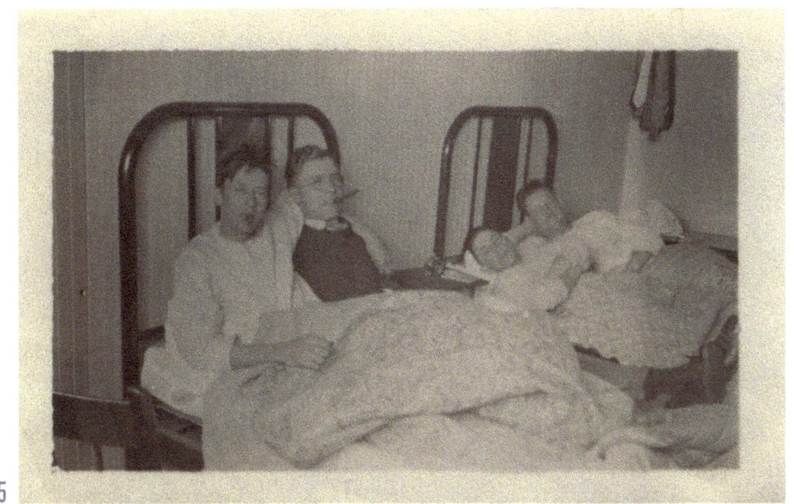

75

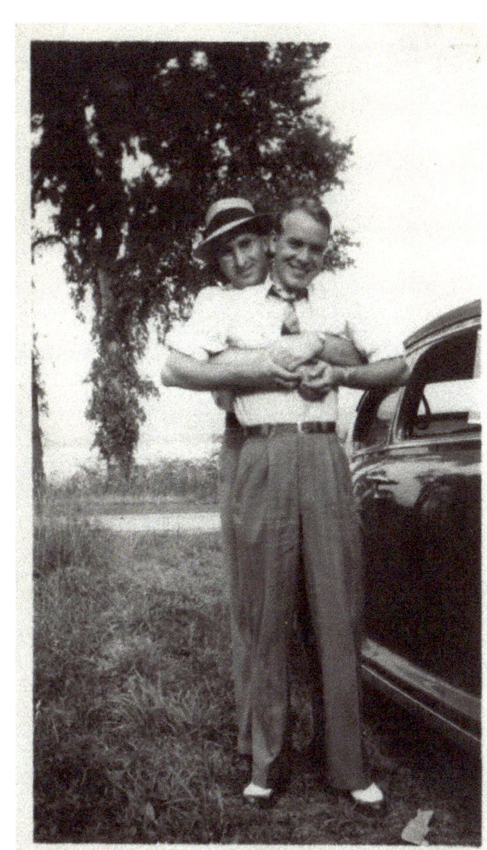

76

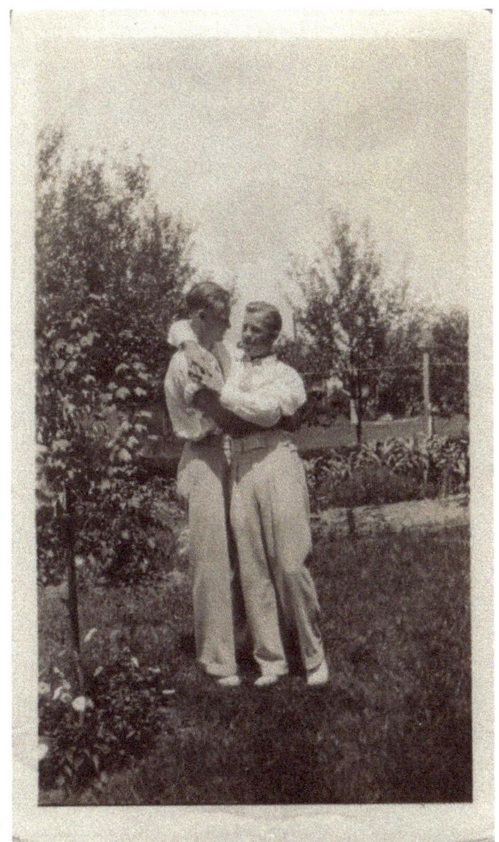

77

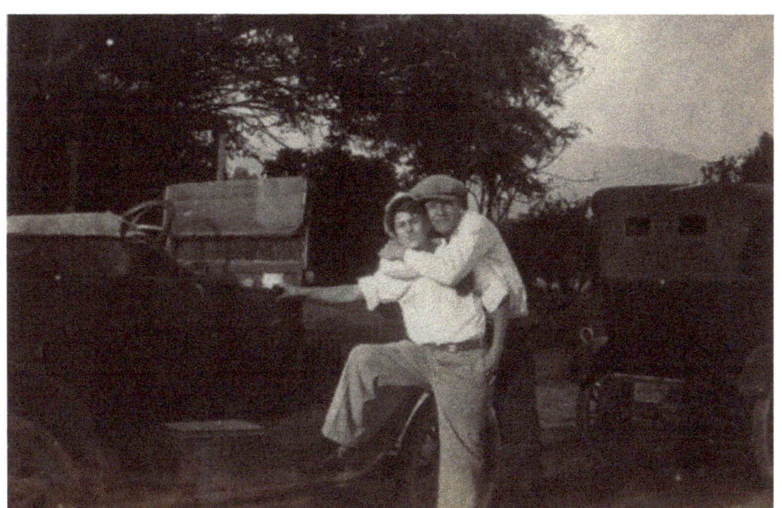

78

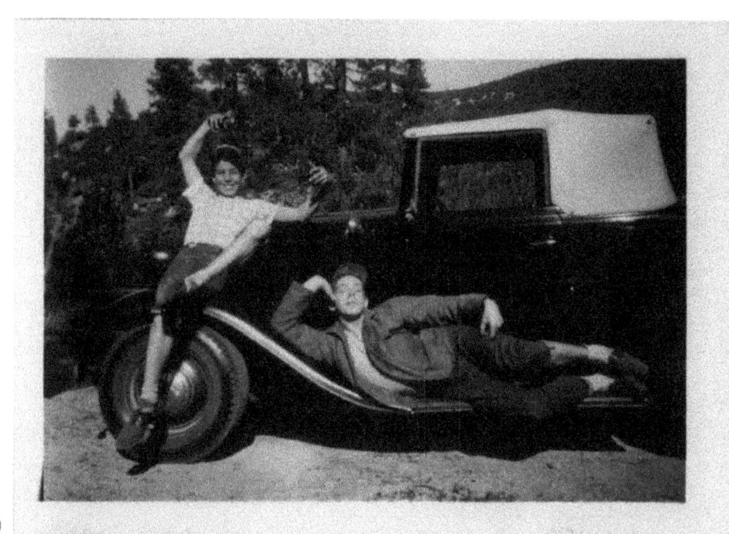

79

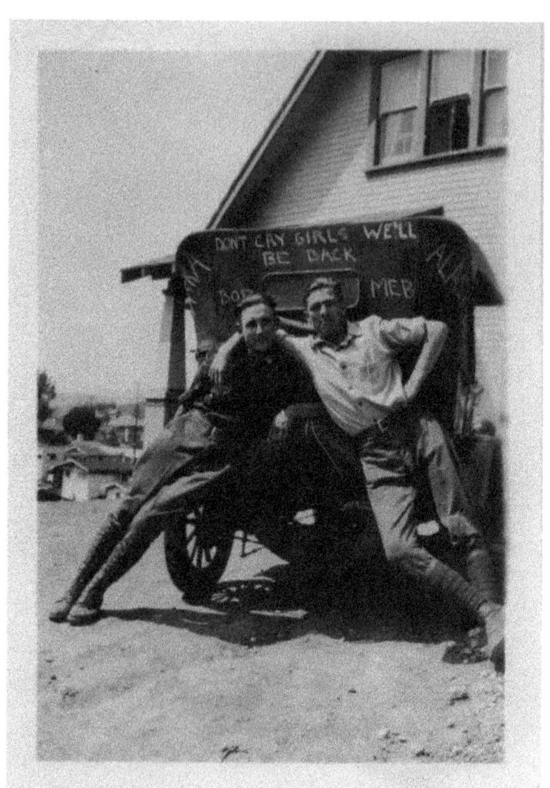

80

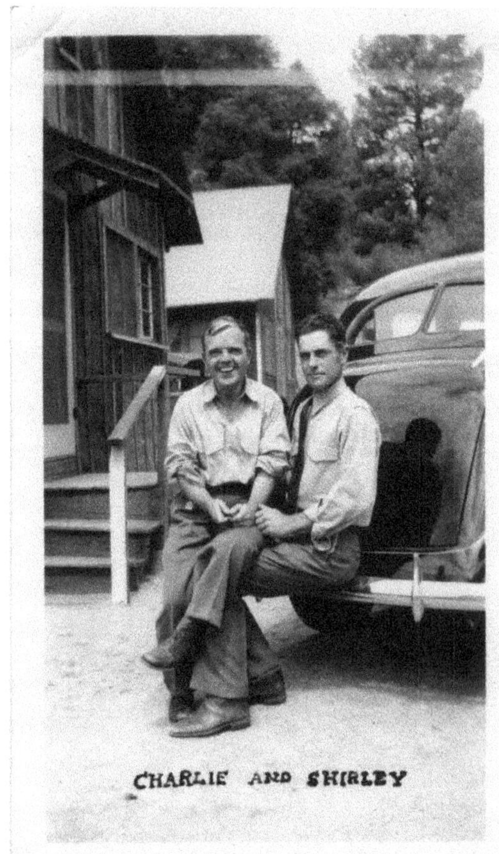

81

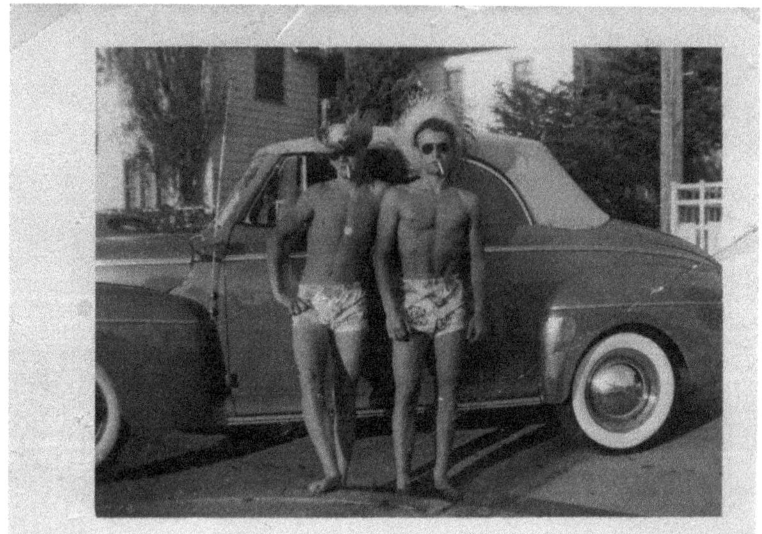

82

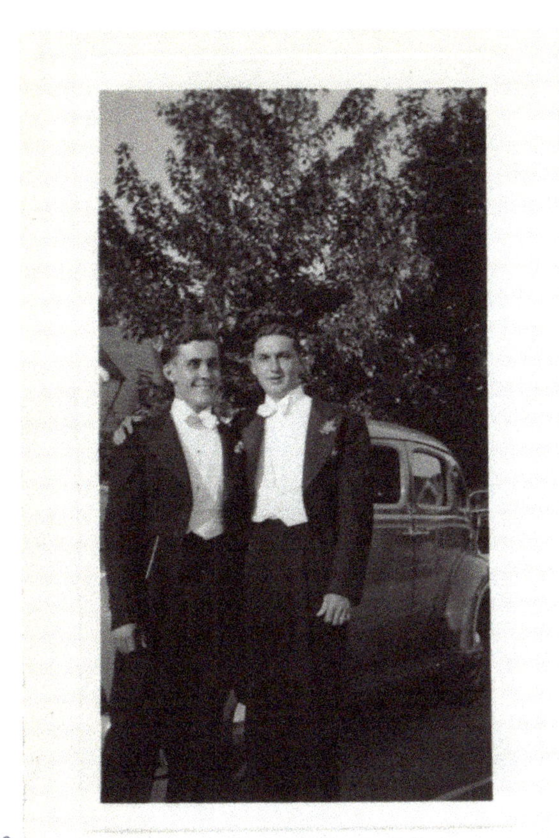
83

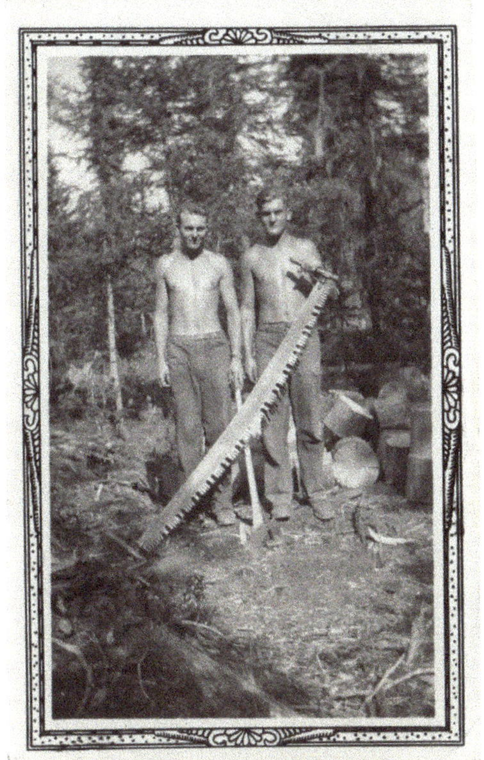
84

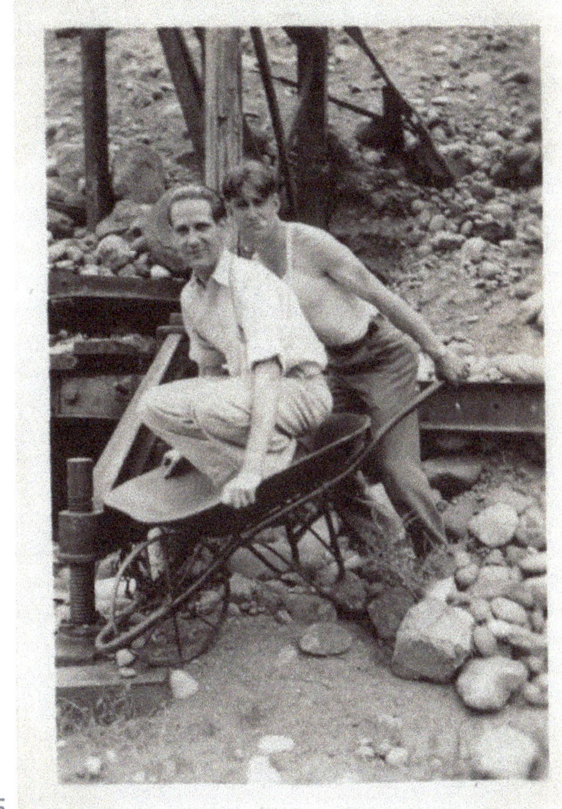
85

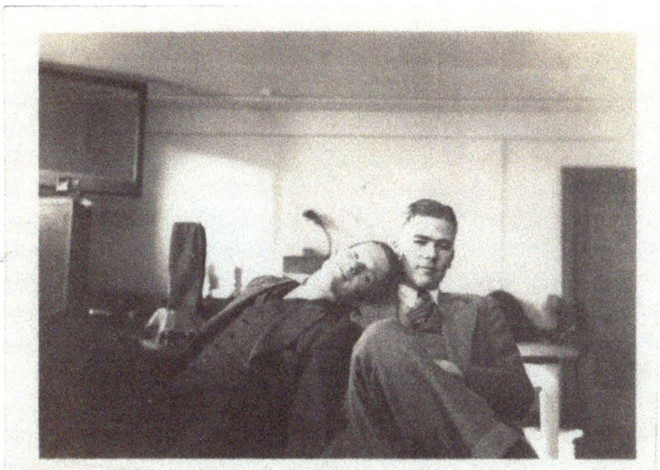
86

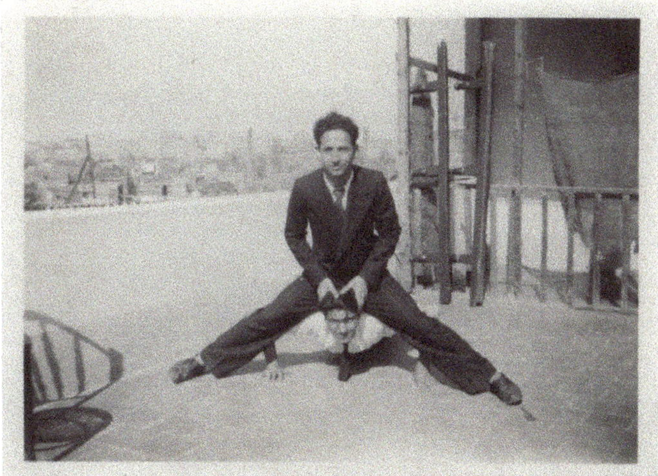
87

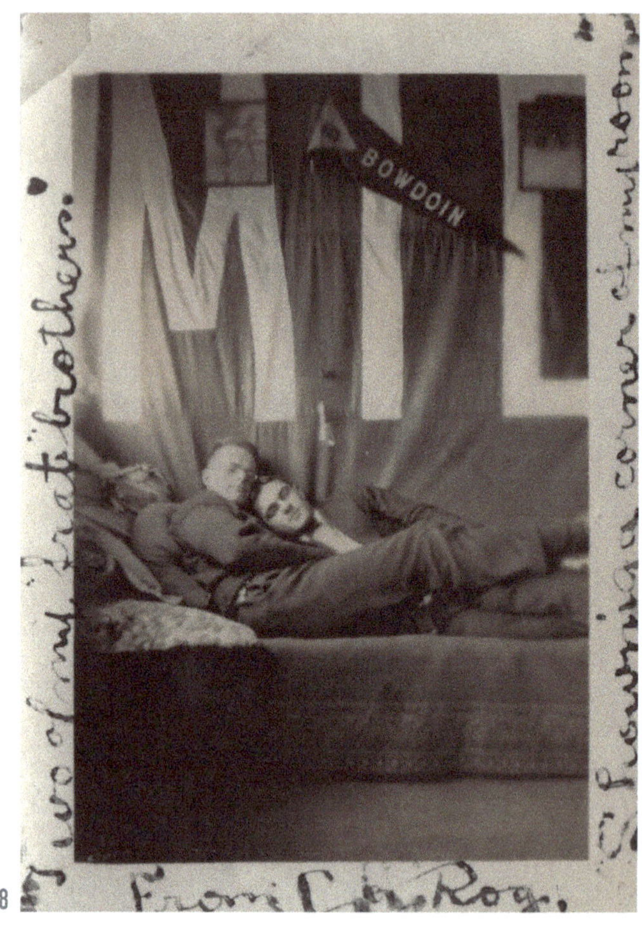
BOWDOIN
Two of my frat brothers.
Showing corner of my room

88

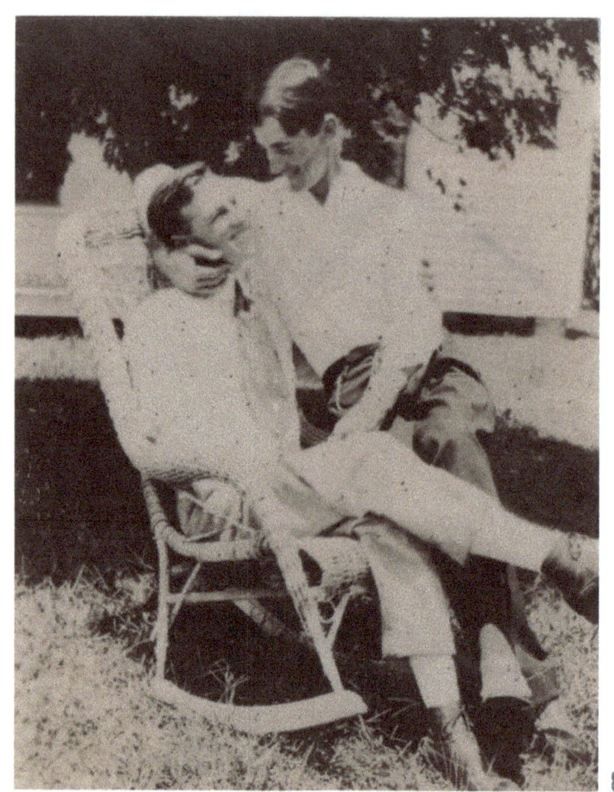

89

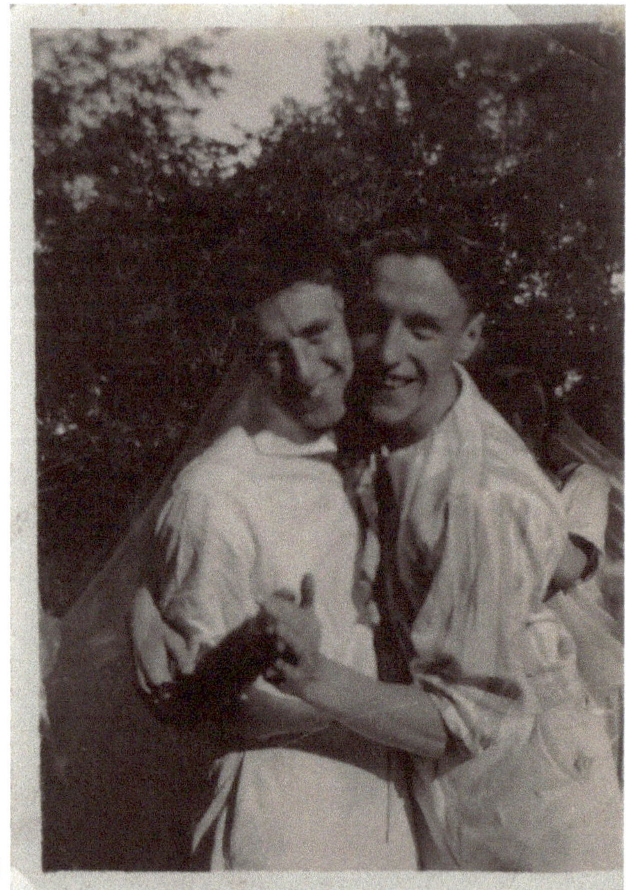

90

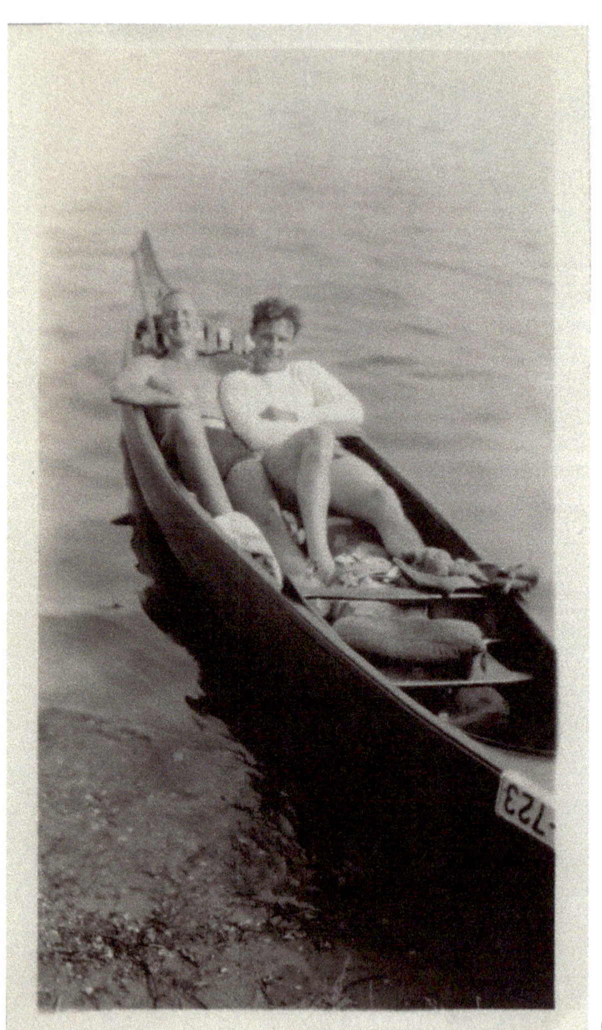
-723

91

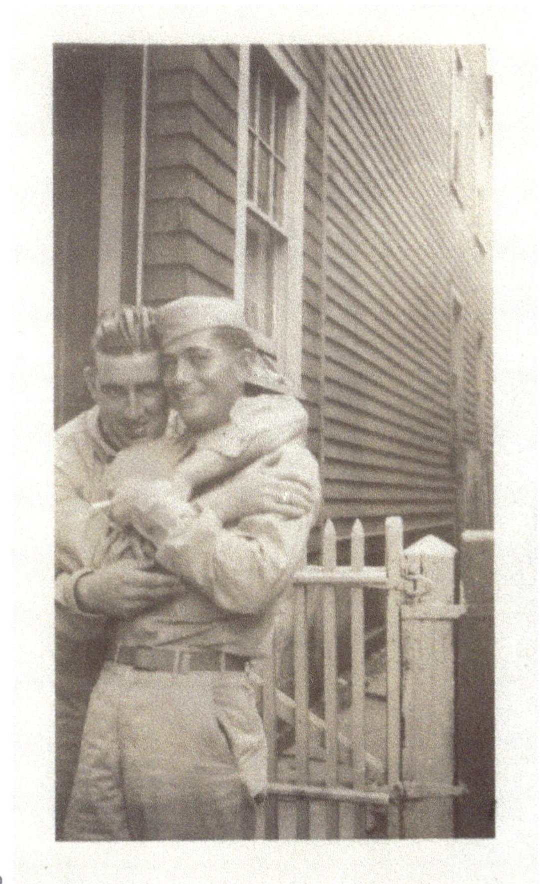

92

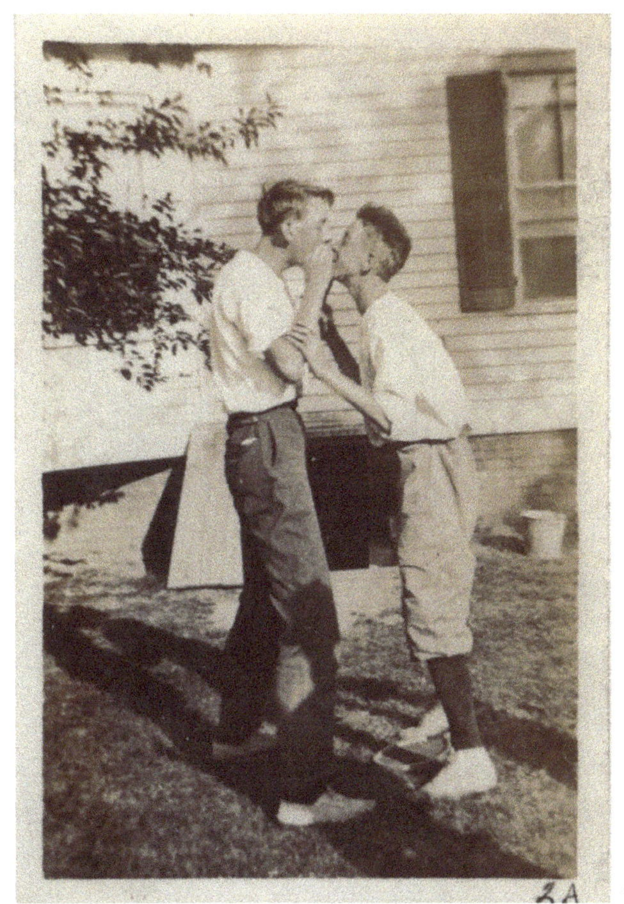

93

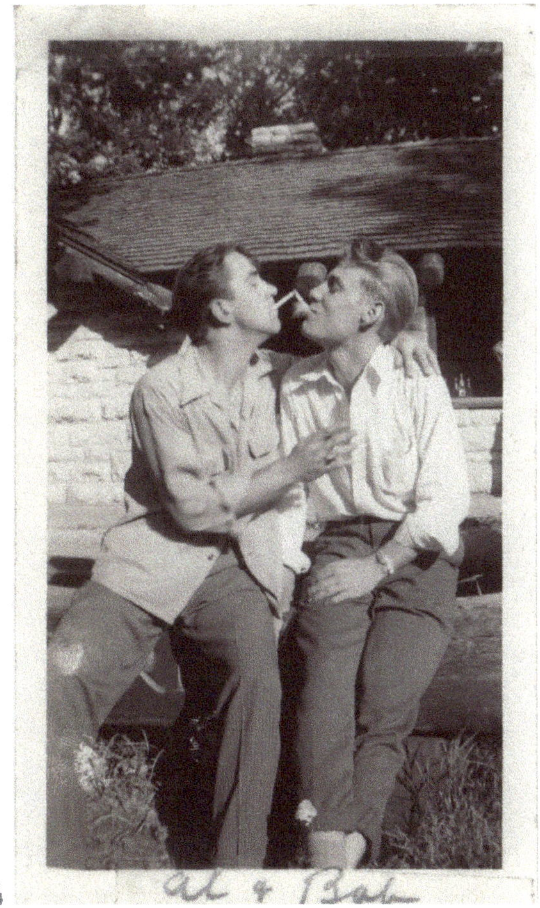

94

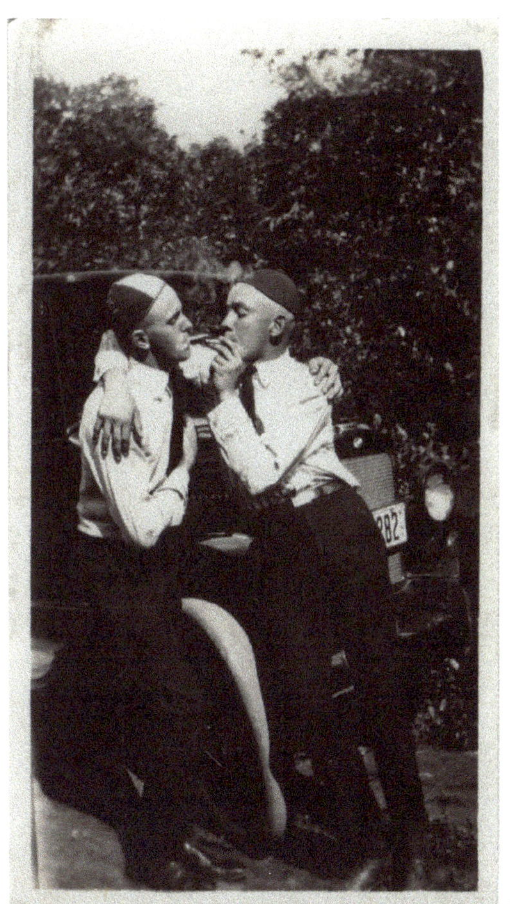

95

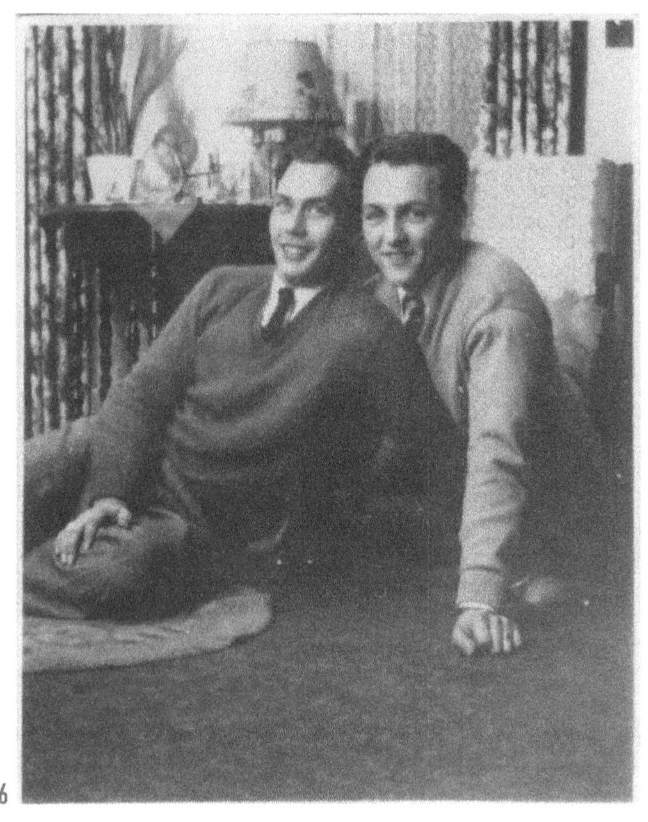

96

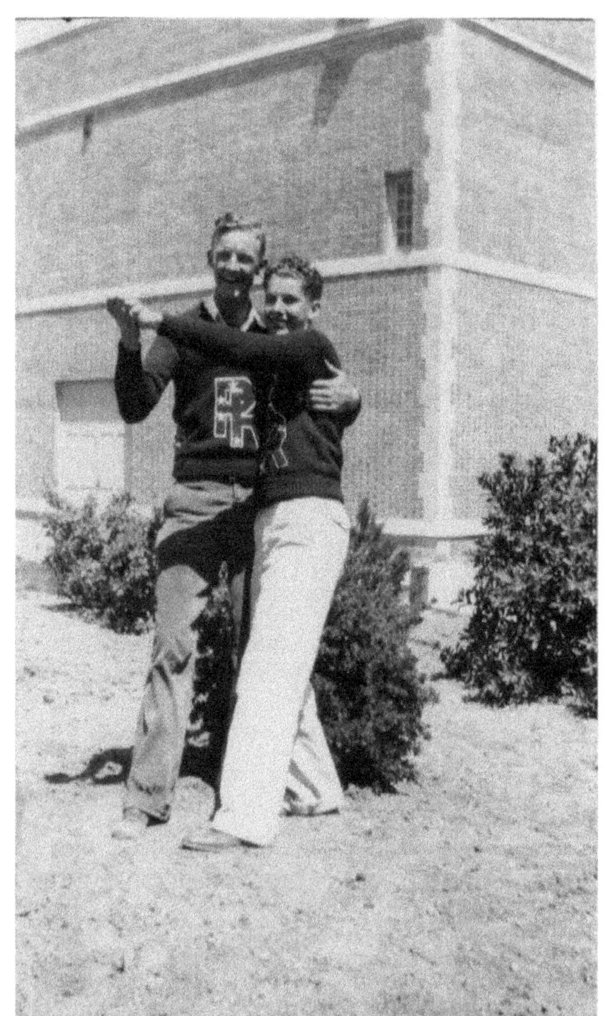

97

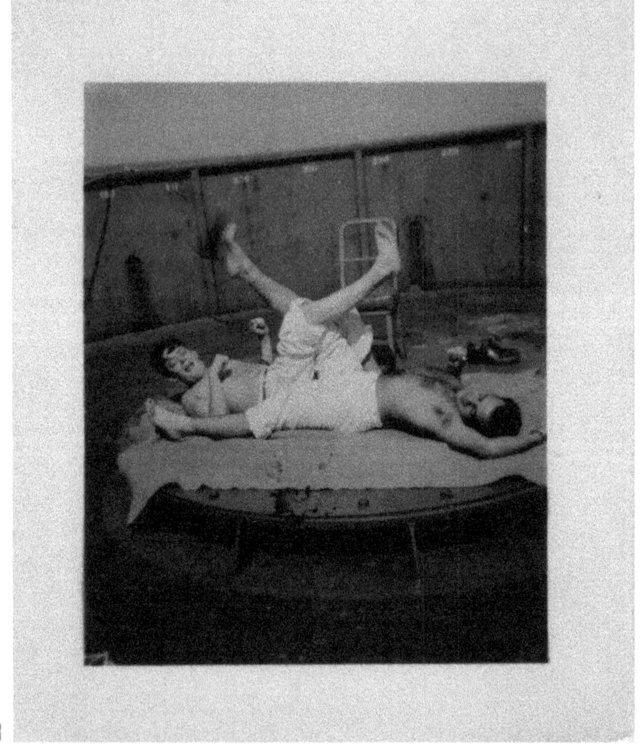

98

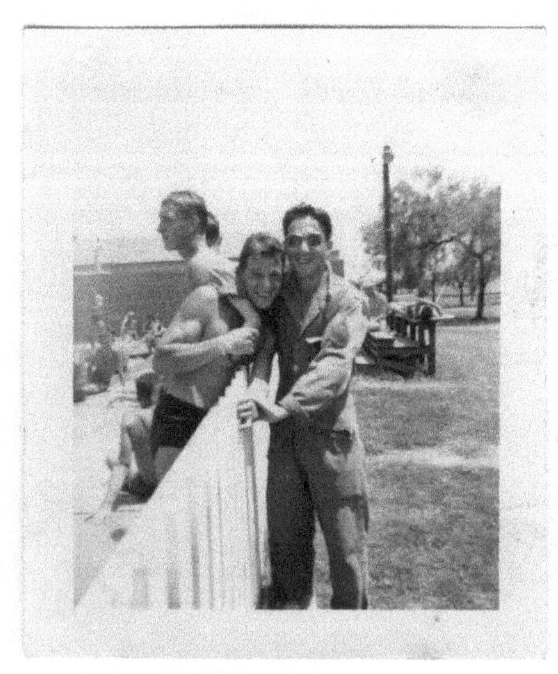

99

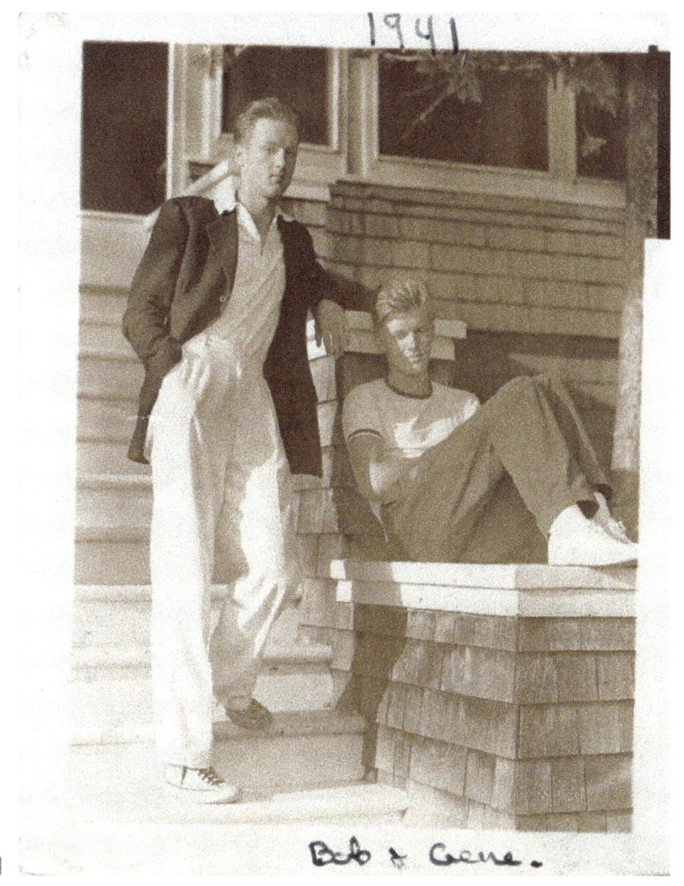

100

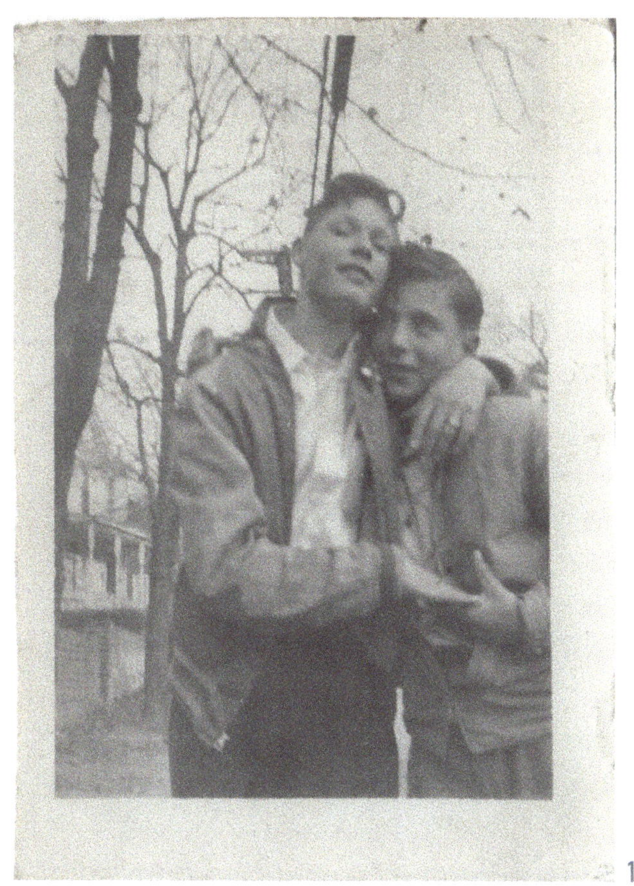

101

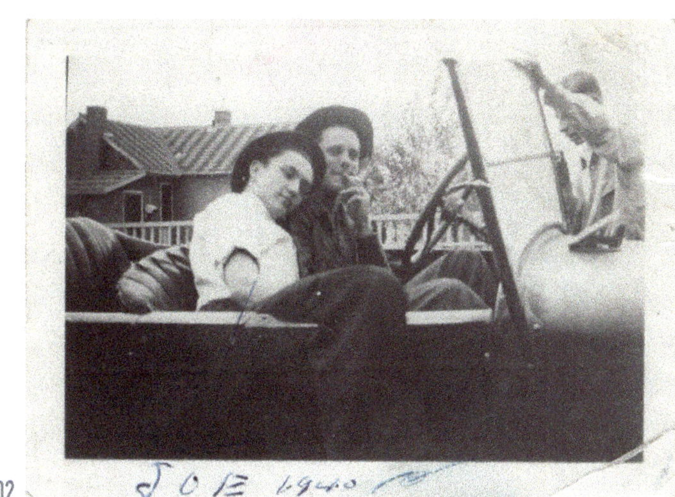

102

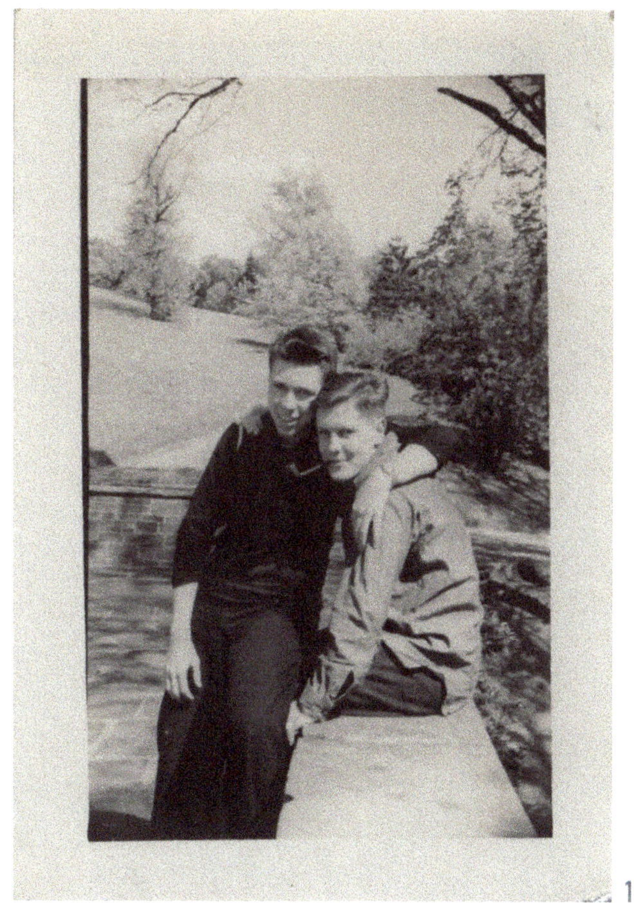

103

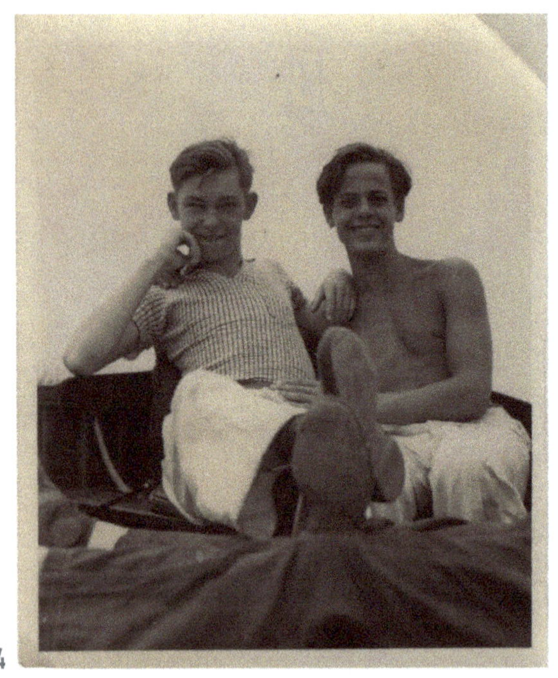

104

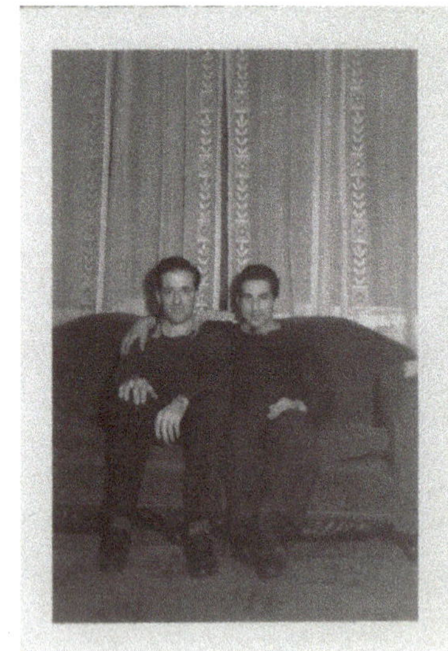

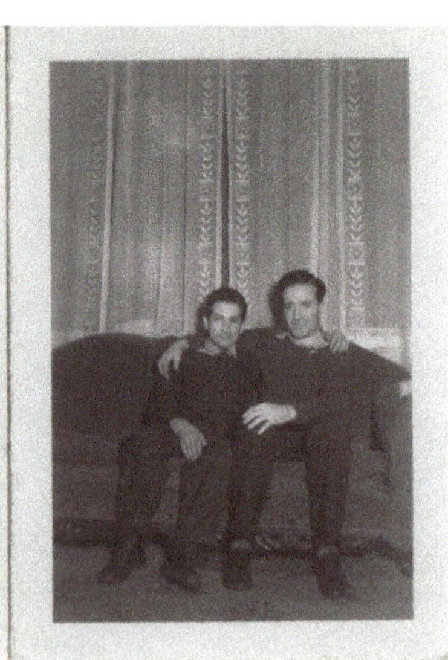

106

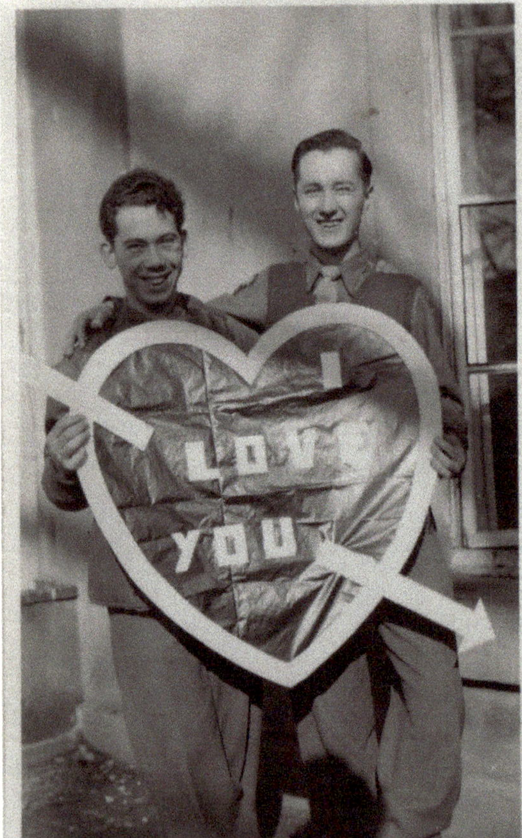

105

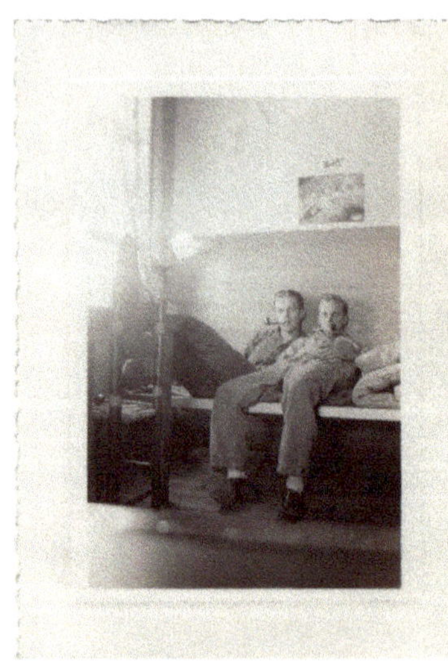

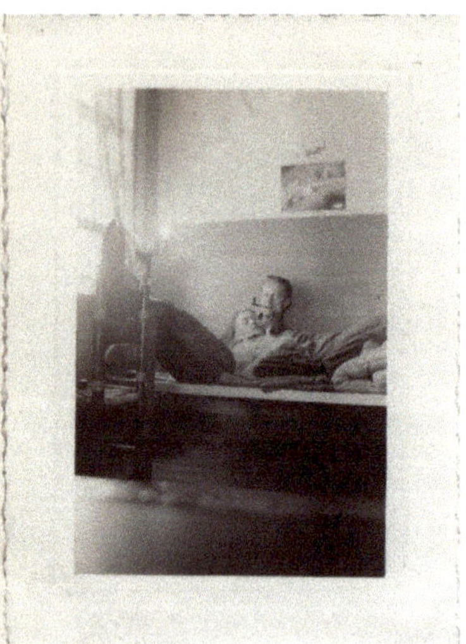

107

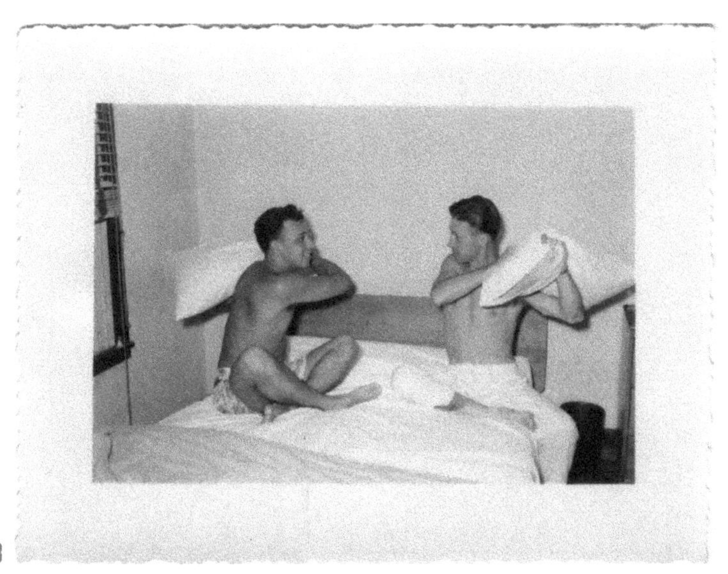

108

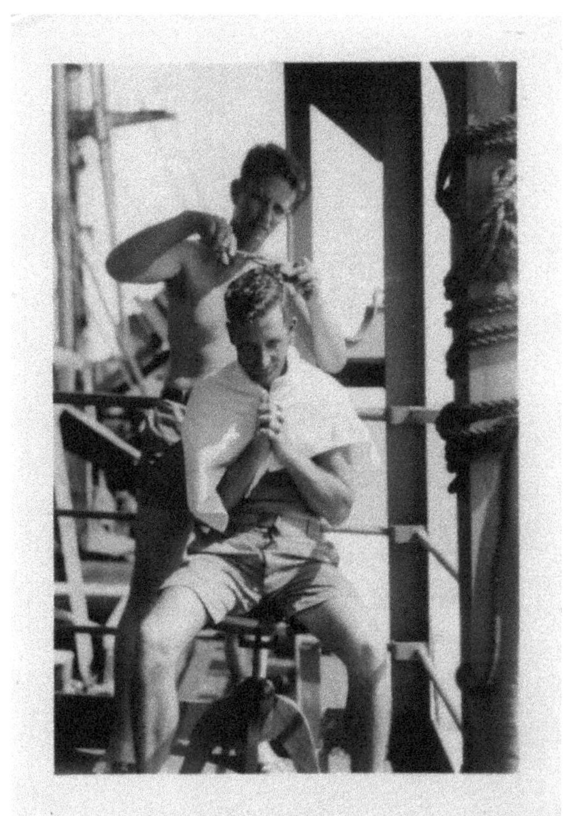

109

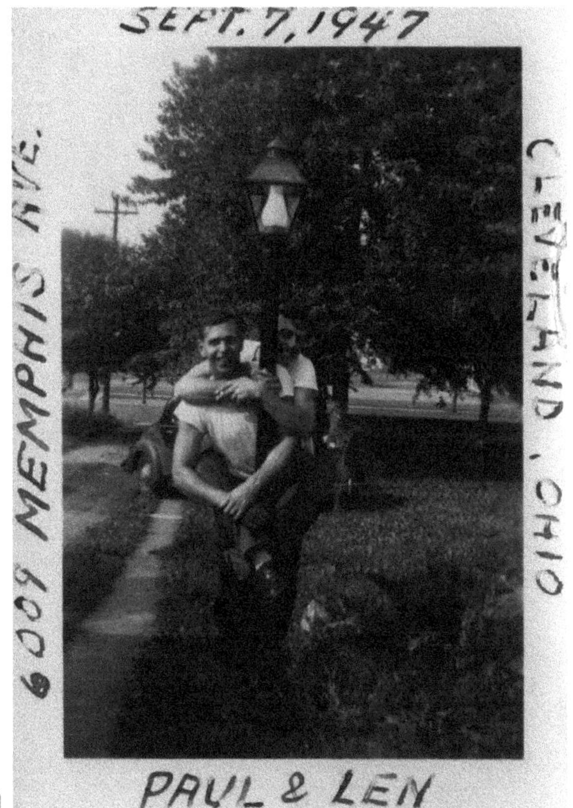

110

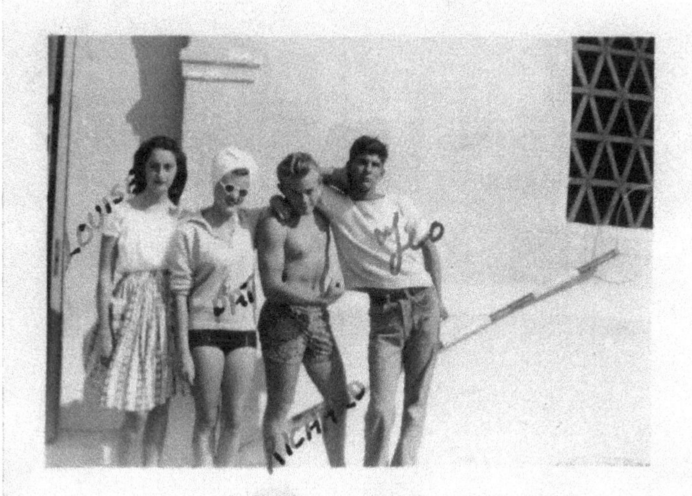

111

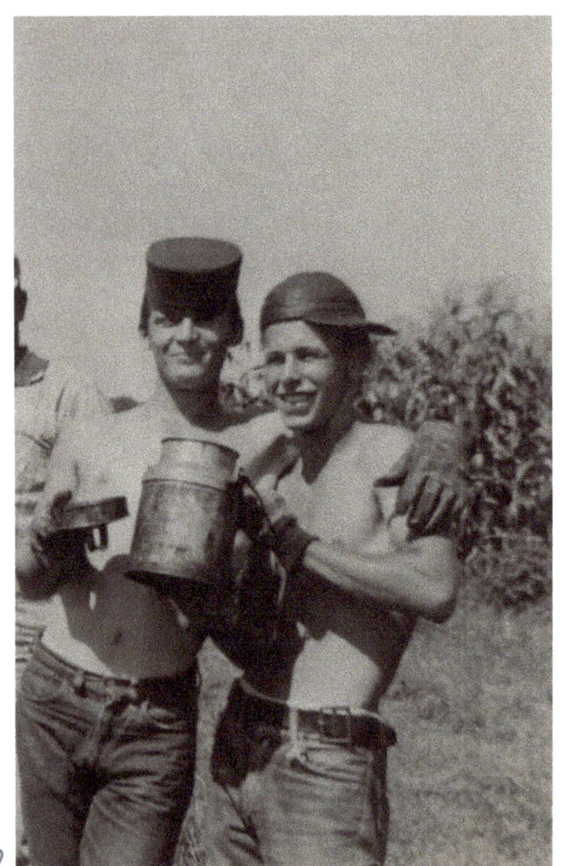
112

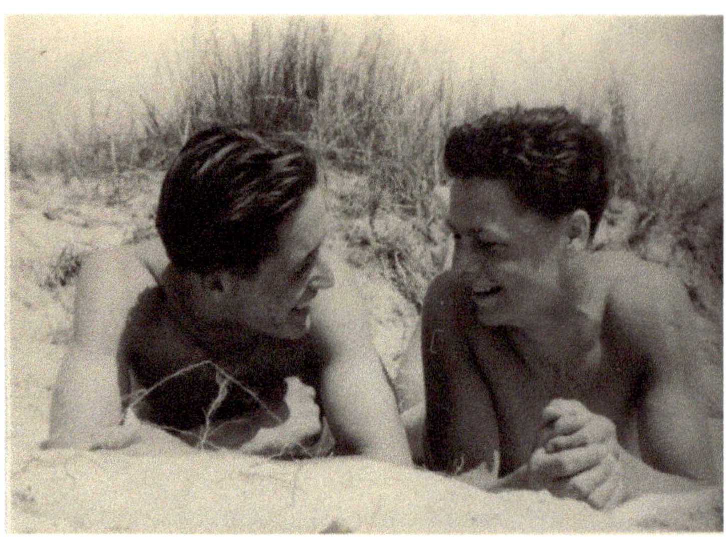
113

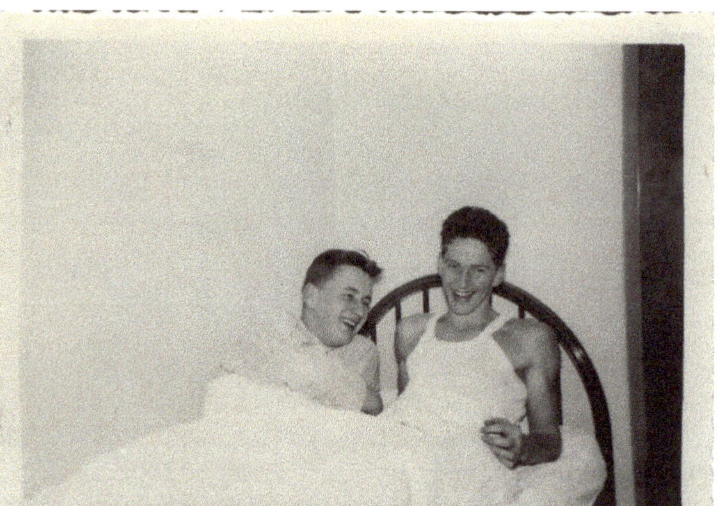
114

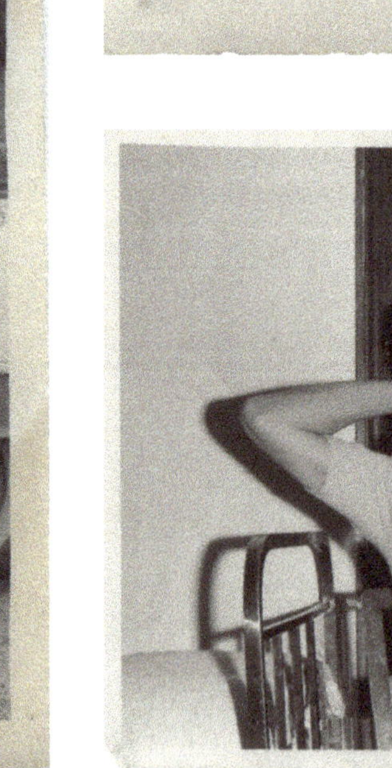
116

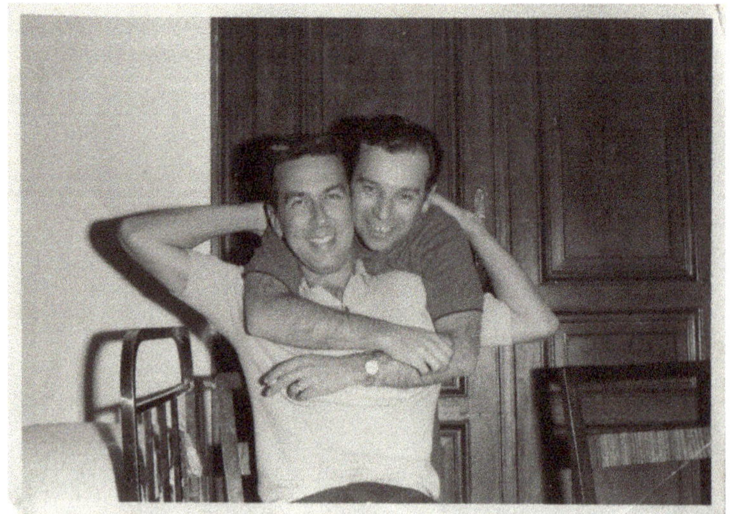
115

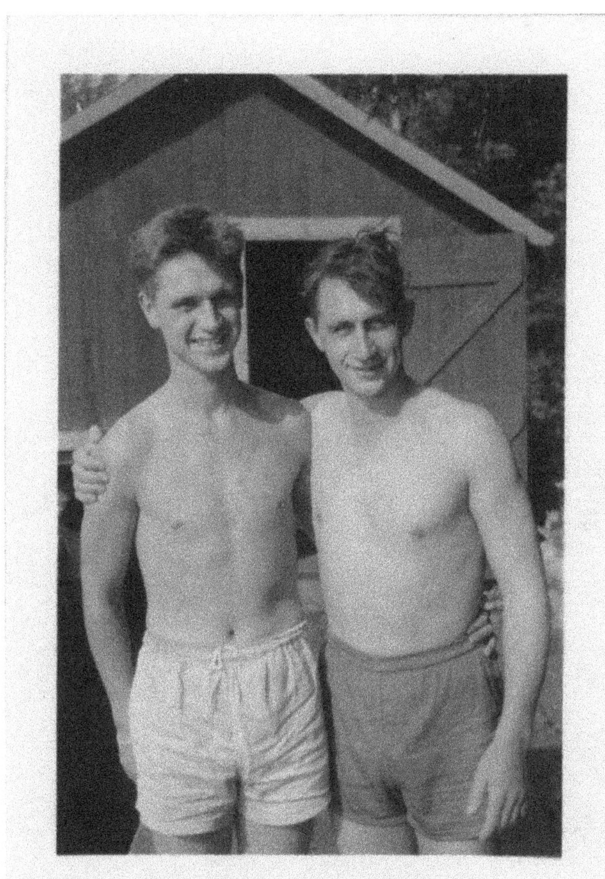
117

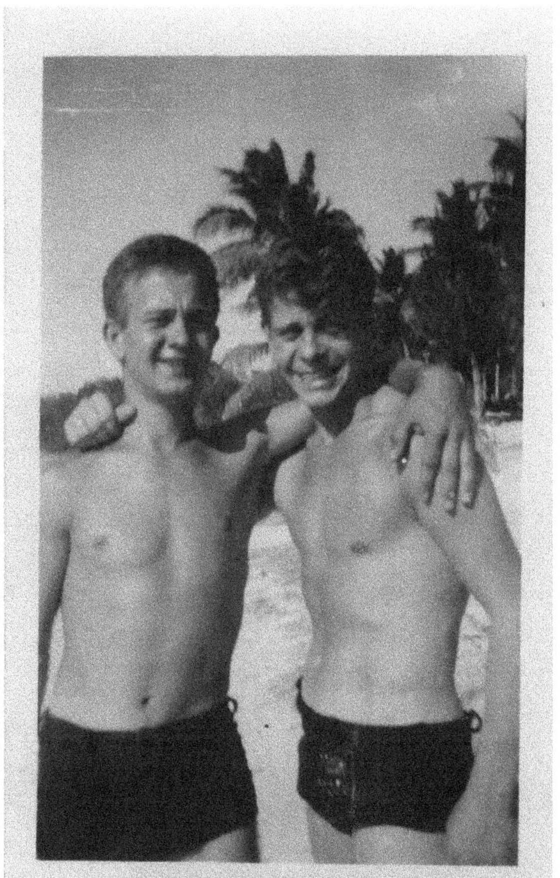
118

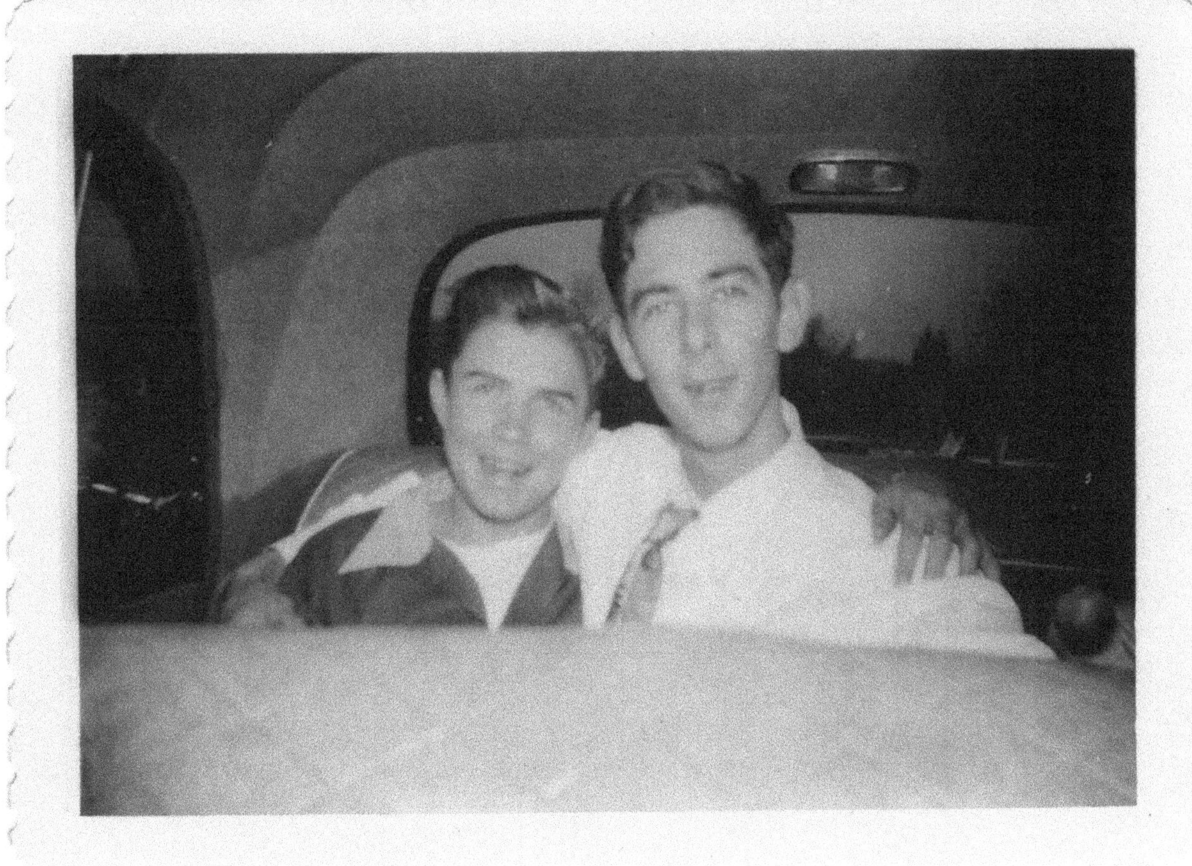
119

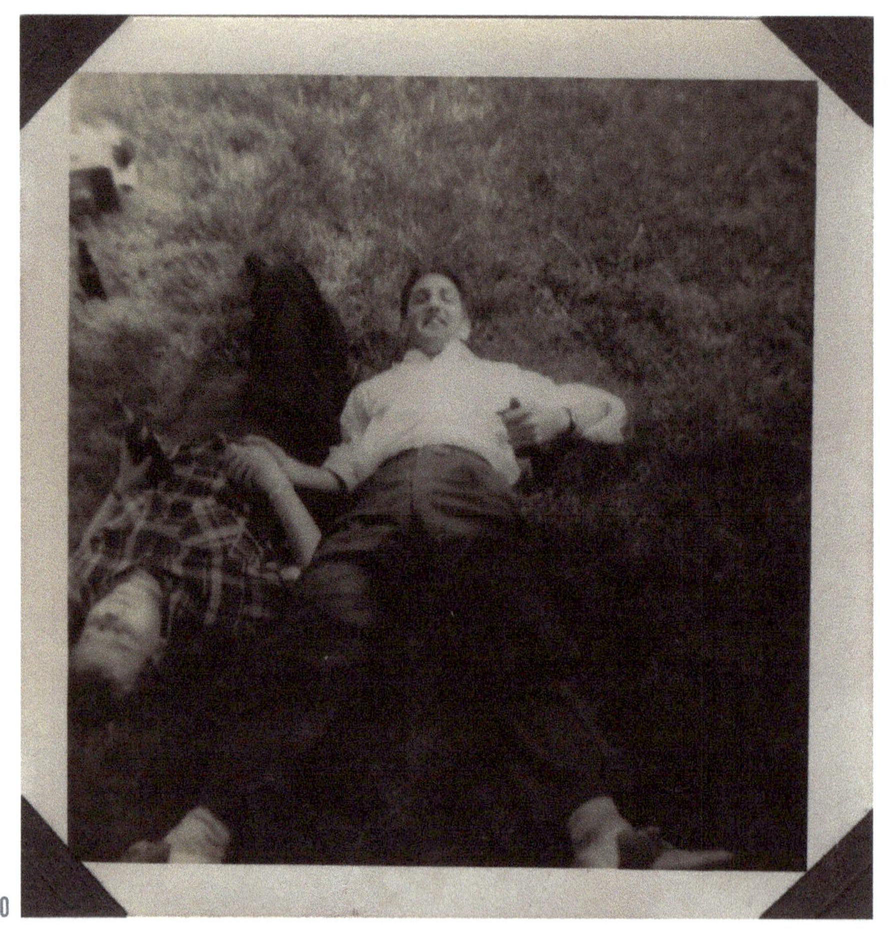

120

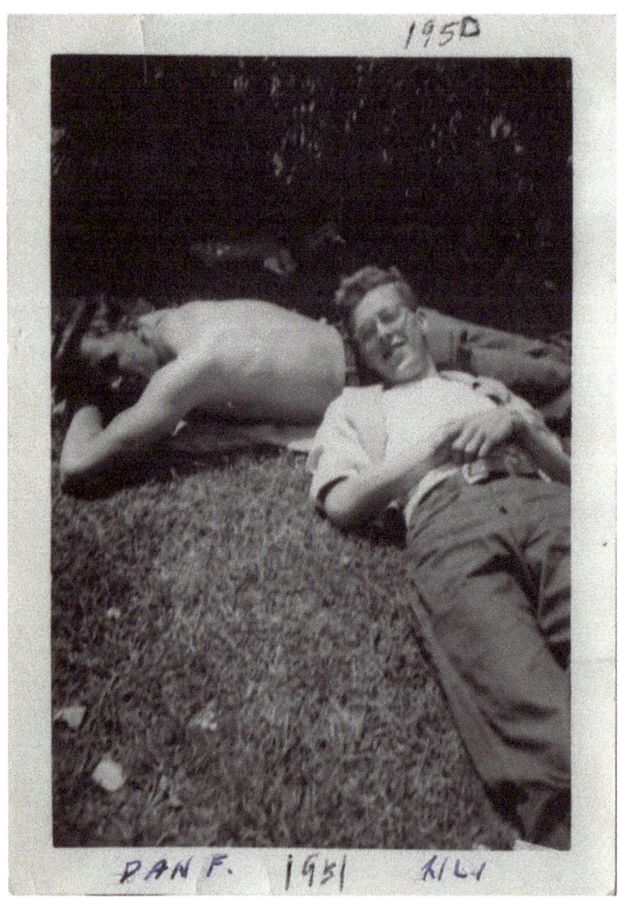

121

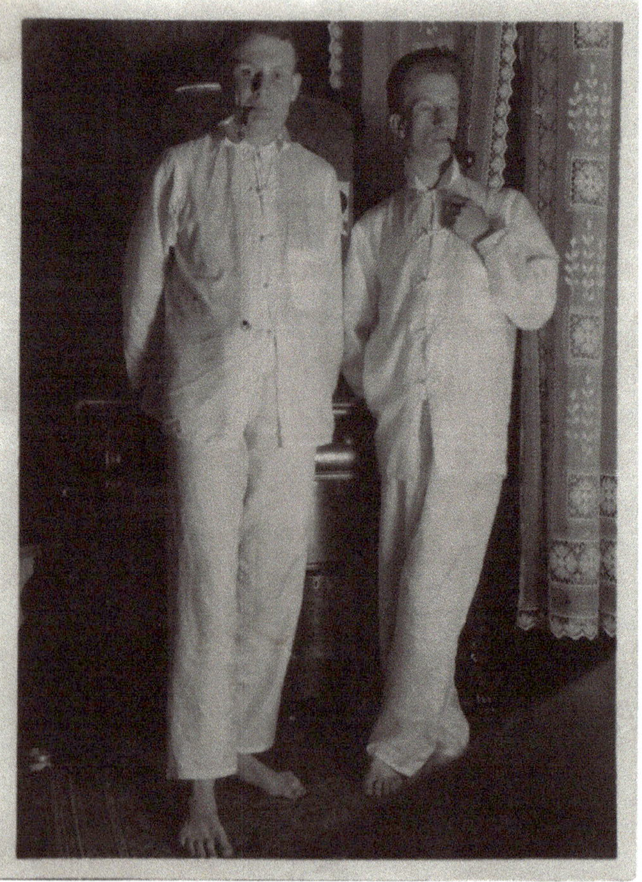

122

CHAPTER 2

MY GUYS

GROUPS OF MEN

This chapter shows that plenty of pleasure came in groups as well as in couples. Boys and men recline together in many of the photos I've collected, but few seem to recline as comfortably as the trio in this chapter's Image 7, an especially attractive and well-preserved photo in the small carte-de-visite format that was popular through the second half of the nineteenth century. Images 18 and 19 show men posing on or around the paper moon that, as noted in the previous chapter, was a common studio prop early in the twentieth century. Men kissing each other, on the cheek or on the mouth, are numerous in my collection; in some the kiss appears to have been for fun, while in others there seems to have been romance or maybe just simple affection involved. Maybe no kissers—nor their observers—are more mysterious than the young males in this chapter's Image 35, though the person behind the kissing pair does seem to be signaling approval of the kiss, perhaps solemnizing a union of the kissers. Such mystery, in my judgment, is a frequent (and appealing) component of found photographs; just what the seven barefoot young males in this chapter's Image 52 were up to, for example, is anybody's guess.

The mystery in many found photos notwithstanding, certain features of such imagery do stand out in my large collection of images of male groups. As did the photos of male couples, group imagery shows the considerable popularity, until about a century ago, of visiting a photographer's studio to have a male relationship memorialized. Examples of photos taken in a studio abound in my collection, as they do in this chapter; especially noteworthy are Images 2–4, 6–8, 14, 18, 21, 22, and 24. The sheer pleasure of being together that I noted in photos of couples is also widespread in those of larger groups, with the photo booth in Image 44 a splendid example. Objects that some would consider phallic reappear, such as the bottles and a revolver in Image 23. A bed is a setting not uncommon, as in Images 25, 26, and 27. Like being photographed in bed together, casual handholding between males was not confined to photos just of couples, as Image 19 suggests.

One often thinks of somber expressions as characteristic of older photographs, but the comparatively lengthy shutter speeds that once were required did not preclude mirth from being a common feature of early images. Simple goofing around was apparently what sometimes made the company of other males so pleasant, as suggested by Images 4, 8, 10, 11, 15, 31, 39, 47, 51, and 53. Rigid postures and standing in orderly rows actually became more common later on, when intimacy among males was culturally less encouraged. Early photos, by contrast, often showed men reclining, sometimes close together, as, for instance, in Images 2, 6, 7, 23, 32, 33, and 41. Sitting on another male's shoulders, holding hands, laying atop each other, even posing casually naked—the groups of males in my collection showed considerable comfort with one another's bodies, as exemplified in particular by Images 12, 13, 17, 19, 20, 24, 29, 34, 36, 37, 40, 42, 43, 48, 49, and 54.

To regret the loss of unselfconscious male intimacy nowadays is not to suggest that American society was better off, say, a century ago than it is now. There is not only a uniformity of sex in this book's photos, but typically monoliths of race, age, and social class as well. Comparatively, the United States was a much more segregated society during the era of these photos. There were then huge cleavages of race, class, and gender—in the workplace, in residences, and in sites of leisure. It wasn't difficult, especially in privileged settings, to gather a group made up exclusively of white males, whether for job openings or a sandlot baseball game. Though, of course, considerable cleavages remain today, and class cleavages have in fact increased of late, the country is nonetheless much more integrated now than it was in the past. The price of the welcome integration by sex, in the workplace and elsewhere, however, needn't have been a loss of the male intimacy so prevalent in these pages. That intimacy was lost, in part, because of homophobia, not an increasing parity between the sexes. ▮

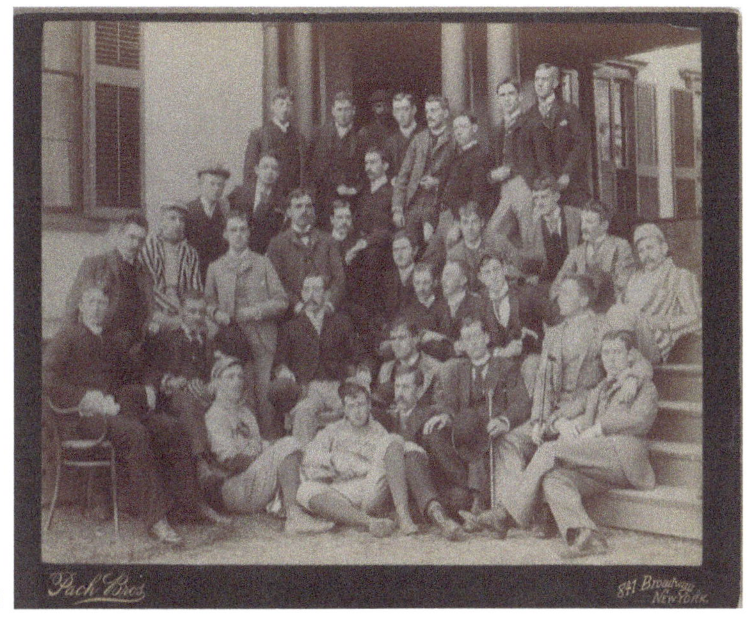

1

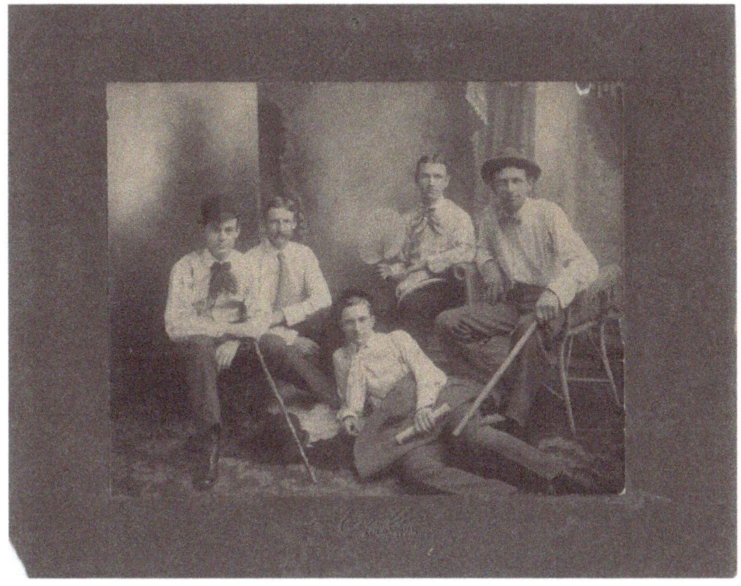
2

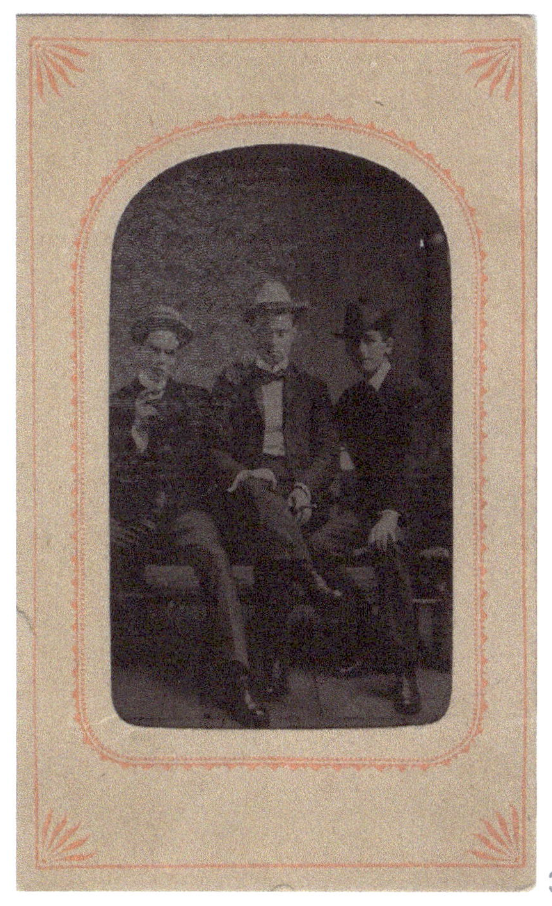
3

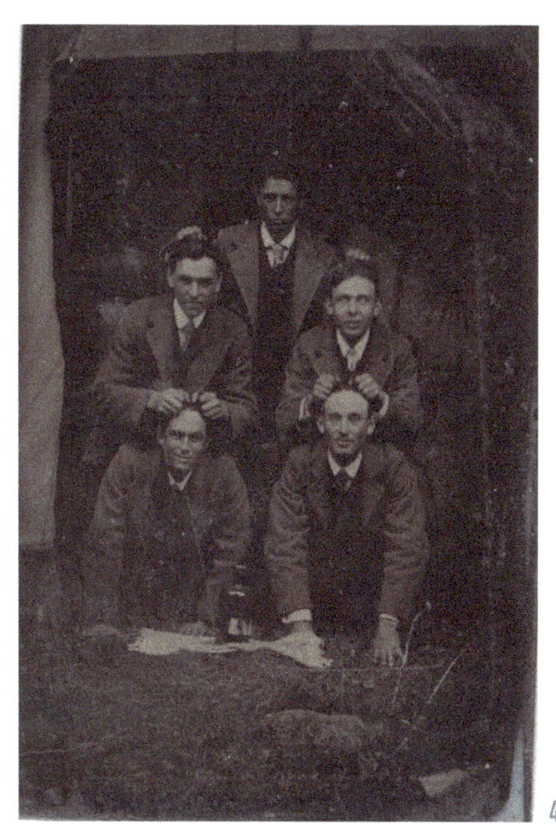
4

5

H. F. Eggert.
STUDIO:
Myers Building,
BETHLEHEM, PA.

6

Dunklee,
Athol,
Mass.

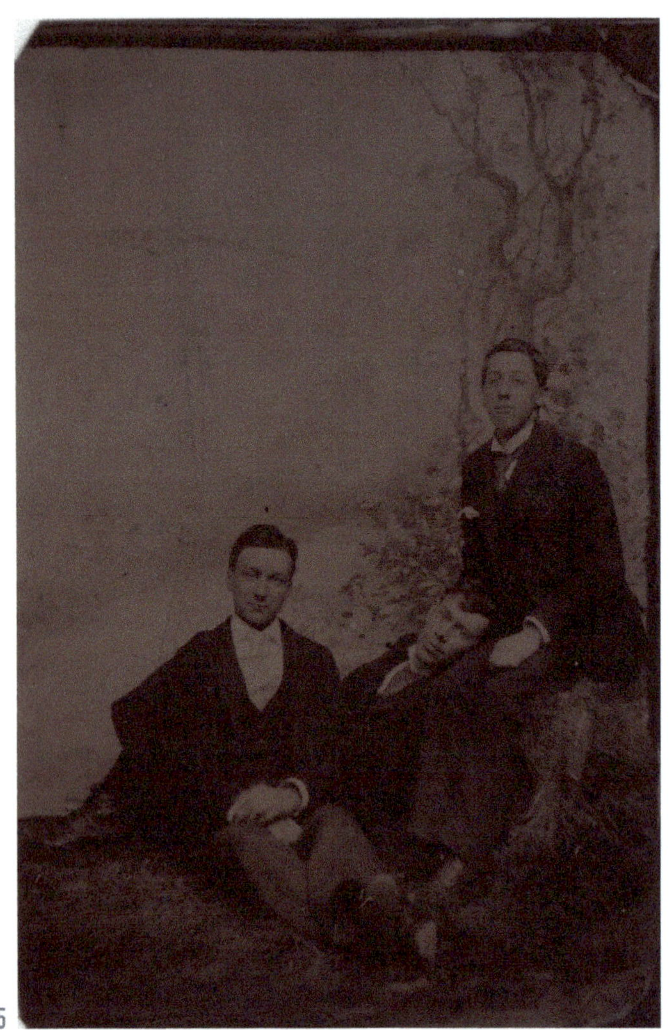

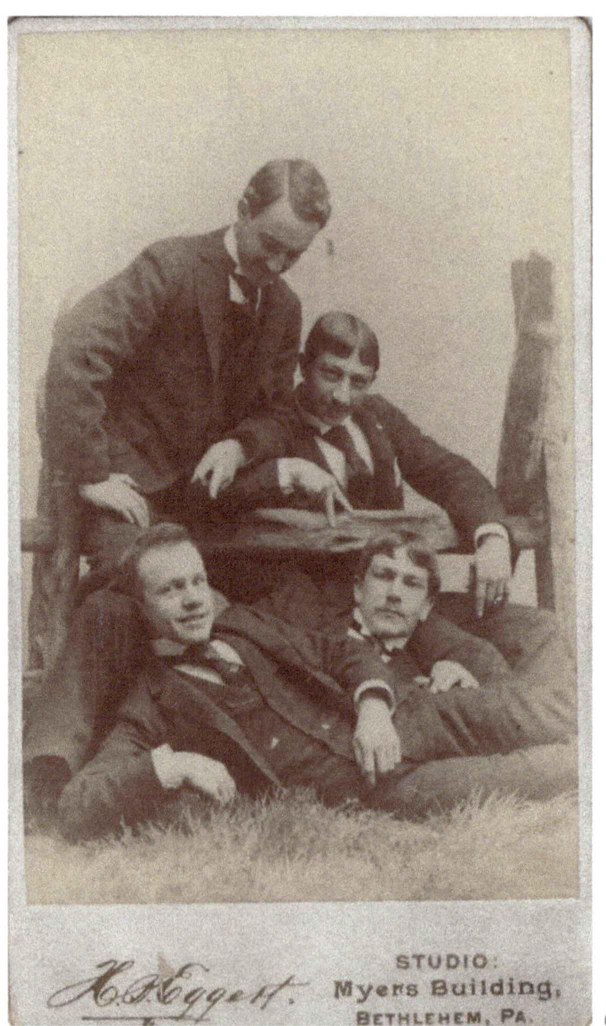

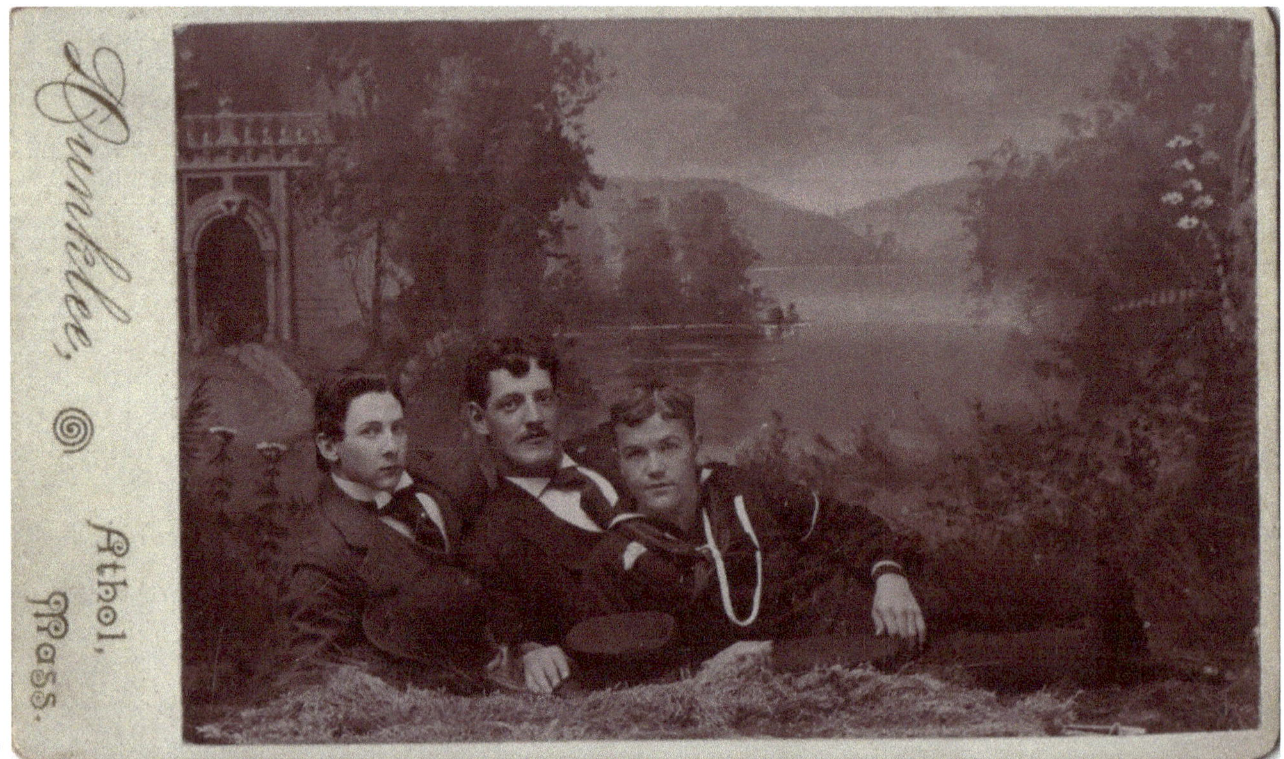

7

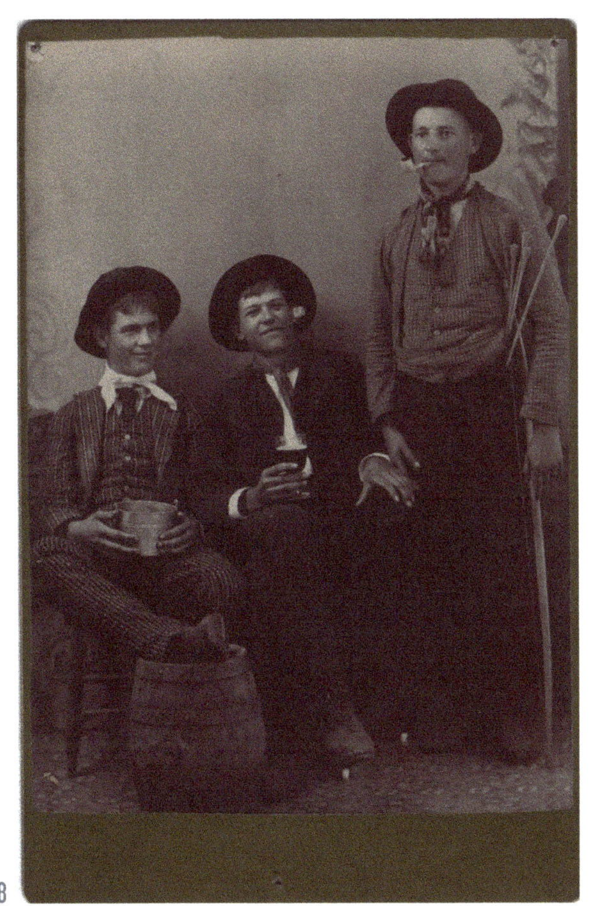

8

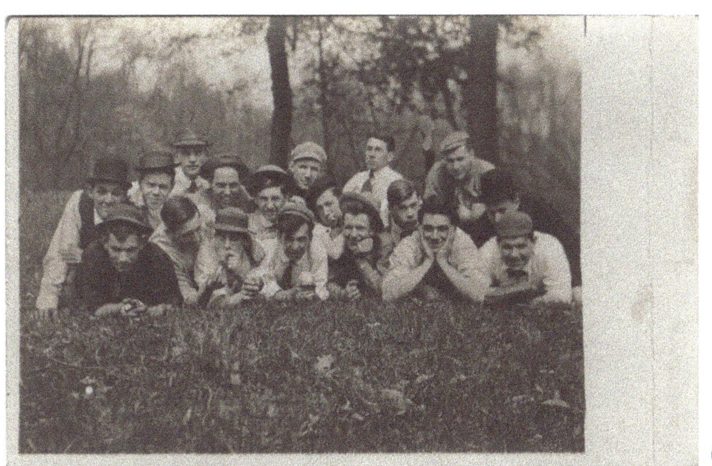

9

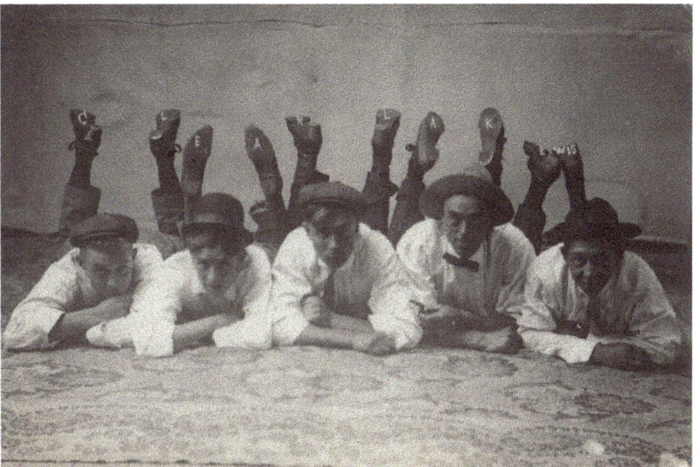

11

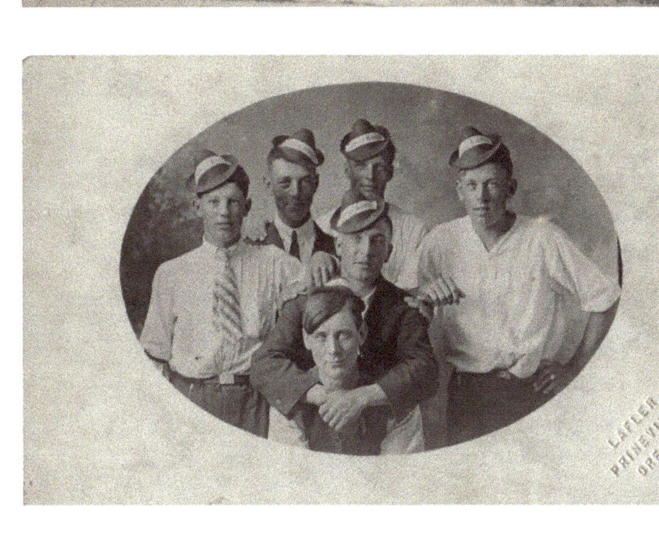

12

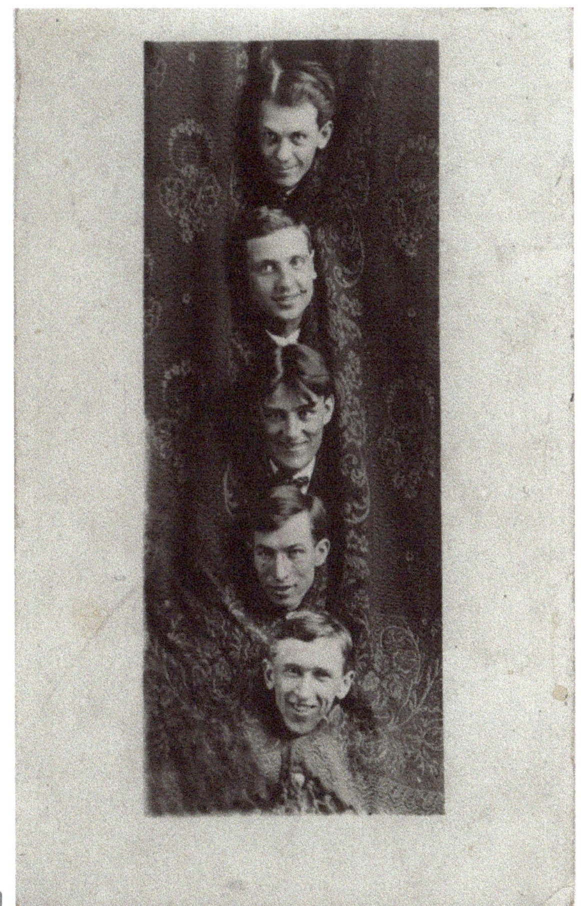

10

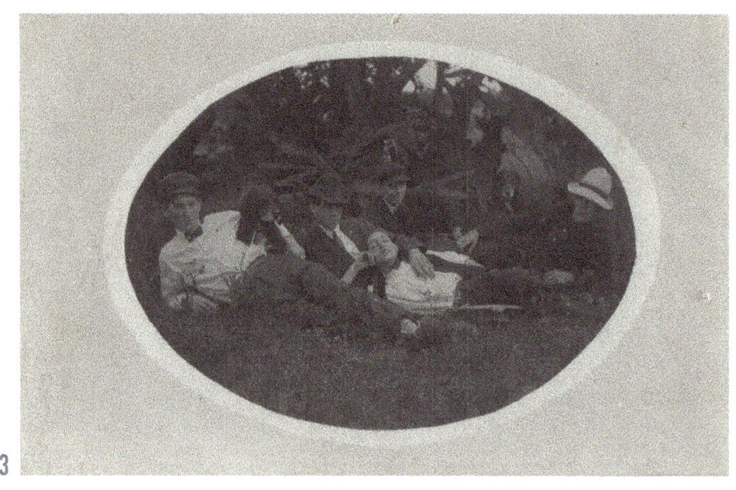

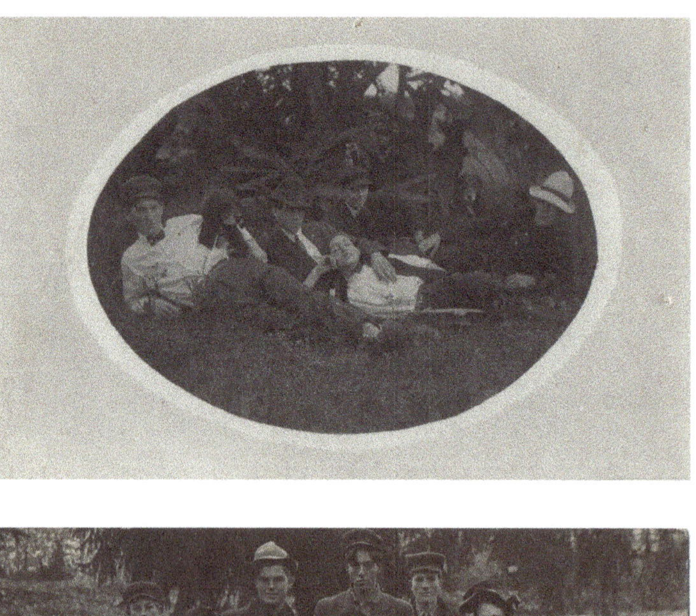

13

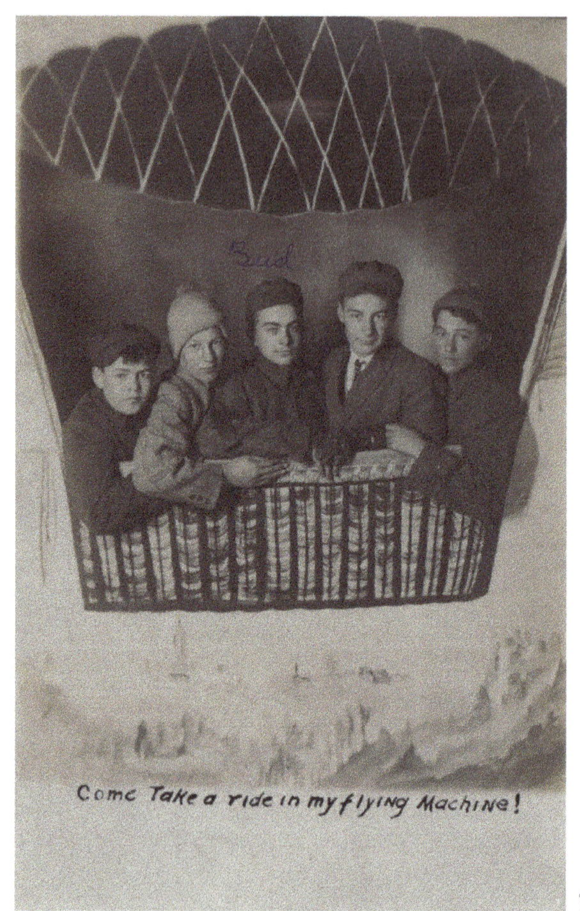

Bud
Come Take a ride in my flying Machine!

14

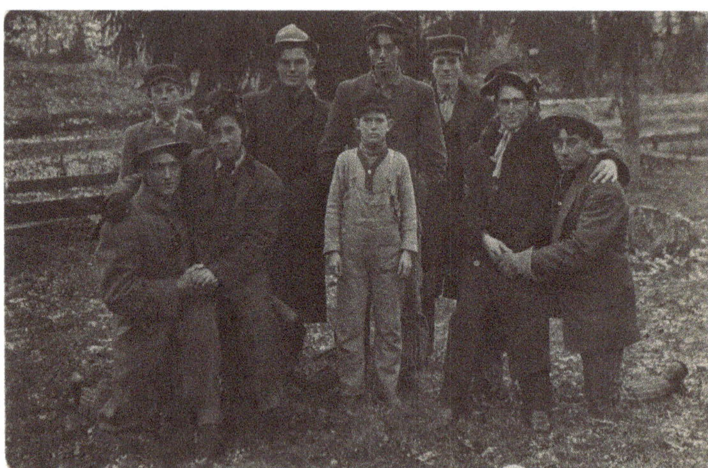

15

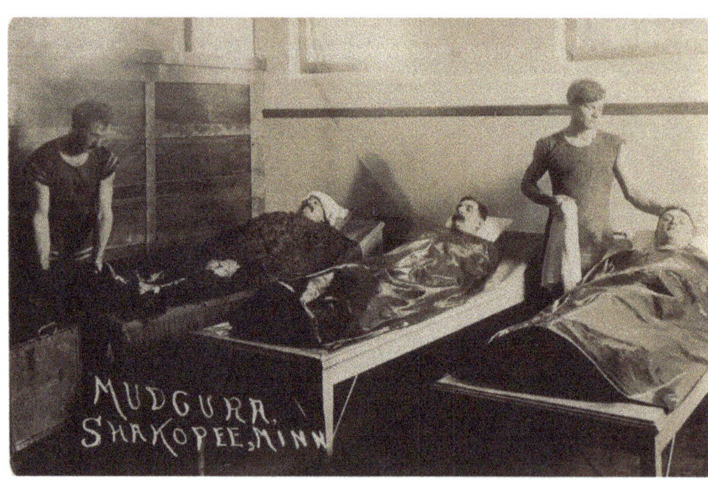

MUDGURA.
SHAKOPEE, MINN

16

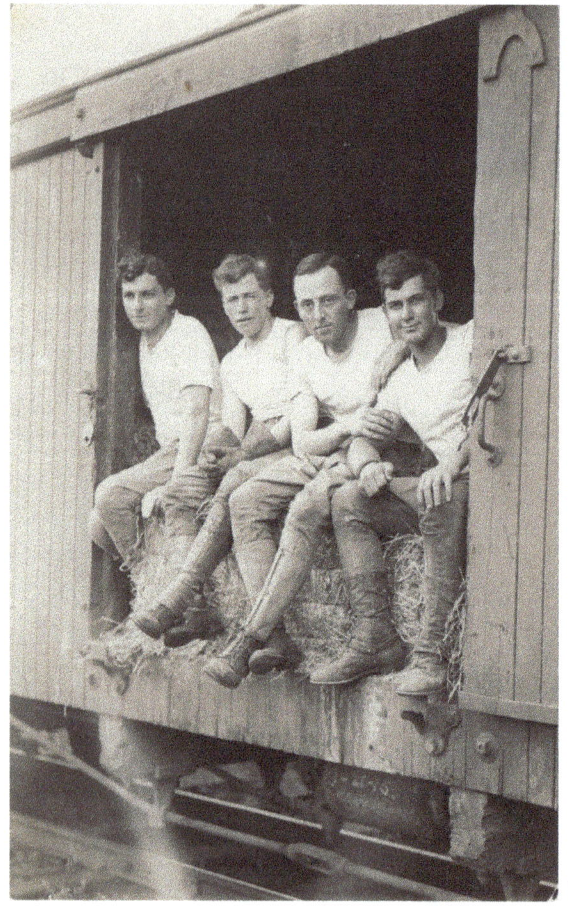

17

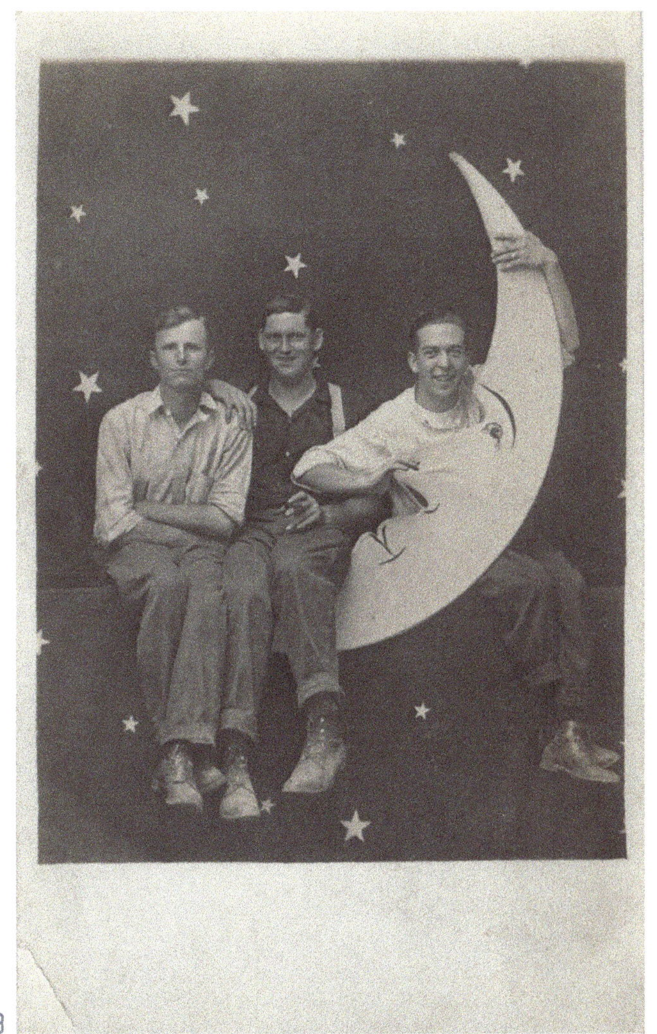

18

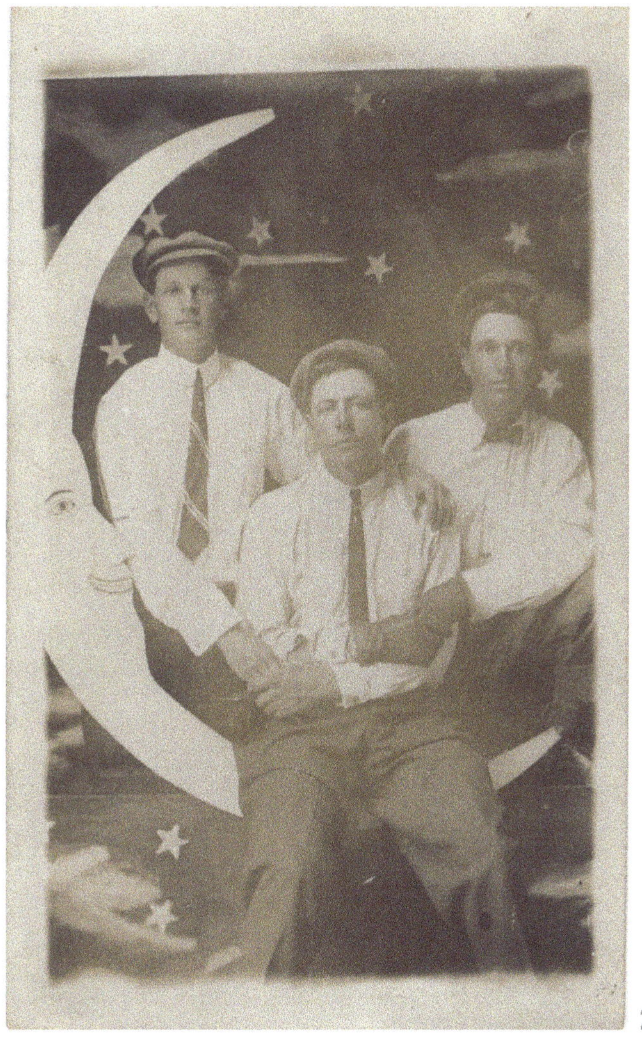

20

19

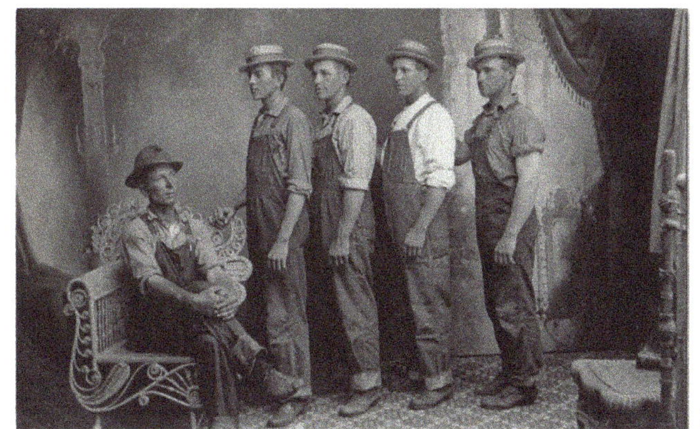

21

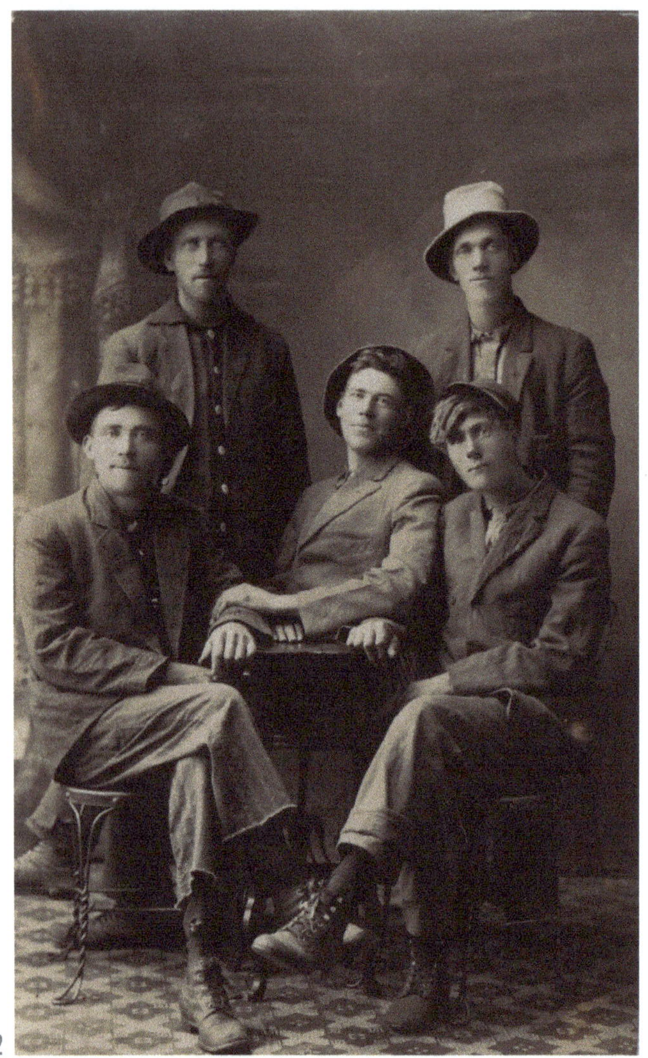
22

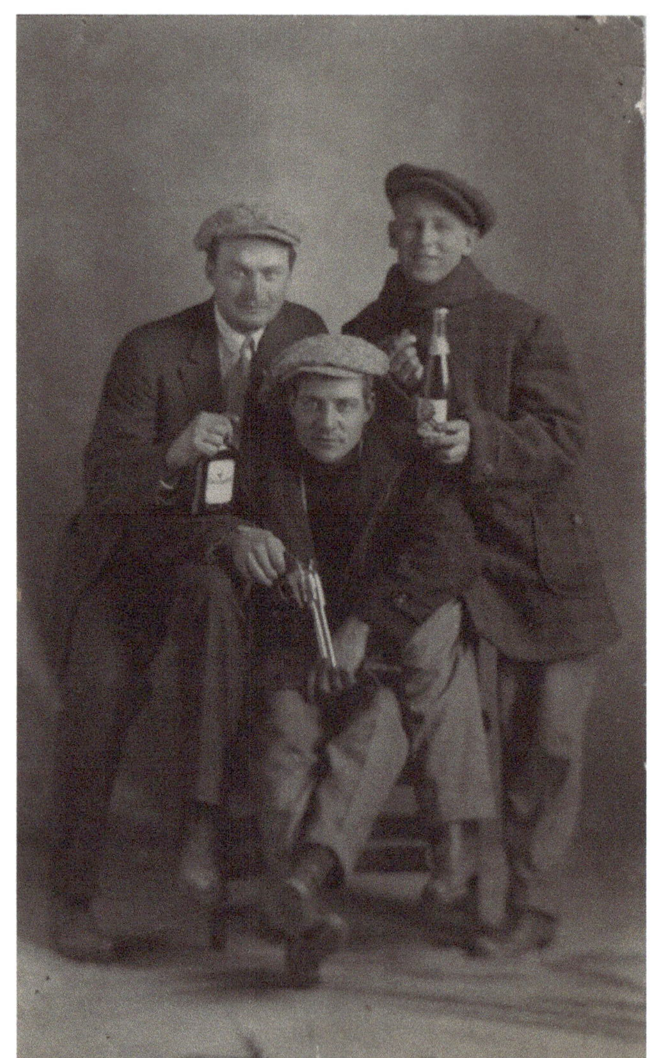
23

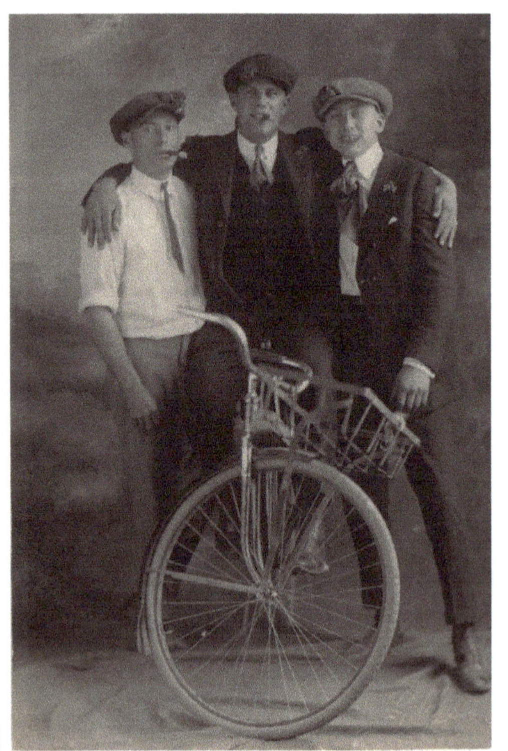
24

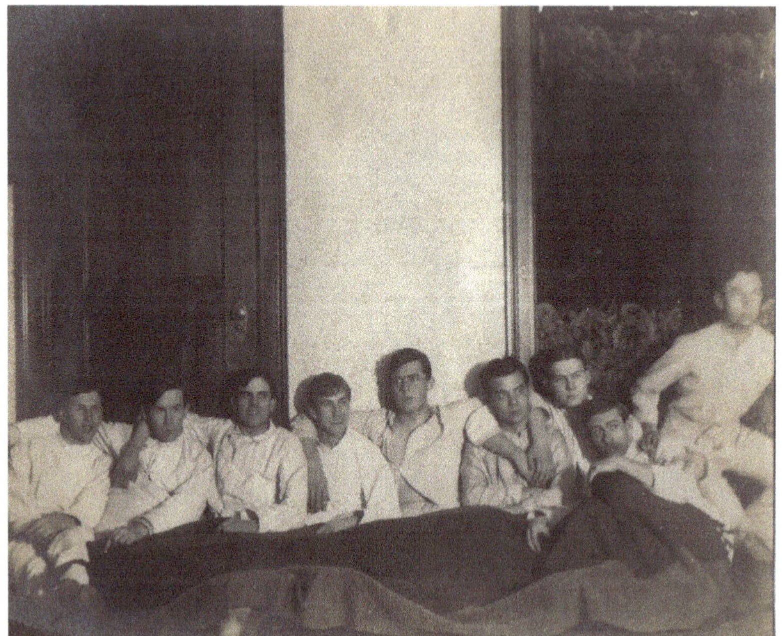
25

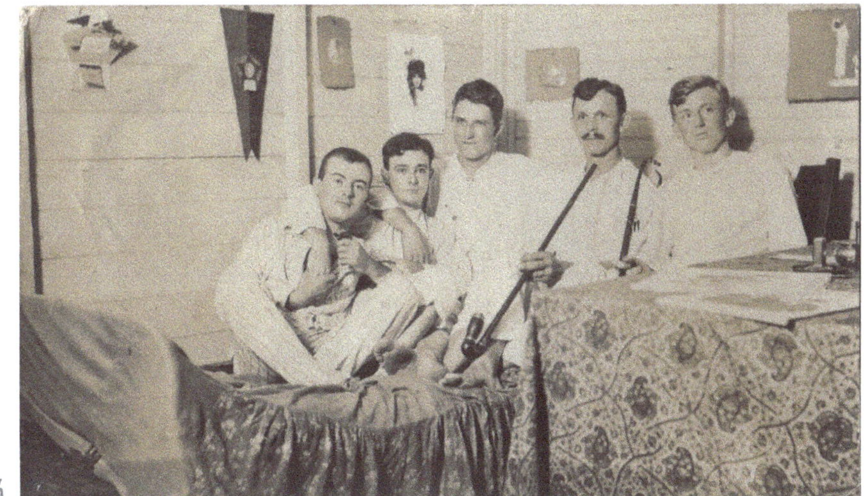
26

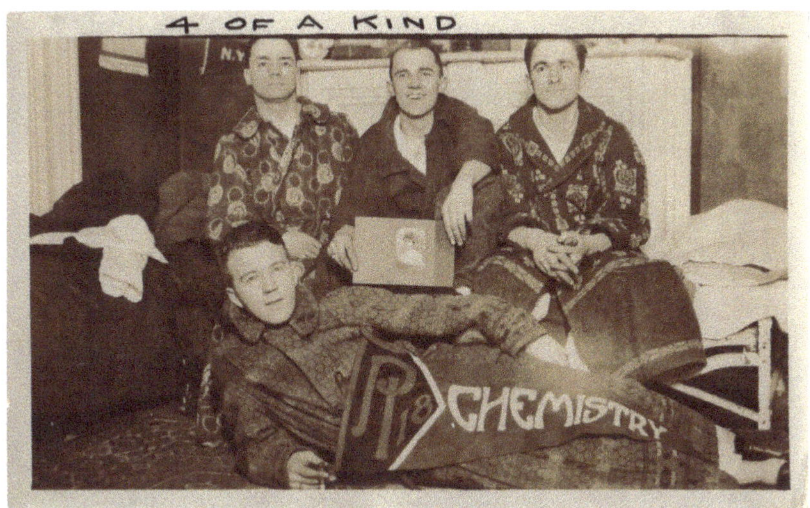

27

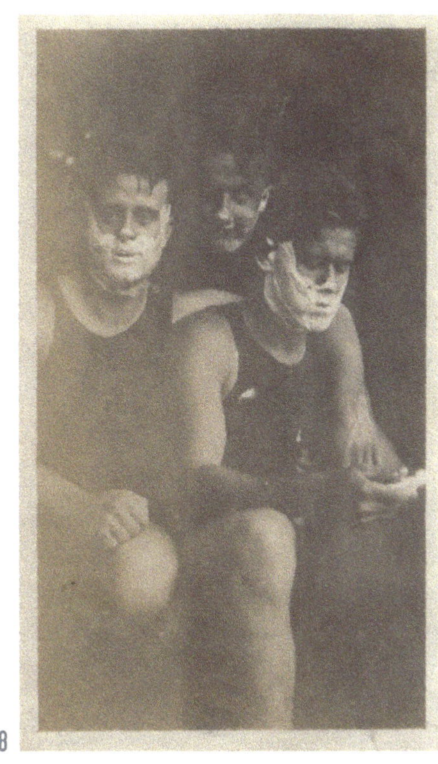
28

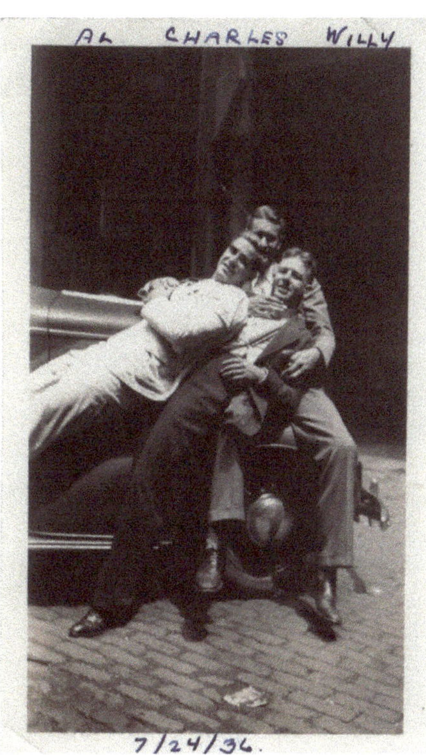

29

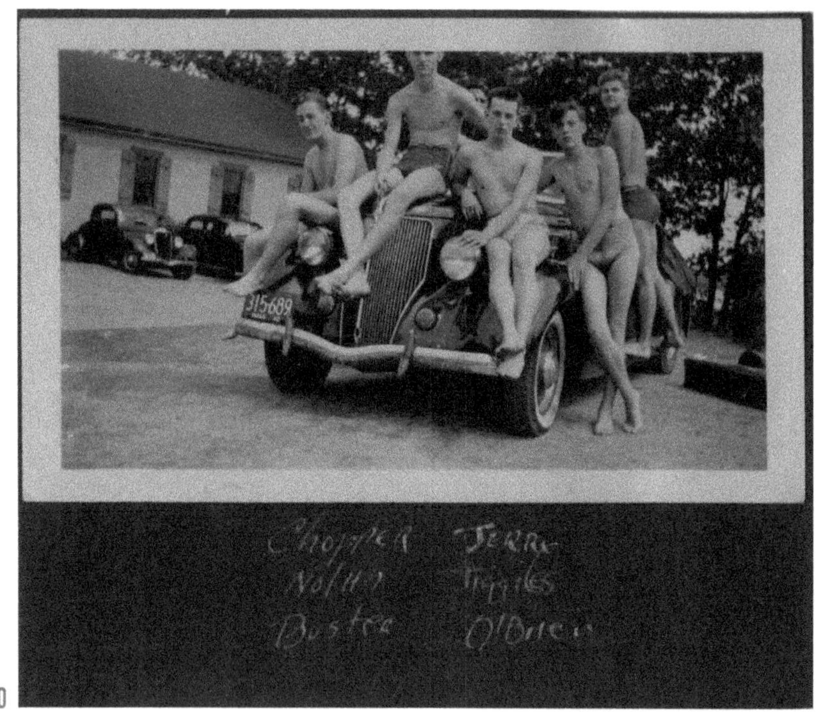

30

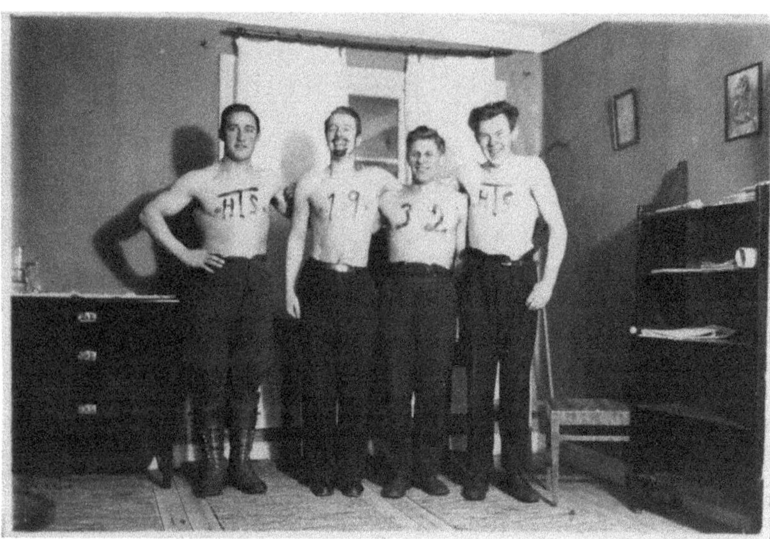

31

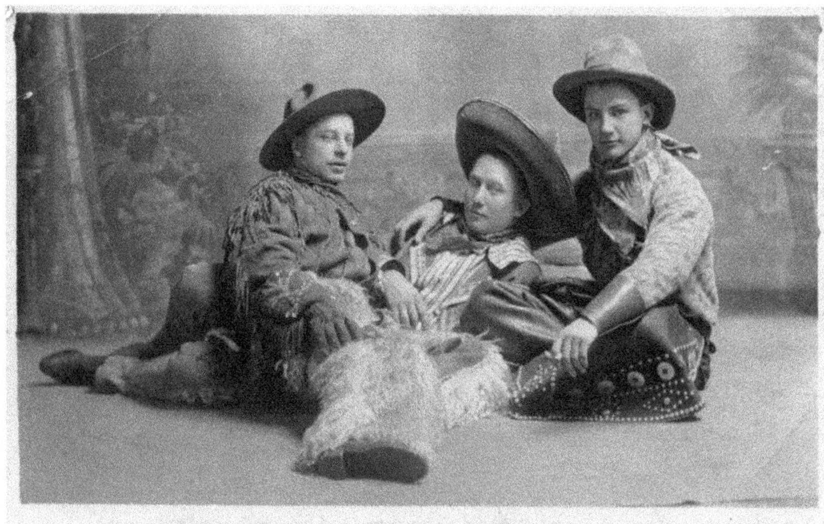

32

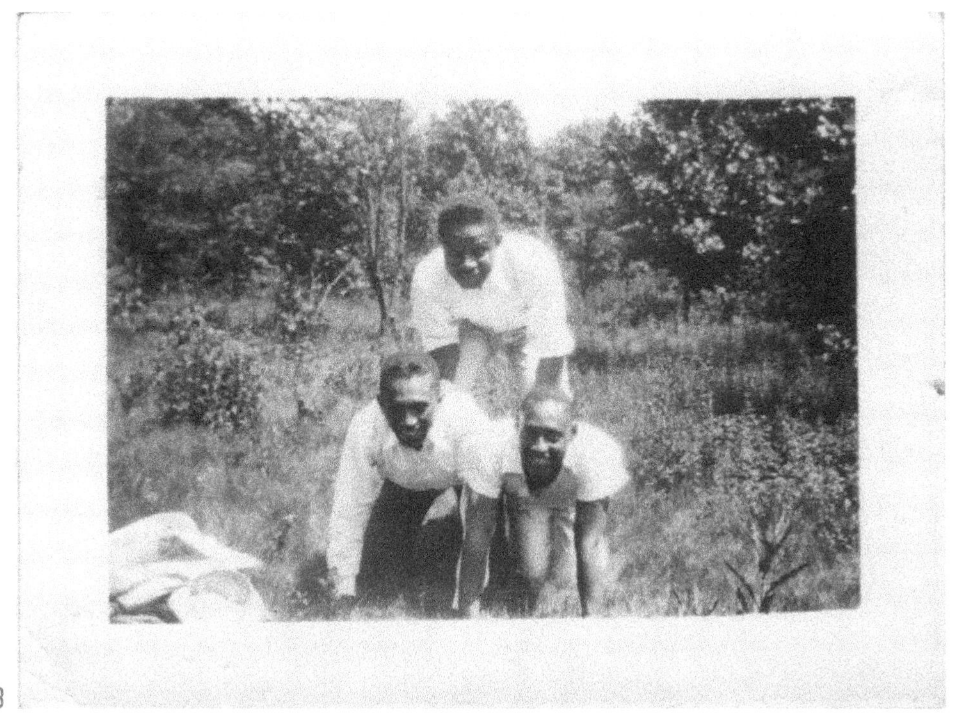

33

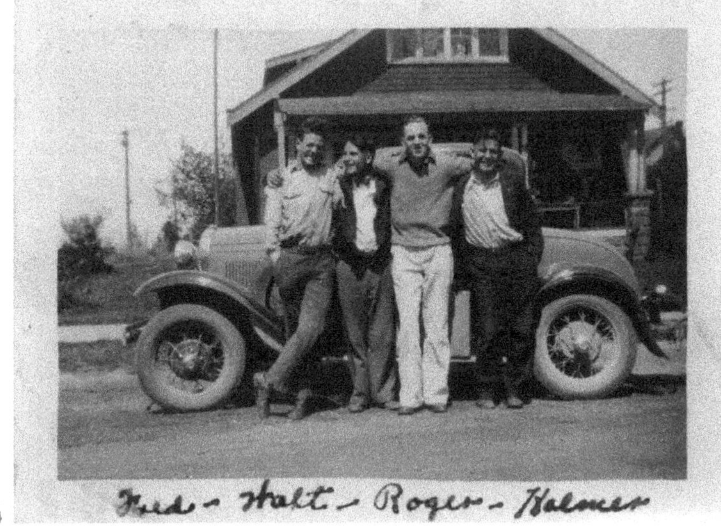

34

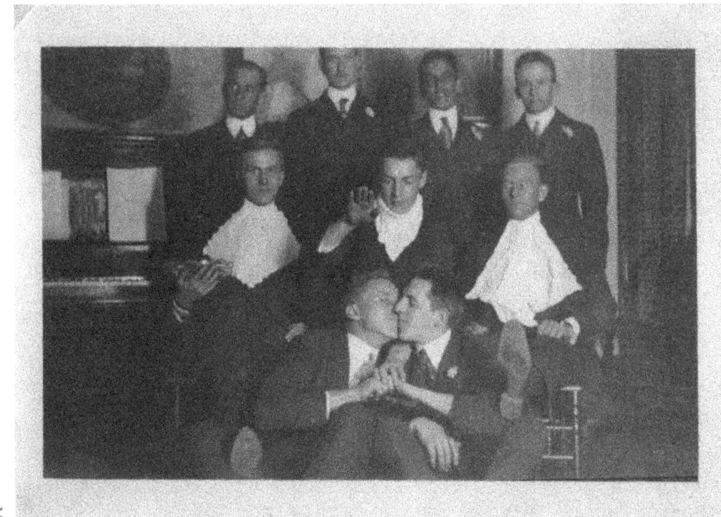

35

36

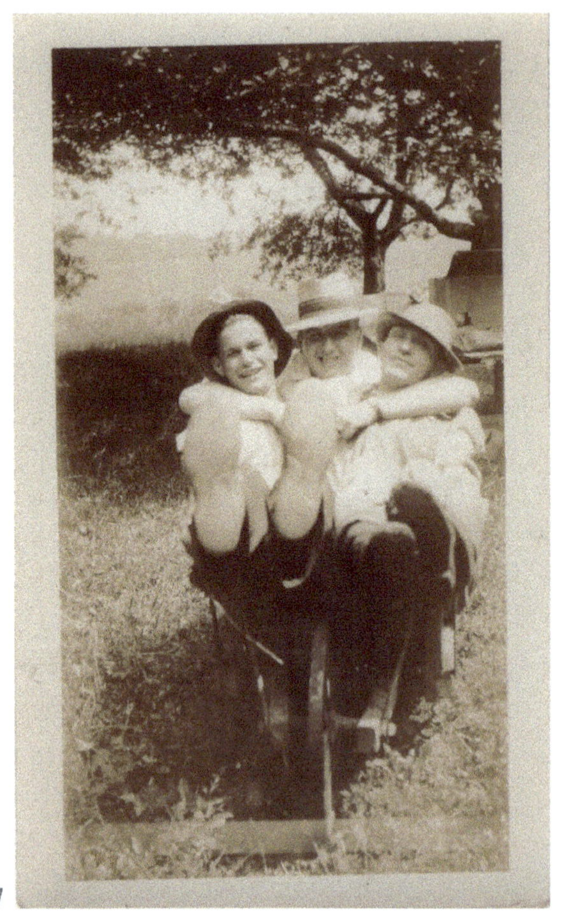
37

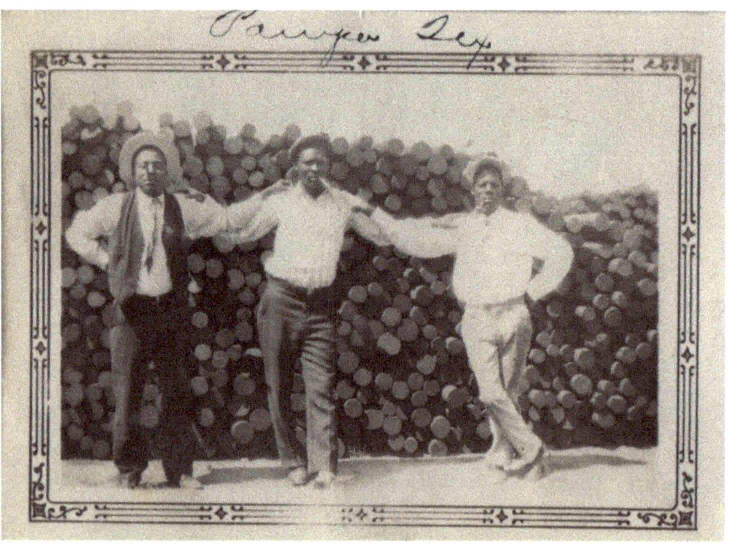
38

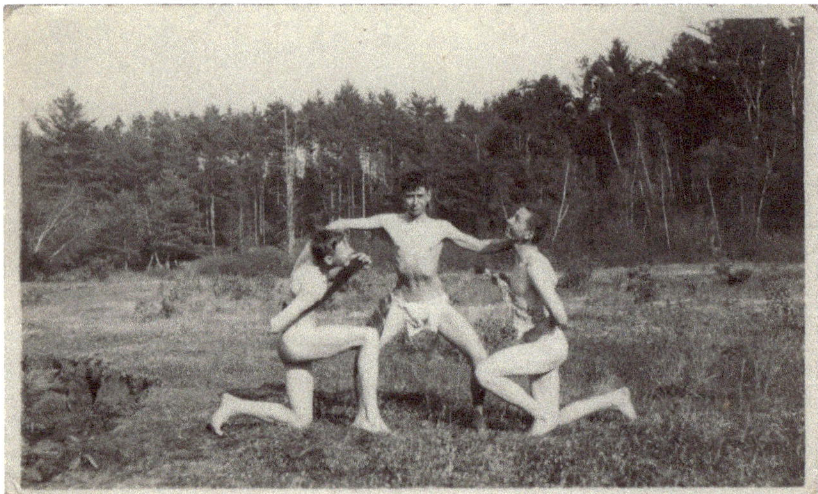
39

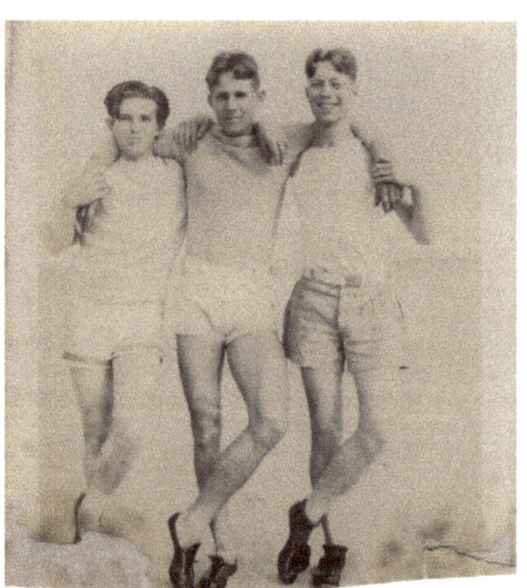
40

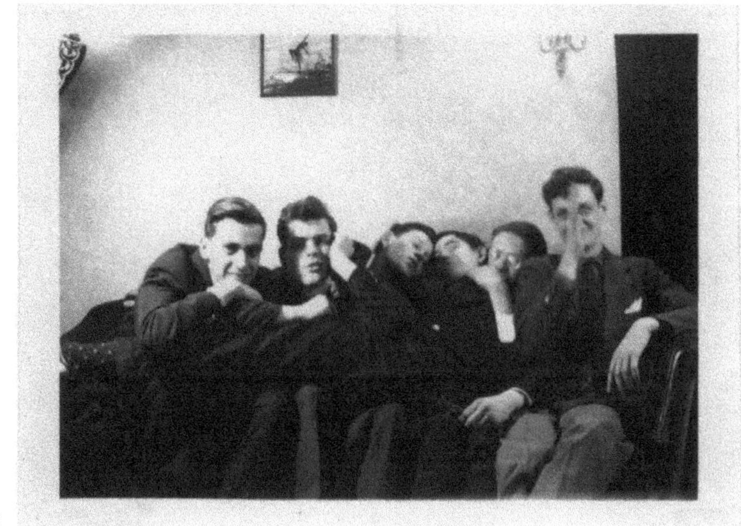

41

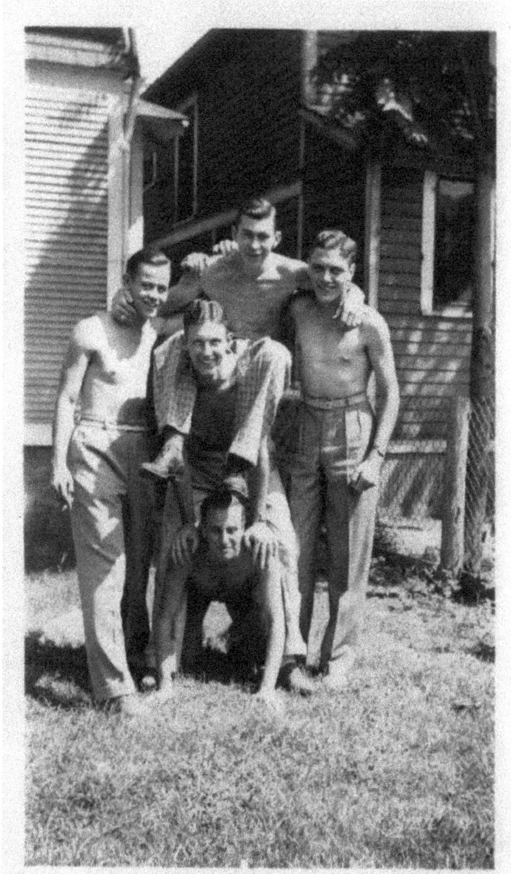

42

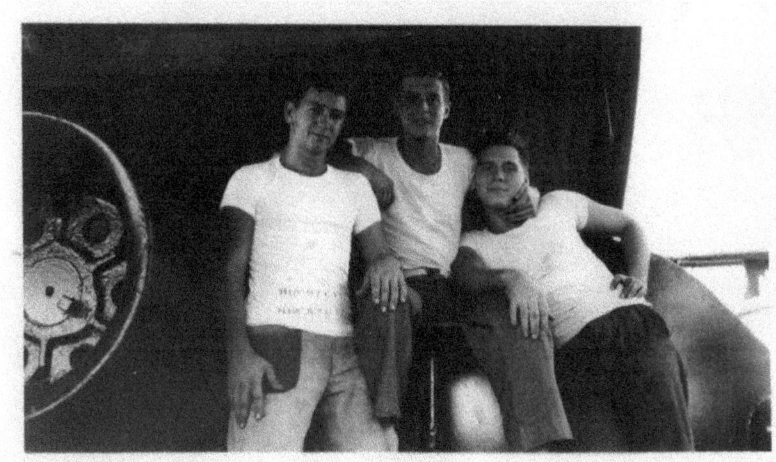

43

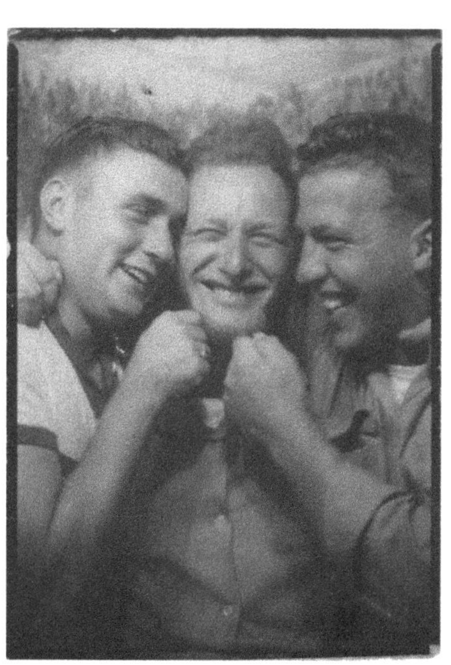

44

C.C.C Camp 38.

45

46

WEOTT
GARBERVILLE 29
SAN FRANCISCO 239
PETROLIA
EUREKA

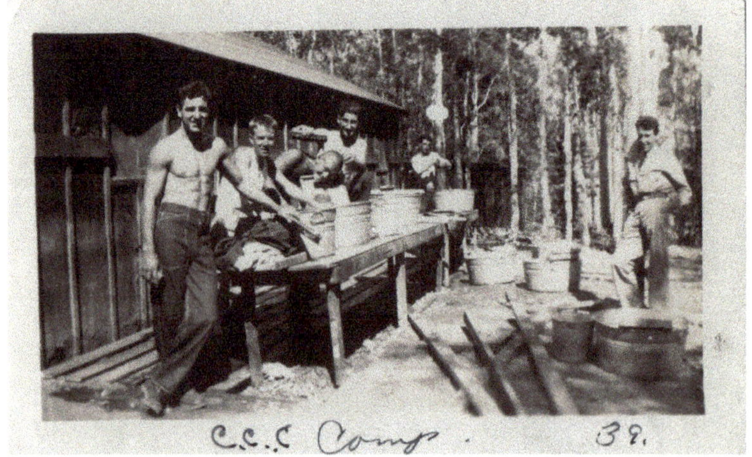

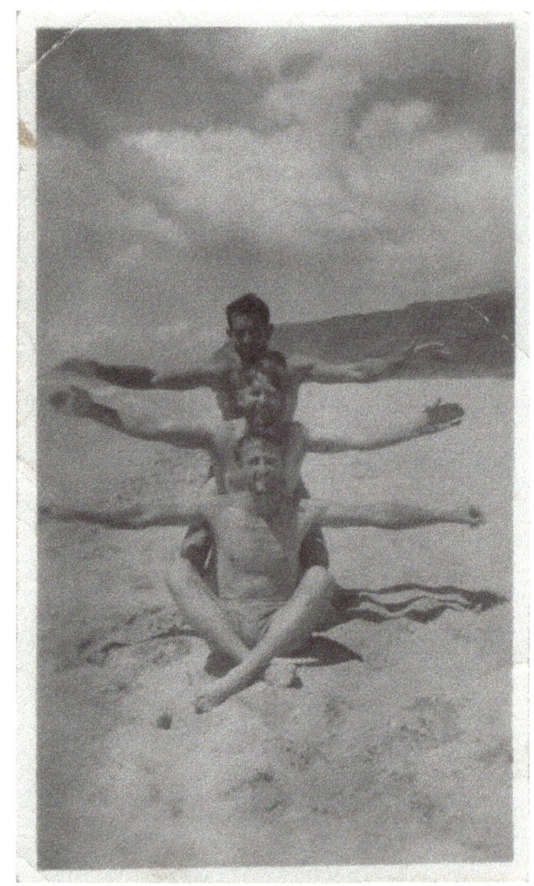

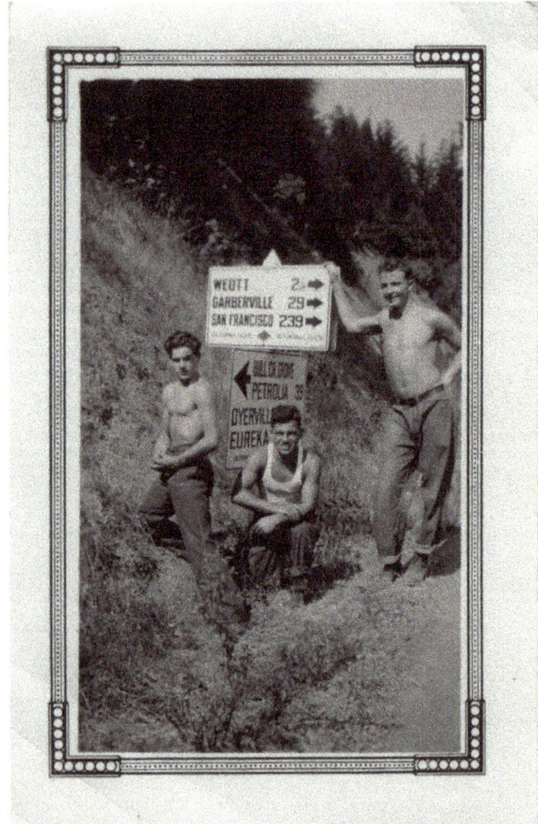

47

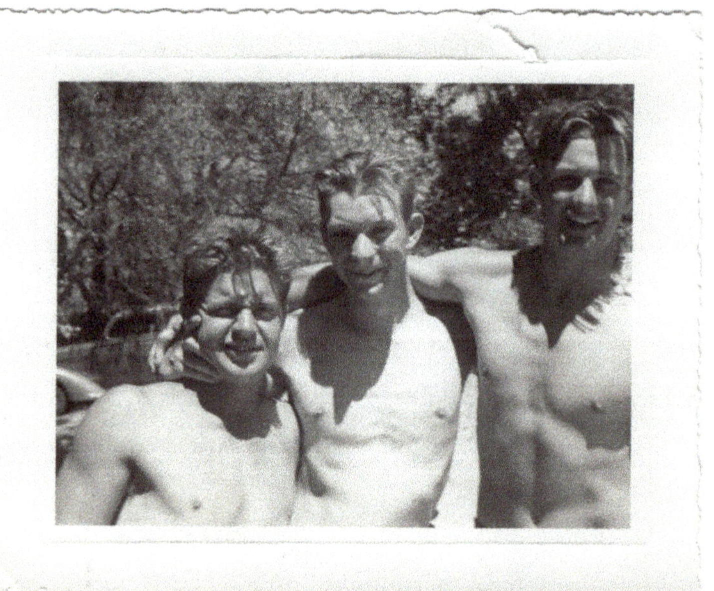

48

49
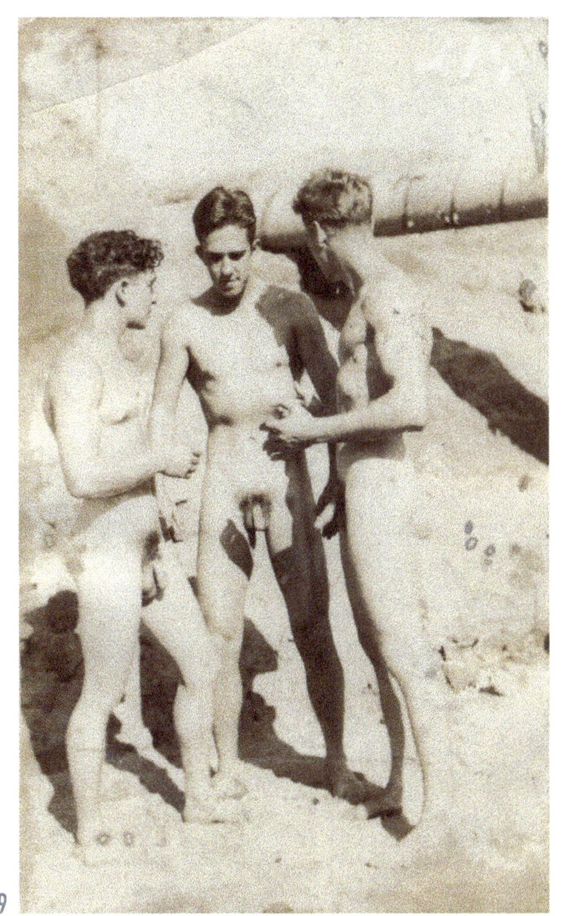

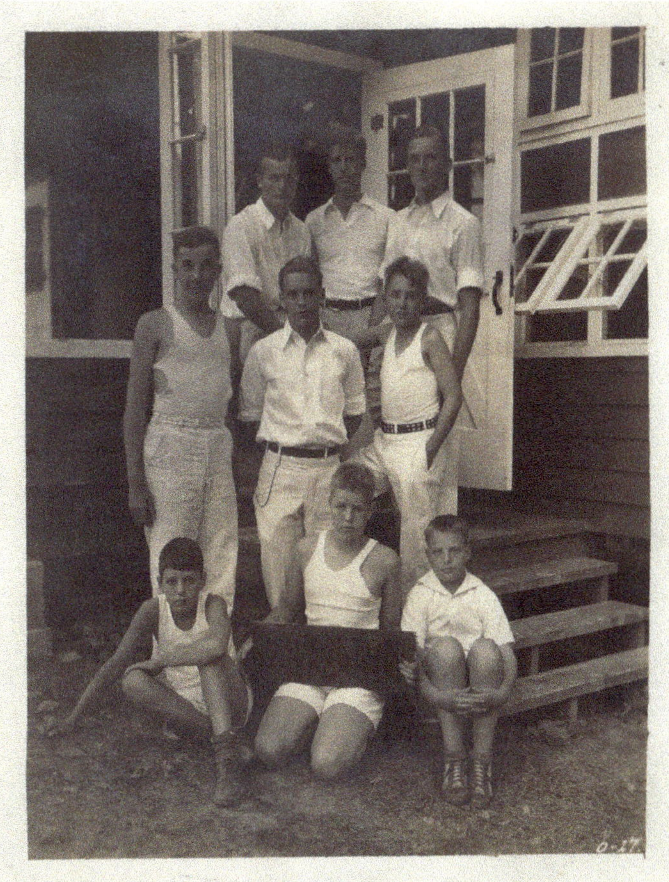

50

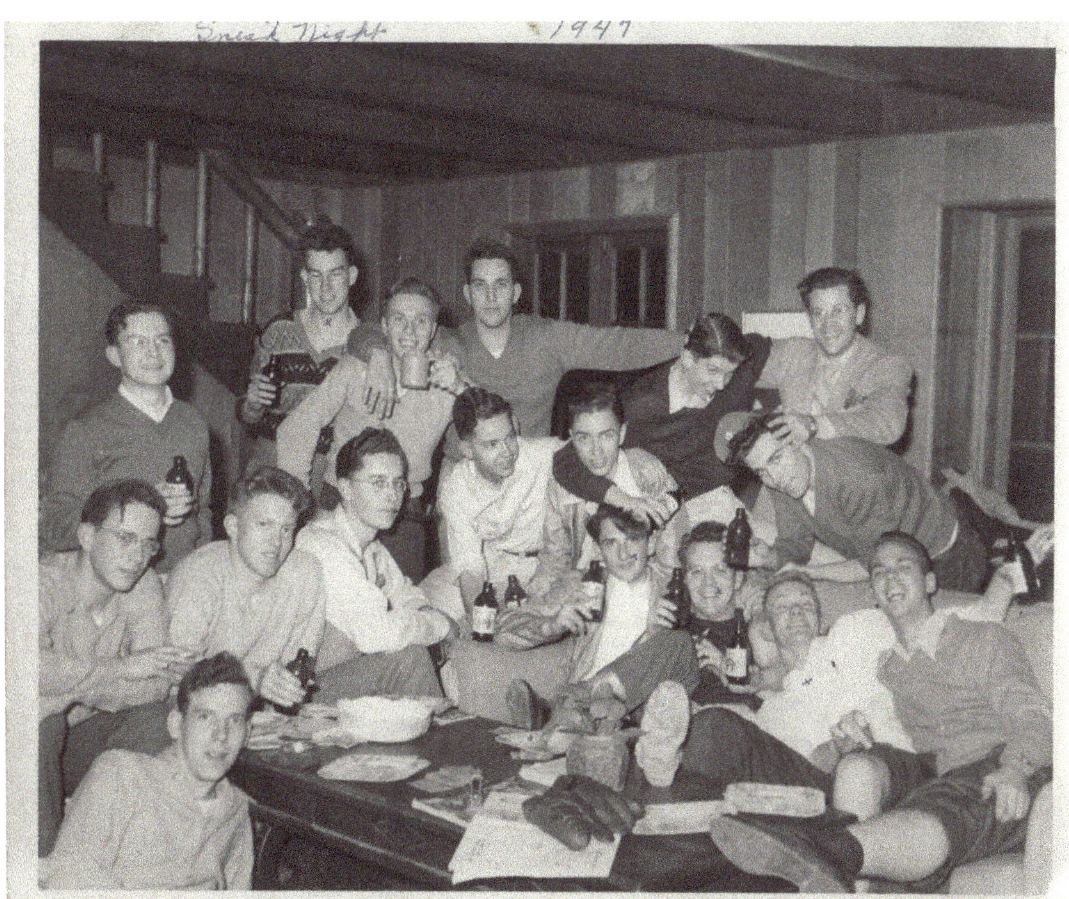

51

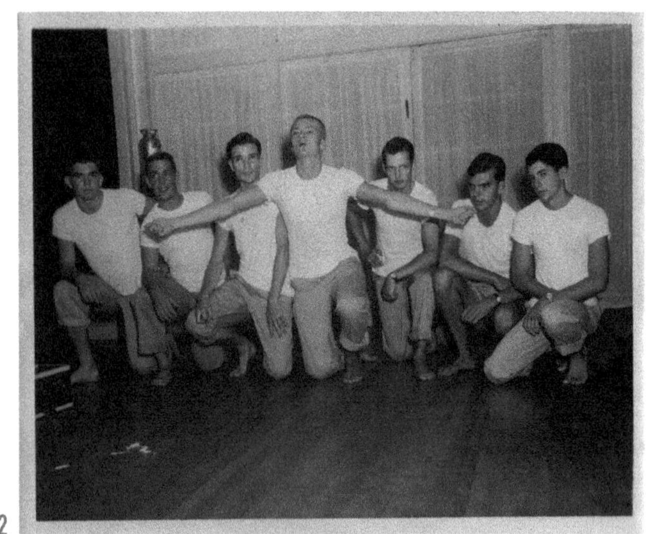

52

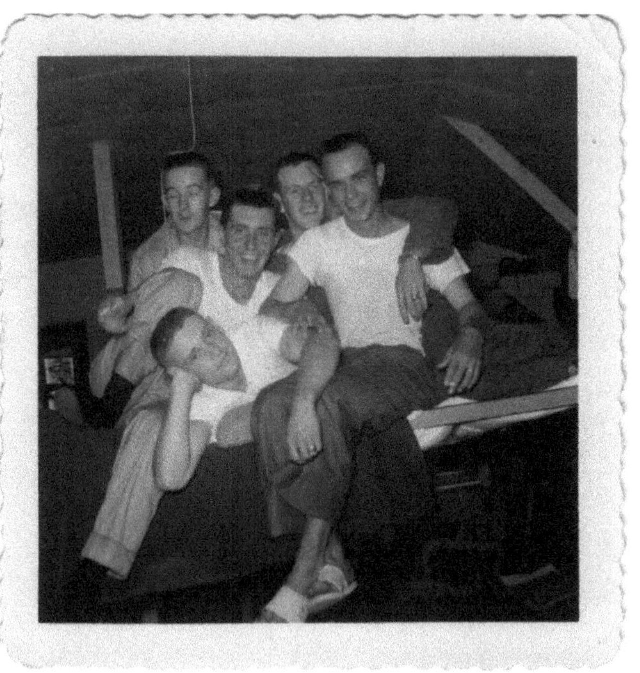

54

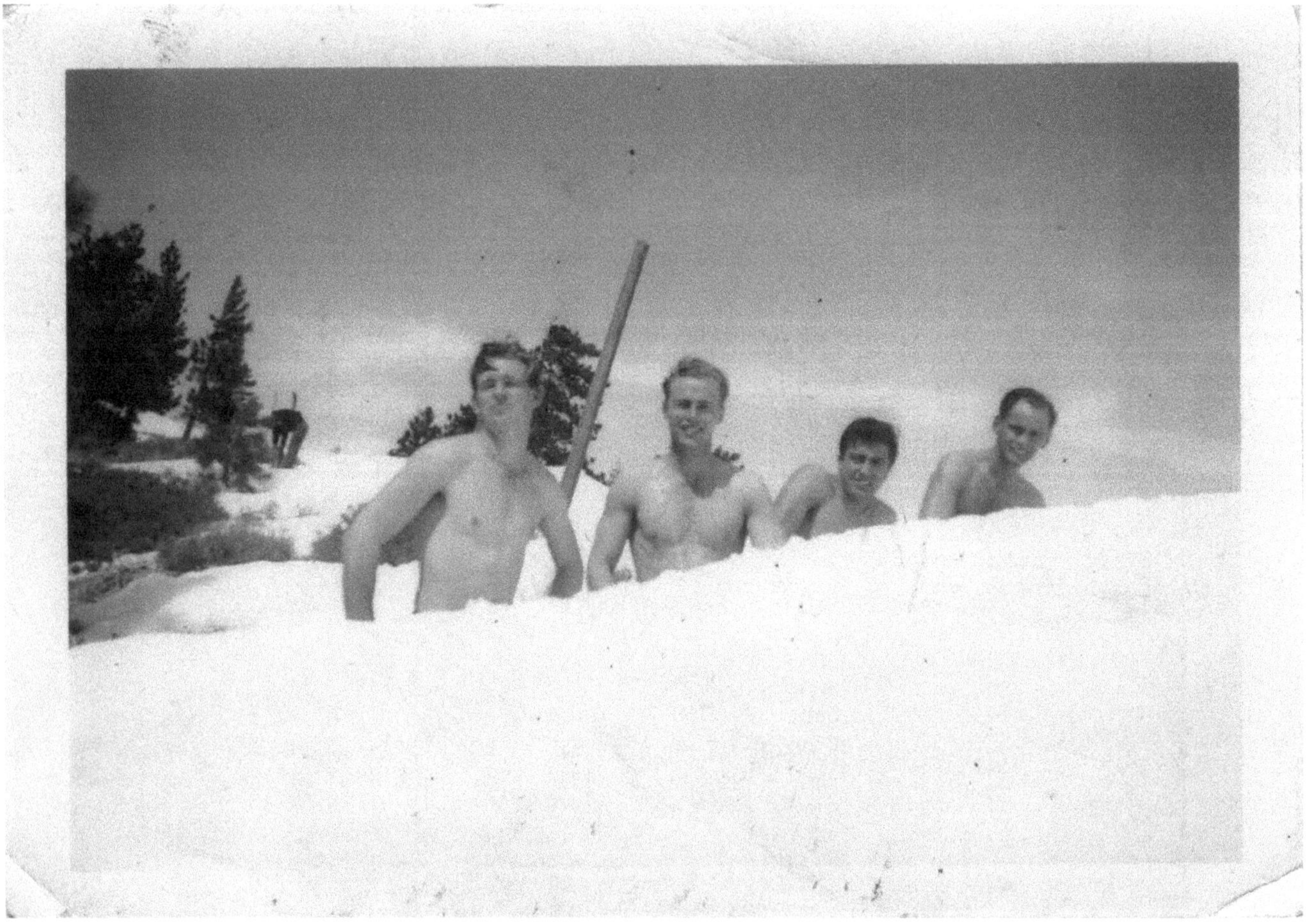

53

CHAPTER 3

BROTHERS IN ARMS

MILITARY PHOTOGRAPHS

The sole focus of this chapter, military photos are numerous in my collection. The spectacle of war was among photography's first subjects, beginning with the Mexican–American War and continuing with the Crimean War and the American Civil War. Roughly half a century later, by the time of the American wars with Spain and in the Philippines, soldiers and sailors were themselves taking photographs, and that practice became even more pronounced during the First World War. Thirty-five-millimeter cameras, notably the Argus C-3, aptly nicknamed "the brick," were available by World War II, and their comparatively small size made their use in the military considerably easier than had been the case with the cumbersome box and folding cameras available during World War I. Even in peacetime, the camera became a popular way for soldiers and sailors to record their experiences and to communicate with friends and family at home.

Not to slight the many women who served earlier, until fairly recently military service in the United States has, of course, been largely a male activity. And military photos are vital cultural documents in the history of American masculinity and male association. Especially during the two World Wars, soldiers and sailors frequently made albums containing photos from their time in uniform, sometimes adding revealing inscriptions beneath a photo about particular people and places. Recognizing photography's significance, the military itself began to provide suitably decorated photo albums. One of these, made available during World War II, was called a "Buddy Album," complete with a page on which to record the buddies' physical measurements, hometowns, and favorite activities. Vendors of military photographs, in and out of albums, typically appeared at gun shows during the decades I was collecting photographs; from these sellers particularly, as well as from eBay vendors, I have put together quite a sizeable collection of military imagery.

I'm particularly fond of the Civil War trio that is this chapter's first photo, a wonderfully preserved cased tintype. The seven sailors in Image 22 posed with relaxed fondness for each other, their affection nicely captured by someone's inscription: "Fond Memories." The sailor couples in Images 17 and 83 are particular favorites of mine, not so much for the images themselves as for the frames in which I found these photos; the frame in Image 83 was homemade, maybe by one of that photo's subjects, using shell casings.

Images 25 through 30 are all from the Neptune Ceremonies, which marked a ship's crossing of the equator. The elaborate ritual was essentially an initiation, sometimes an outright hazing, of pollywogs—those crossing for the first time—by shellbacks (sailors who had crossed before). The two-day ritual featured complex roleplaying, costumes as well as nudity, female impersonation, intimacy, and roughhousing that often became violent. King Neptune, Roman god of the sea, sometimes played by the ship's captain himself, presided, accompanied by his "wife," a sailor done up as Greek sea goddess Amphitrite, and sometimes by sea spirit Davy Jones. Sailors have photographed this ritual extensively, from the earliest days of snapshots, sometimes devoting entire albums to the ceremony. There were even empty leatherbound albums available with a specific ship's name on the cover. My Neptune collection is notably large, with 525 loose snapshots and more than 100 additional mounted in albums, 61 of those in a US Navy "Log Album." Images 25 through 29 are representative of many in my collection, but Image 30, from the *USS Colorado*, is distinctive, especially with its inscription on the back: "Kissing the Equator Romeo of the South Seas."[26]

I particularly like the two snapshots that comprise Image 39, taken at Indian Point Park, New York, in 1944. The young men's silly and affectionate behavior in front of two women who may be their mothers is endearing enough, but also in my collection are two more photos from the same day and location that show the uniformed male sitting on the other's lap and the two of them lying close together on the grass, arms around each other. Incredibly, I found these pairs of photos at different photo sales from different vendors. The other two images appear in my book *The Mourning After.*

Image 42, a photo of tender kissers, tempts me to adopt the approach of Nini and Treadwell, of which I was previously critical, and say that it's surely a photo of two men in love. Instead, it simply reminds me of remarks I made in my book *Men without Maps: Some Gay Males of the Generation before Stonewall*:

> Yet if World War II saw a revival of men's romantic association on a scale approaching what I suggested in *Picturing Men* and *The Mourning After*, it seems no exaggeration to say that the end of the war signaled the end of many a love affair between two American males. Juxtaposed alongside the iconic photograph by Alfred Eisenstadt of the returning male sailor enthusiastically kissing a female nurse on the streets of New York, much to their countrymen's delight, we might imagine two other photos: one of a pair of sailors standing apart, knowing that no such public enthusiasm would greet a similar public embrace between them; another of a sailor alone, with his wartime lover killed in battle or his wartime romance already dead from the from the hostile fire of American culture.[27]

That melancholy imagining of mine notwithstanding, Image 42 reminds us that, if not in Times Square, male lovers in the service could sometimes find a good place for some kissing. The frequently romantic quality of many military photos, particularly those from the Second World War, is obvious, underappreciated, and, I believe, very significant.[28]

Images 44, 46, 59, and 85 are favorites of mine, not only because of some appealing poses and—in the case of Image 59—those mysterious props, but also because of their regrettable rarity in my collection—photos of men of color. The reasons that such photos have largely eluded me remain unclear. In the nineteenth century, before snapshots, there may have been so many more white people, mostly men, working as studio photographers in our highly segregated society that African Americans had fewer opportunities to be photographed. Though tintype photographs, sometimes taken in makeshift "studios," were quite inexpensive, they may still have seemed luxuries beyond the means of many African Americans. Or photographs may have had less cultural significance to persons of color, resulting in fewer photos being taken. Conversely, perhaps families of color have held onto their photographs more often than white families have, with a smaller proportion of images ending up for sale to collectors. Or certain notions of masculinity may sometimes have kept men of color away from the camera more frequently than white males. There is also the fact that, because of their relative scarcity, photos of persons of color are quite collectible nowadays, comparatively more expensive yet more quickly purchased, and, hence, harder to find.

Lastly, among the military photos are several—Images 67, 68, 70, 72, and 73—that show males wearing what was common attire in photos taken during World War II in the Pacific: a grass skirt. As Images 69 and 71 show, leaves might be worn instead, though much less often. So numerous are such photos from World War II, there must have been few ships in the Pacific without grass skirts aboard. As Images 72 and 73 especially suggest, wearing the skirt permitted a sort of homoerotic play that more typically male attire might preclude. Though nobody wore a grass skirt, dressing in female garb also seemed to permit homoerotic play in the two photos that comprise Image 79, though two of the sailors in the photo on the right remind us that cross-dressing wasn't necessary for two sailors to pose affectionately.

The next chapter is devoted to photos of various male performances for the camera, both in the military and among civilians. ■

26 Though the Neptune Ceremony received some superficial attention by journalists during the early 1990s' debates over "gays in the military," I am aware of only one scholarly analysis of this ritual: Simon J. Bronner's brief, but suggestive, *Crossing the Line: Violence, Play, and Drama in Naval Equator Traditions* (Amsterdam: Amsterdam University Press, 2006).

27 *Men without Maps* (Chicago: University of Chicago Press, 2019), 14.

28 I devote an entire chapter in my *Picturing Men* to "Men Set Free: World War II and the Shifting Boundaries of Male Association," 158–95. An expansion on that theme, my *Mourning After*, examines the war's lasting legacy in American meanings of masculinity.

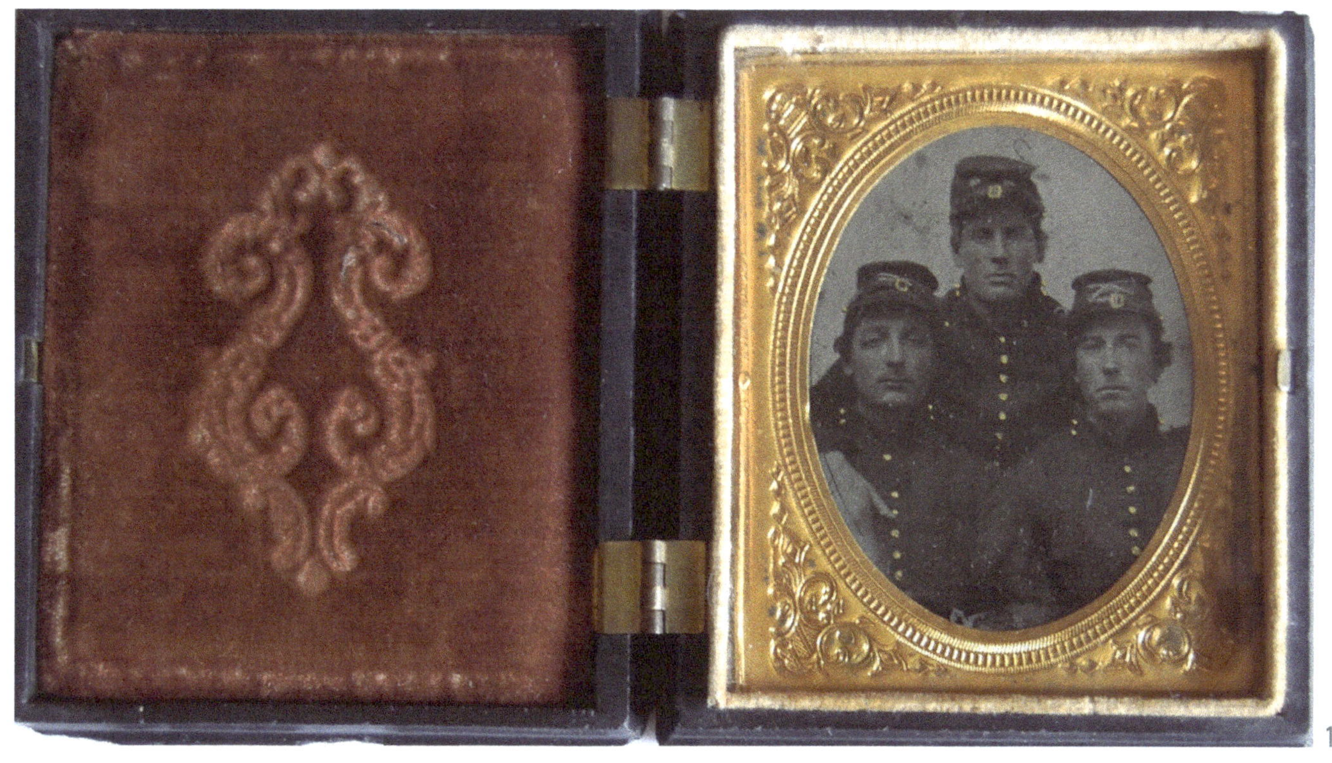
1

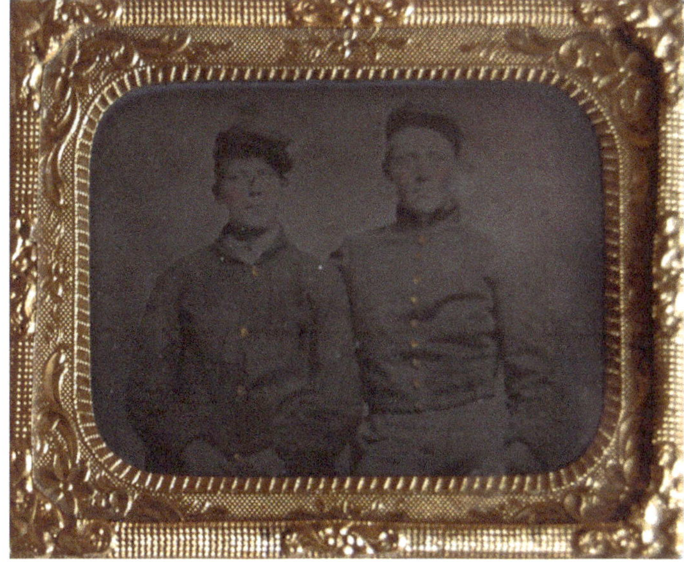
2

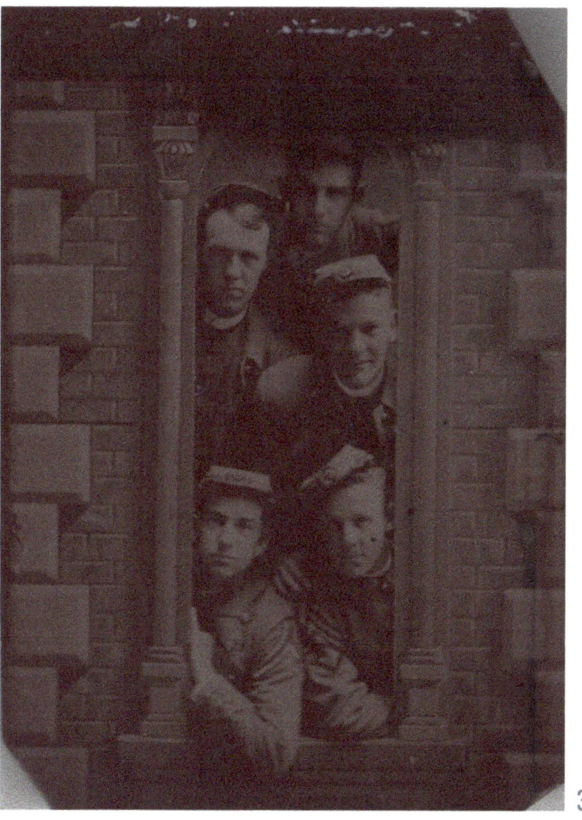
3

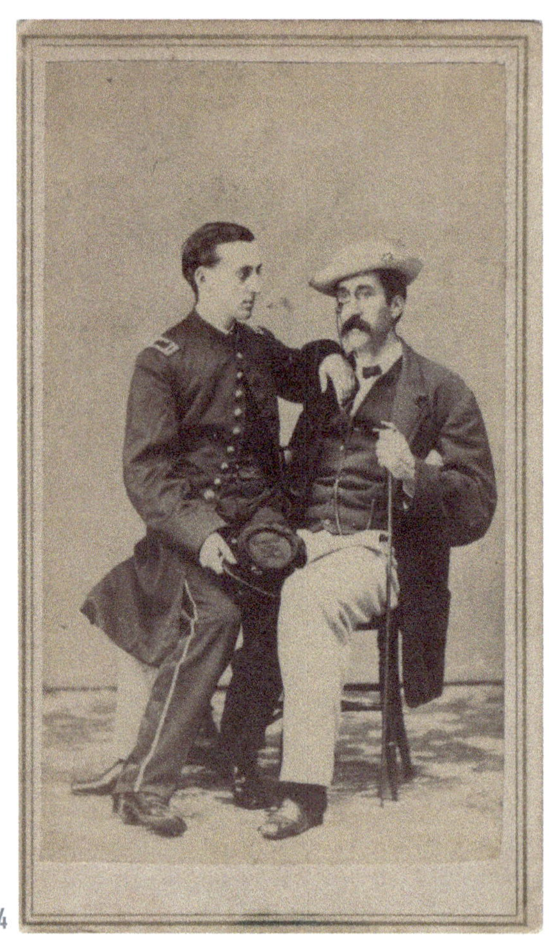
4

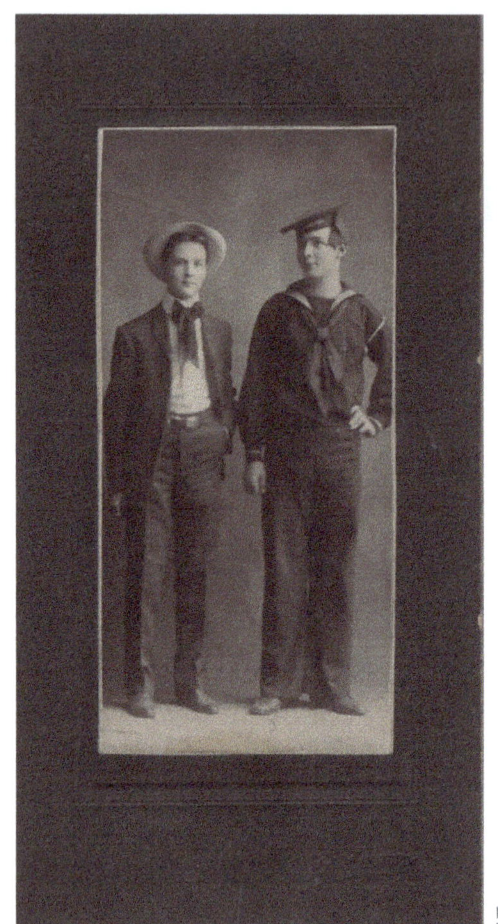
5

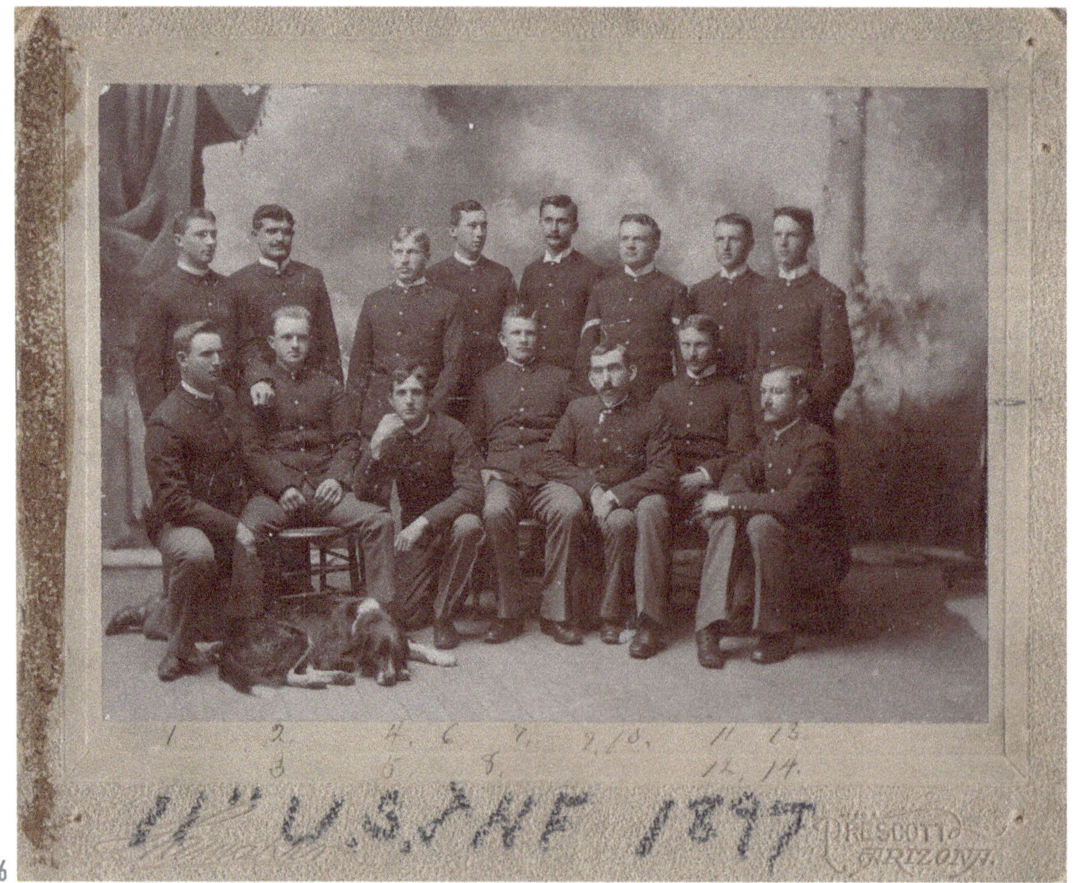

6

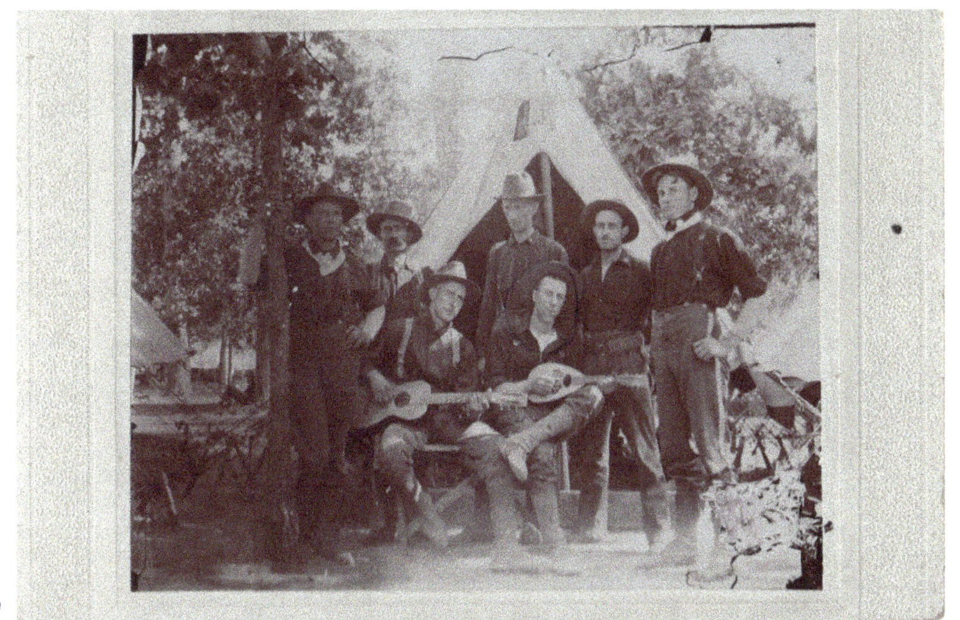

7

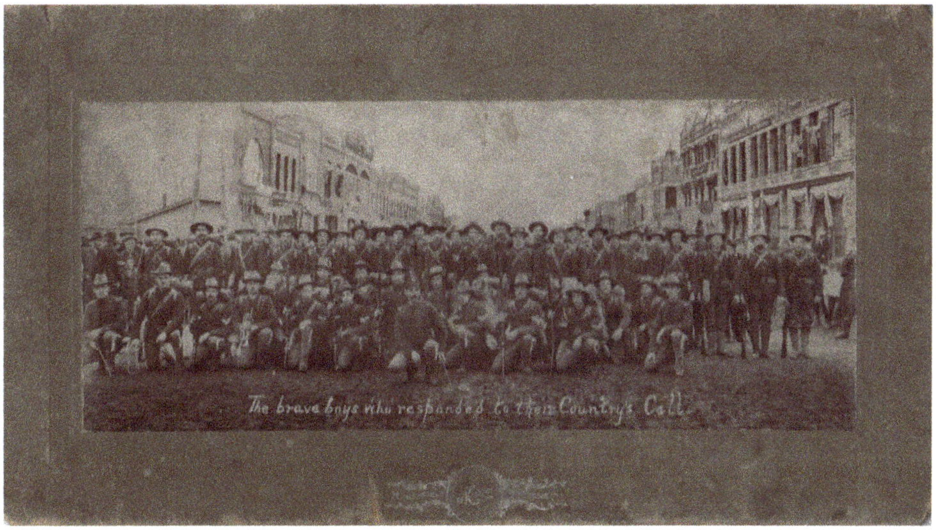

The brave boys who responded to their Country's Call

8

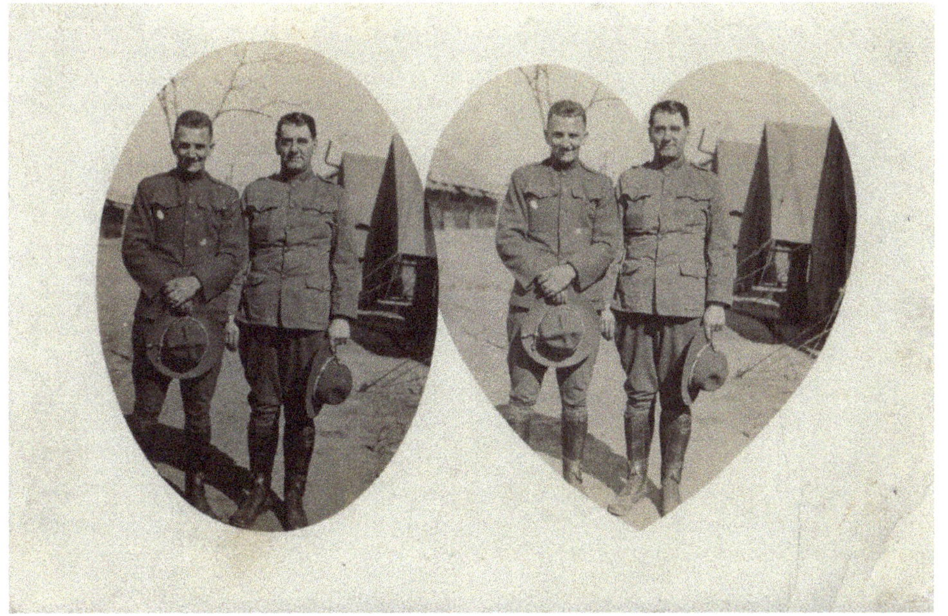

9

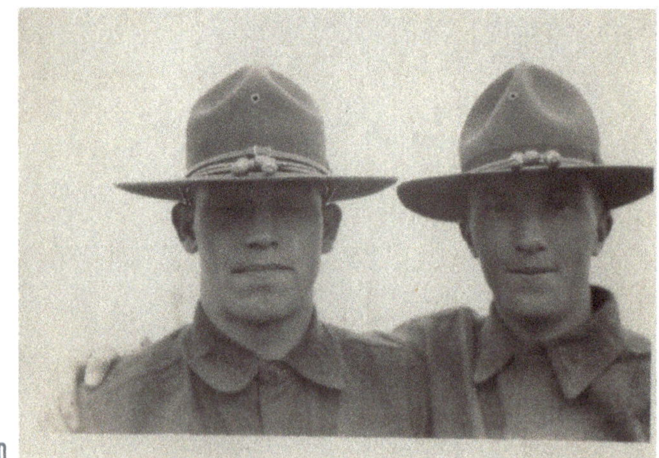
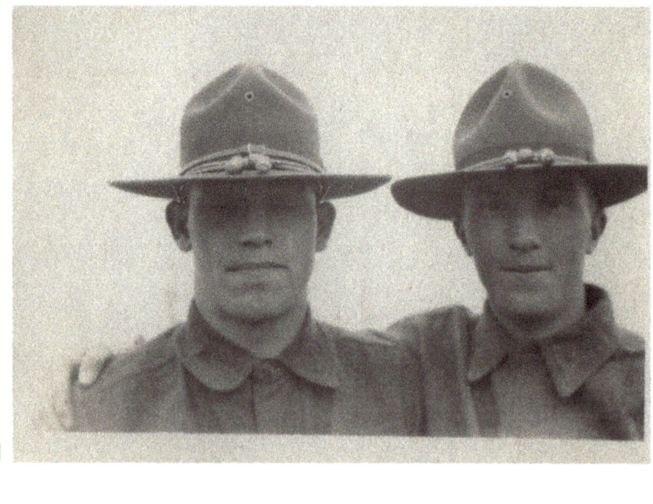

10

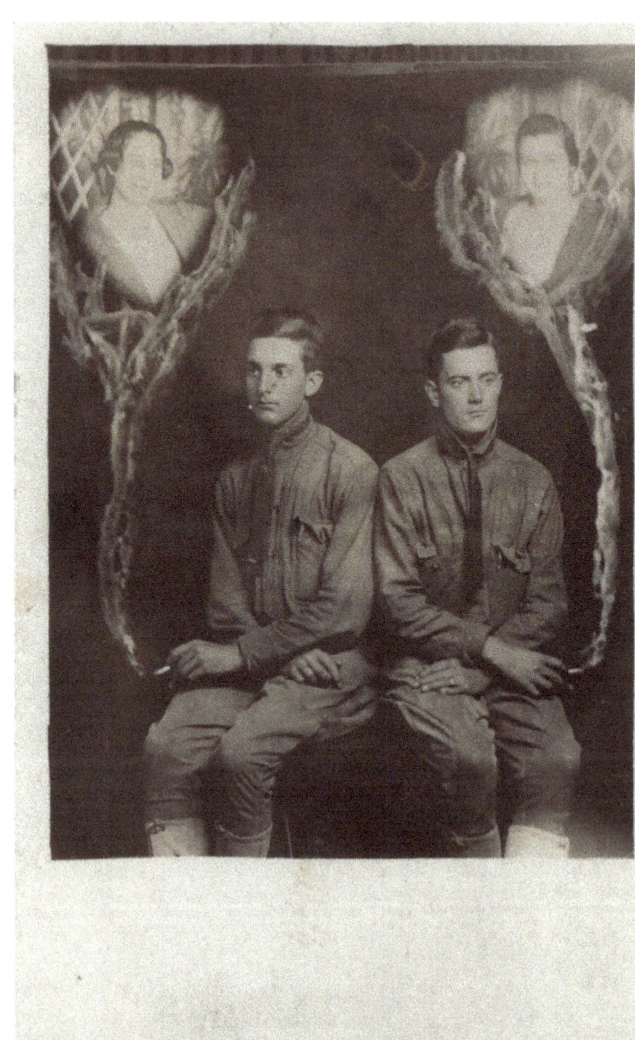

12

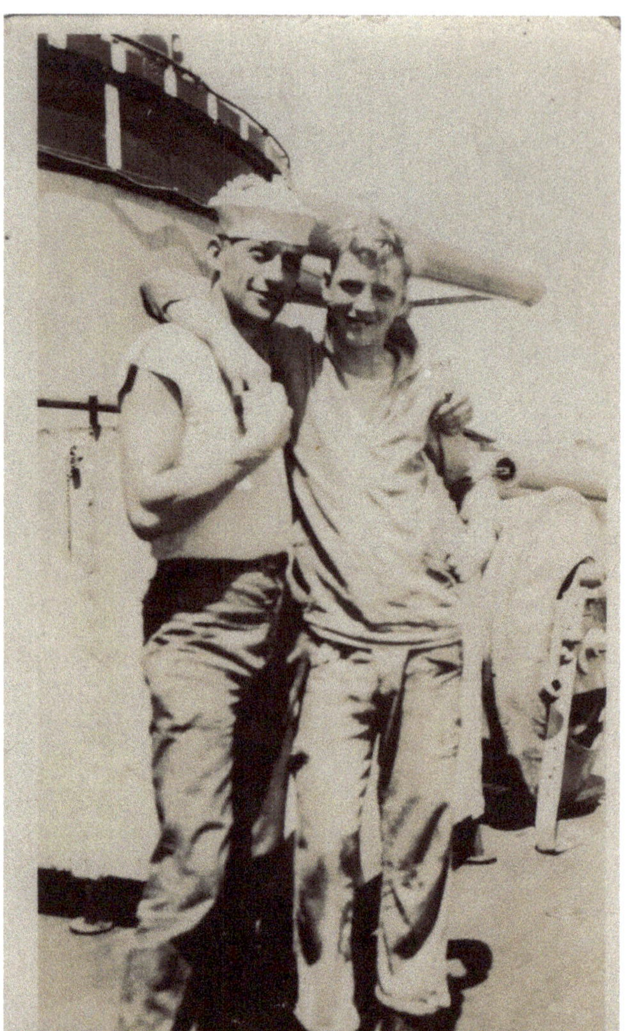

13

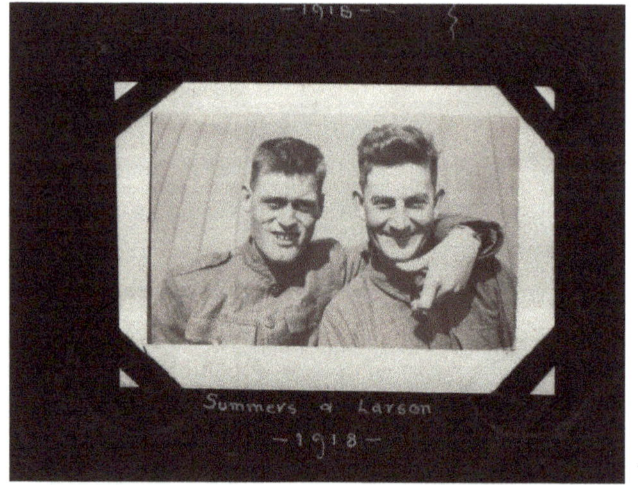

11

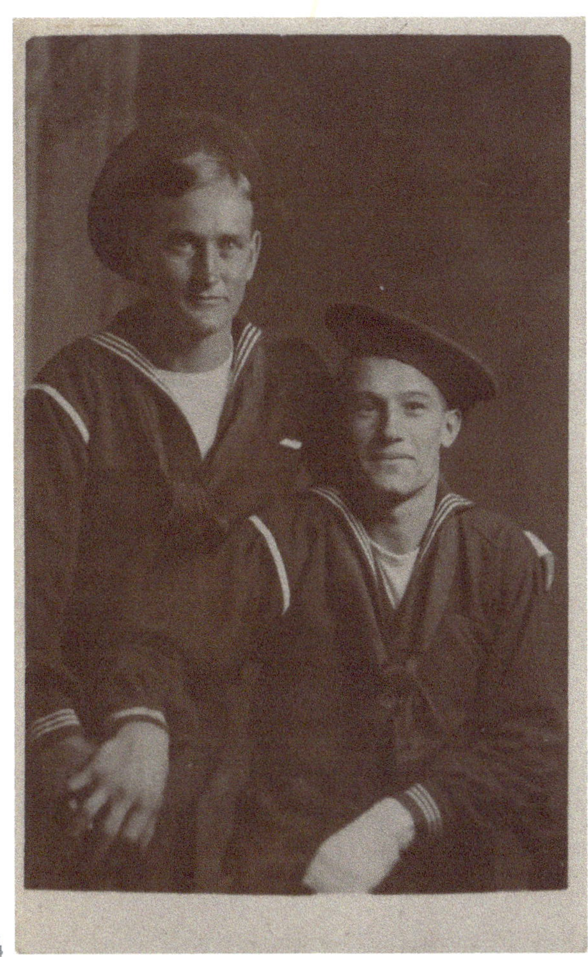

14

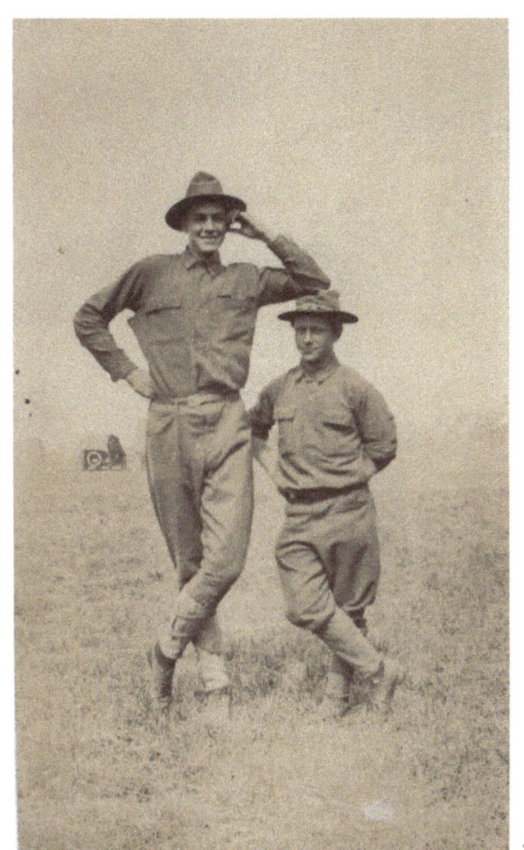

15

16

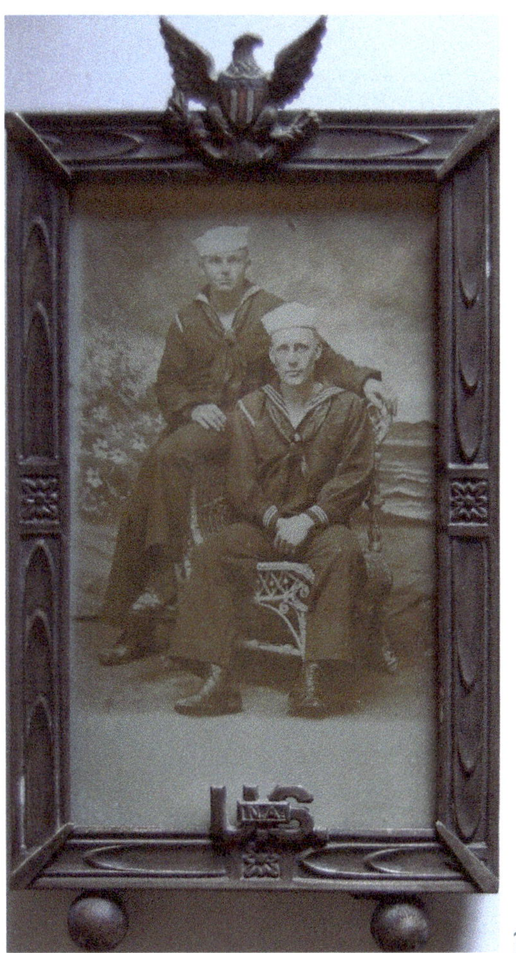

17

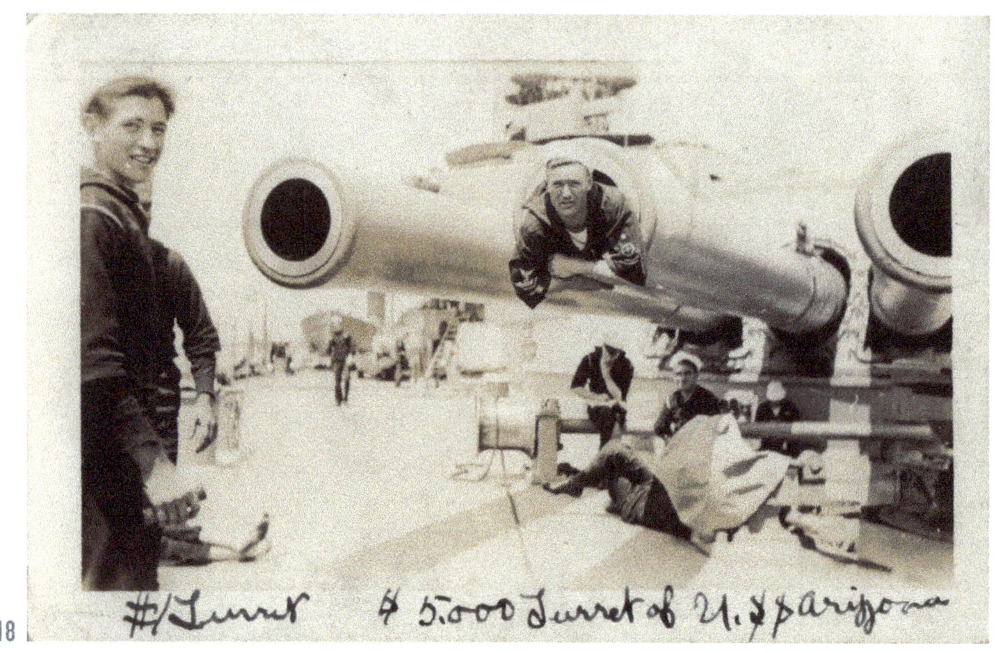

18

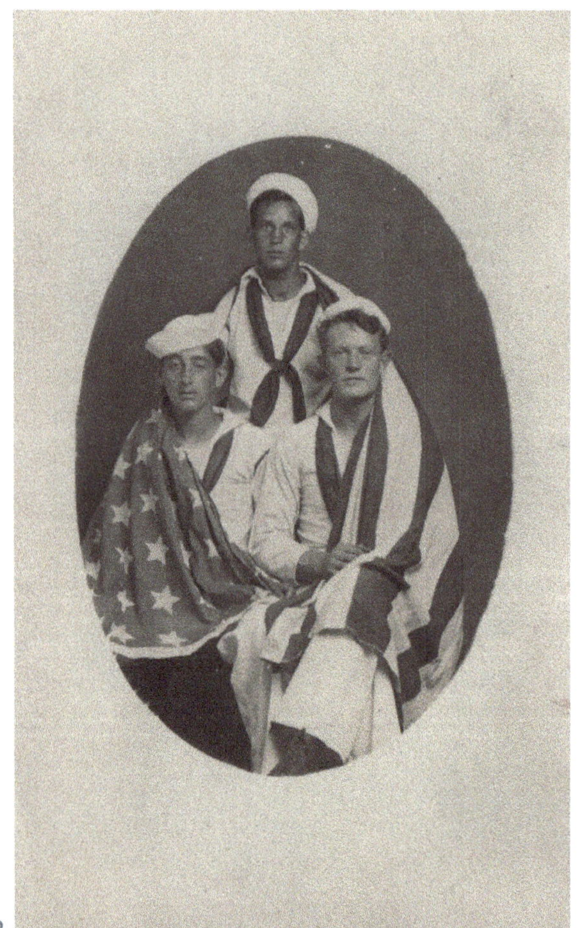

19

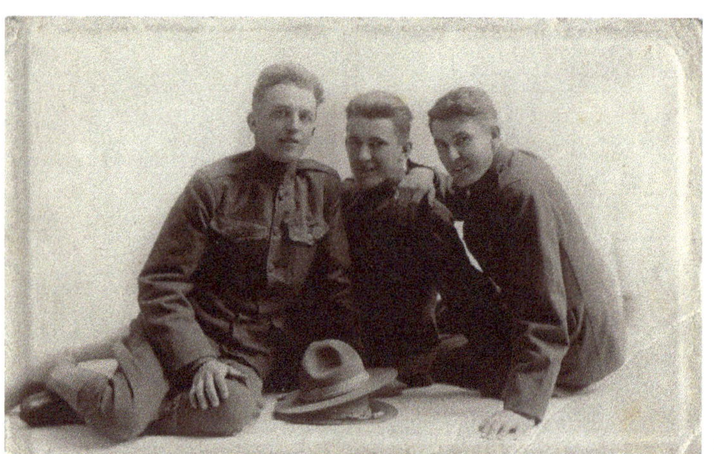

20

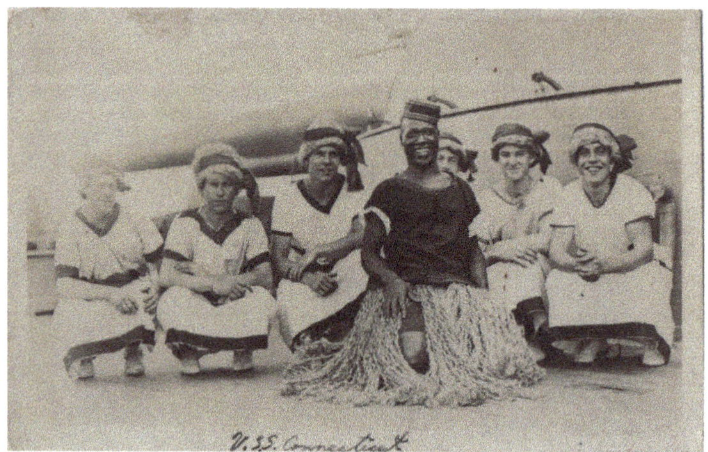

21

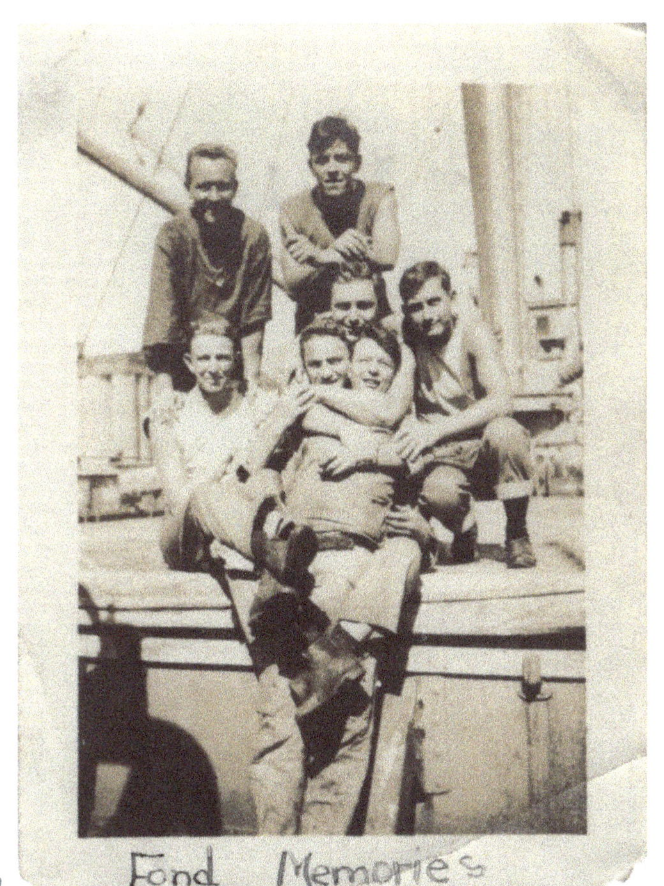
Fond Memories
22

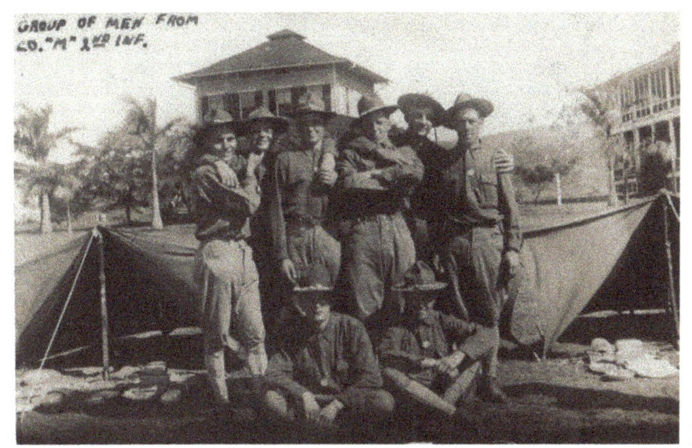
GROUP OF MEN FROM
CO. "M" 1ST INF.
23

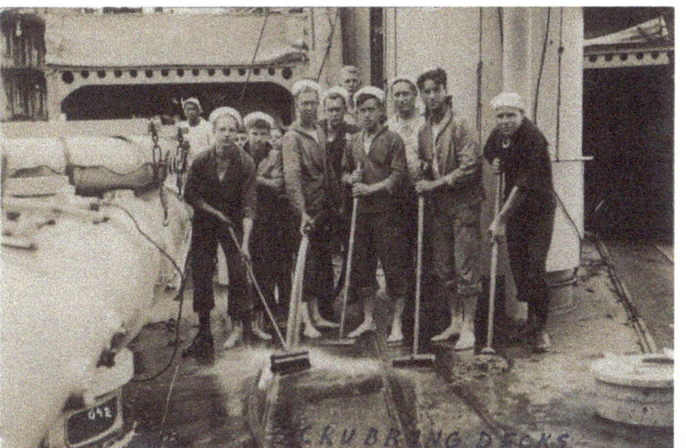
SCRUBBING DECKS.
24

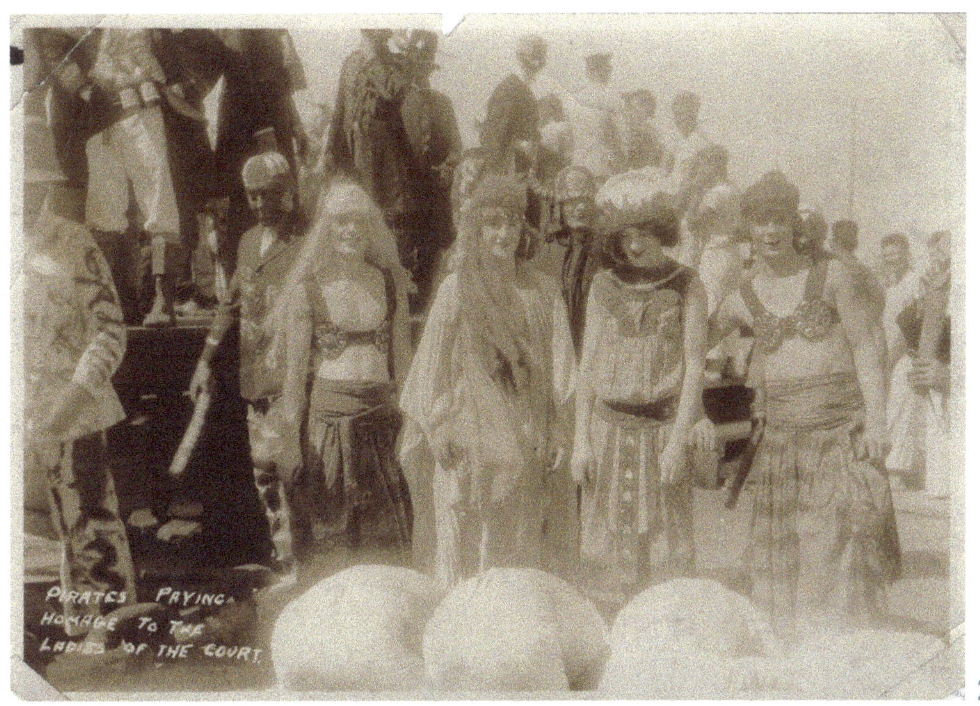
PIRATES PAYING
HOMAGE TO THE
LADIES OF THE COURT
25

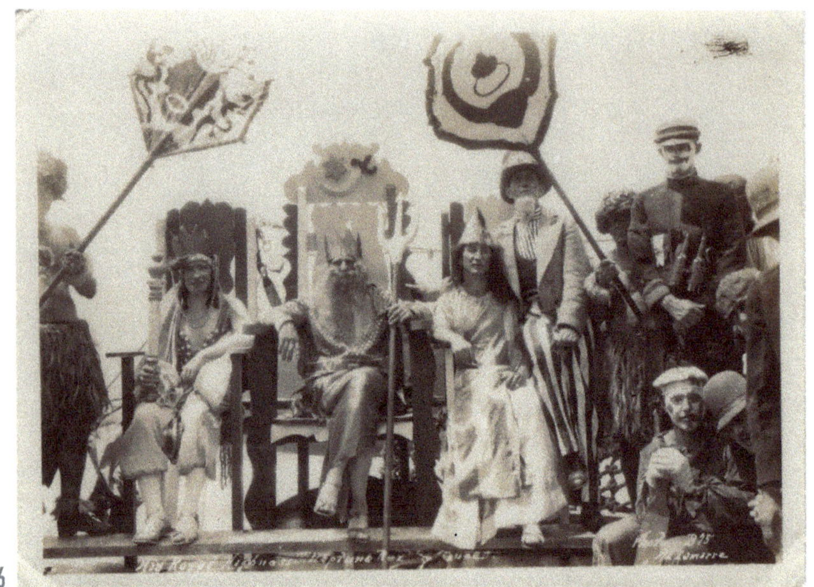

26

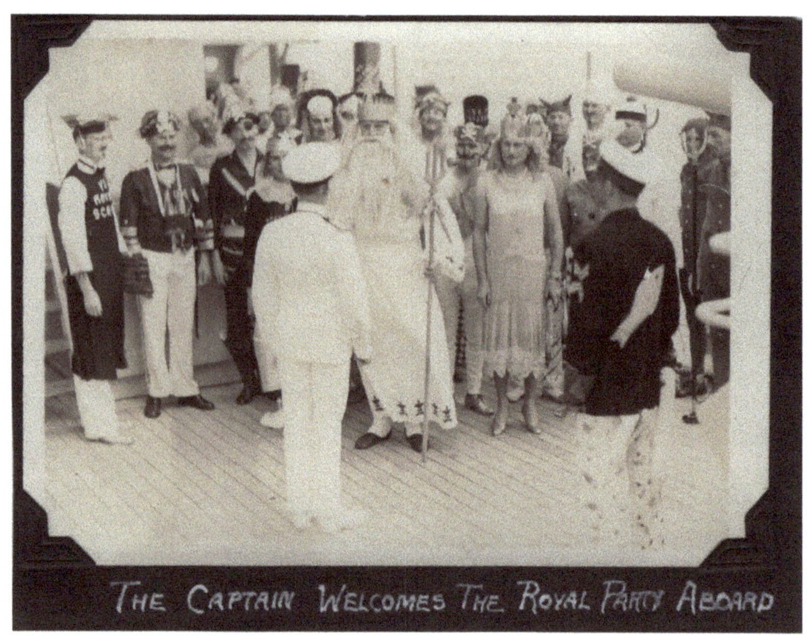

27

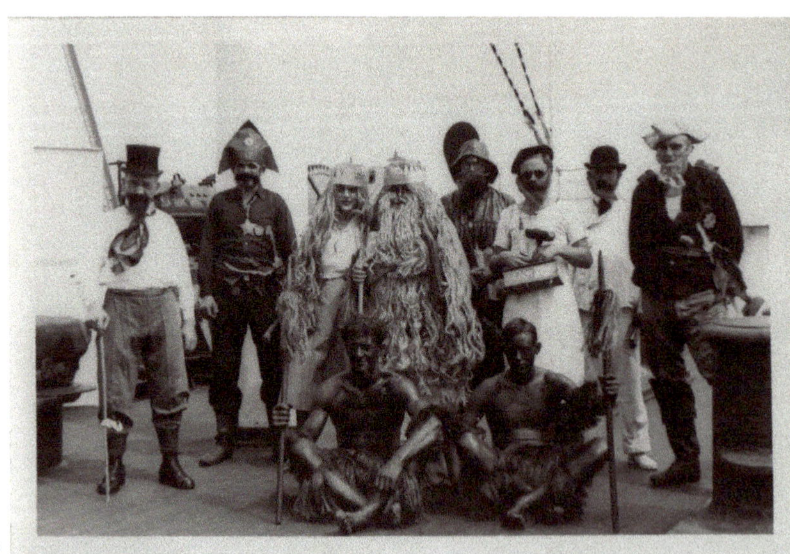

28

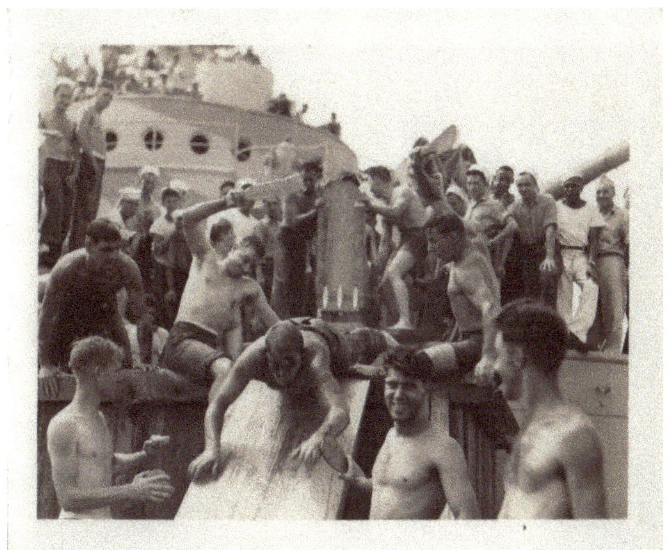

29

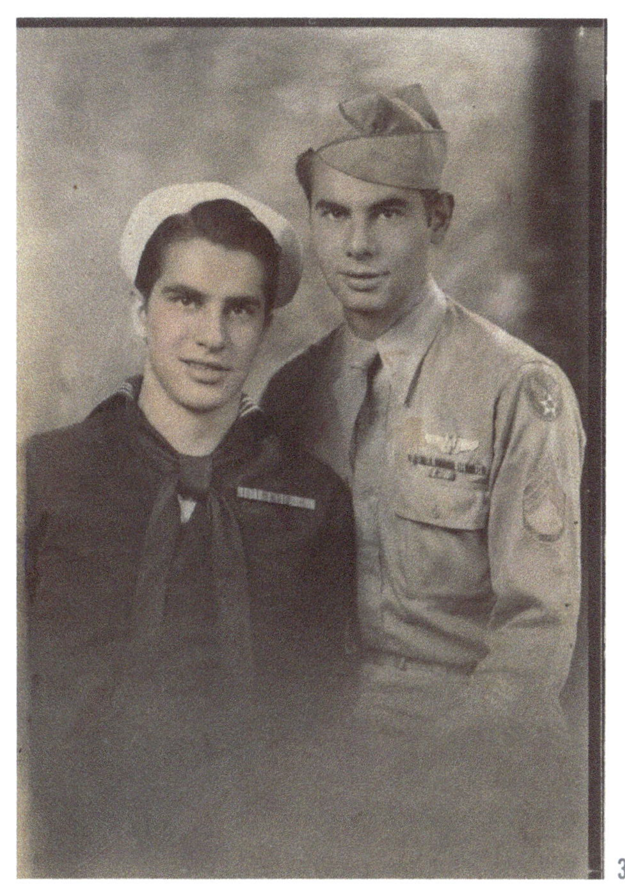

31

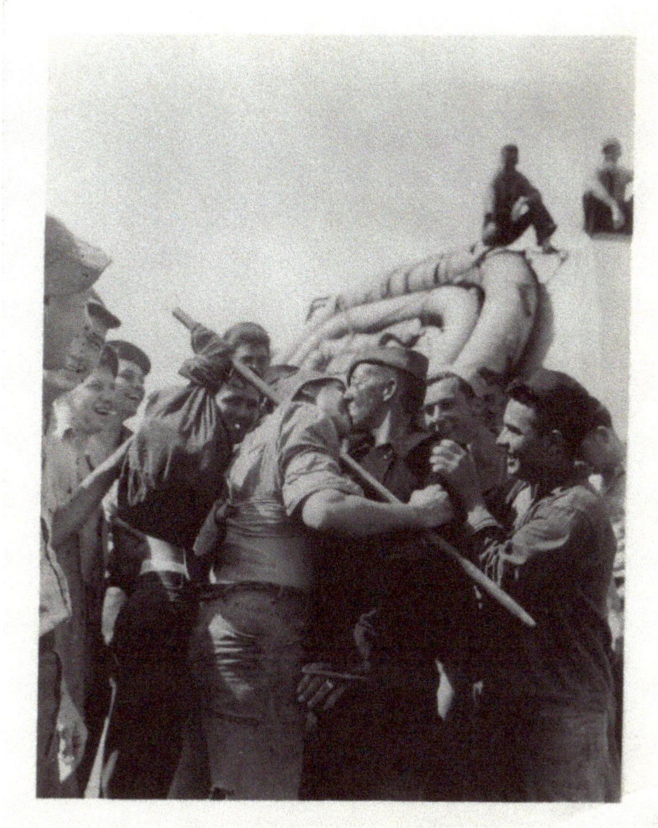

30

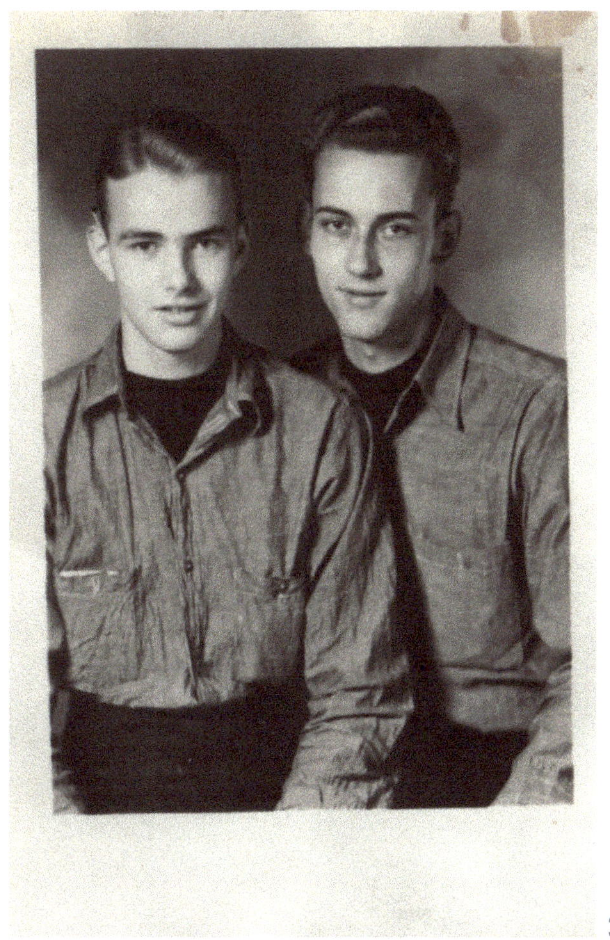

32

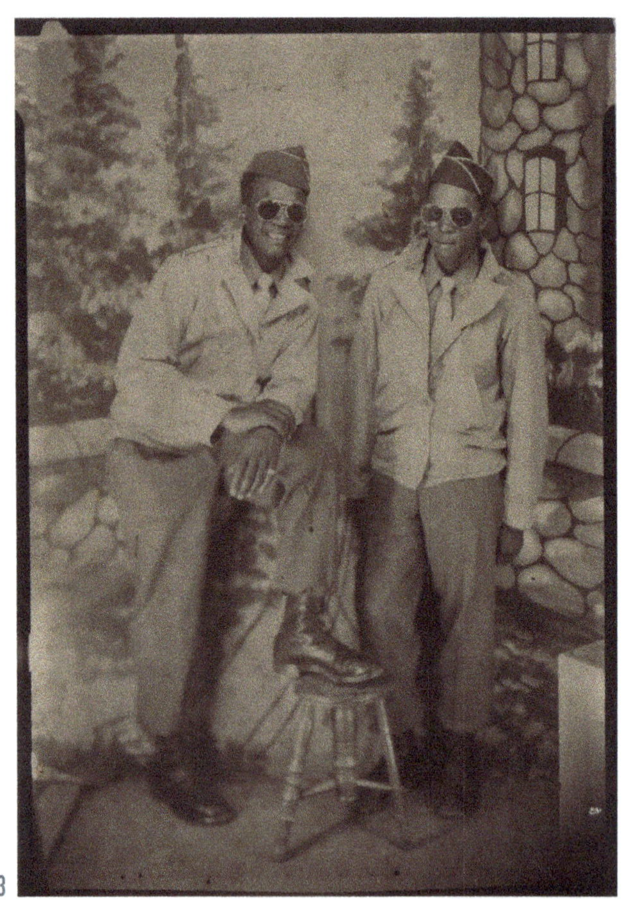

33

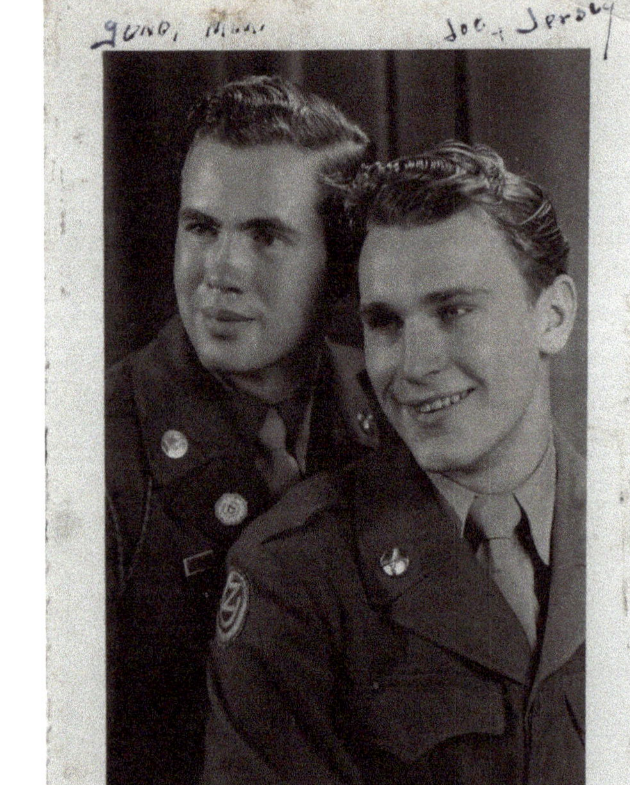

34

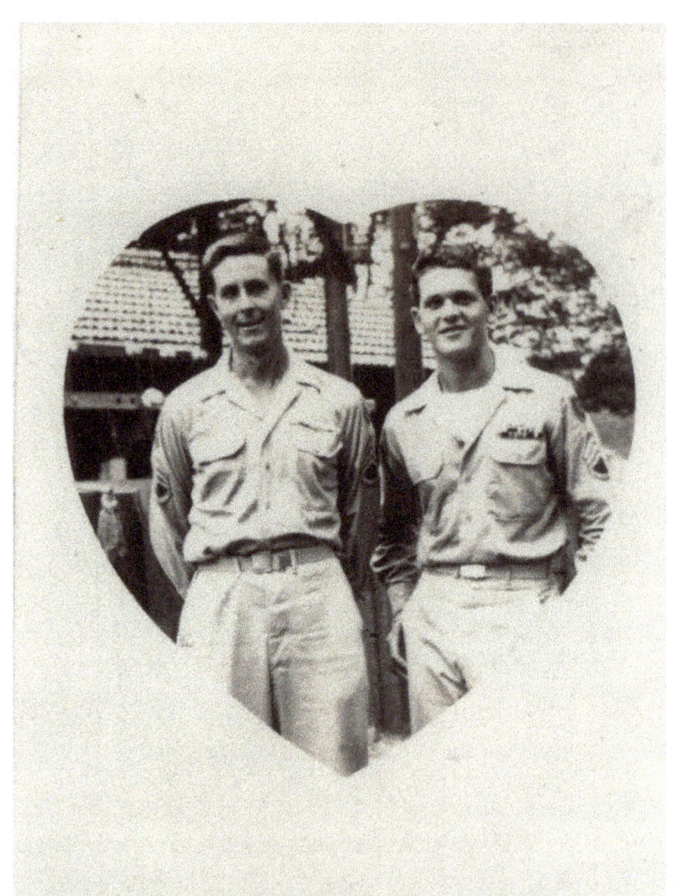

35

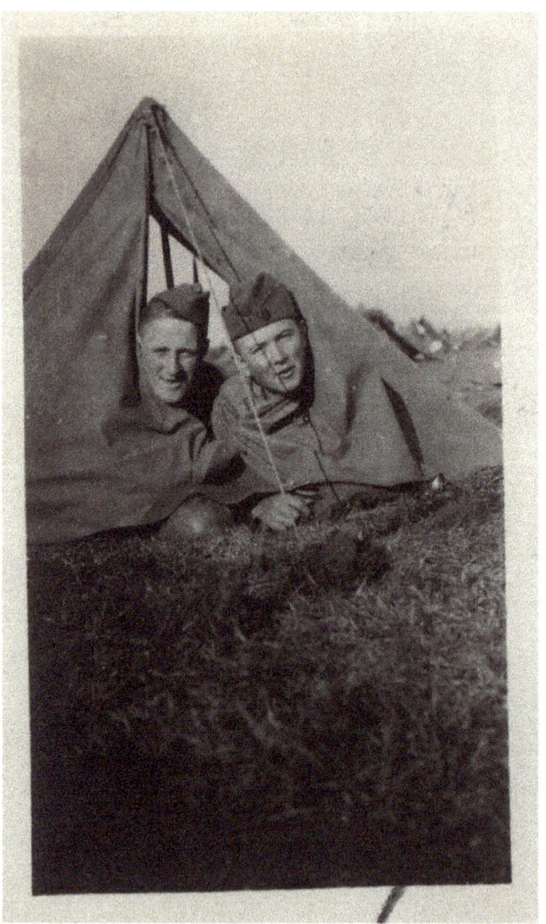

36

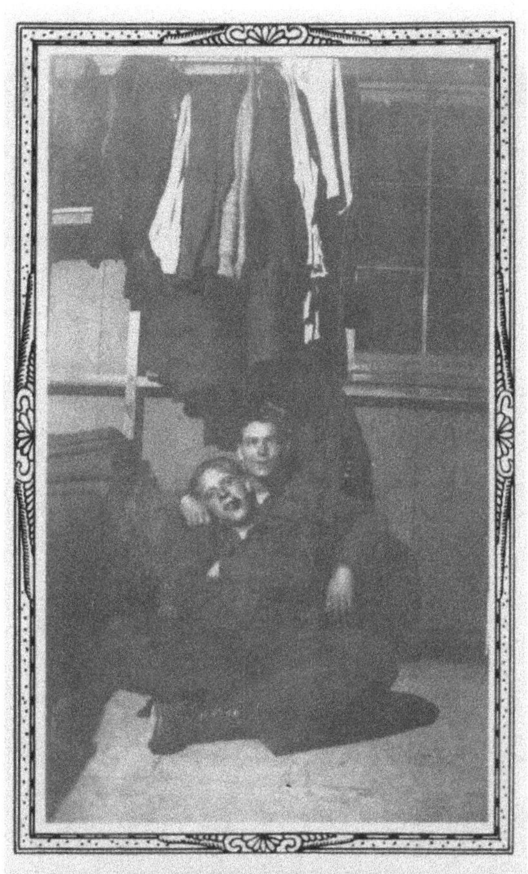
37

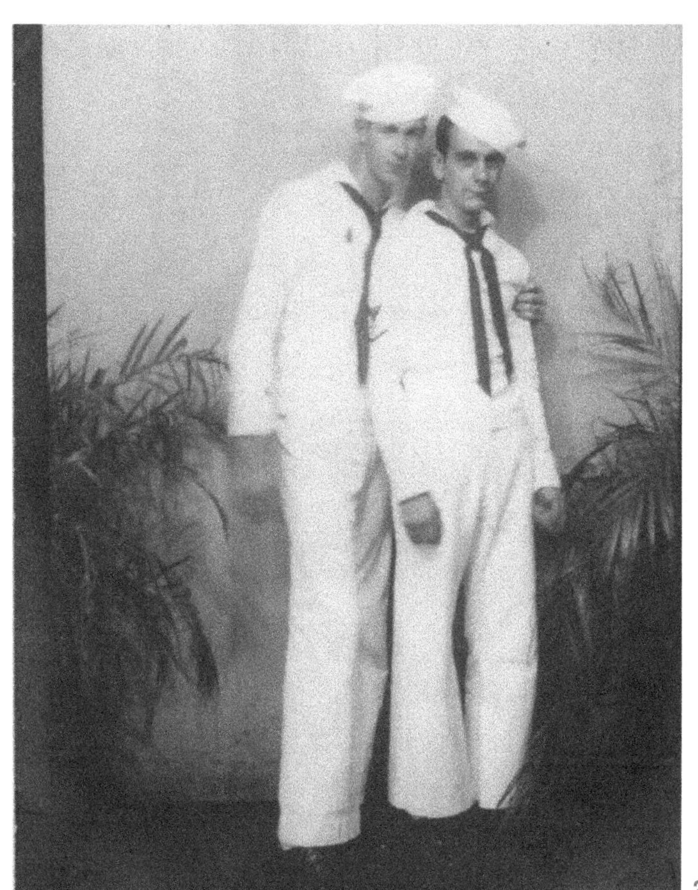
38

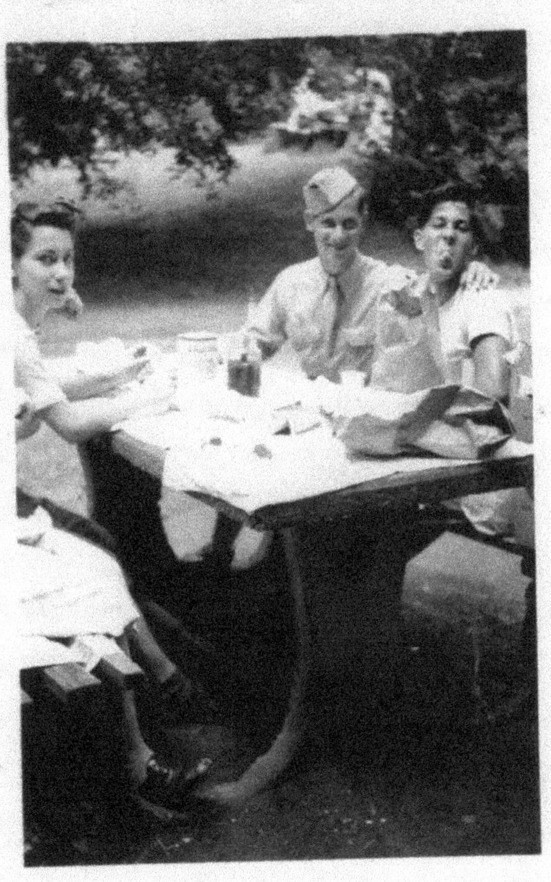
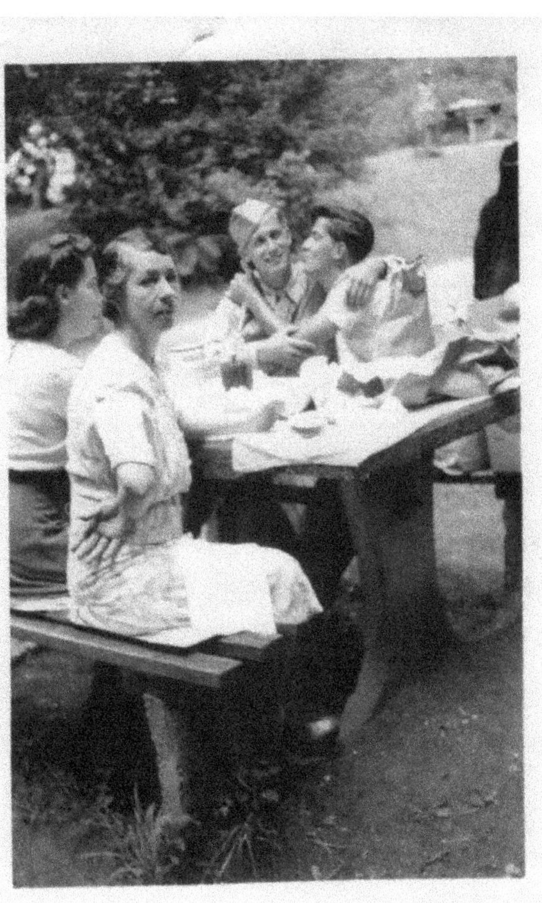
39

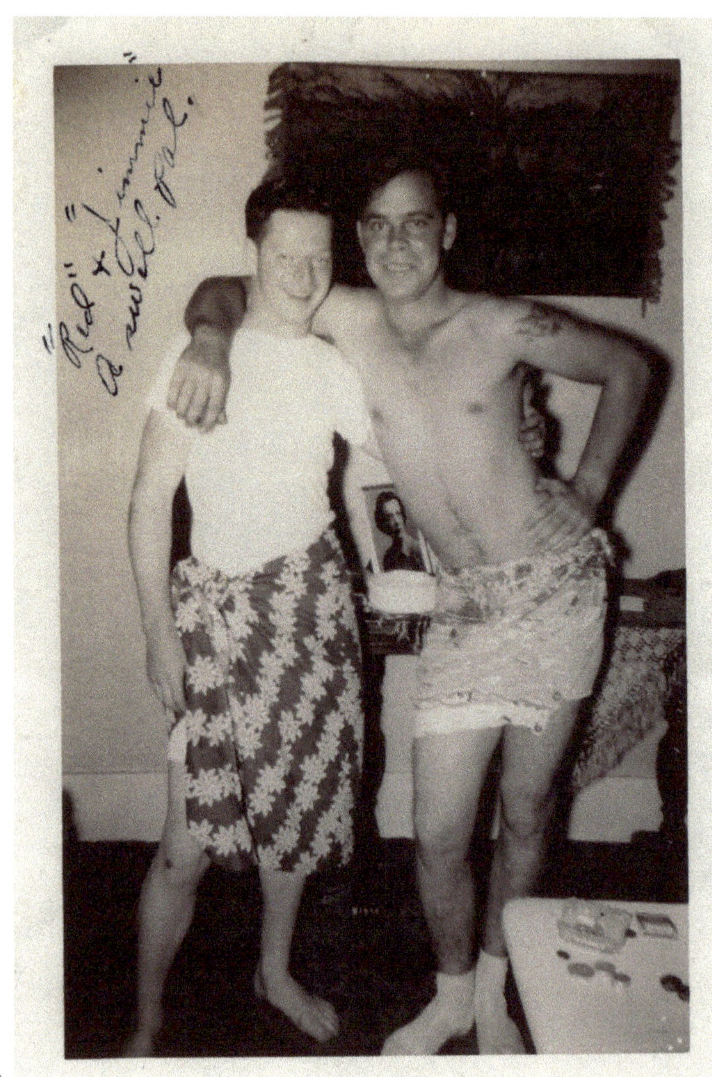

40

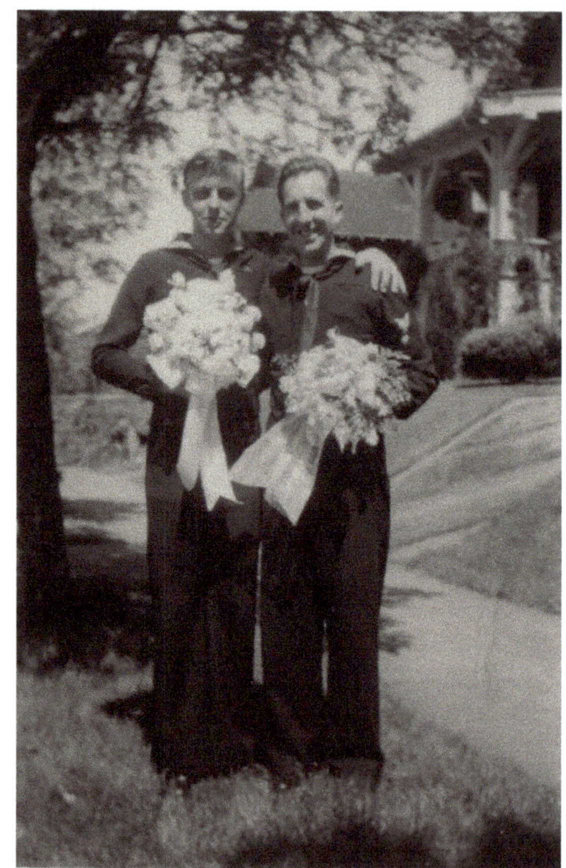

41

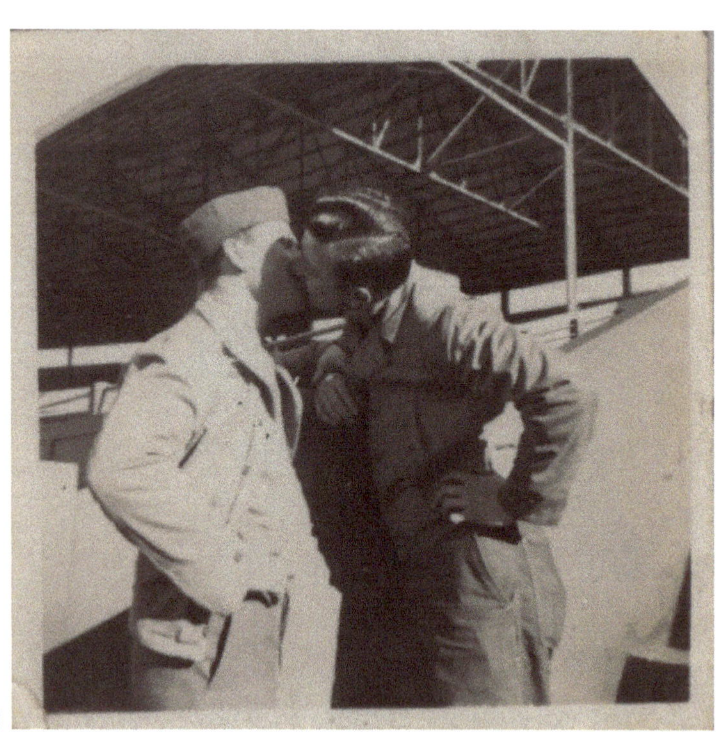

42

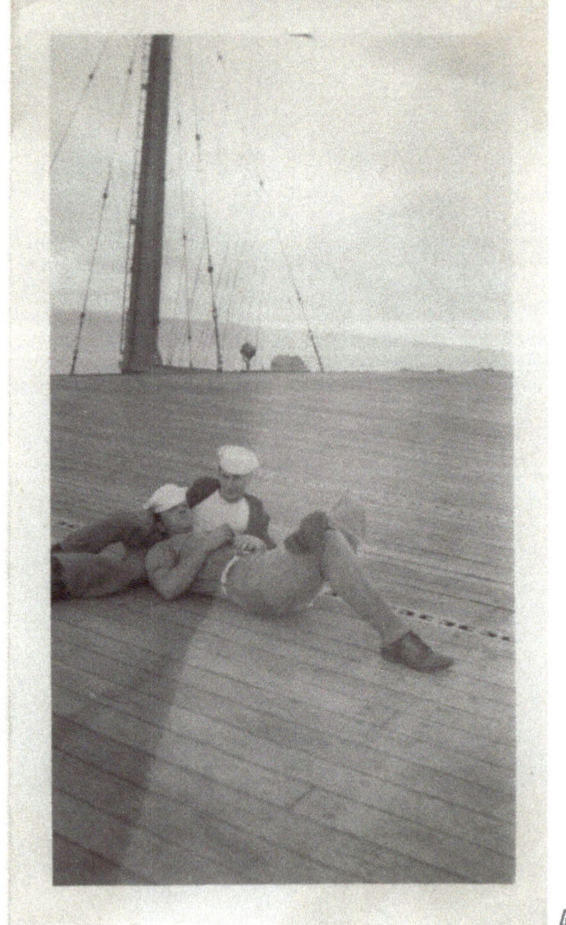

43

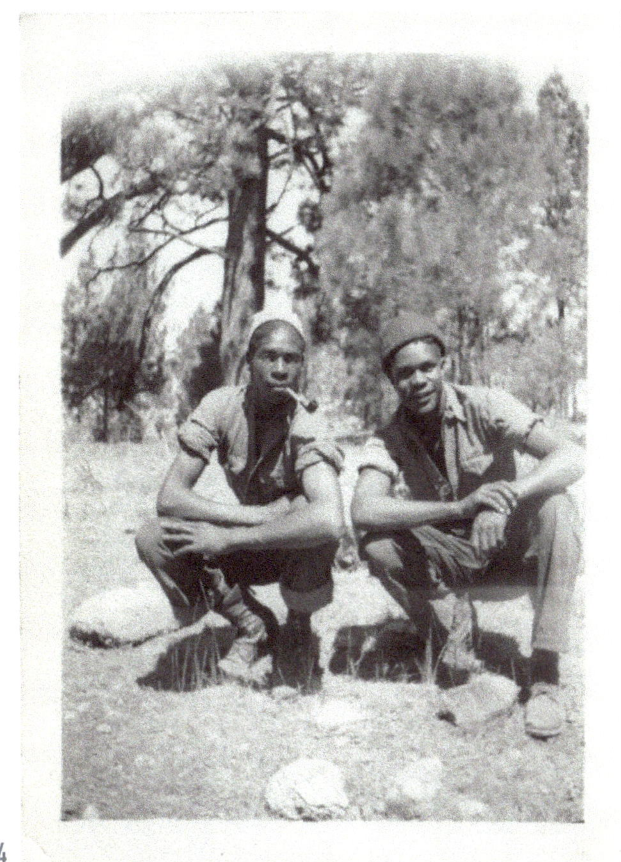

44

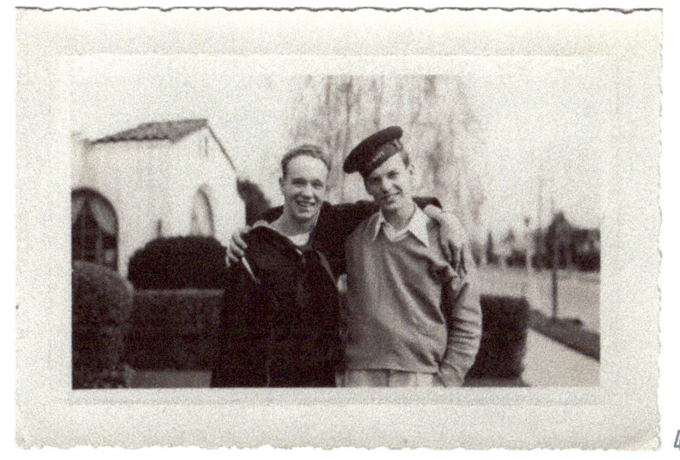

45

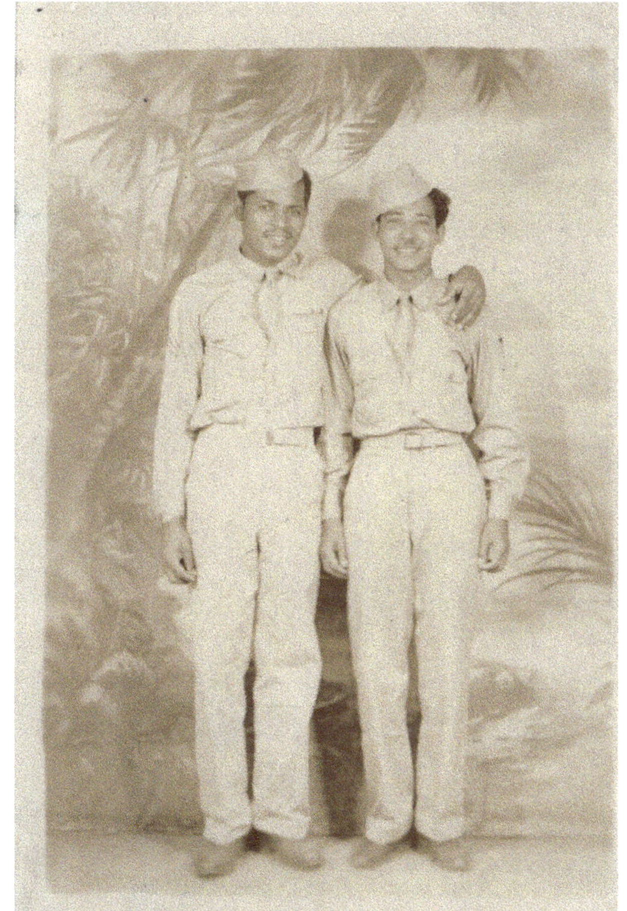

46

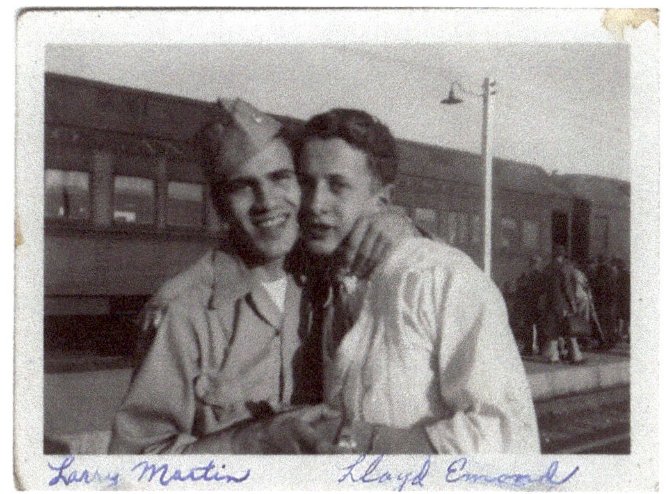

47

48

Denny & Friend from Detroit
Bob Hilty

49

SOUVENIR OF THE
TRIANON
BALLROOM
CHICAGO, ILL.

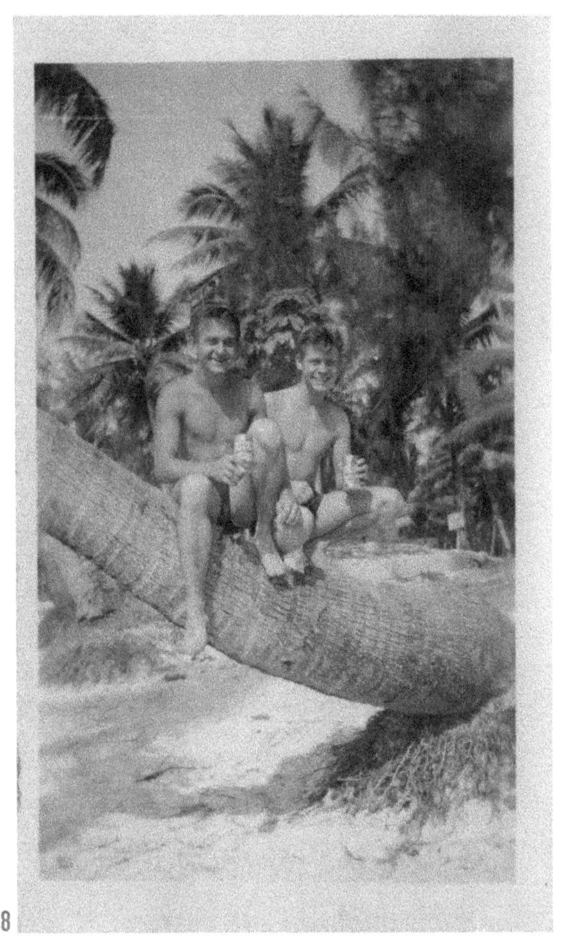

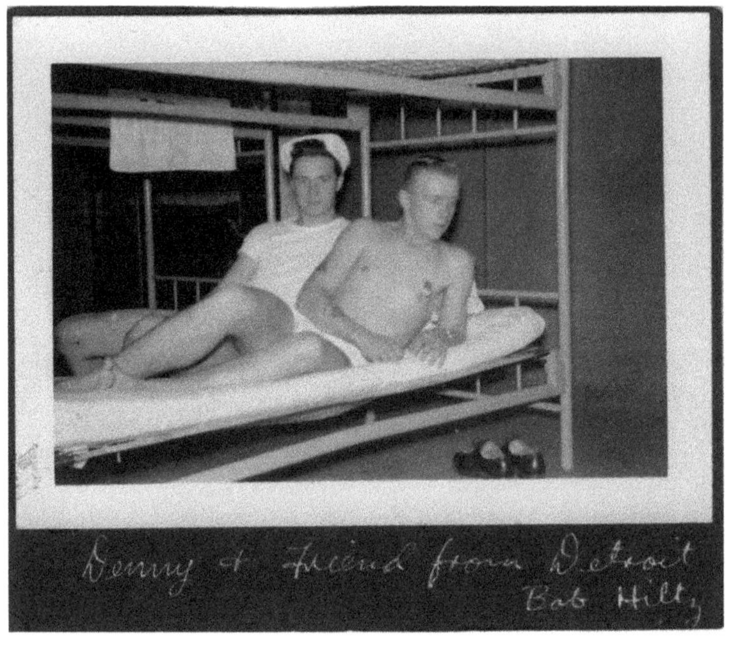

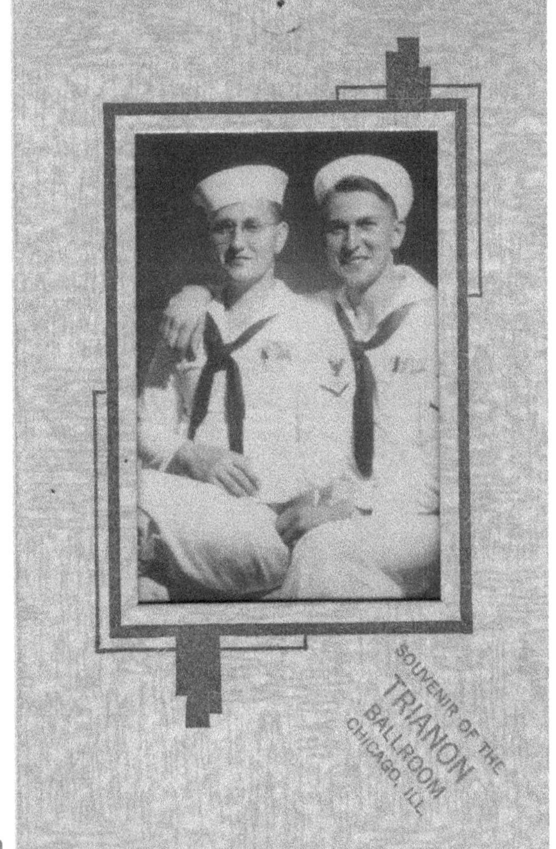

50

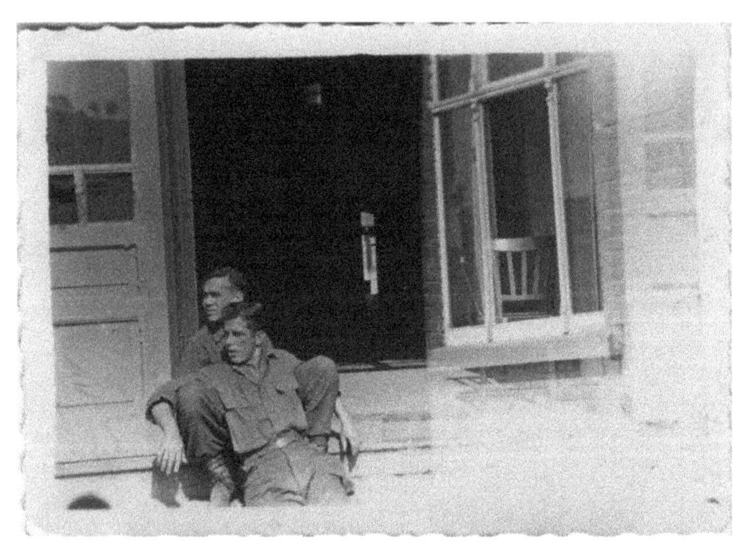

51

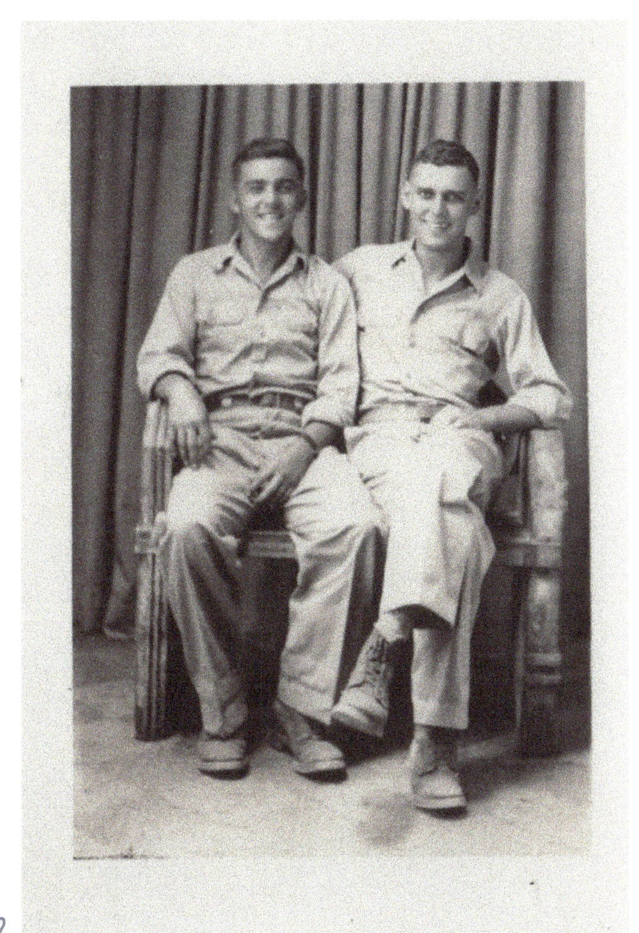
52

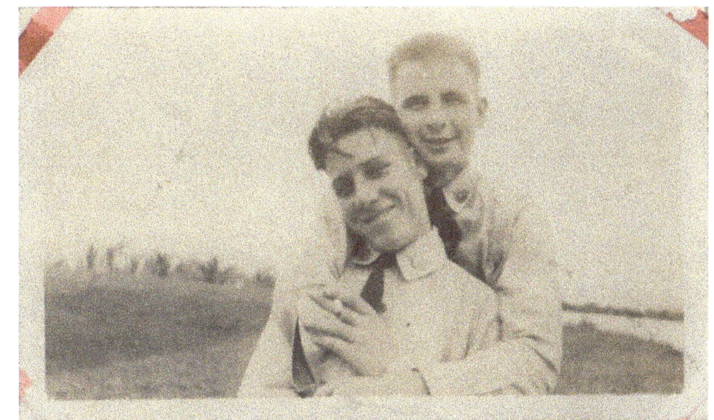
53

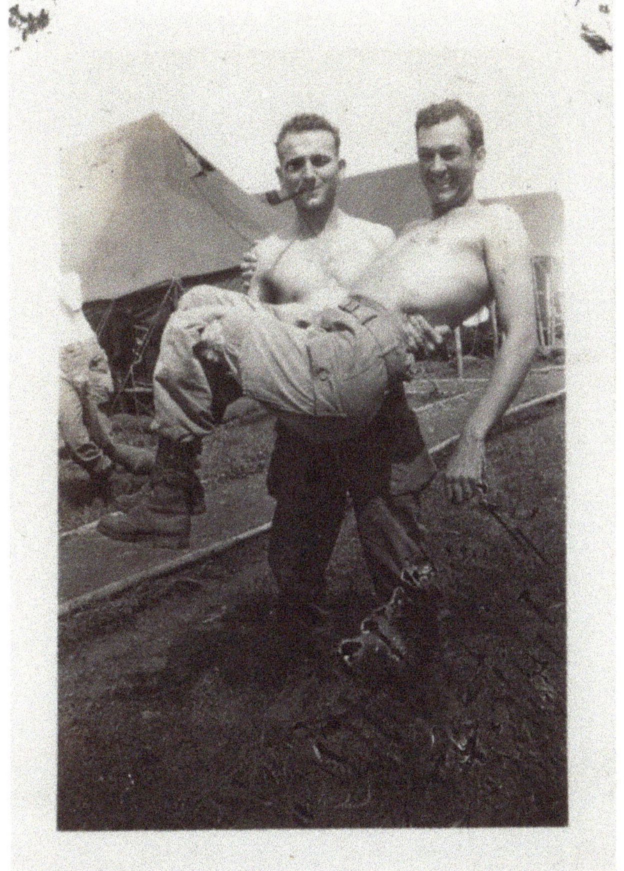
54

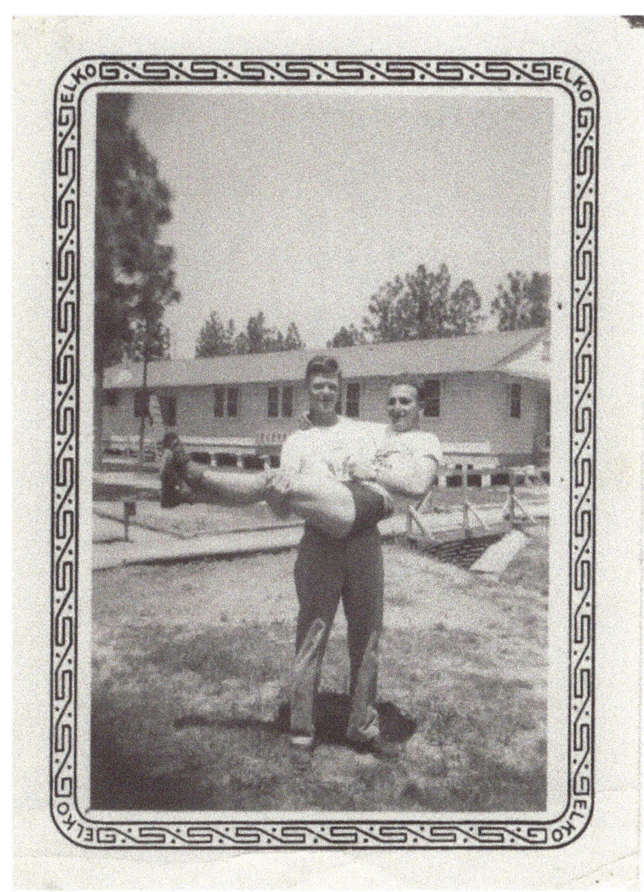

55

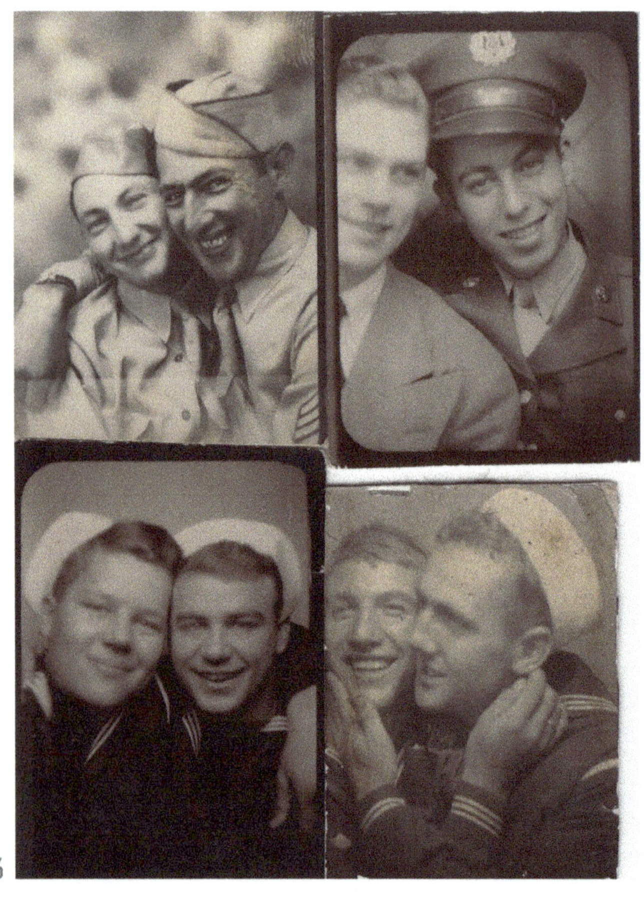
56

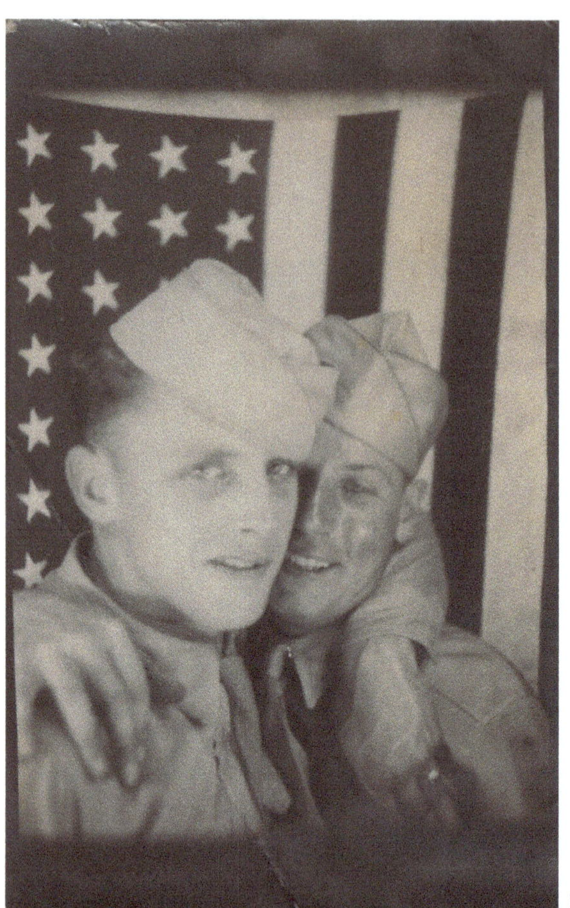
57

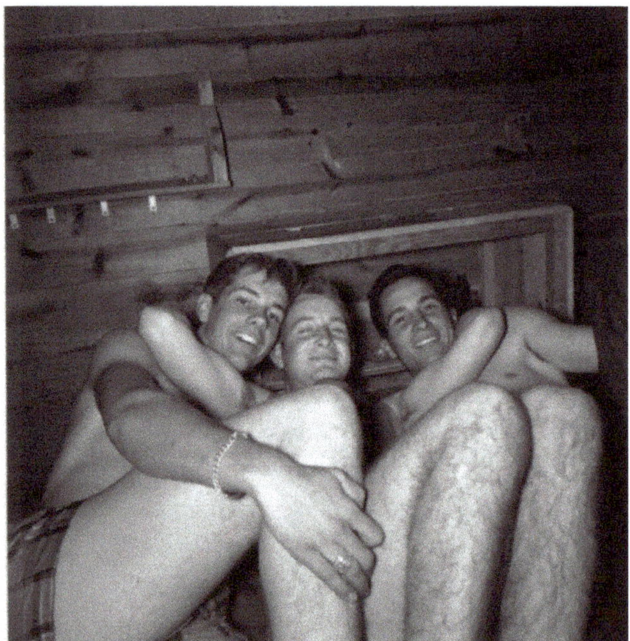
58

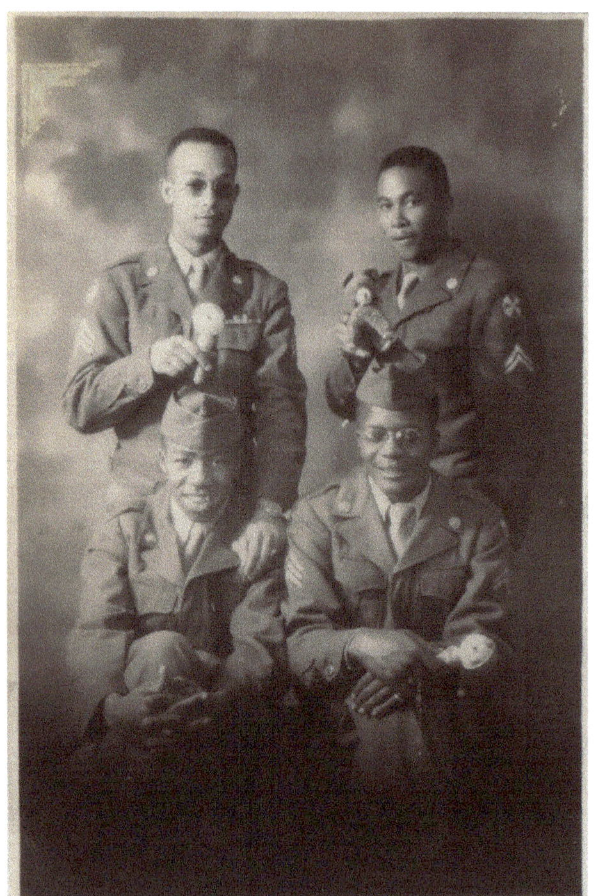
59

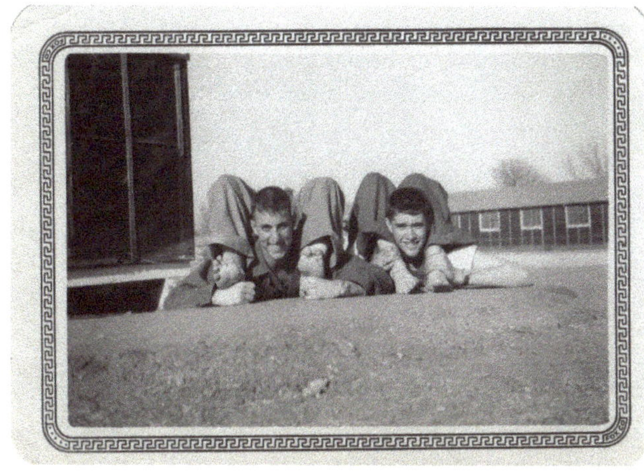

61

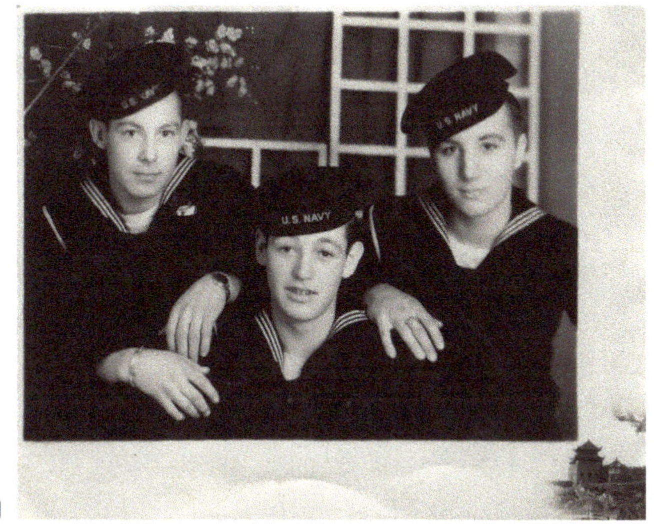

60

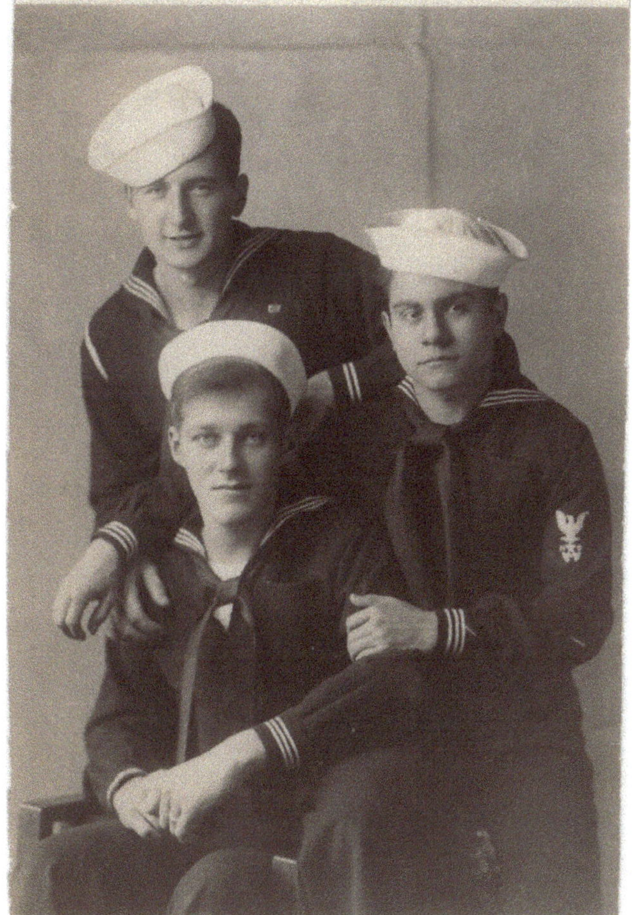

63

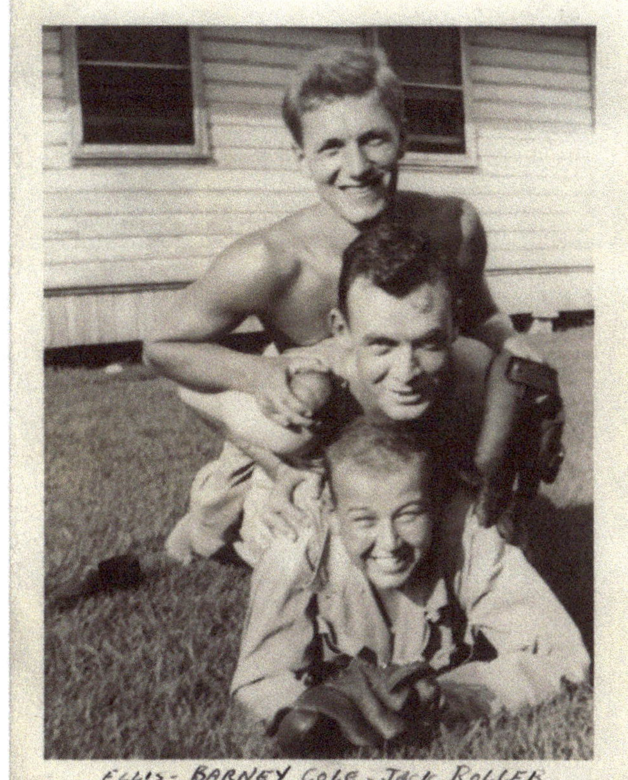

62

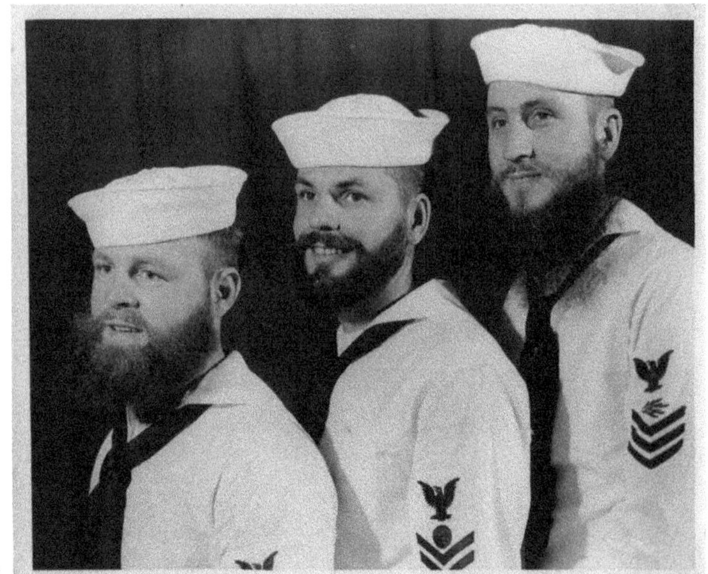
64

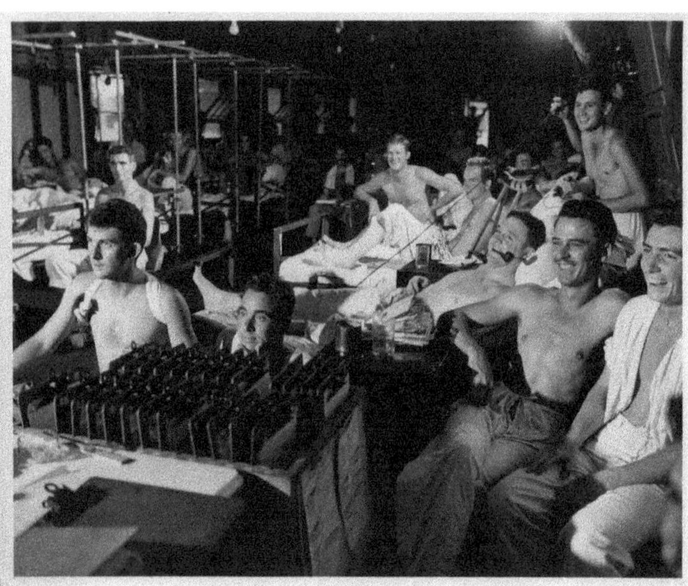
65

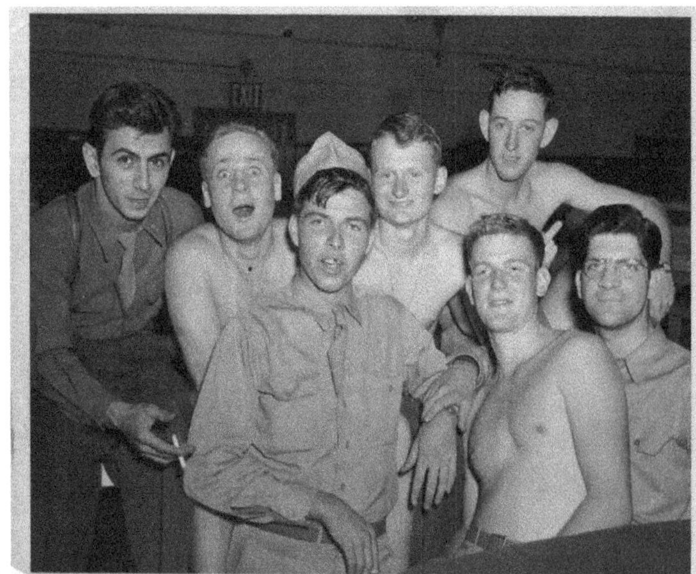
66

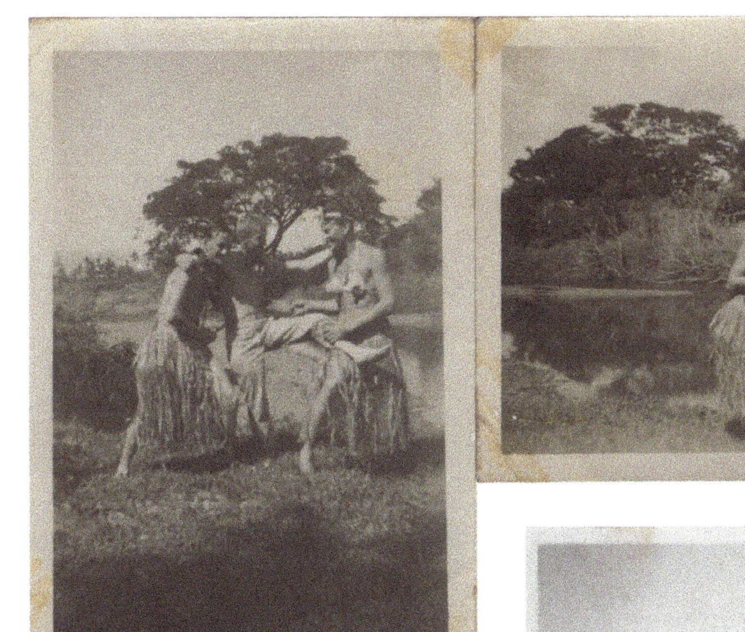

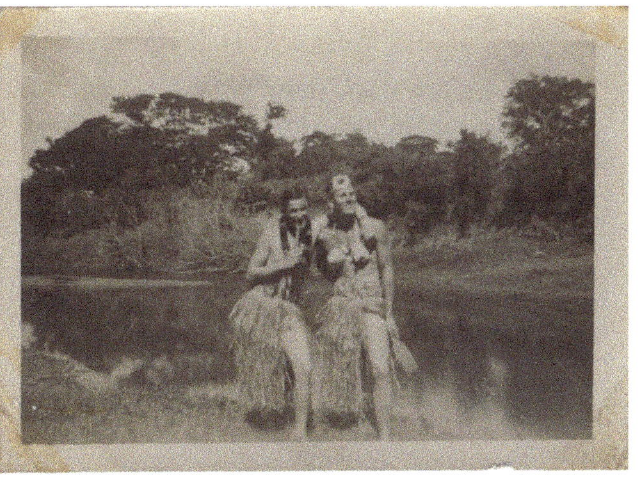

67

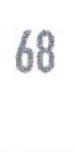

68

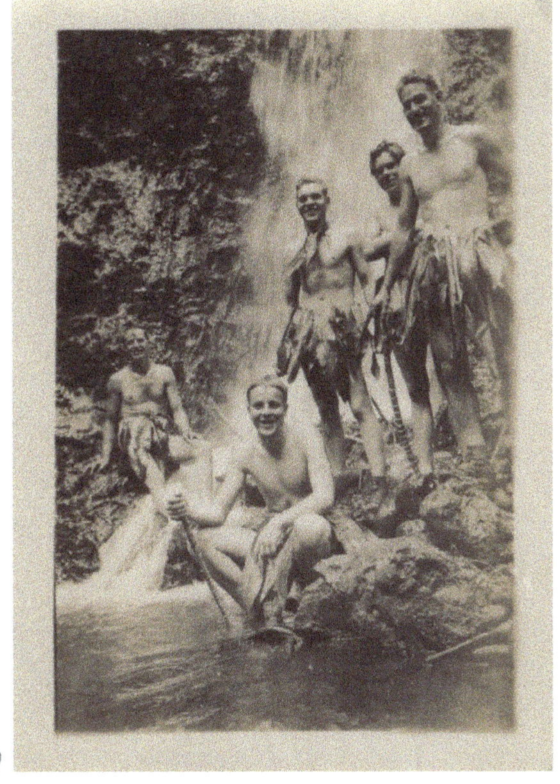

69

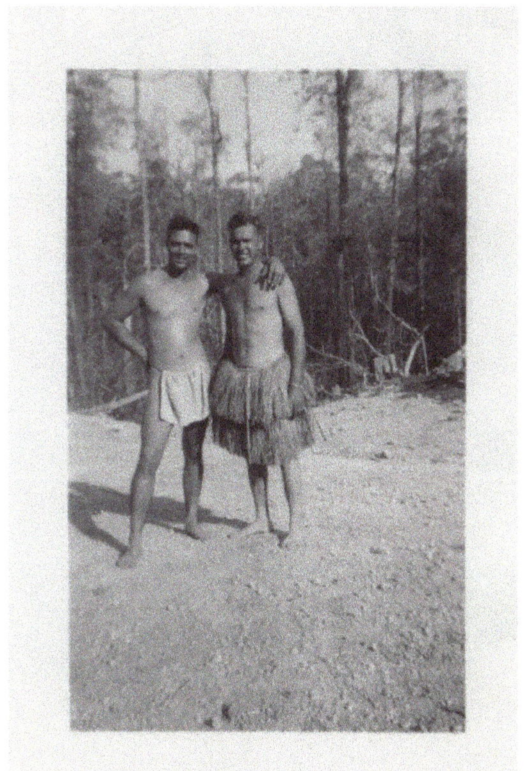

70

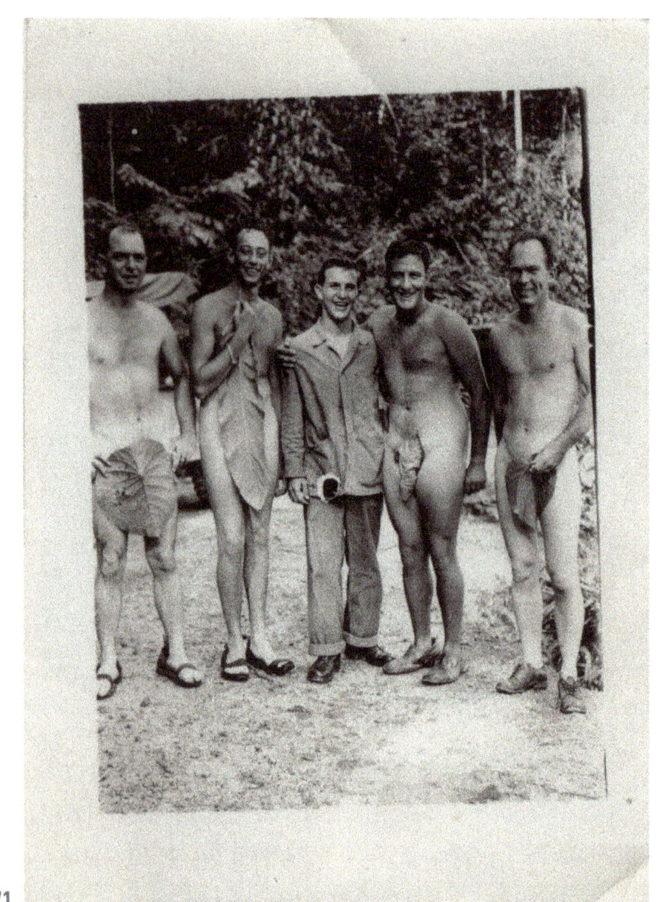
71

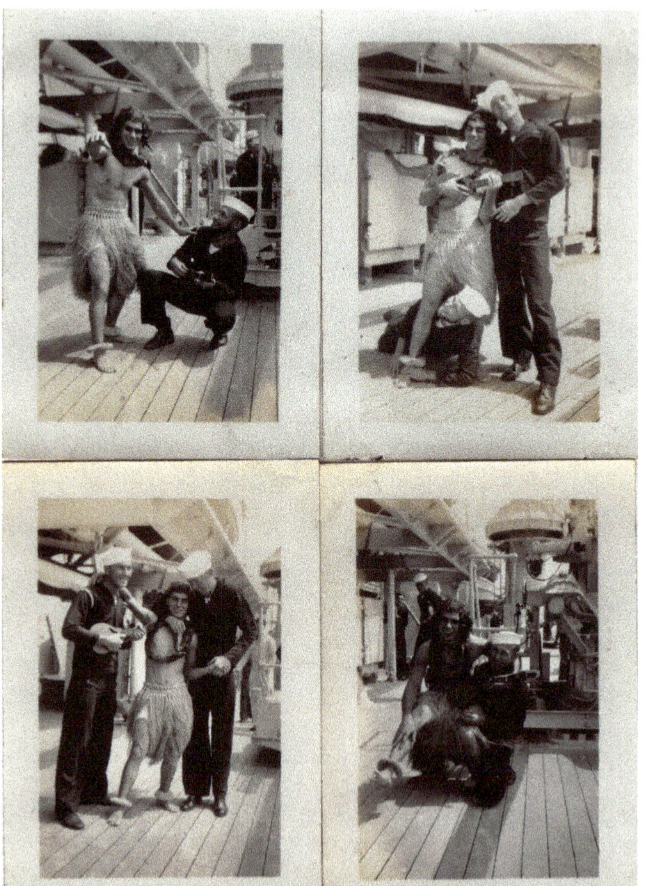
72

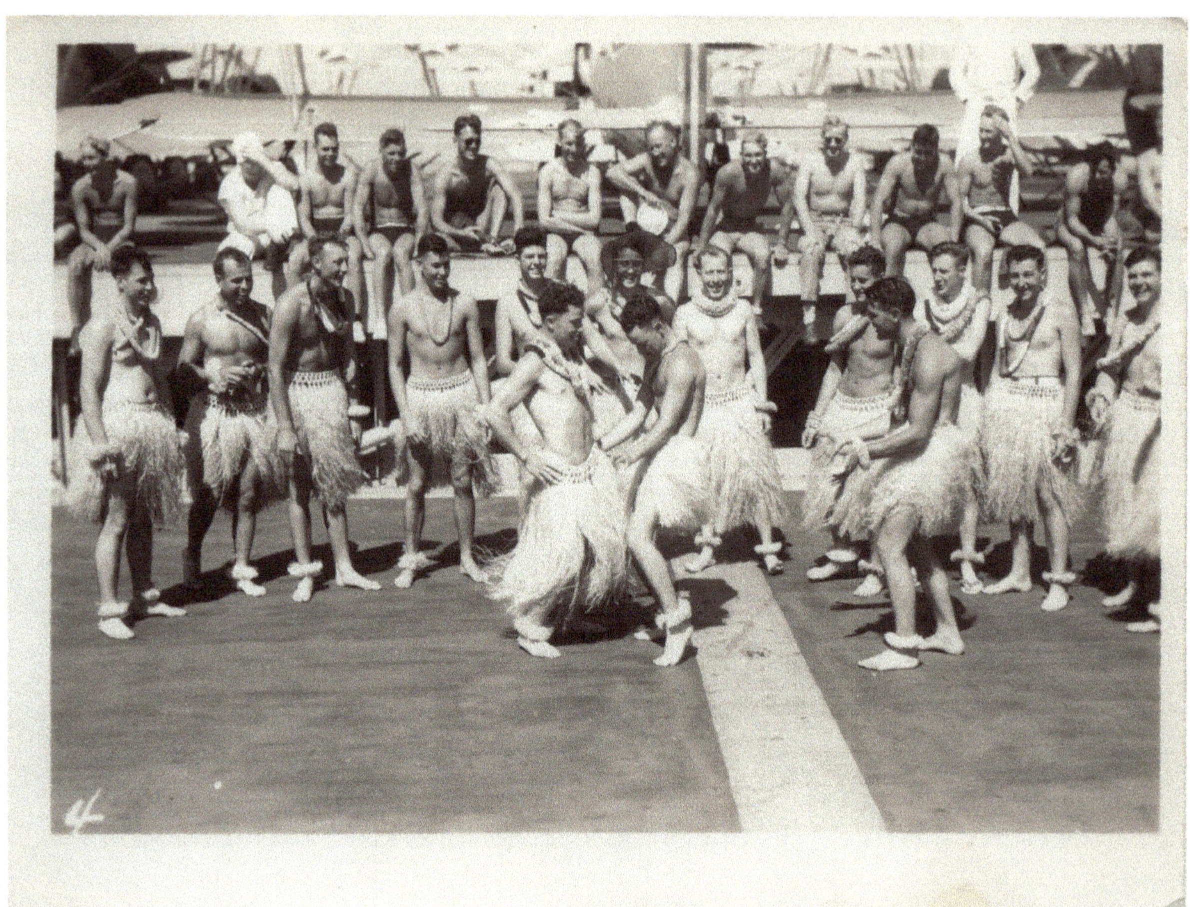
73

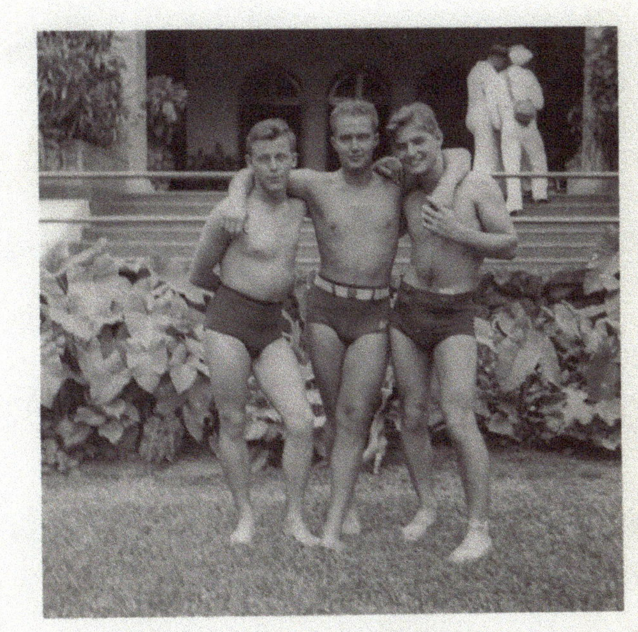

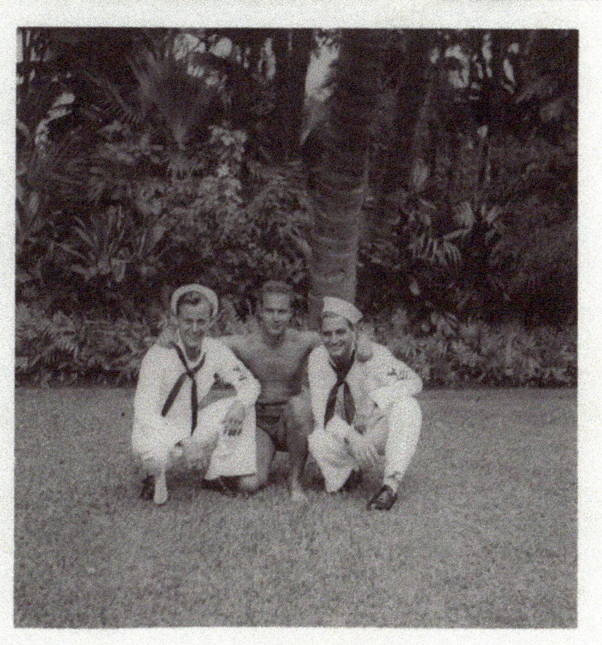

74

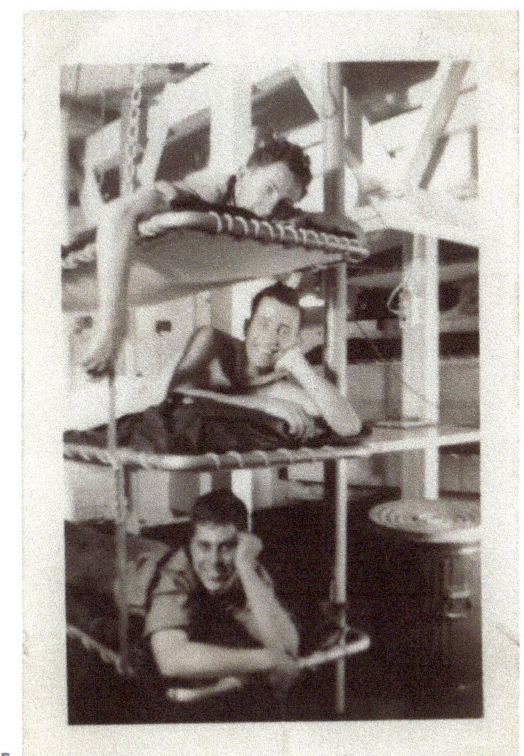

75

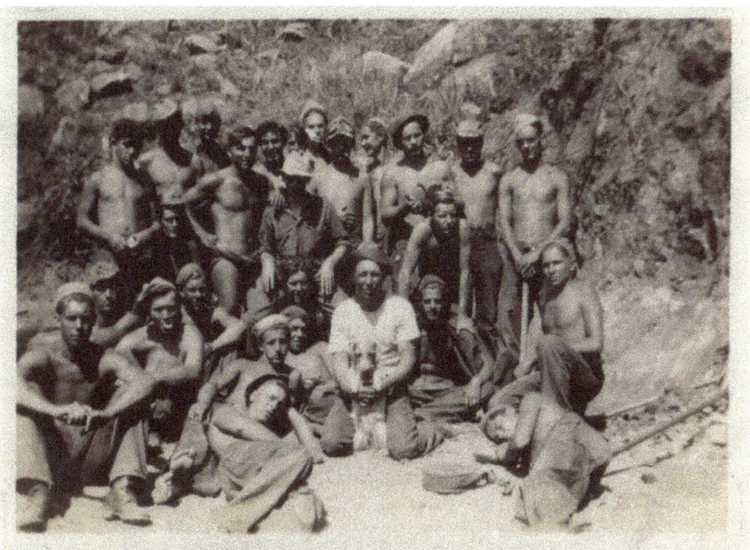

76

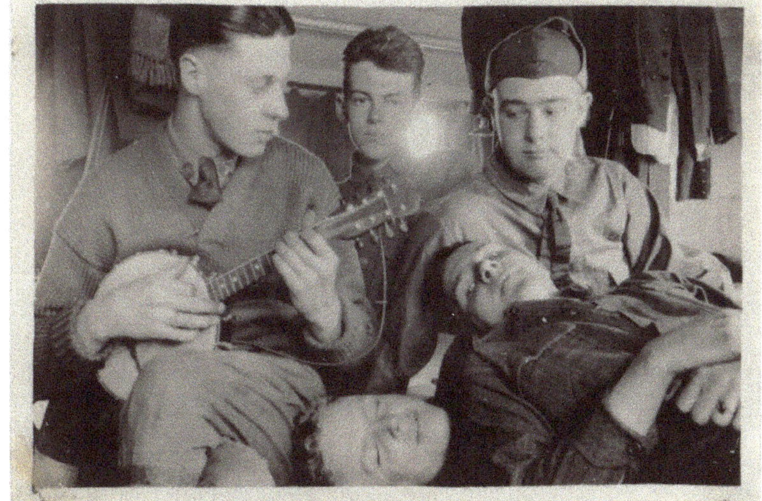

77

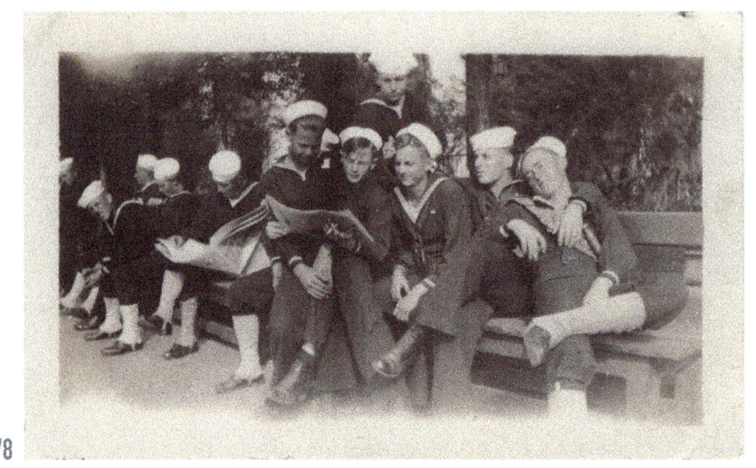

78

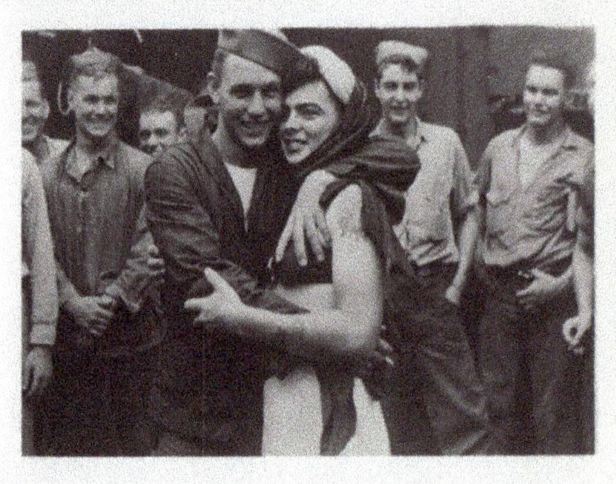

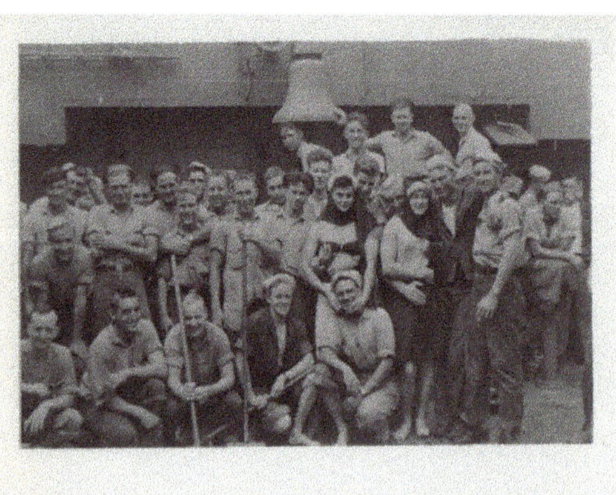

79

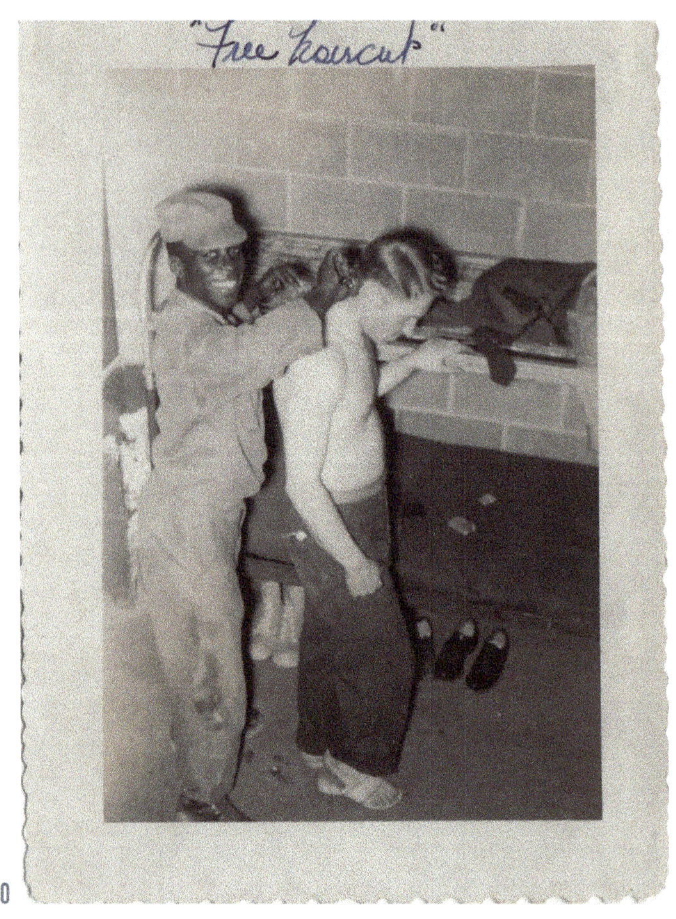

80

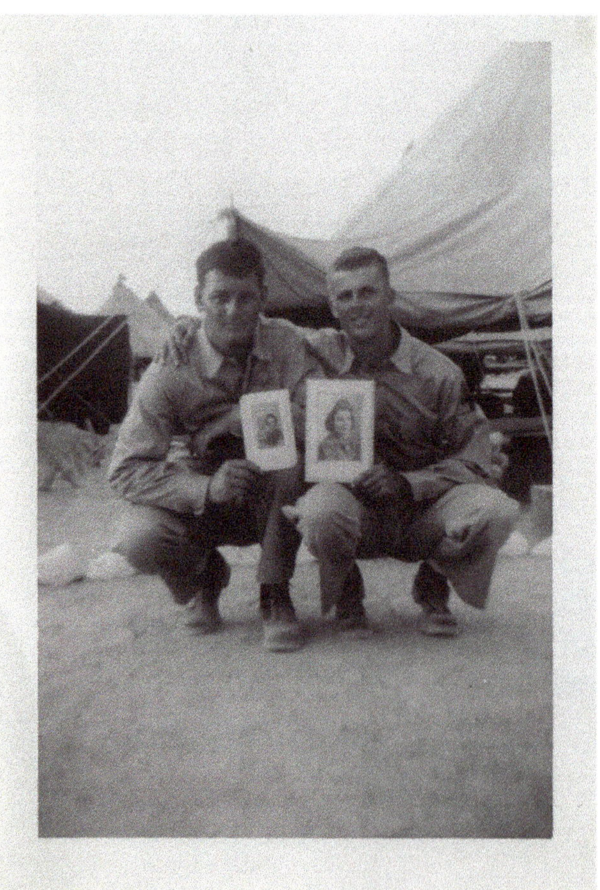

81

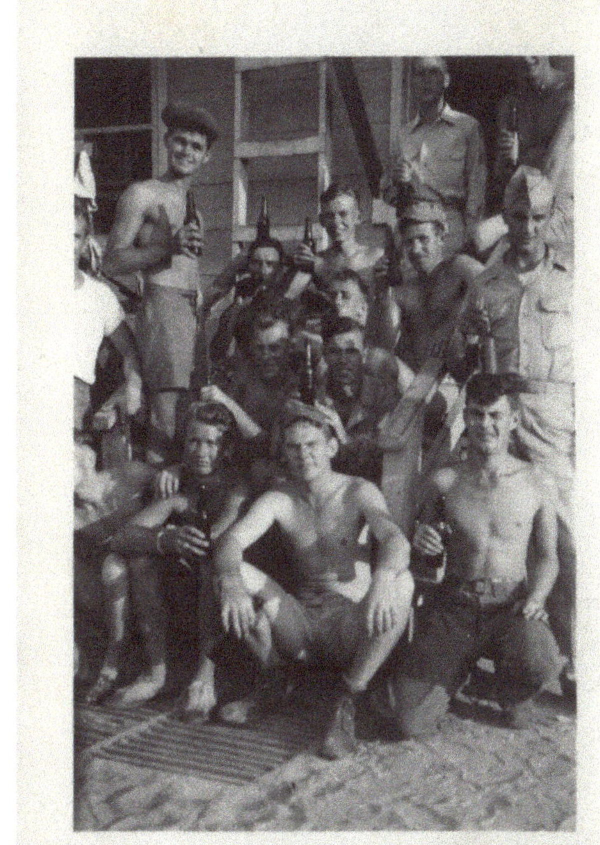

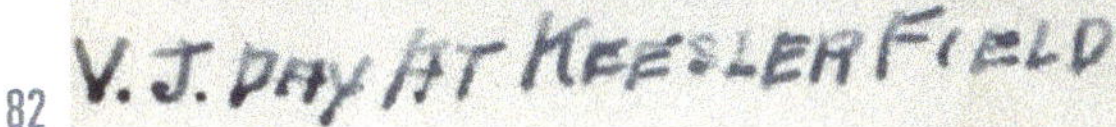

82

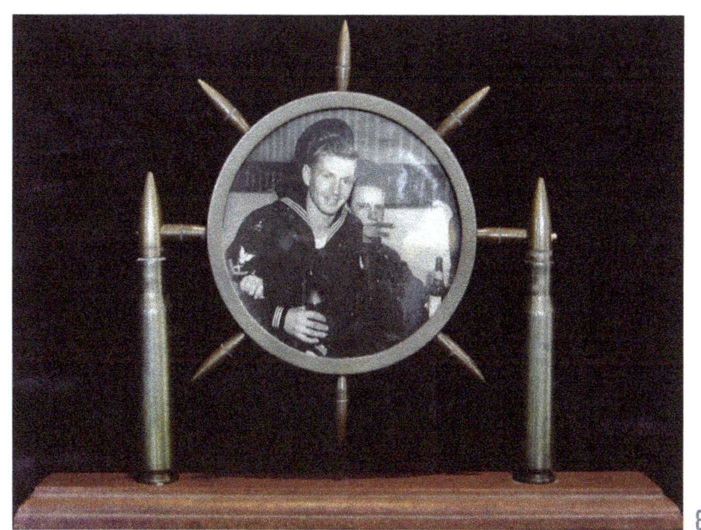

83

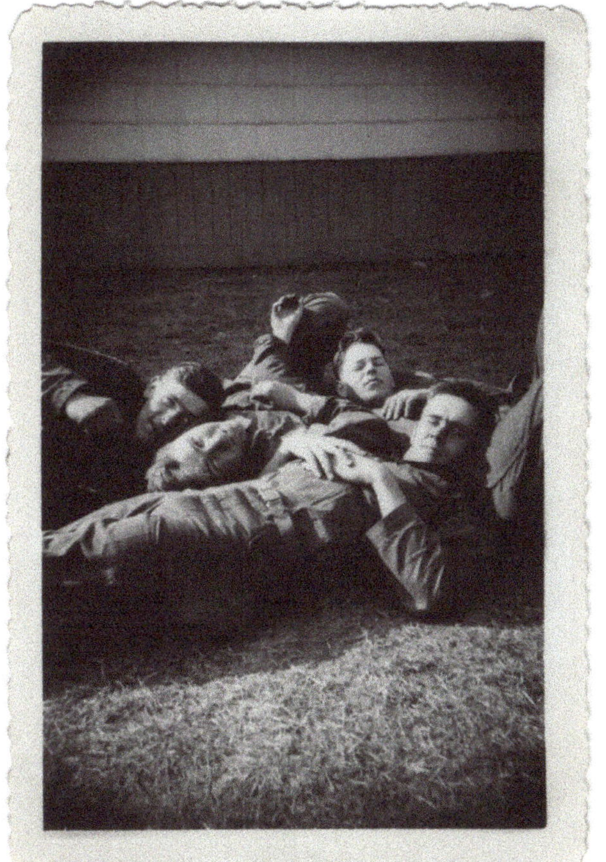

84

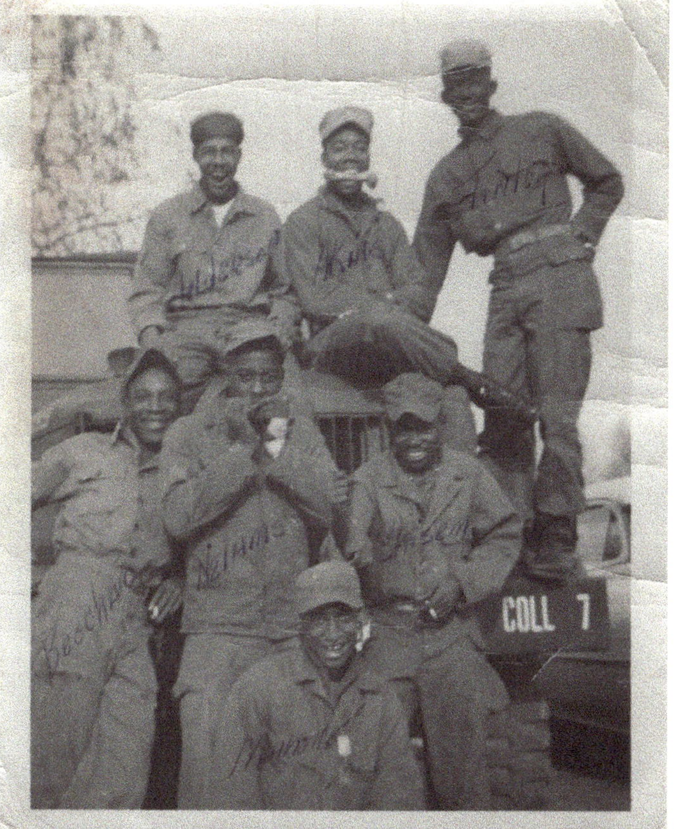

85

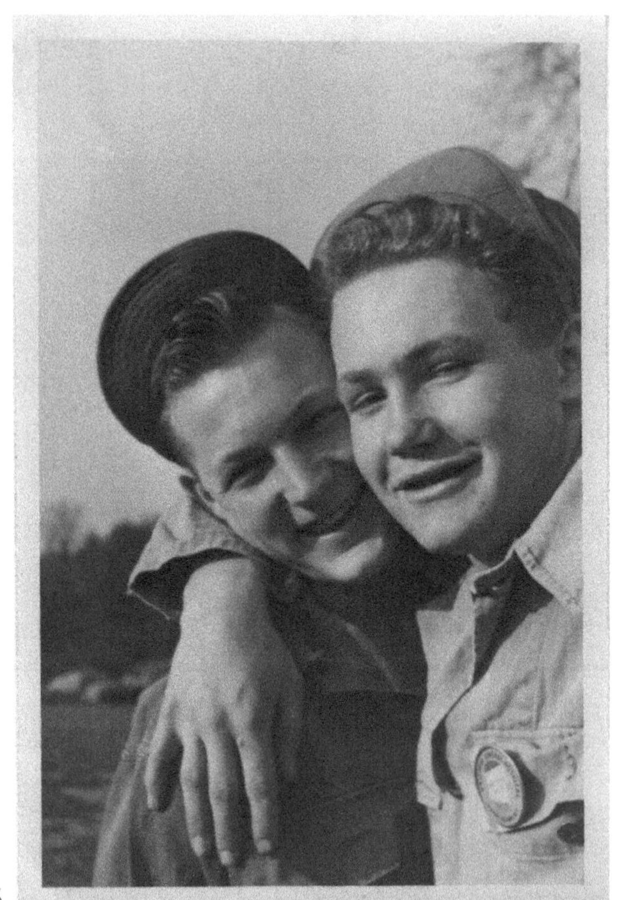

86

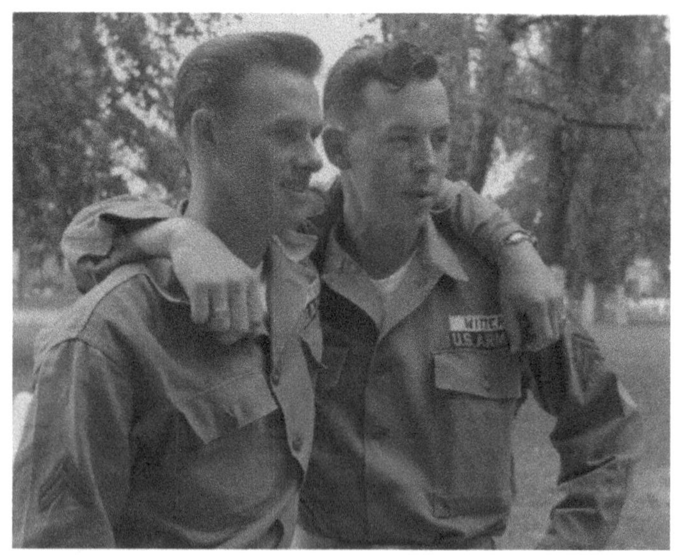

87

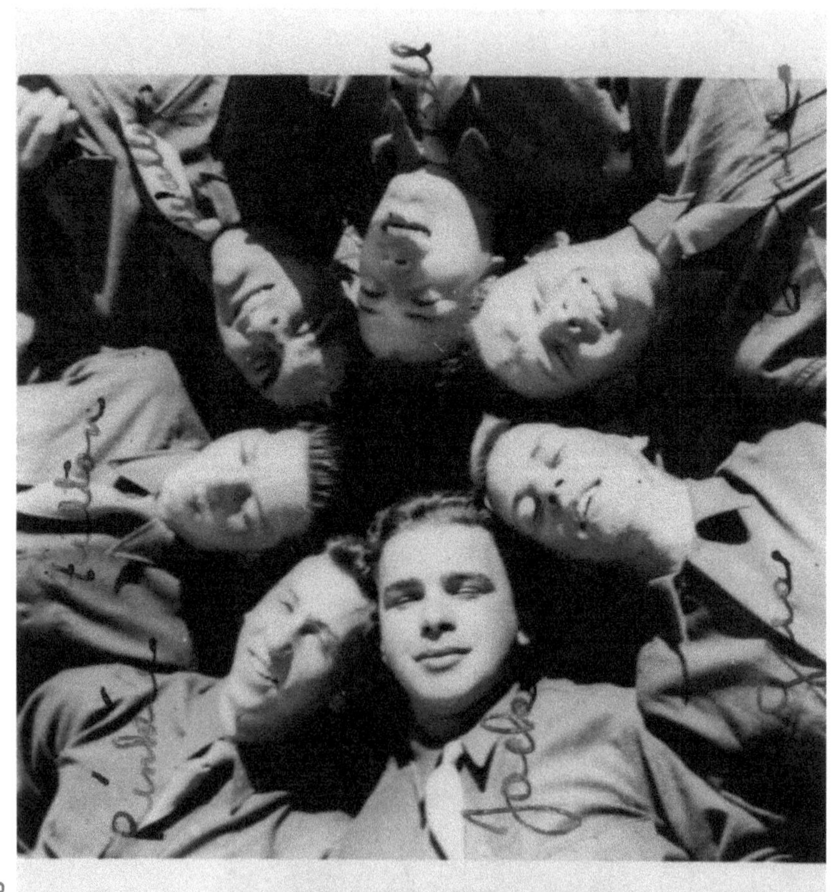

88

CHAPTER 4

ACTING FOR THE CAMERA LENS

MALE PERFORMANCE IN PHOTOGRAPHS

A photograph of one or more persons is frequently a performance of some sort, an acting-out for the photographer or for a subsequent viewer of the image. The performative intent of some photos is utterly central, however, and such images are this chapter's subject. Images 3, 4, 5, 6, 8, and 9 show how often humor—simply enjoying themselves, as noted in chapter 2—was the purpose of the studio portraits that men had taken in the late nineteenth century. Photographers had certain costumes and props at the ready for what, in *Picturing Men*, I called "pageants of masculinity." Numbers 19 through 21 all feature an especially popular costume at the turn of the century, that of the cowboy with pistols, bandanas, hats, and chaps. Gambling is staged in Images 31 through 34; the young males in Images 27 and 28, a studio portrait and a set of snapshots, act out a boxing match; and the two in Image 29 point pistols at each other.

Performances of toughness—adopting a fighting stance, as well as pretending to be a gun-toting cowboy or a gambler—became extremely common photographic poses among males of all ages in photos at the turn of the century and beyond. The simpler, gentler pleasures seen in the older studio photos appearing earlier in this chapter were no longer as common, though by no means did gentleness and obvious enjoyment of each other's company disappear from male photographic performance. The appearance of symbols of strength, even with hints of violence, anticipates how some twentieth-century males would increasingly seek reassurance of various sorts whenever they experienced affection or simple togetherness with other males. Were these "toughness" photos perhaps the predecessors of today's sad outcry of "no homo"? It was, after all, as I've already noted, early in the twentieth century that Americans were increasingly coming to think of sexual attraction between persons of the same sex as the sign of a particular orientation, a specific identity, an identity that for men was equated in mainstream culture with weakness. Affection between men sometimes became conflated with sex, and both were scorned. Especially with overt affection being taboo, men's affection for each other might of necessity be present only in sublimation, in symbolic representation in a photograph. The abundance of phallic imagery in this chapter's photographs—cigars, rifles, pistols, fishing poles, and liquor bottles, for instance—is at least noteworthy.

Paradoxically, some of the same young males who might want to perform toughness while costumed in a photographer's studio might live with other young males in an urban boardinghouse or rooming house. These males were part of an army of bachelors, often new arrivals in a city, farmers' sons who had left rural America or rural settings abroad to do the work—in factories and offices—demanded by a rapidly growing urban industrial economy. It may be such a group that is seen in the set of three photos comprising Image 24, showing that in the privacy of domestic space, whether a boardinghouse or a college dormitory, a relaxed, affectionate togetherness could survive.[29] And if an audience and a setting were supportive and private enough, some males of the early twentieth century might perform more than simple affection, as did the kissing males in Images 39 and 40 and the dancers in Images 49 and 50.

More than kissing or dancing might occur. From photography's earliest days, and surely with a variety of motives and satisfactions, males have taken what would usually be seen as a female's role in performing before the camera while wearing women's clothing. Images 41 through 46 and 51 through 61 are but some of the better photos in my collection of males in drag. Images 63 through 66, however, show a particular sort of drag performance: two males pretending to be a bride and groom, a common occurrence if the number of such photos in my collection is an accurate indication. The "wedding" being performed onboard a ship in Image 67, on the other hand, captures something quite different: the union of two sailors, with no attempt to dress one of them up as a woman. Few photos in my entire collection make me wish more strongly that more information accompanied found photographs. The mystery of that photo, though, is part of its charm; it's definitely a favorite.

Concluding chapter 4 are three photographs of another sort of nuptial performance, the Womanless Wedding (Images 68 through 70), an all-male ritual that is rarely, if ever, performed today, yet once was common, especially in the South, at events such as county fairs and church and charity fund-raisers. The event was an all-white activity; at least one wedding "guest" was often in blackface. Anthropologists and historians are familiar with various "inversion rituals," events in which a community's traditional roles are temporarily reversed. The result of these rituals, so the customary explanation would have it, is a reaffirmation of tradition, the everyday status quo. Womanless Weddings may have been just such a ritual, an actual endorsement of heterosexual marriage in a time when same-sex marriage was simply unthinkable—making a wedding without women seem outrageous enough to be highly amusing, genuinely deviant. Or perhaps more was being transacted. Various drag performances, like minstrel shows, may have more psychological complexity than the simple "role reversal" explanation suggests. At least some participants may have derived a satisfaction beyond simple amusement or ridicule when they disported themselves as "the other."[30] ▮

29 On this influx of bachelors and their residing in boardinghouses, see especially Howard P. Chudacoff, *The Age of the Bachelor: Creating an American Subculture* (Princeton: Princeton University Press, 1986), 31, 33, 34, 39, 76, 77, 79, 84, 85, 91–96, 98.

30 One of the few scholarly analyses of the Womanless Wedding is Craig Thompson Friend, "The Womanless Wedding: Masculinity, Cross-Dressing, and Gender Inversions in the Modern South," in Friend, ed., *Southern Masculinity: Perspectives on Manhood in the South Since Reconstruction*, 219–45.

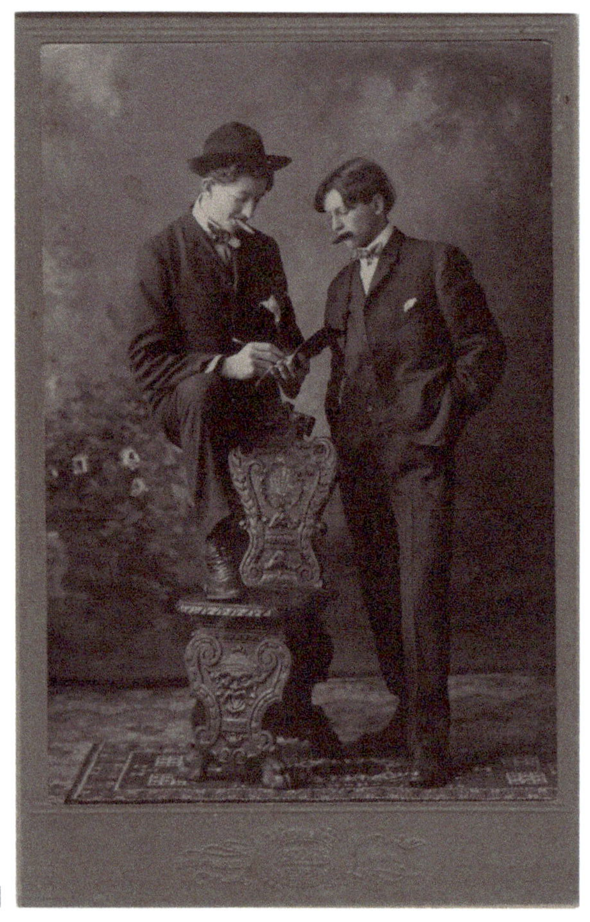
1

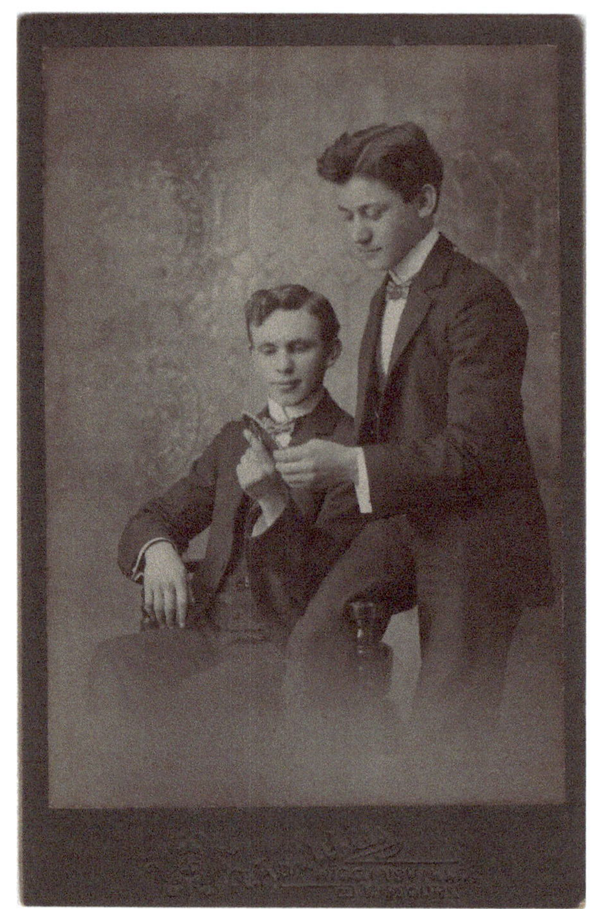
2

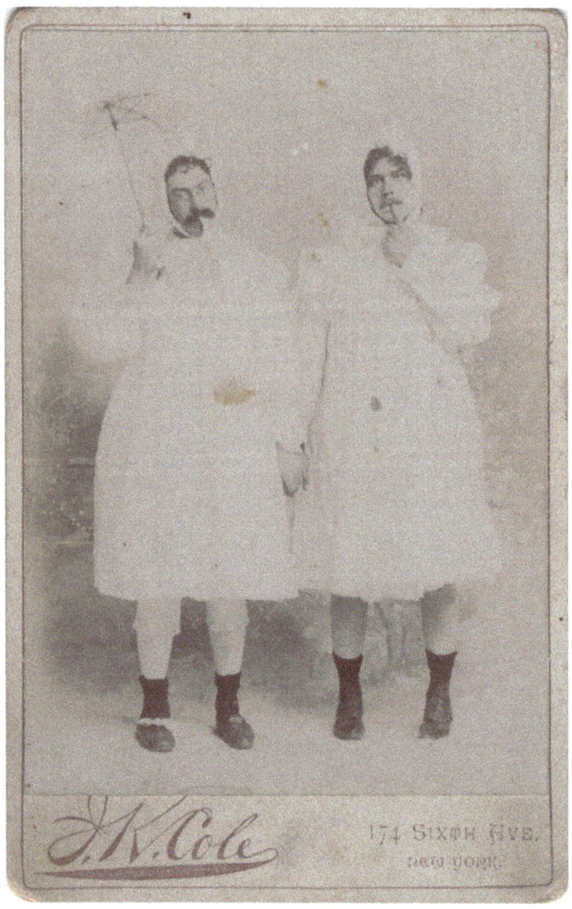

3

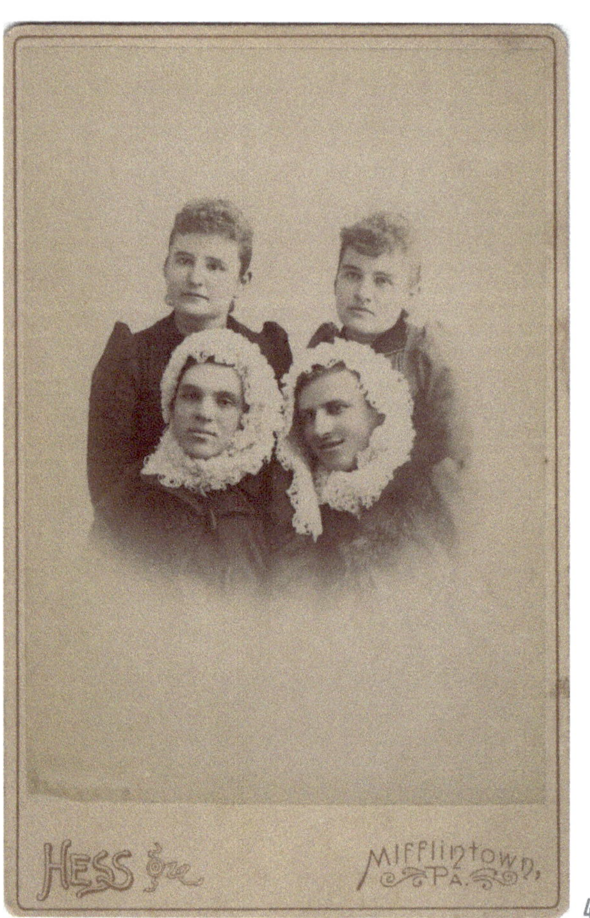

4

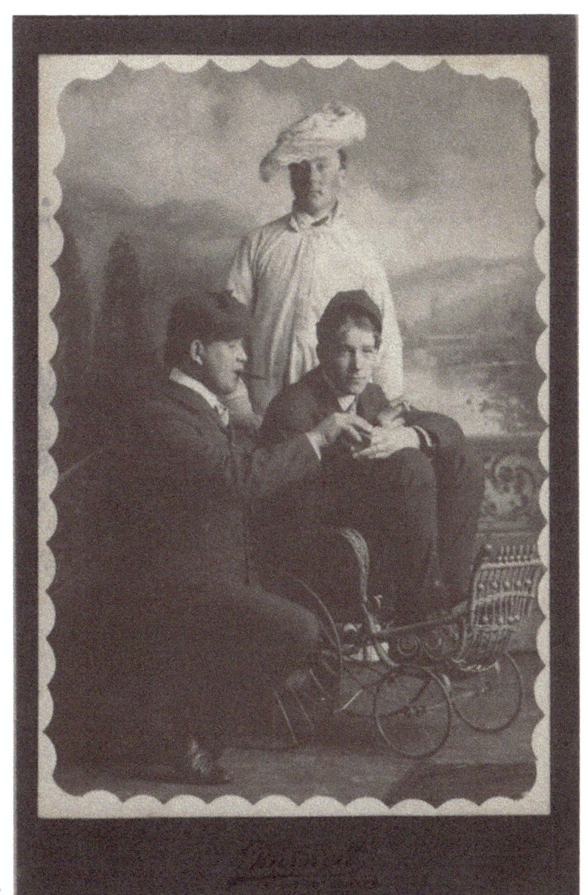
5

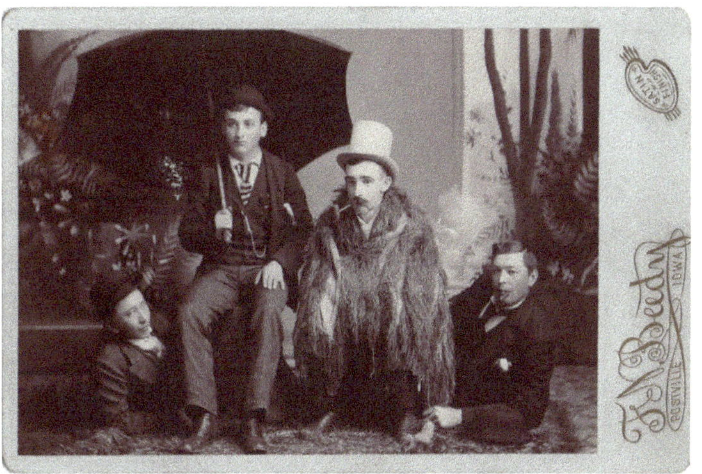
6

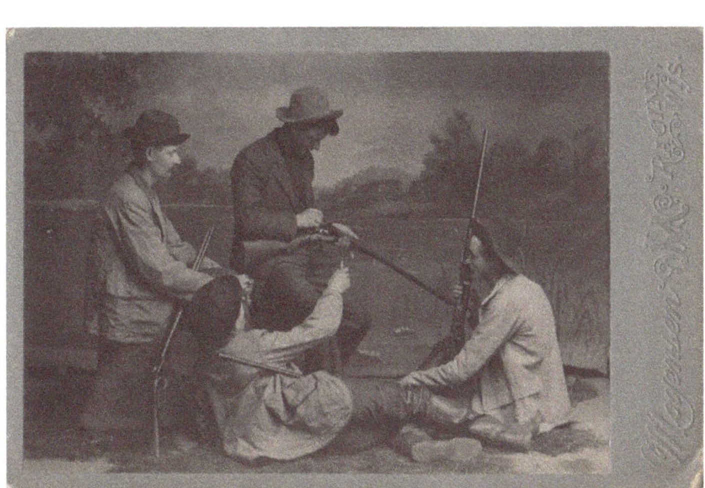
7

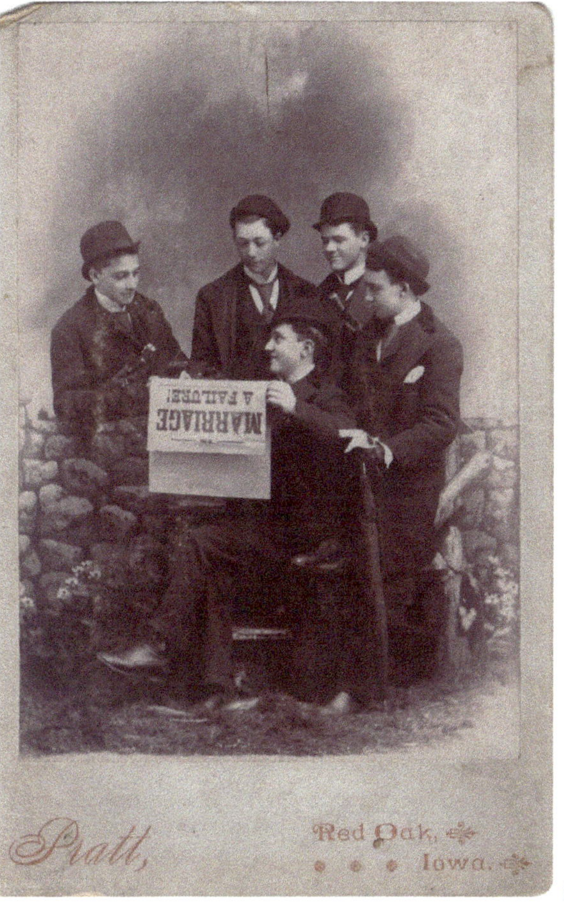

8

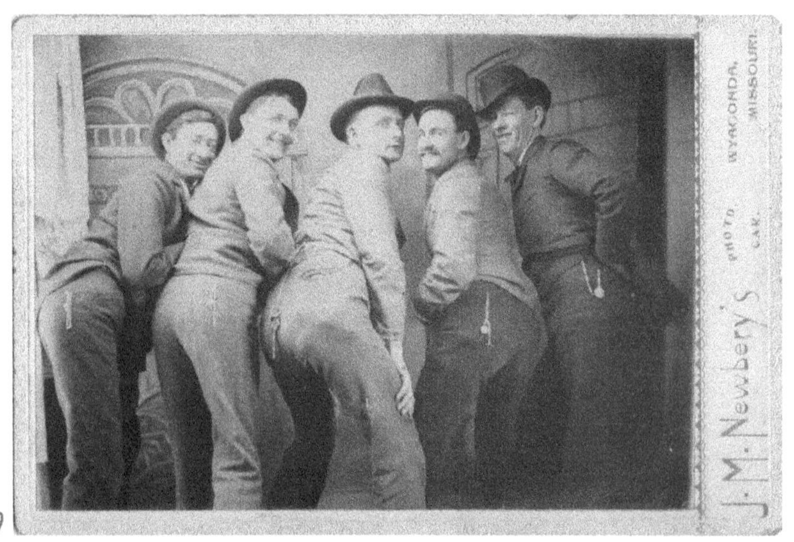

9

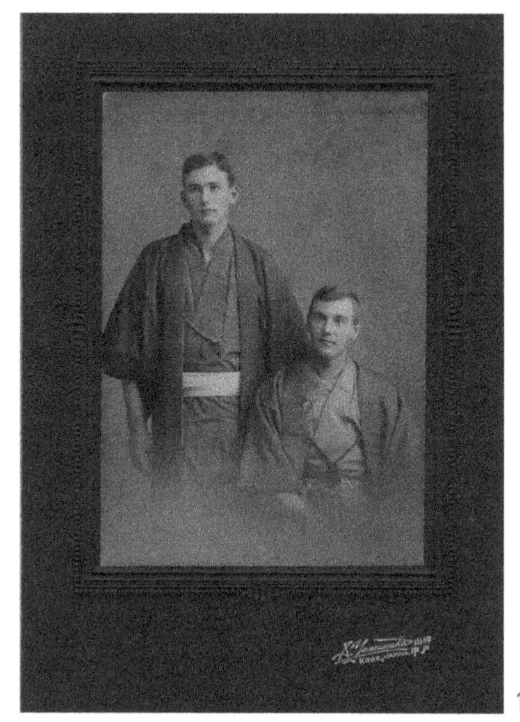

10

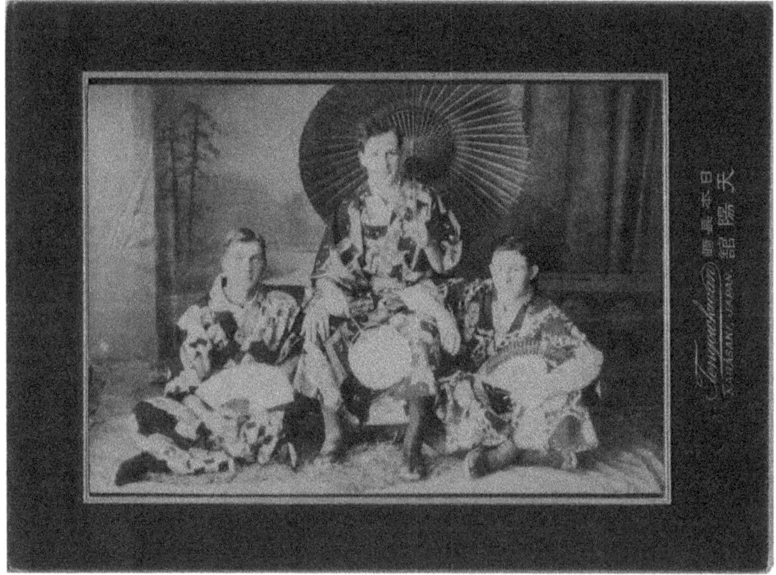

11

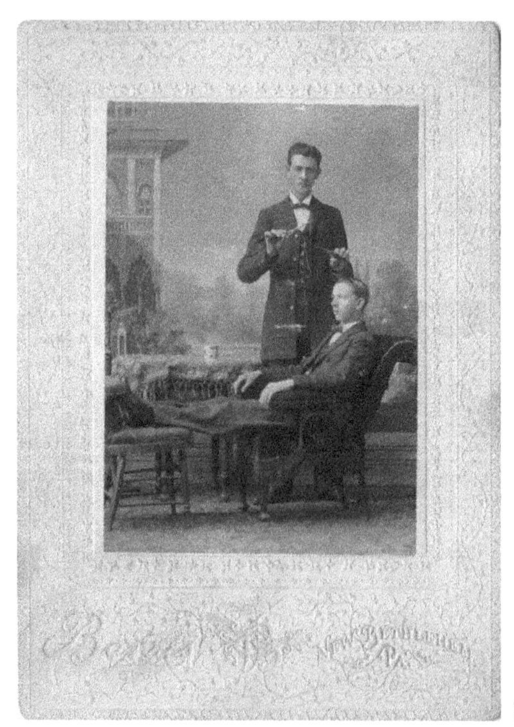

12

THREE MEN AND THE BABY!
13

14

McGillivray
Forest City Gallery
Ithaca, N.Y.
15

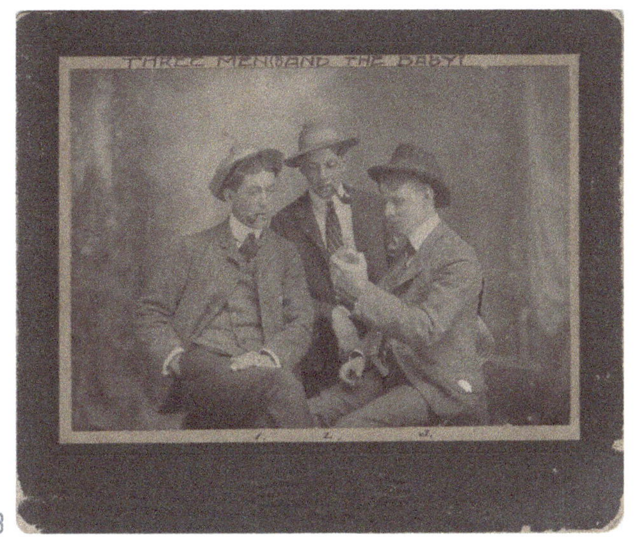

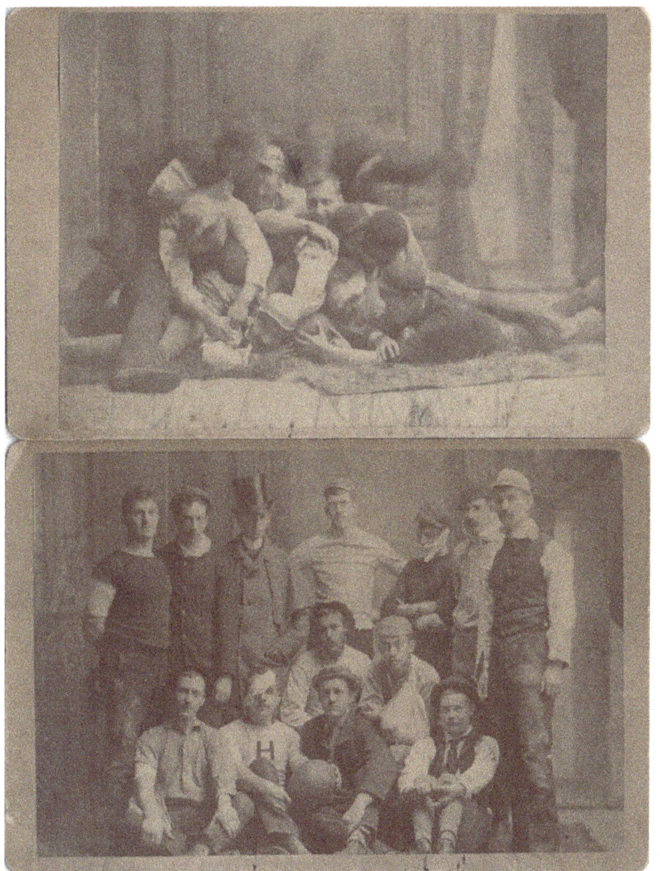

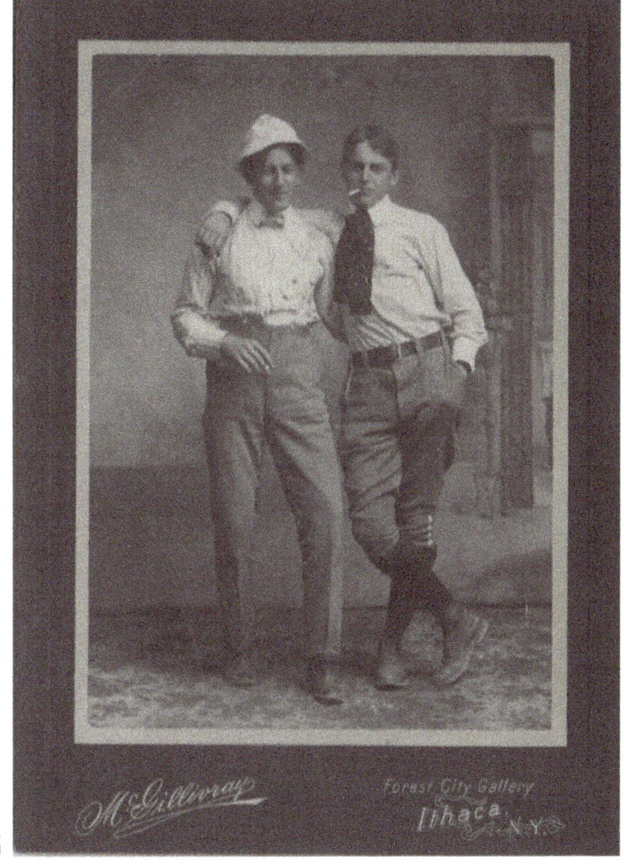

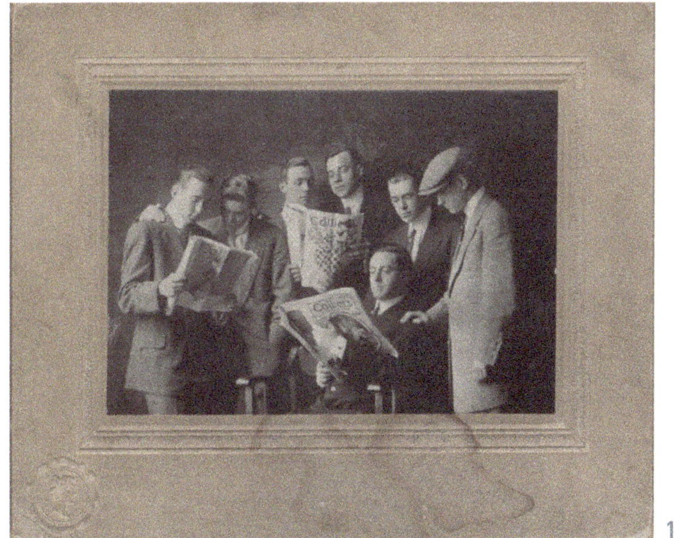

16

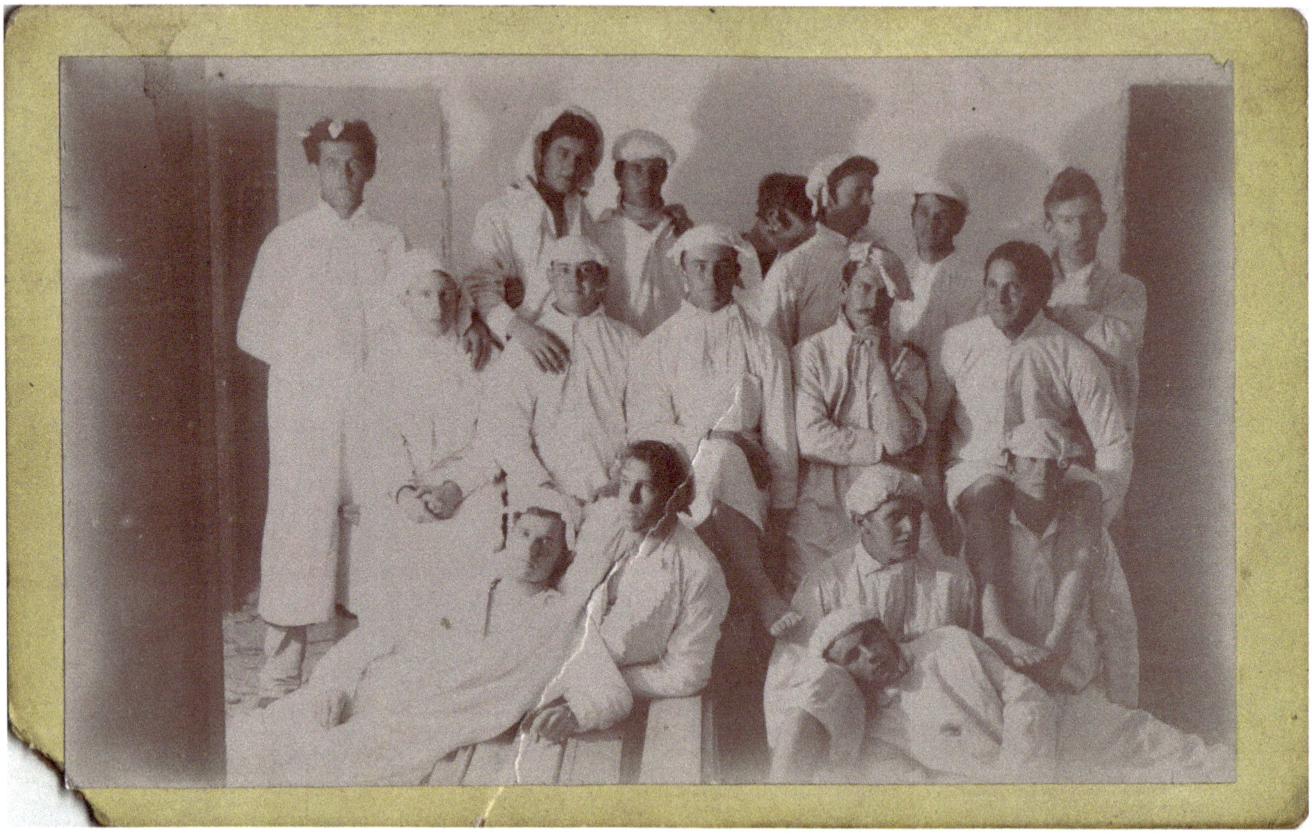

17

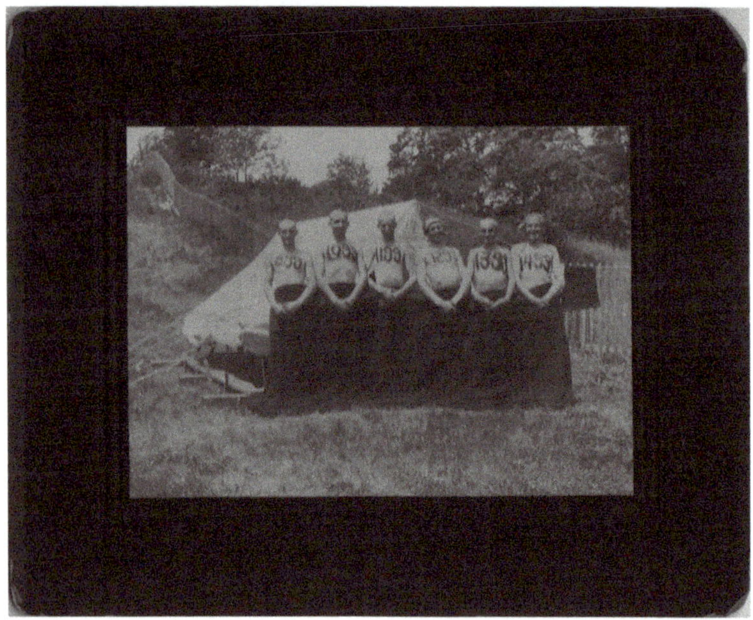

18

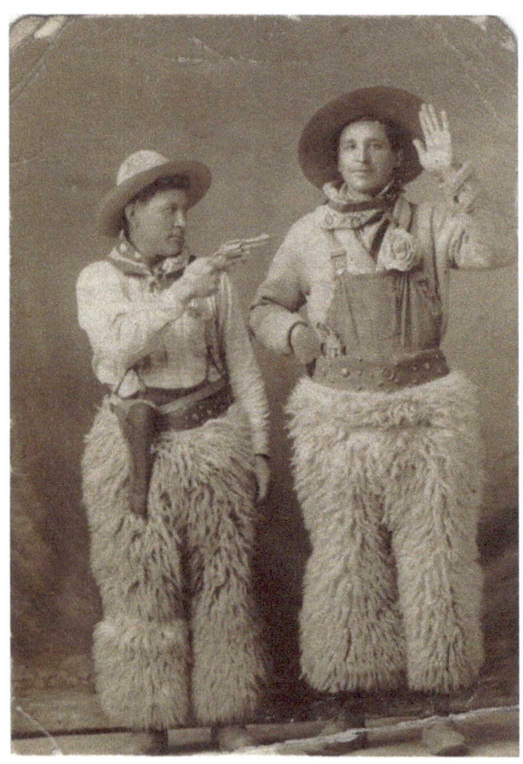

19

20

Lets Pretend!

22

SALOON
MASKIRATE BALL
NEXT WEEK
AT THE TIVOLI HALL

21

A Midnight PARTY

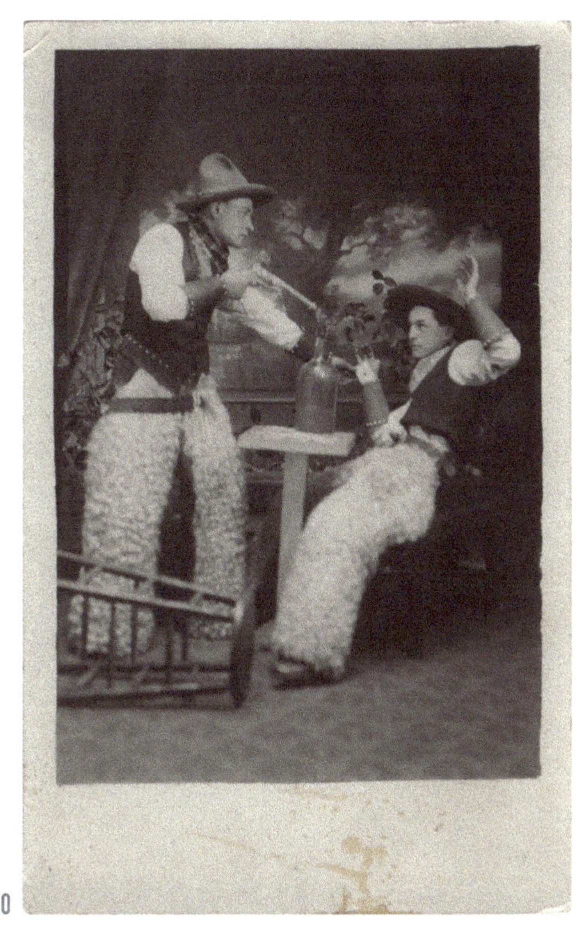

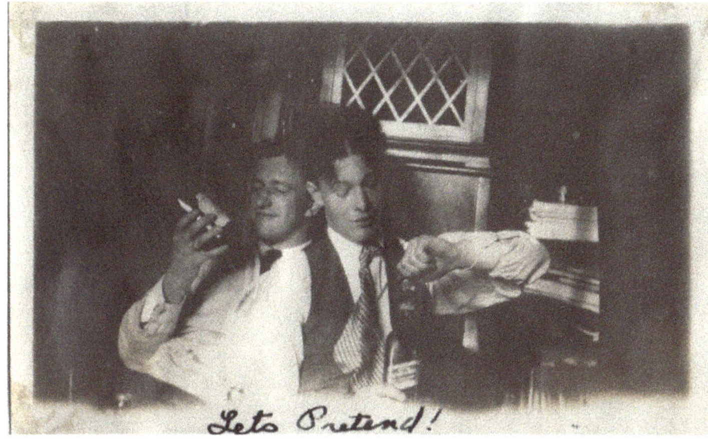

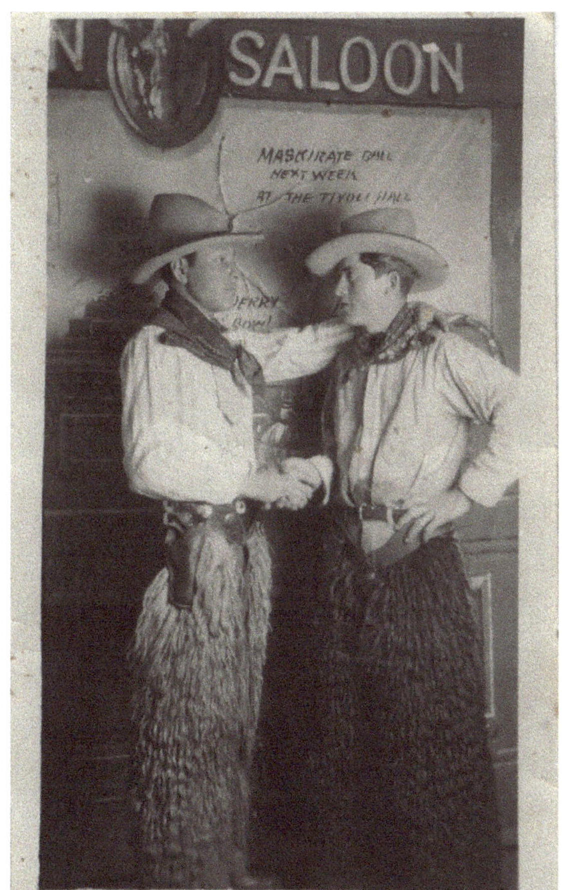

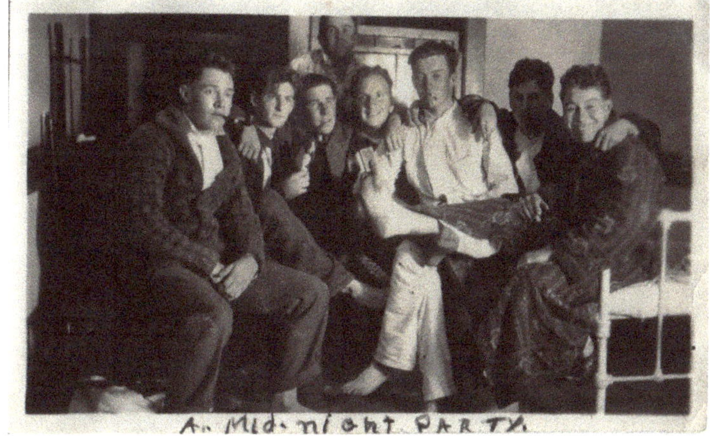

23

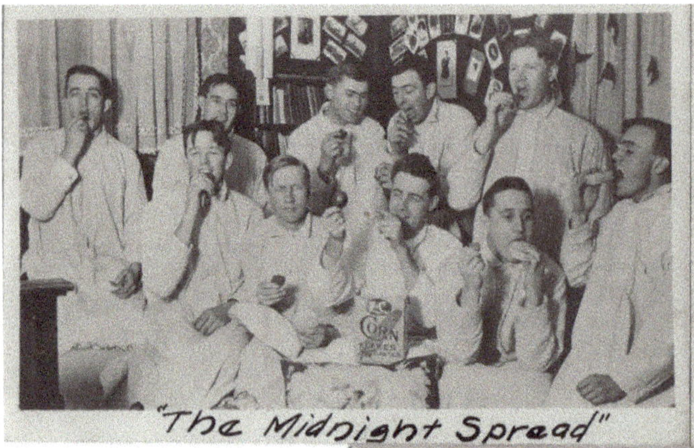

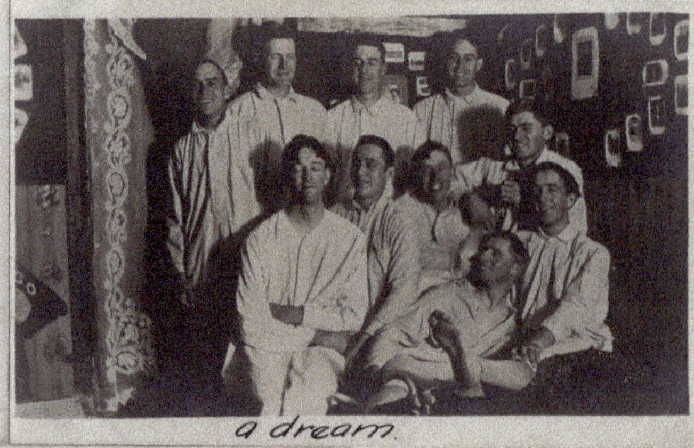

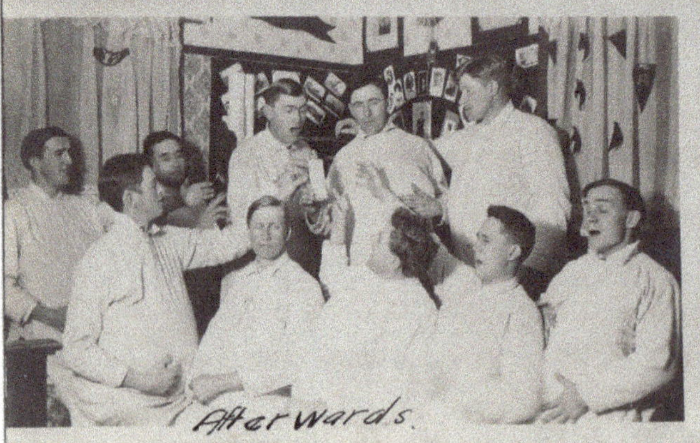

24

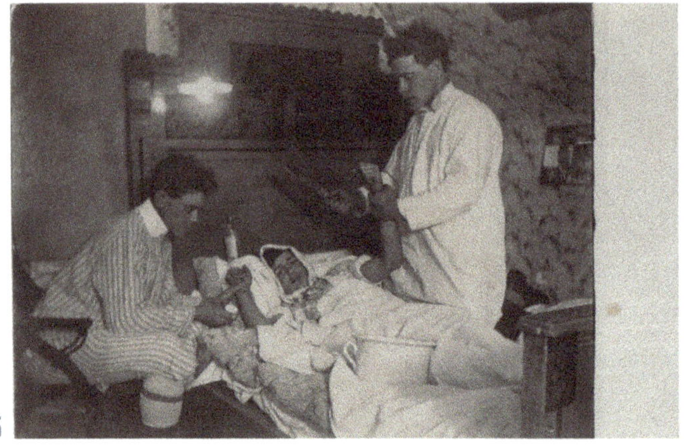

25

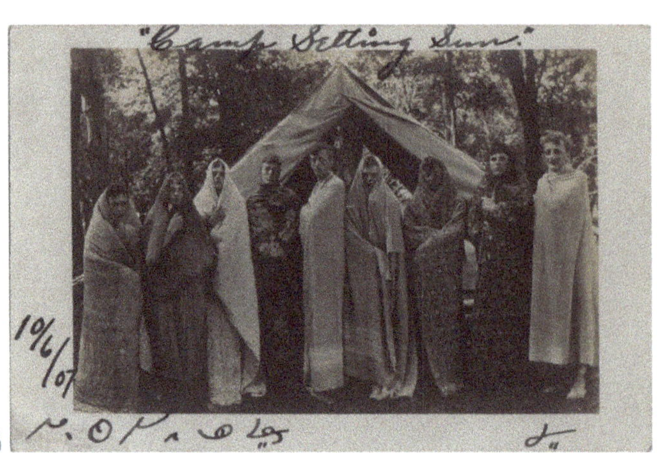

26

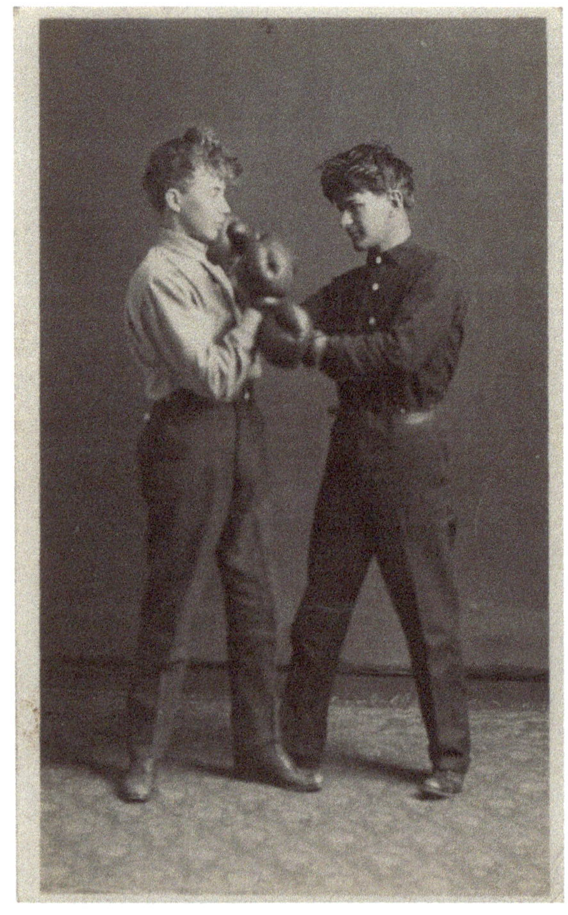

27

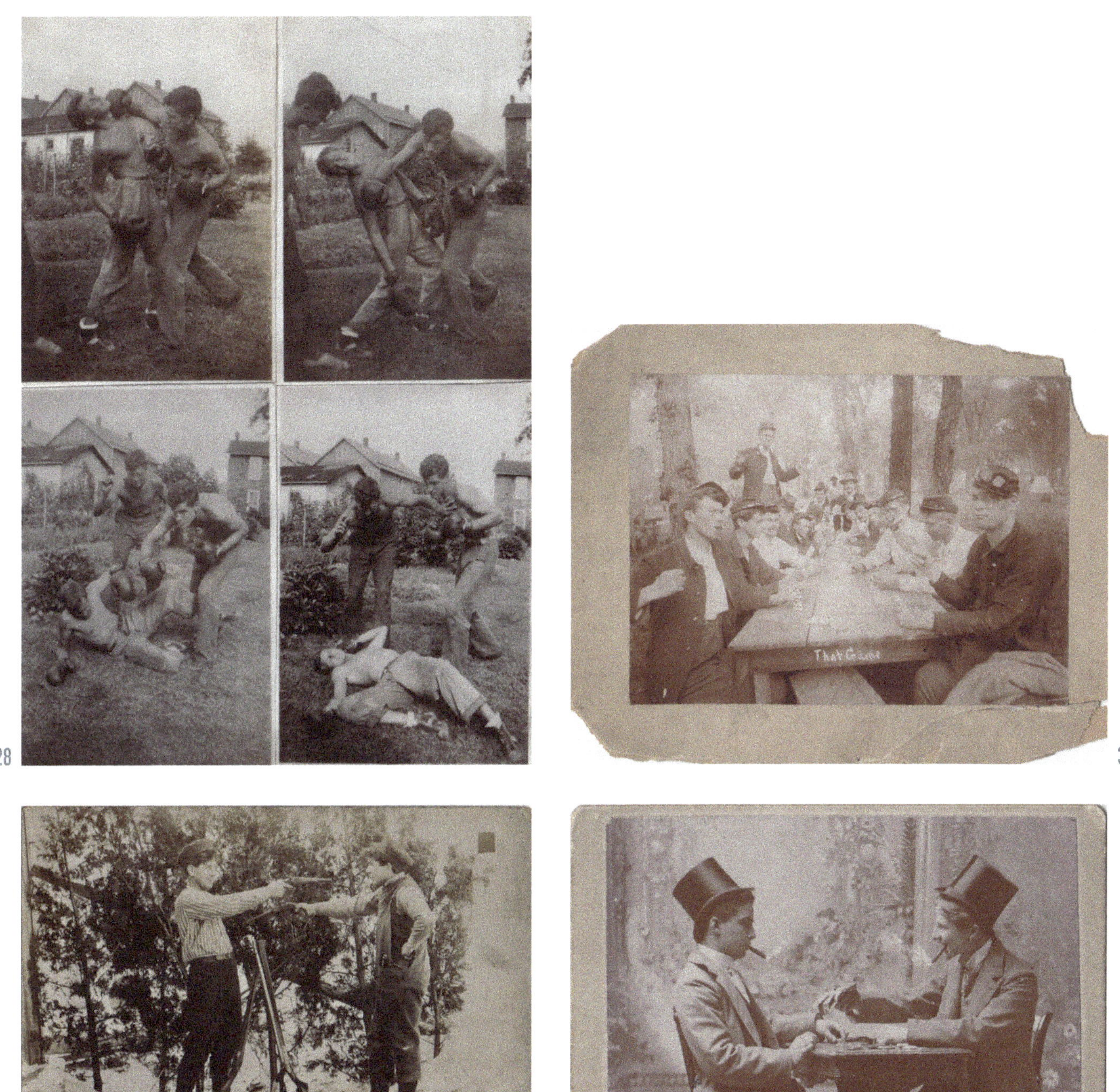
28
30
That Game
29
31

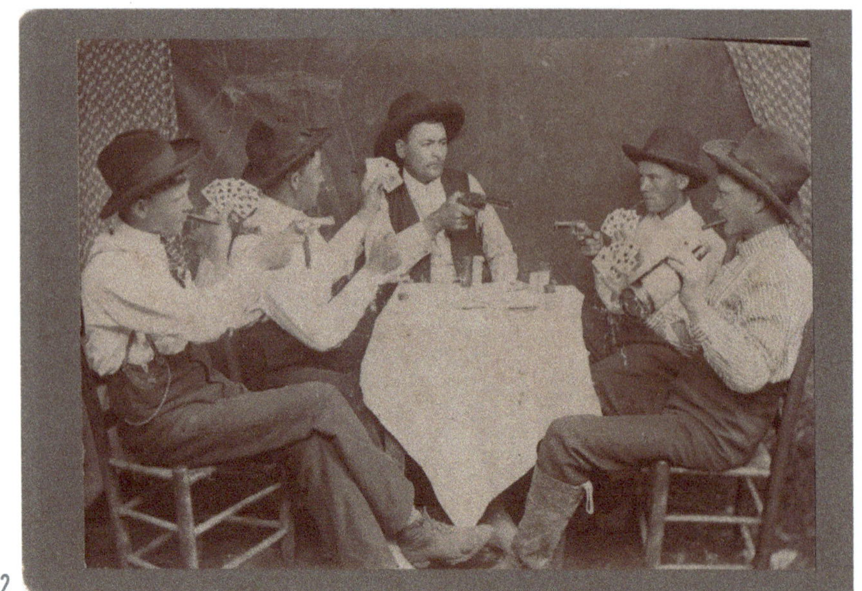

32

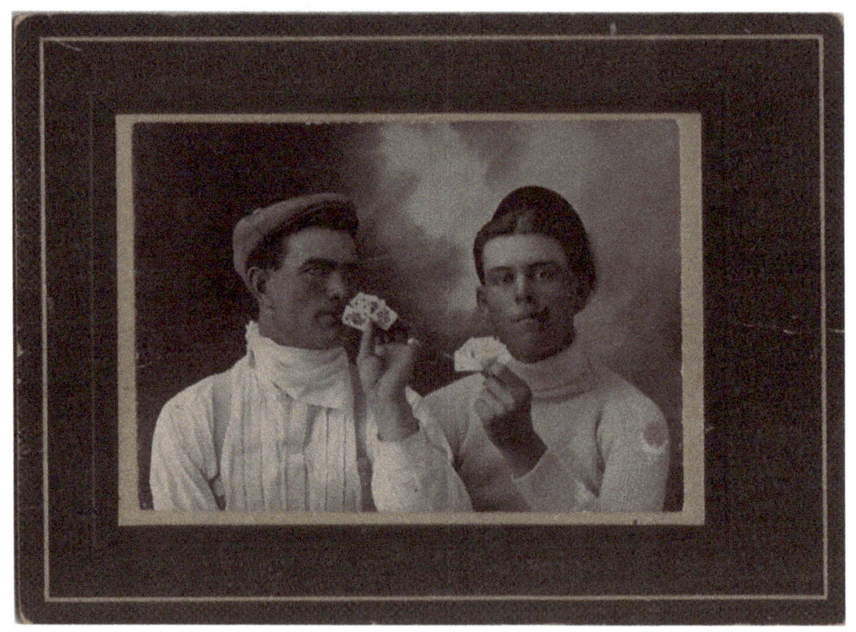

33

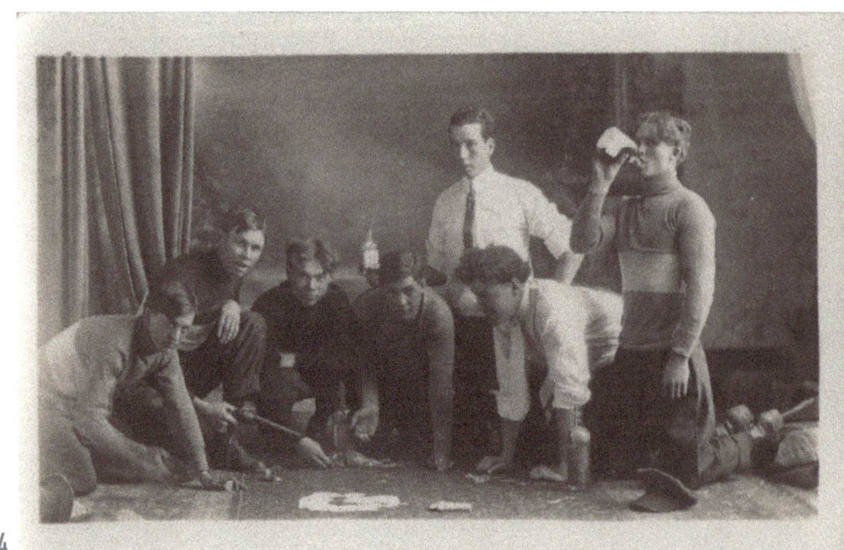

34

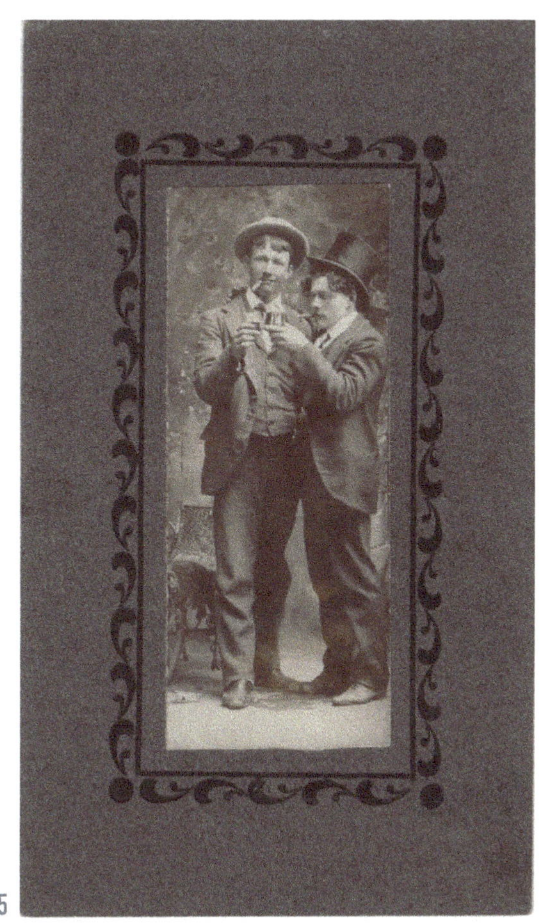
35

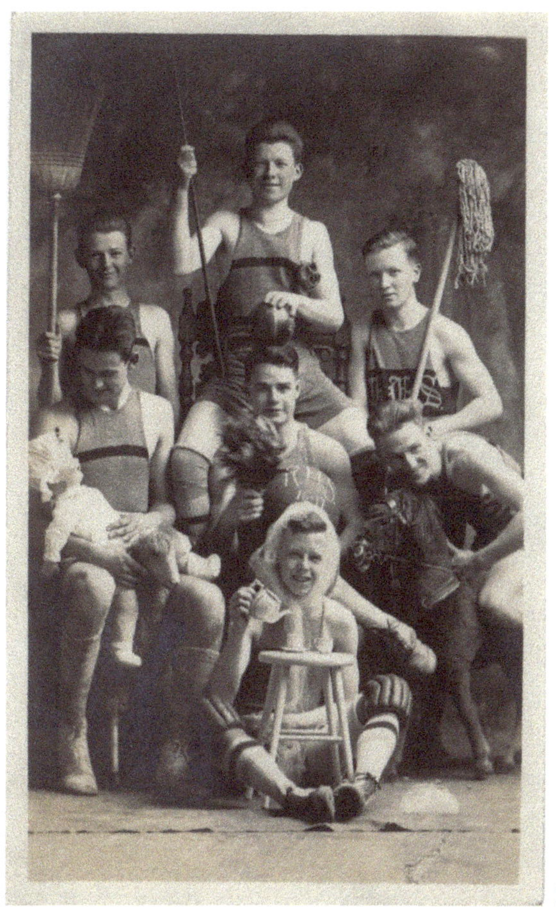
36

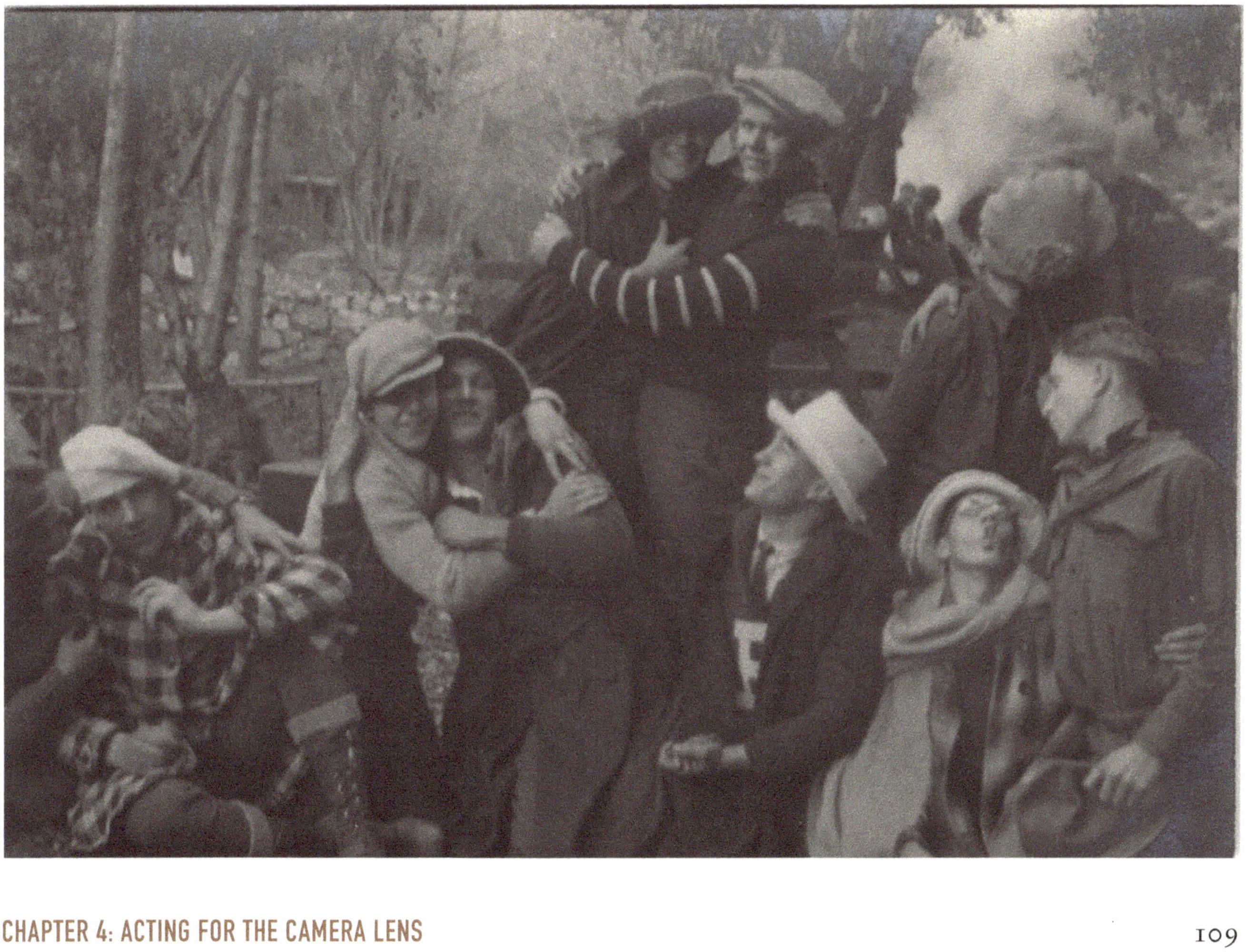

37

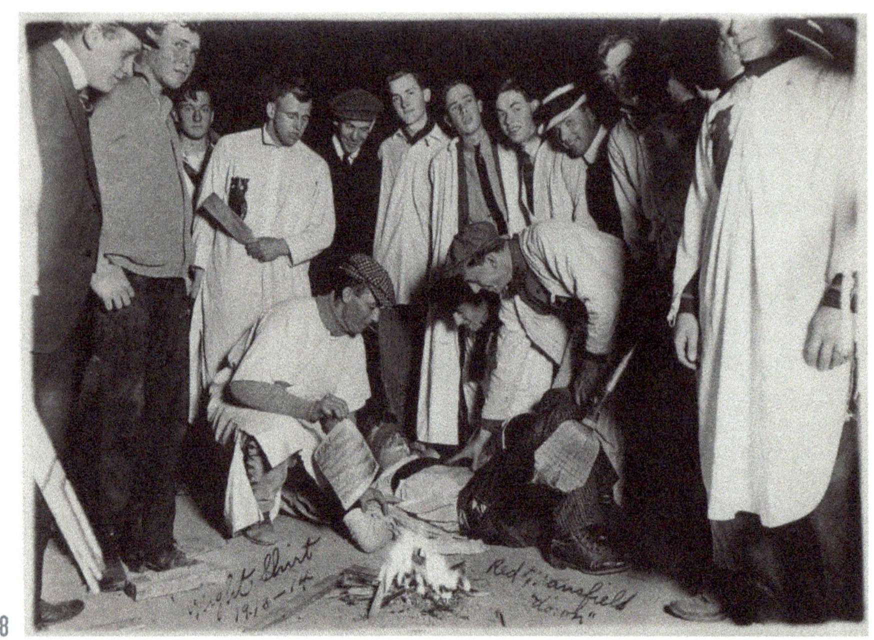

38

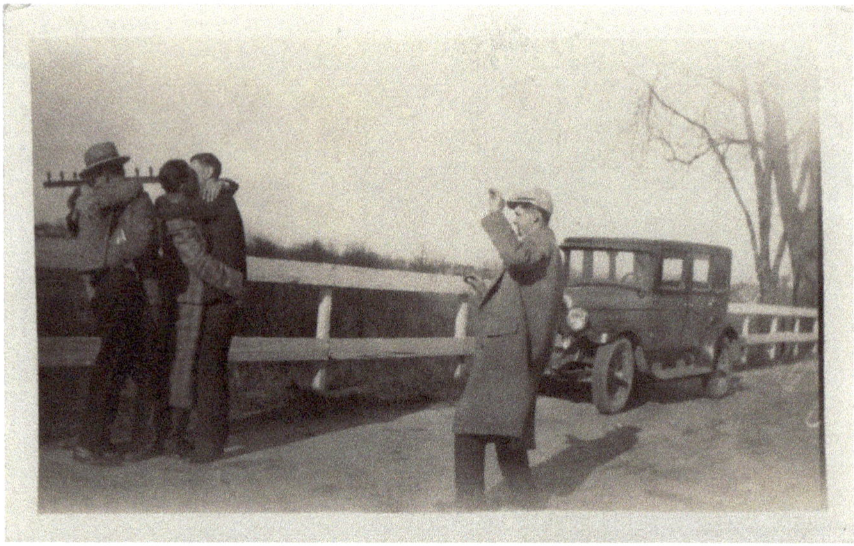

39

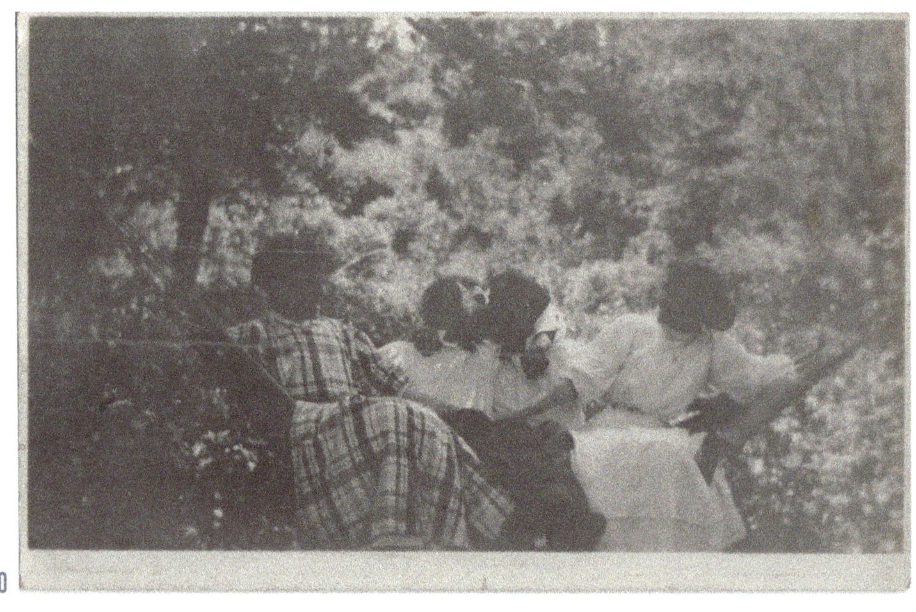

40

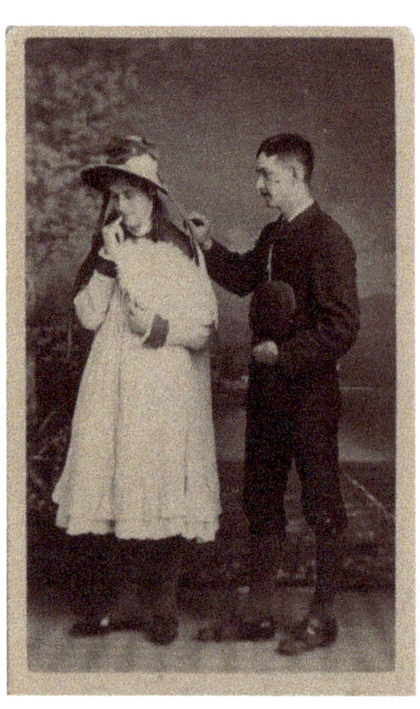

41

42

43

Love knows no
crowd.

44

REGULAR MEAL'S 75¢
CHICKEN 4 BITS
NO
Treat-
Trade
or
Travel.
Furnished
ROOMS
with beds.
FOR THE CAPTURE OF
RED MIKE

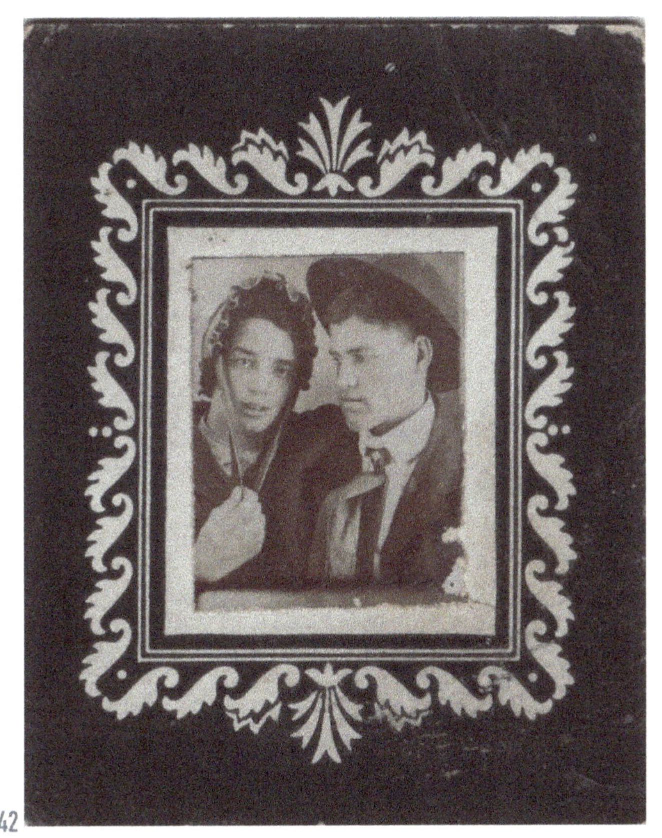

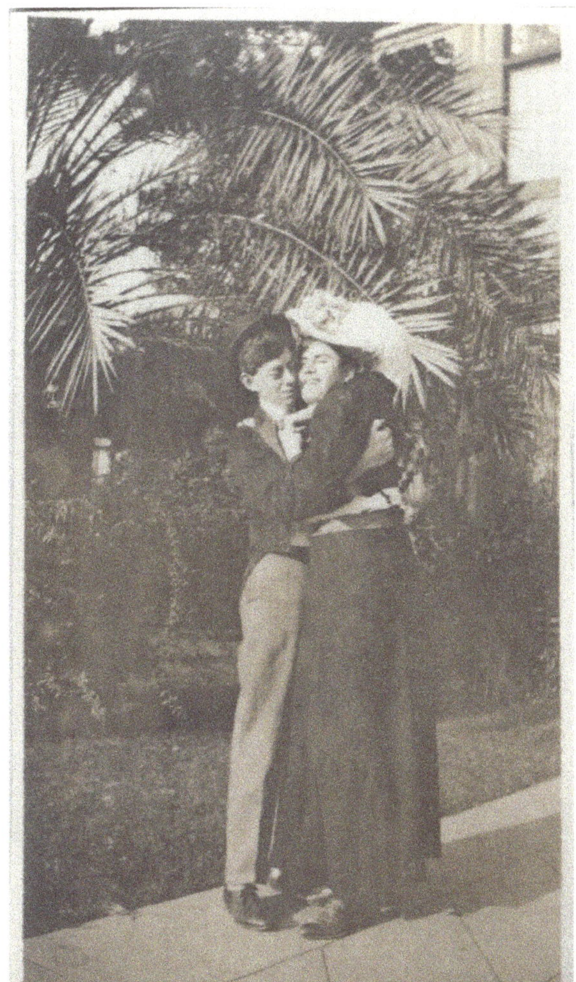

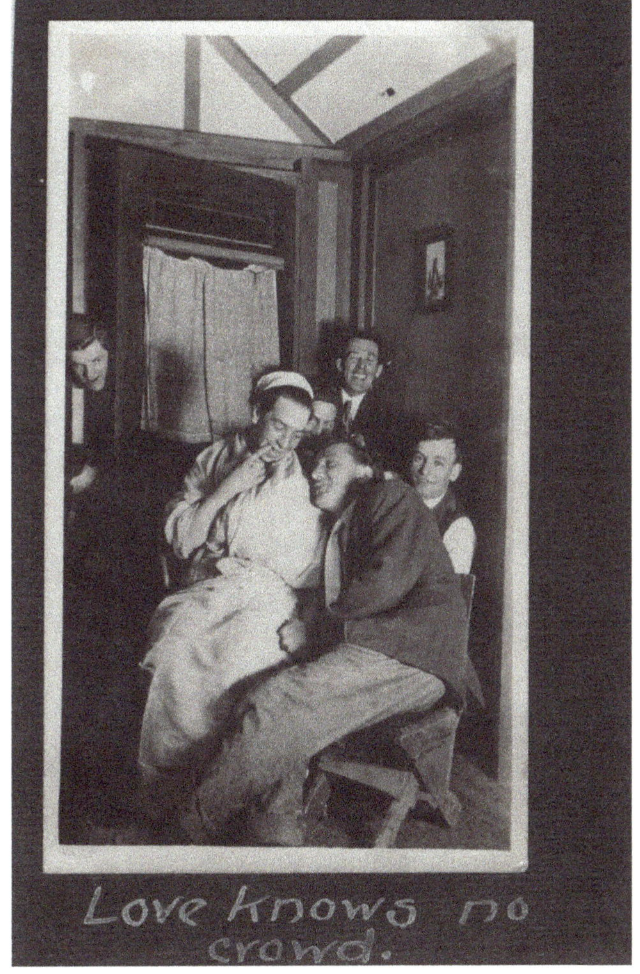

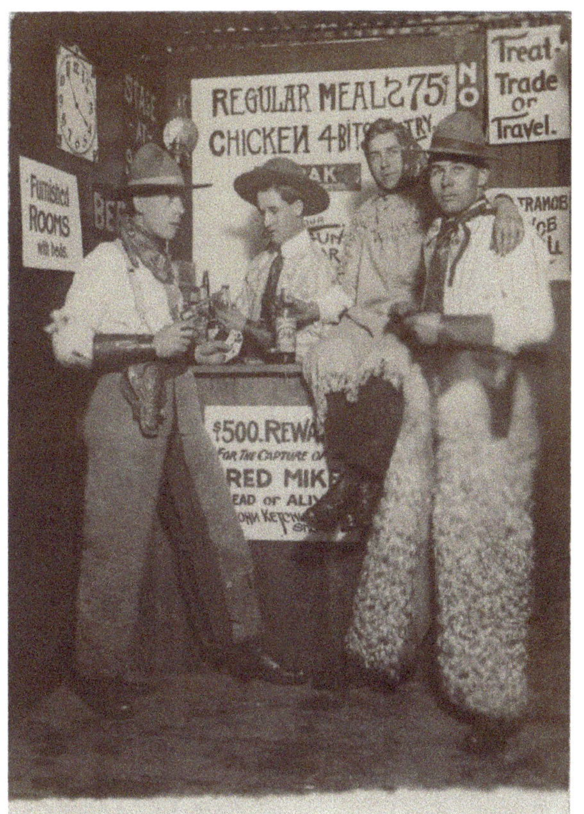

45

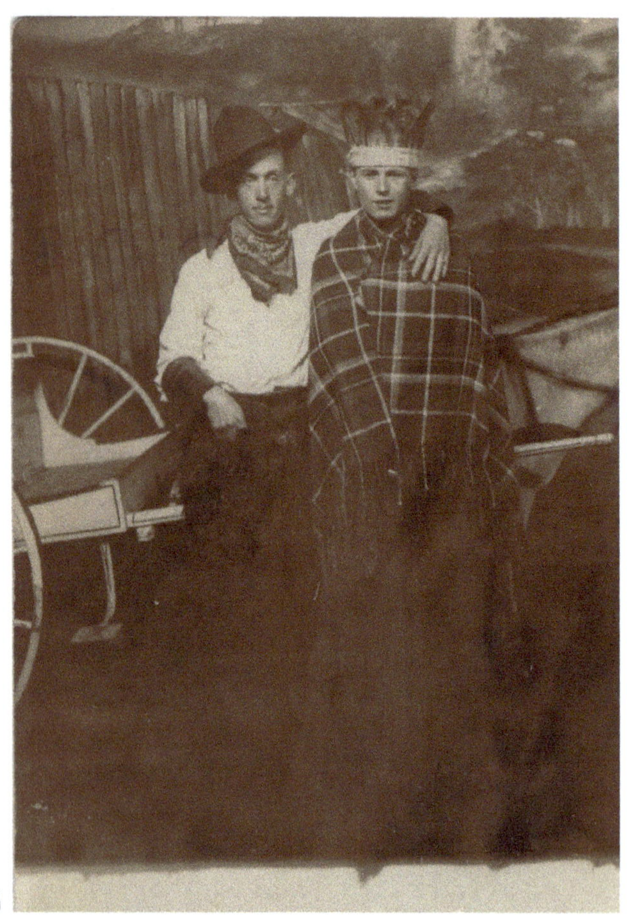
46

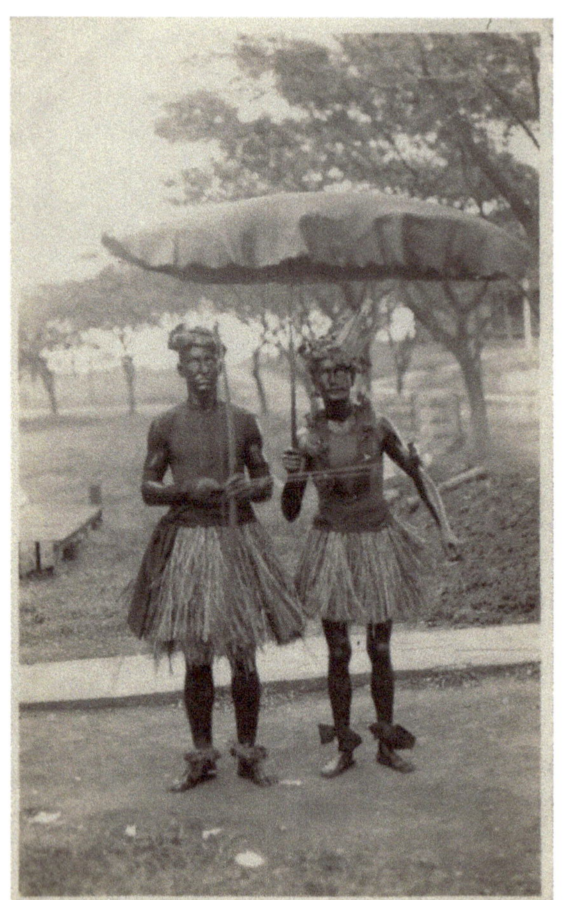
47

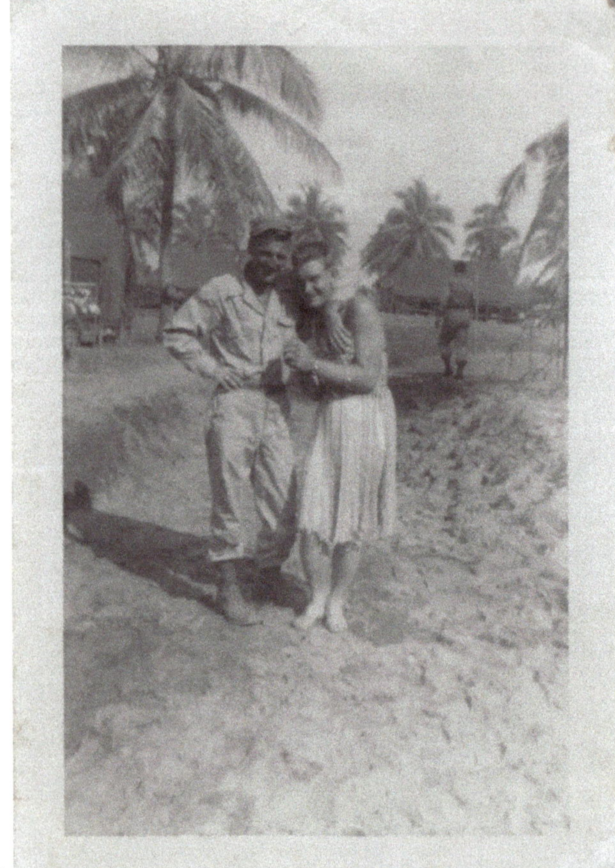
48

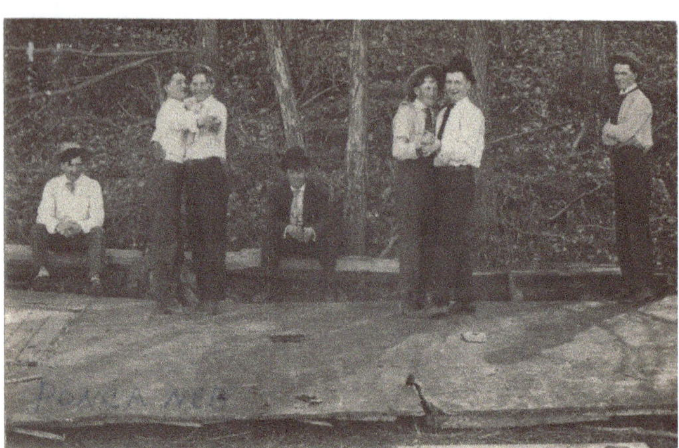
49

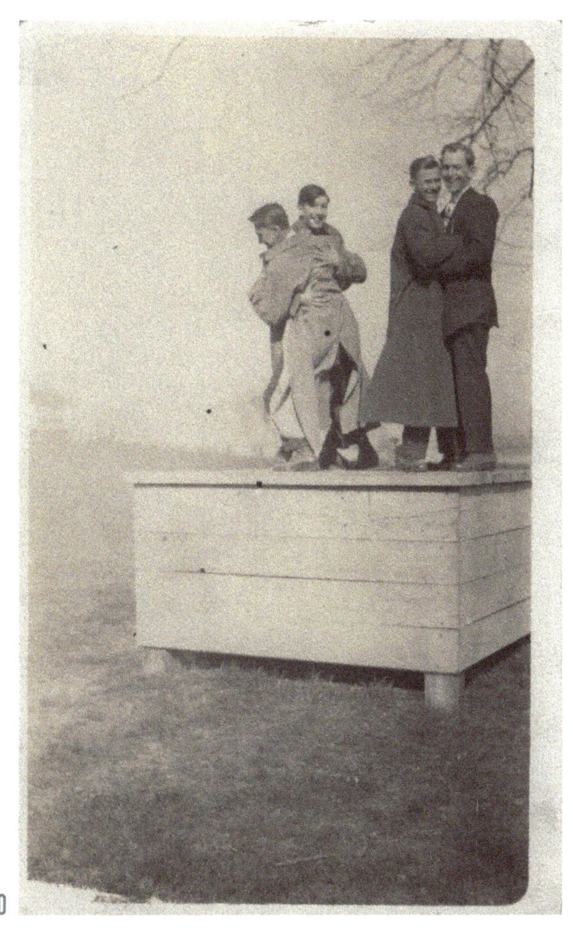

50

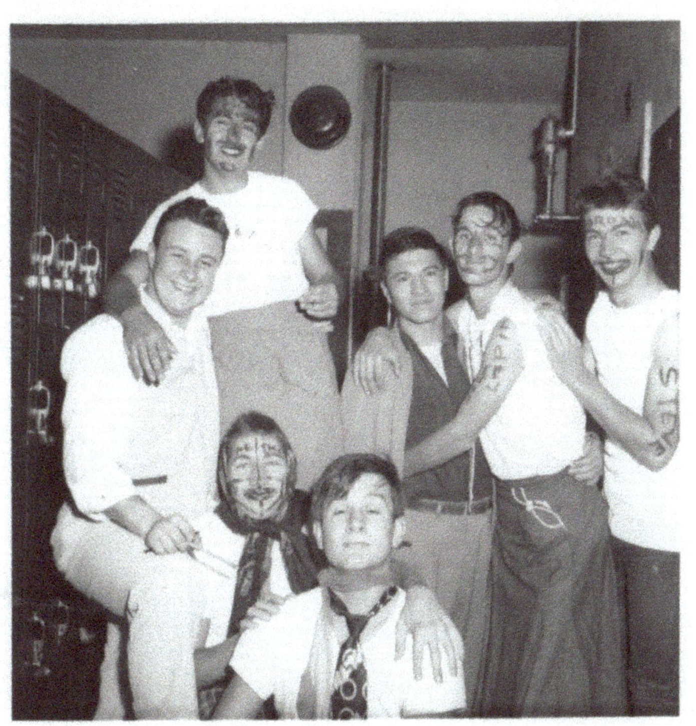

51

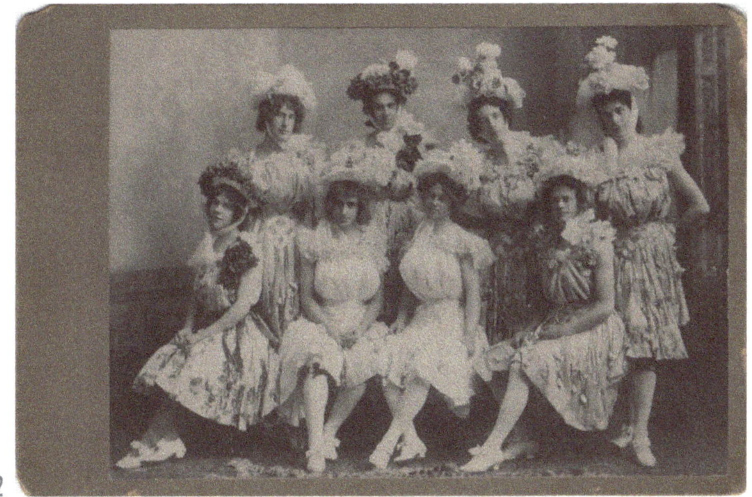

52

Hula! Hula! Cuba.

53

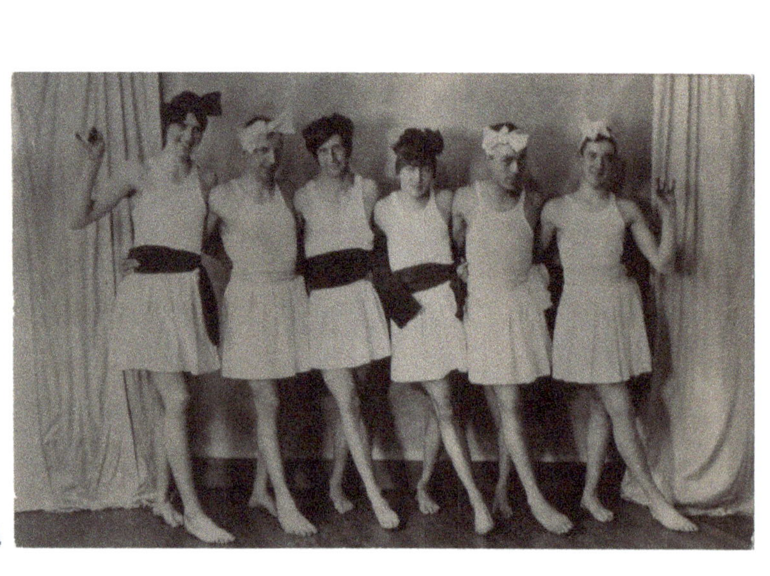
54

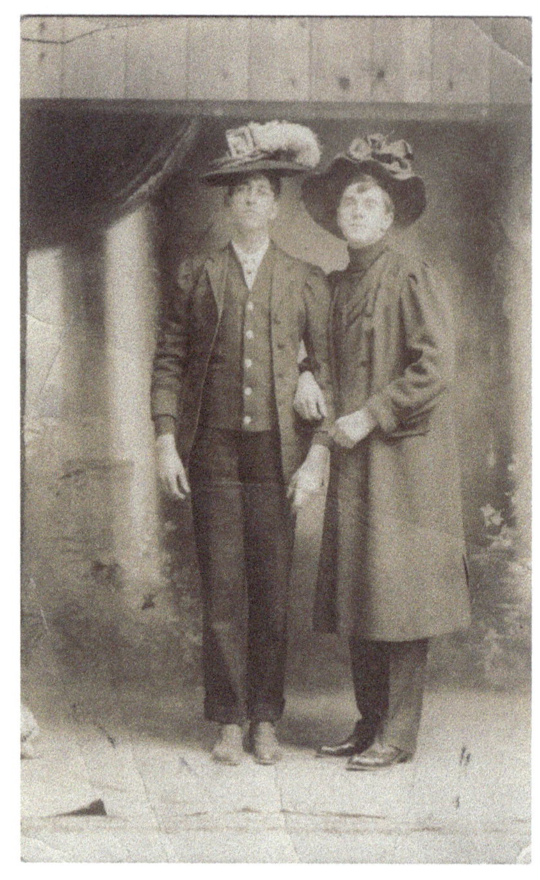
55

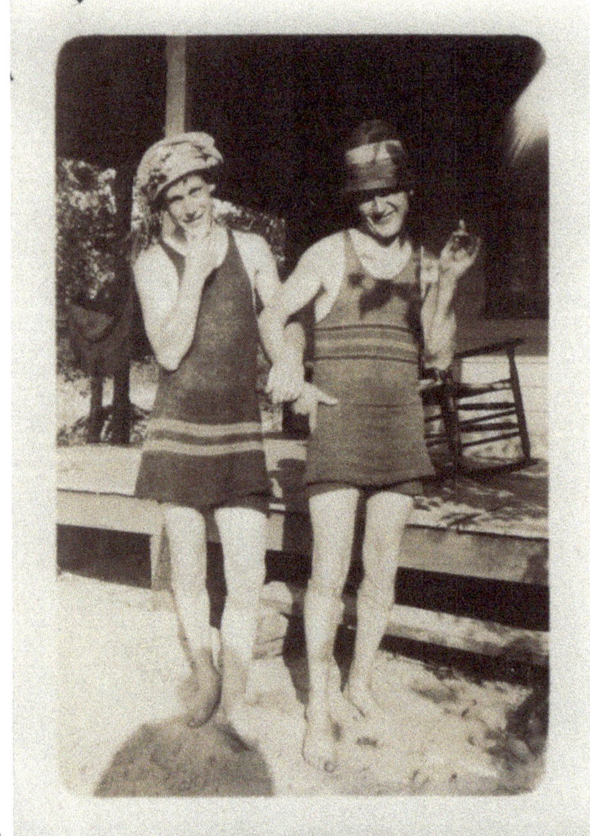
56

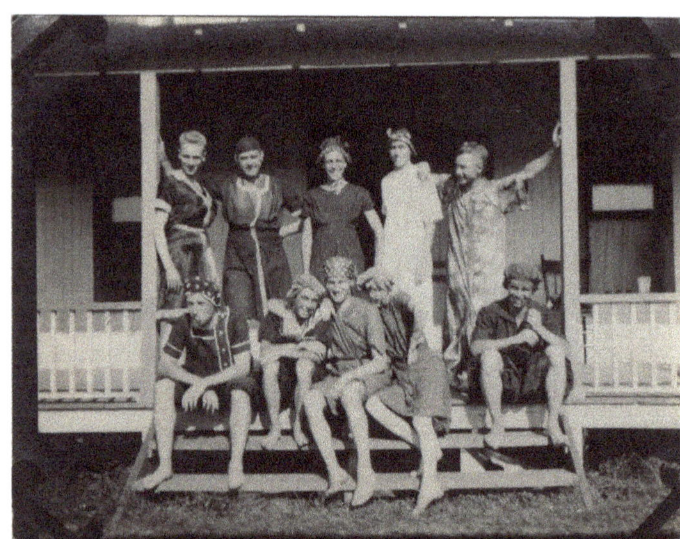
57

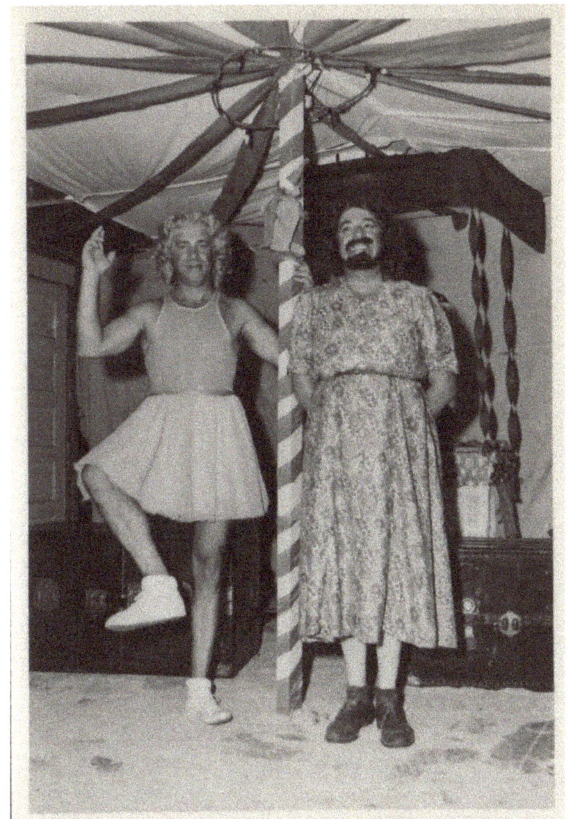
59

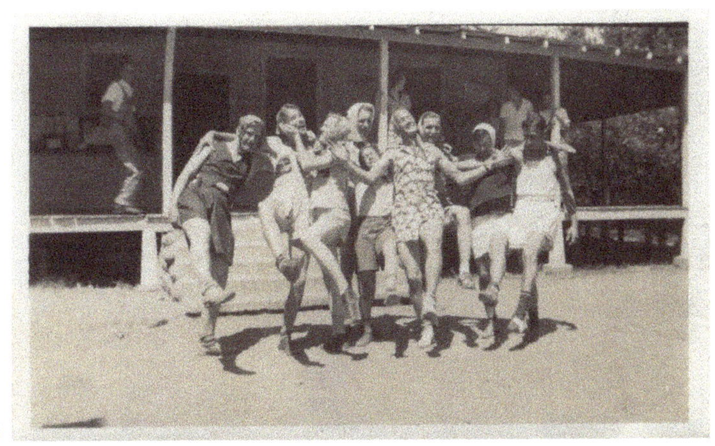
58

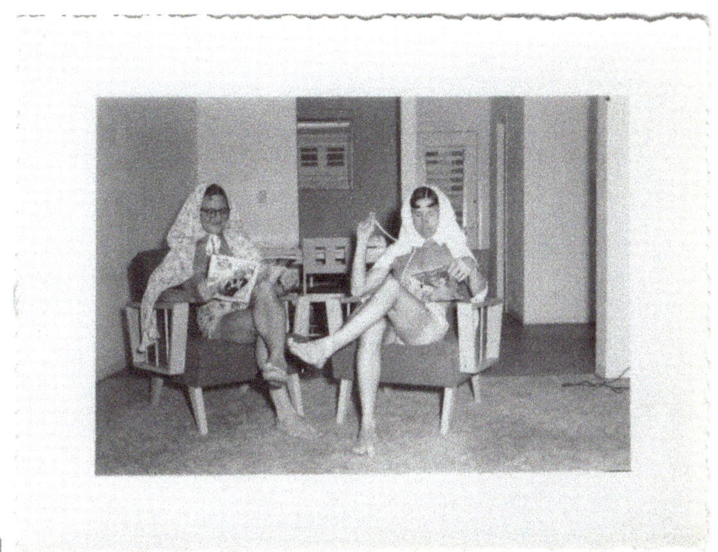
60

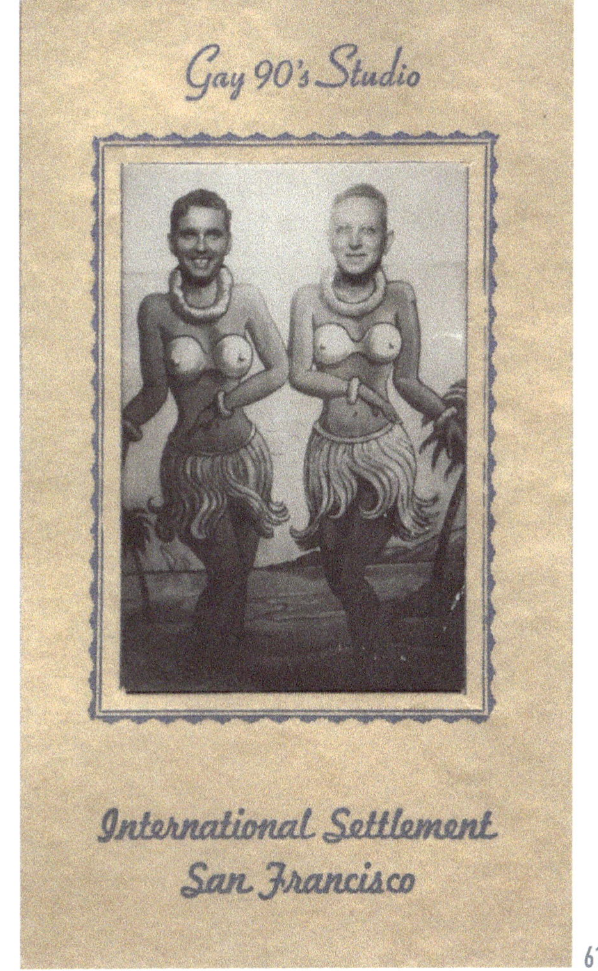

61

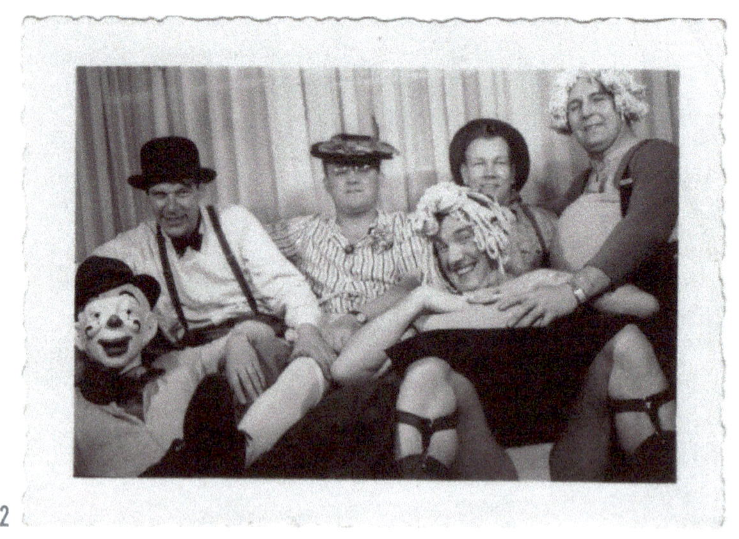

62

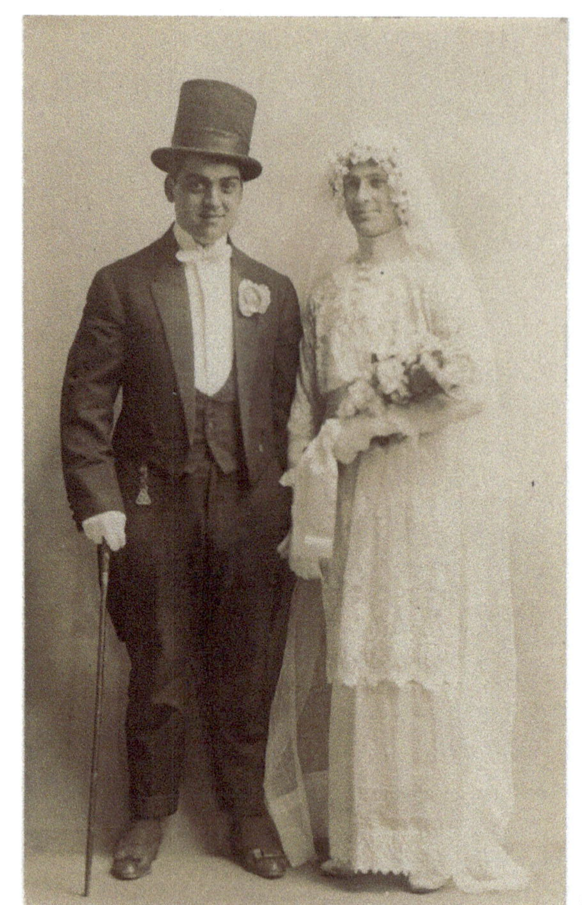

63

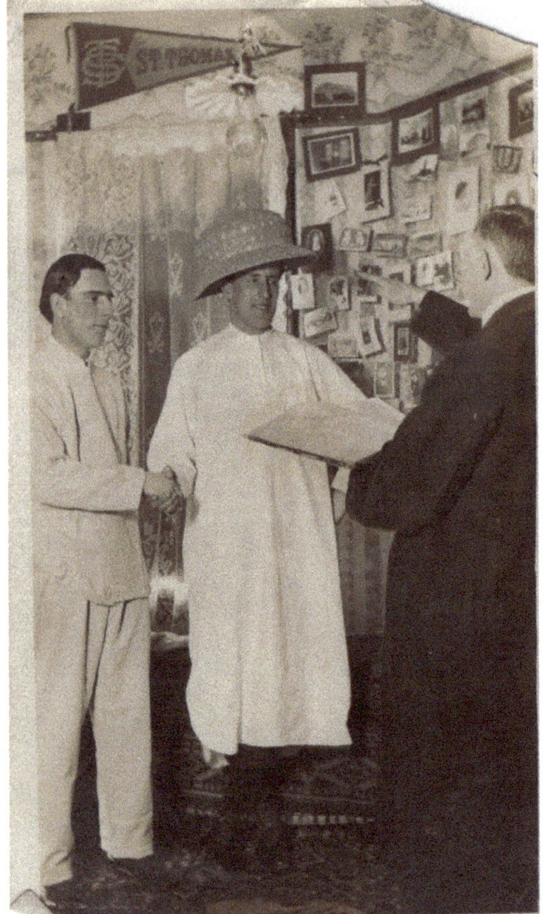

64

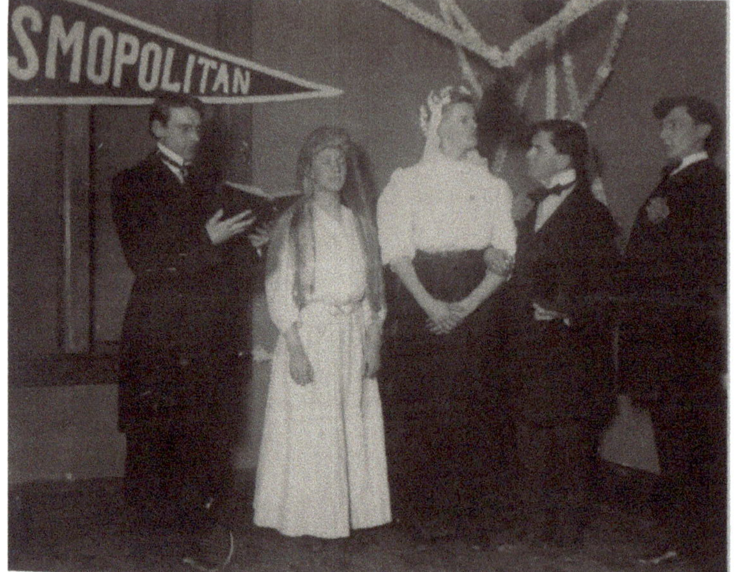

65

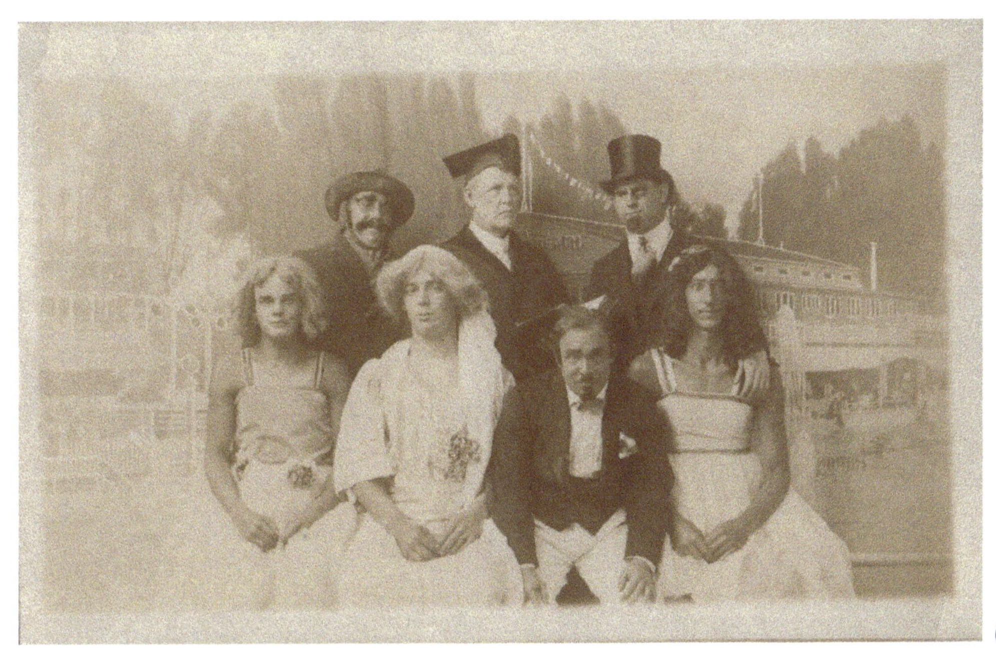

66

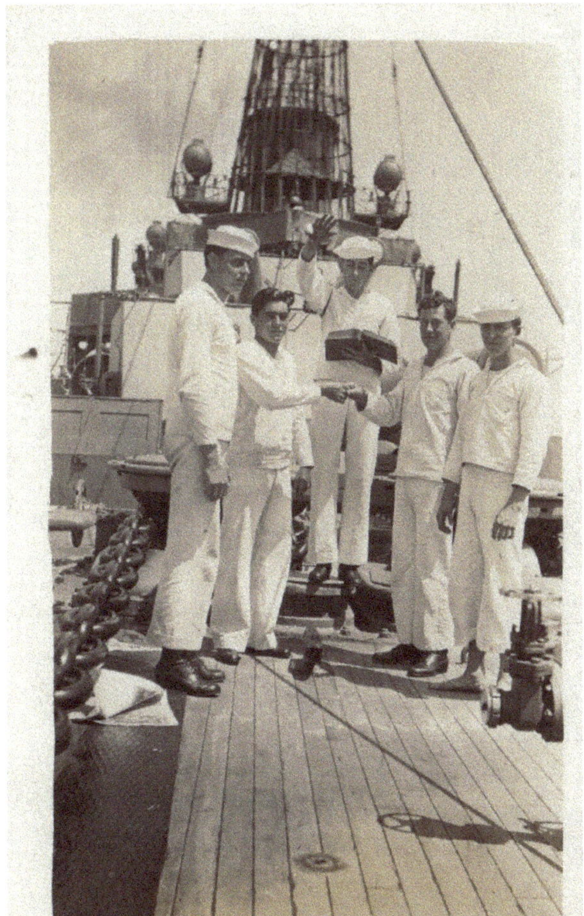

67

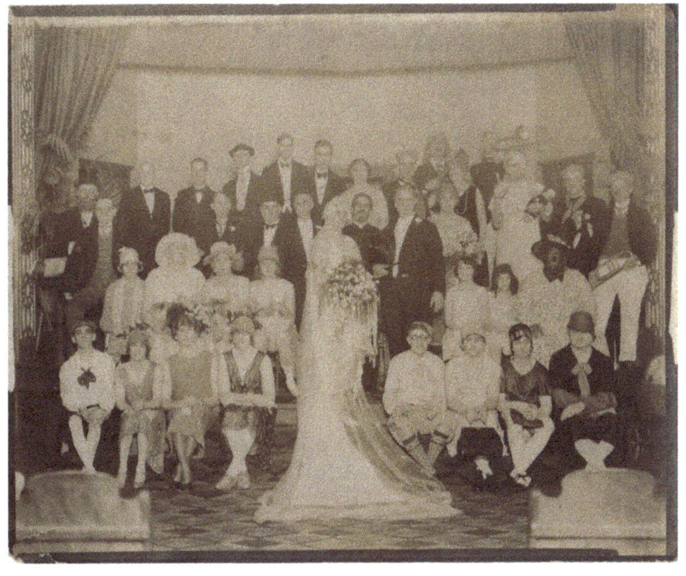

68

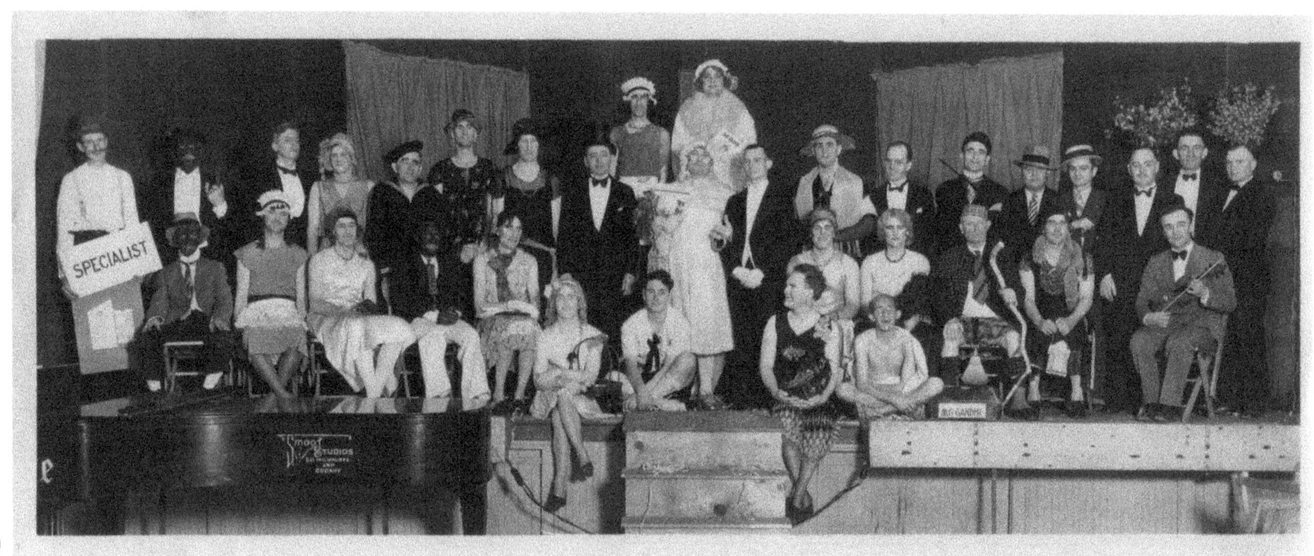
SPECIALIST

69

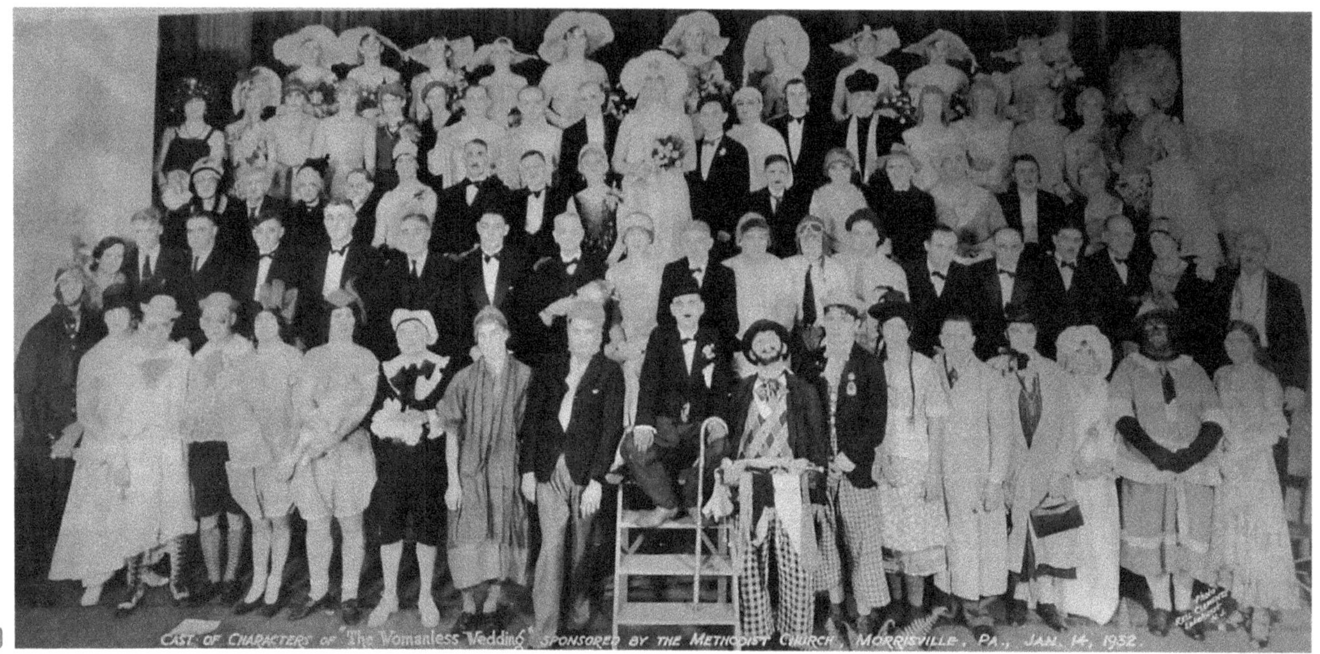
CAST OF CHARACTERS OF "The Womanless Wedding" SPONSORED BY THE METHODIST CHURCH, MORRISVILLE, PA., JAN. 14, 1932.

70

CHAPTER 5

PRESERVING THE SPECIAL OCCASIONS

MALES AT WORK AND PLAY

To further show the range of my collection, this final chapter presents five types of imagery of American masculinity's "special occasions": boyhood; sports; men at work; fraternal organizations; and males enjoying themselves at a beach. Some previous publications of mine have featured numerous photos of American boys, displaying how boys experienced a gradual distancing and a certain increasing somberness in how they posed together from the late nineteenth century to the mid-twentieth. The few photos in chapter 5a, on the other hand, are there simply because I think they capture so well the pleasure of a moment, the strength of an attachment, or, in the case of Image 15, the mystery, the untold story, that often accompanies a found photograph.

Sports imagery, especially team photos, have also appeared extensively in earlier works of mine. Team photos showed a pronounced shift from a relaxed intimacy in the late nineteenth century and the very early years of the twentieth to a joyless regimentation by the mid-1910s, an orderly formality that has lasted. Such images received an entire chapter of display and interpretation in *Picturing Men*.[31] The sports photos comprising chapter 5b in this book are there, in most cases, either because of an unusual pose or what I considered an artful composition. The brevity of this section of a chapter, however, is not an accurate reflection of how numerous photos there are of males playing or at least suited up for a game, or, as in Image 4, displaying the results of hunting or fishing. From the late nineteenth century forward—the era when basketball was invented, boxing became wildly popular, and colleges were expected to field a team for as many sports as possible—sports and mainstream masculinity have been culturally joined, tightly bound. The boy who didn't play was an outsider. Not to be in a team photo might, for some boys, be a painful exclusion, while to be pictured in a team photo might be considered a sure sign of masculinity.

Another sort of imagery closely associated with masculine identity in American culture is the subject of chapter 5c: photographs of men taken at their places of work or else in photographers' studios dressed in the uniform of their occupation. Such photos—in factories and offices, for instance, or in the woods among lumberjacks—were once so common that among collectors they have the special designation of "occupationals." That these photos were so frequently taken surely attests to the significance the workplace had come to have for many men. Interestingly enough, as did team photos, photos of men at work eventually became displays of regimentation, as Image 6 clearly shows. They also became much less frequently taken at all, attesting perhaps to a diminished significance of the workplace as a male space and a source of identity.

Membership in an organization that featured regular in-person meetings; at times, secret passwords and ceremonies as well as rites of initiation; and, very often, also a uniform or costume, has been a significant part of many American men's lives even since before there was an ability to take photographs of the members. Photographs of the members of a few such organizations comprise chapter 5d: a church group, something called "The Wild Sons Club," a college fraternity, the Knights of Pythian, an automobile club of some sort, and three societies of unknown name and purpose that featured highly distinctive costuming (Images 1 through 8). Some organizations have been more exclusive than others, steadfastly devoted to excluding certain other men and all women from their ranks. Not only was the gender boundary enforced by these groups, but boundaries of race, religion, and social class might also be involved. Some organizations were guardians of privilege, with membership serving as an avenue to economic advantage. Other groups were designed primarily for companionship, a family of sorts, in an otherwise lonely urban environment. The racial segregation of American society is painfully obvious in the racial uniformity in the photographs of these organizations—indeed, in the rarity of mixed-race photos throughout my collection.

As the doings of the Ku Klux Klan and the hazing rituals of some college fraternities remind us, some of these groups have engaged in reprehensible behavior. Even groups with much more benign intentions and activities have typically been undemocratic agencies of exclusion, a means of dividing "us" from "them," their secret rituals and costumes providing a feeling of distinctiveness to males who apparently needed to feel that way. Except for organizations, such as the Klan, that wanted to keep their membership a secret, photos such as those in chapter 5d might be tokens of belonging. Even the Klan at times allowed photos, as long as the members wore their hoods.

Chapter 5e, the final section, shows men and boys at what has been a favorite site of male play: a seaside or lakeside beach (or, as in Images 1 and 2, a simulated beach; or, in Image 7, a swimming pool). If photos are a guide, for a time the beach seems to have been largely a male space, or at least a place segregated by sex. It is highly noteworthy how often males were photographed at a beach with no females present, at least until the 1950s. American males were expected to wear tops to their swimming attire until the 1930s in most parts of the country, but even then, more of their bare bodies could be exposed and touched than in other public settings, except for public bathhouses. When tops came off, opportunities for intimacy might increase. In more remote, often rural, settings, as well as in the pools of some organizations, swimming naked was the norm, as was the case in Image 5. A camera often accompanied males to the beach; it was a setting frequently photographed. ■

31 *Picturing Men*, Chapter 5, "Straightening Up: The Evolution of the Team Portrait," 98–117.

FOUND PHOTOGRAPHS OF AMERICAN BOYHOOD

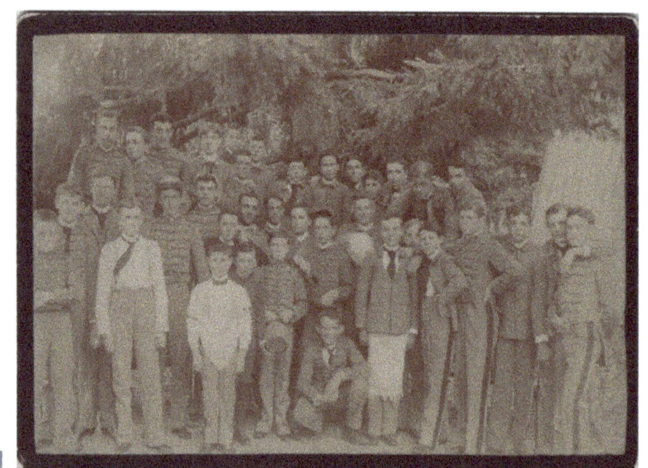
1

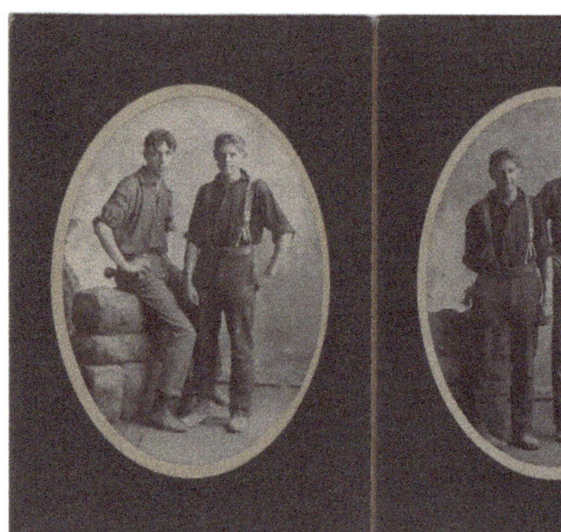
2

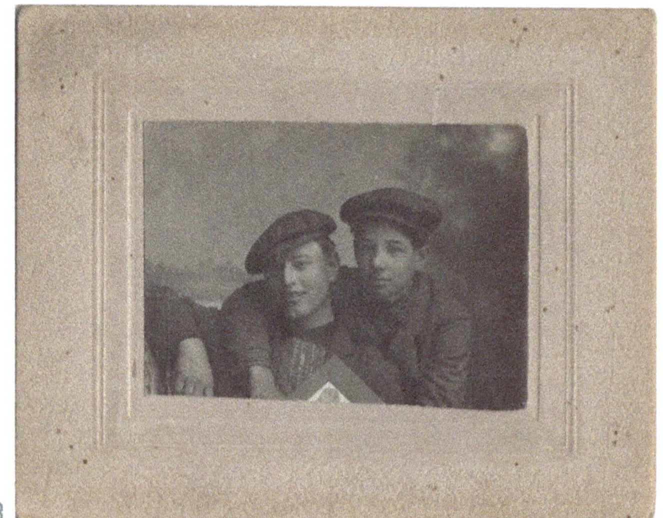
3

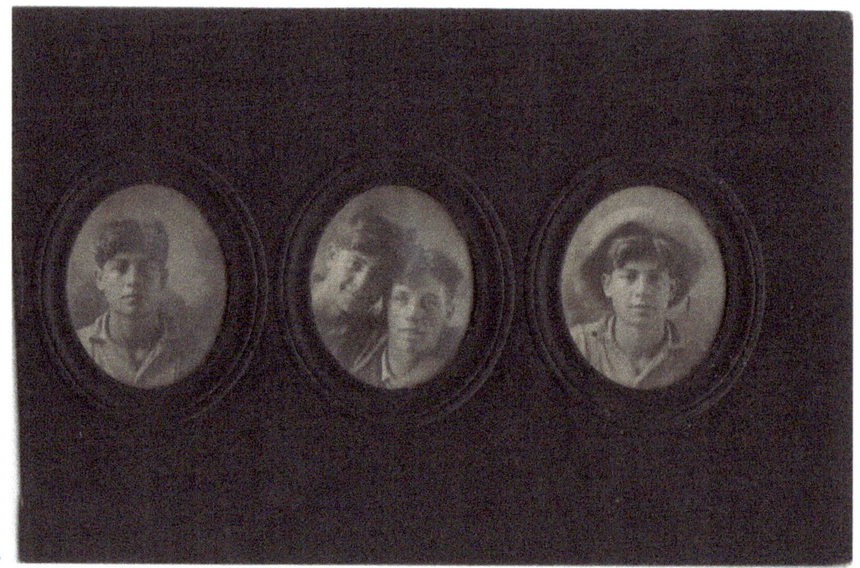
4

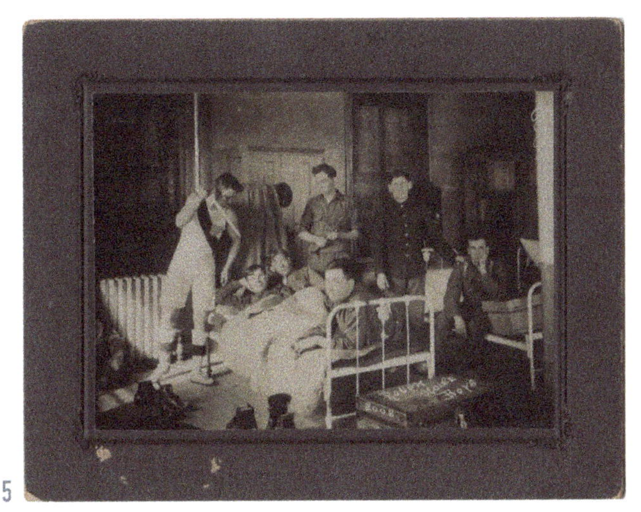
5

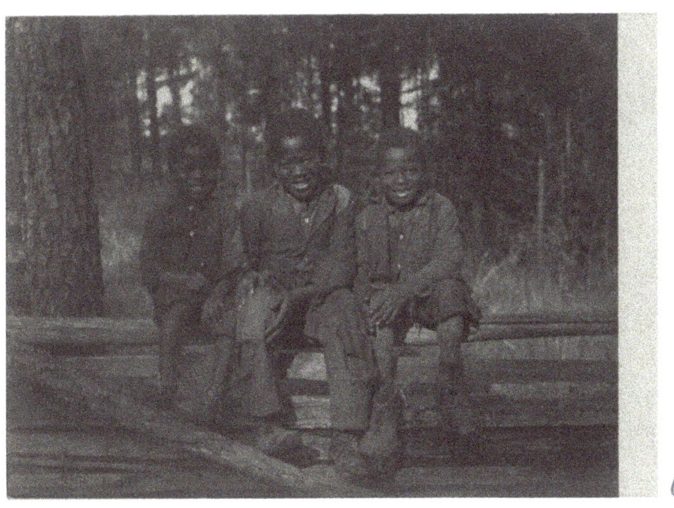
6

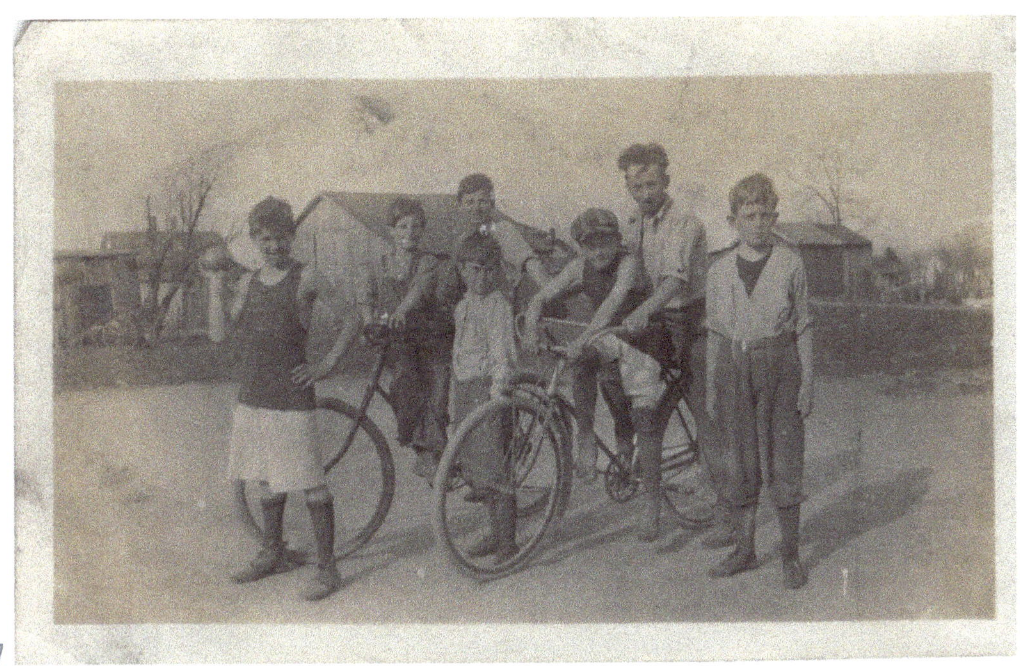
7

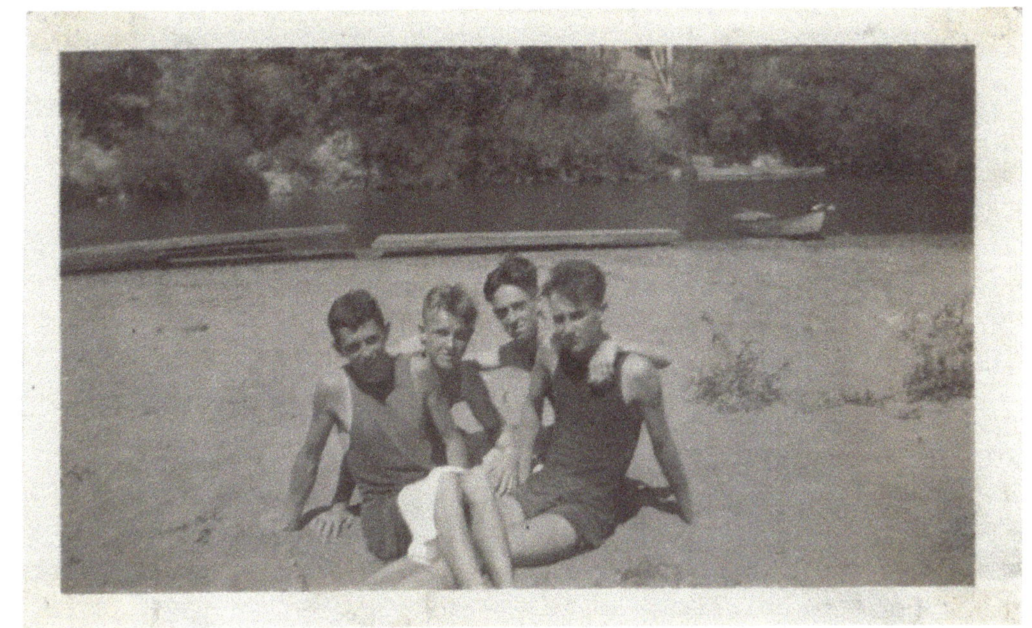
8

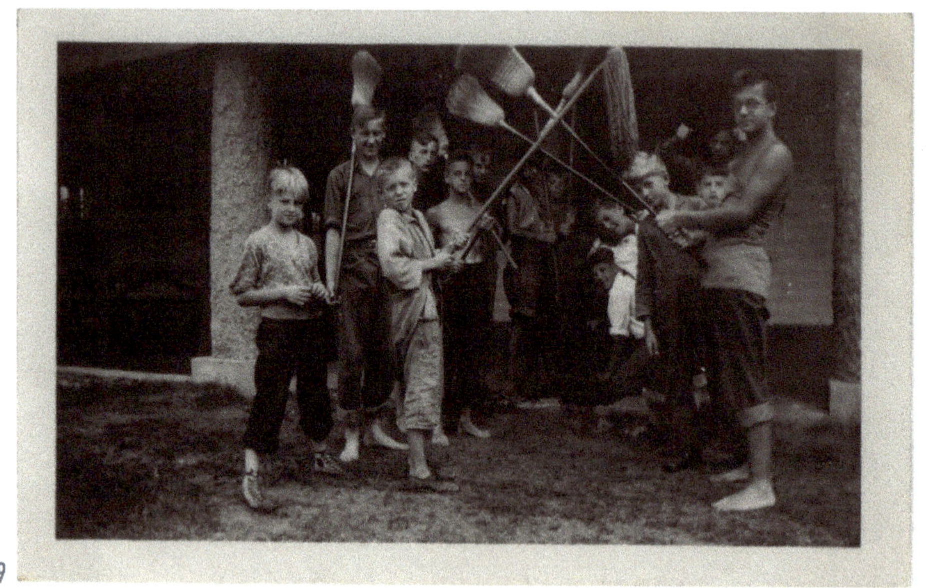
9

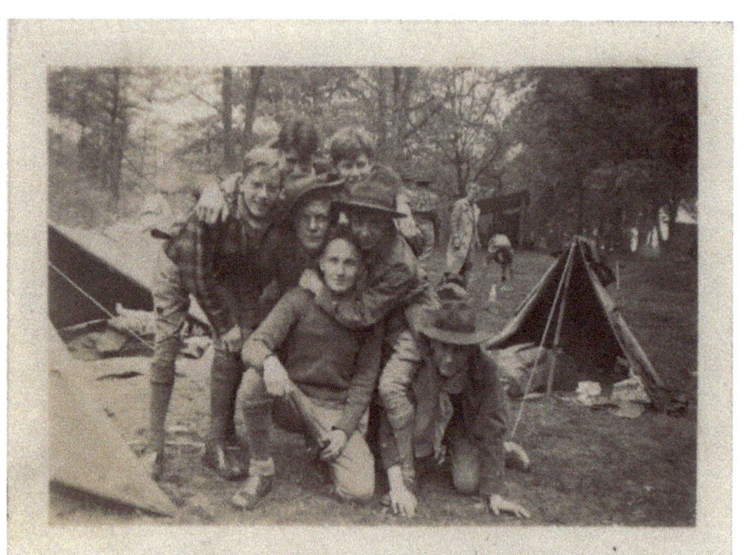
10

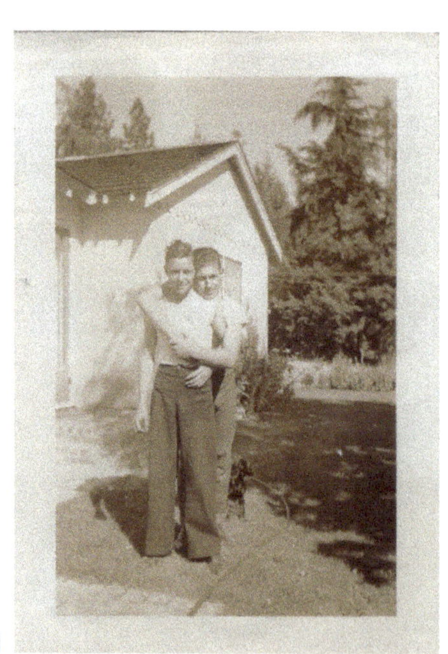
11

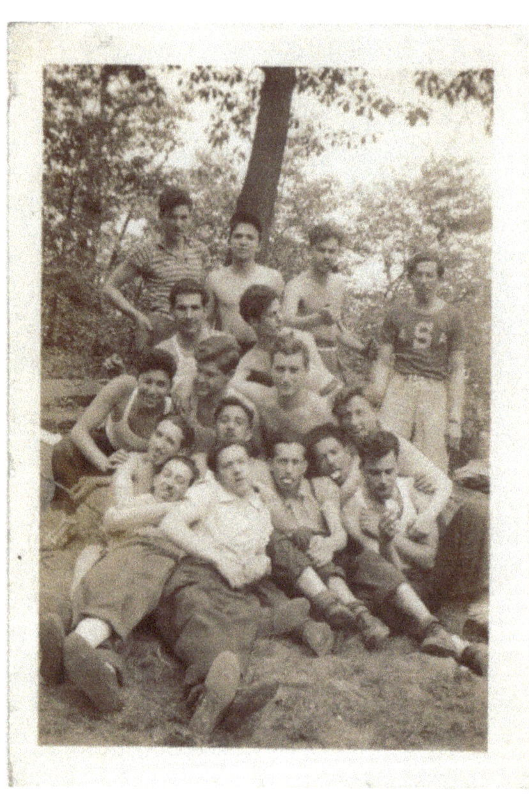
12

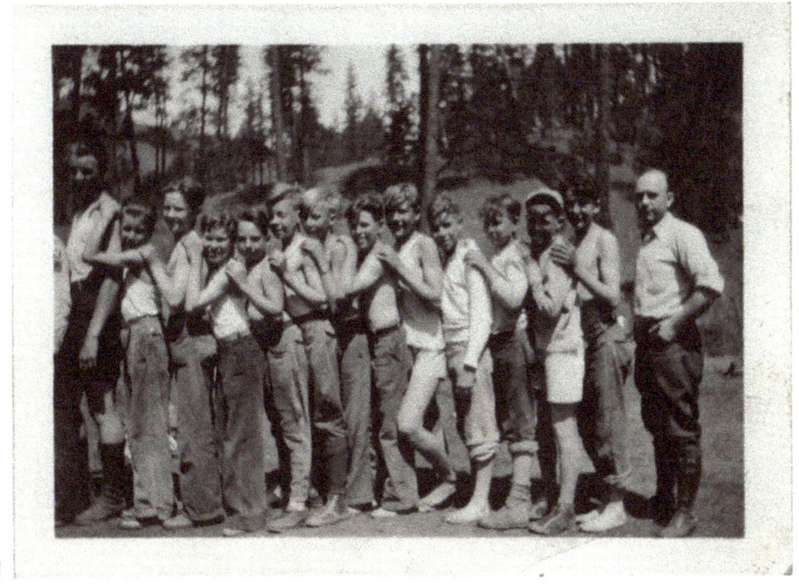
13

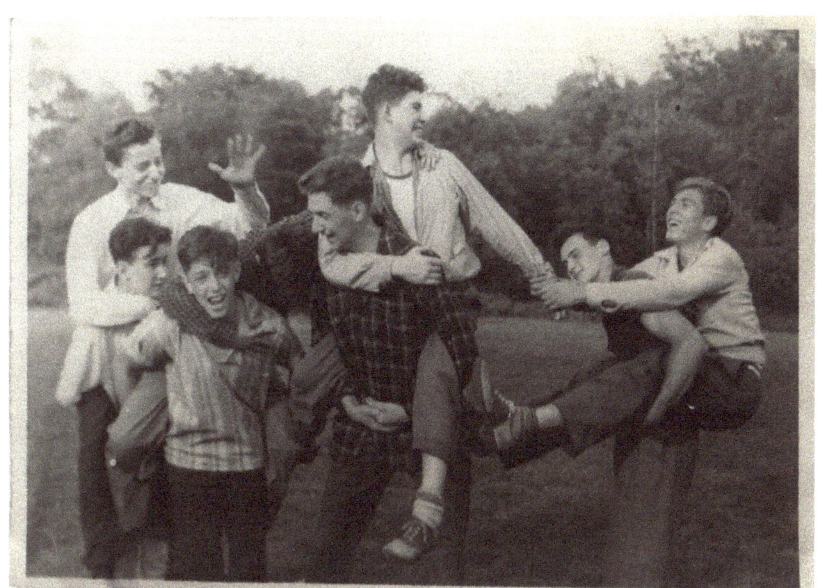
14

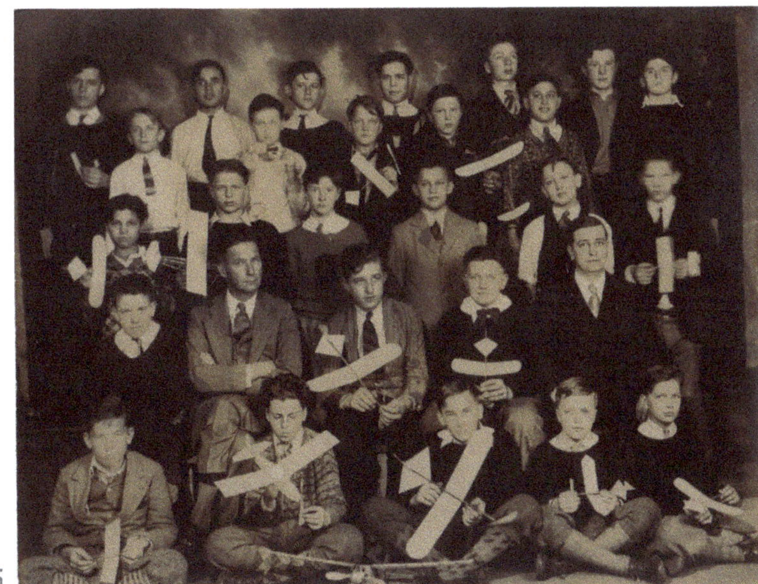
15

THE TEAM PHOTO AND AMERICAN MASCULINITY

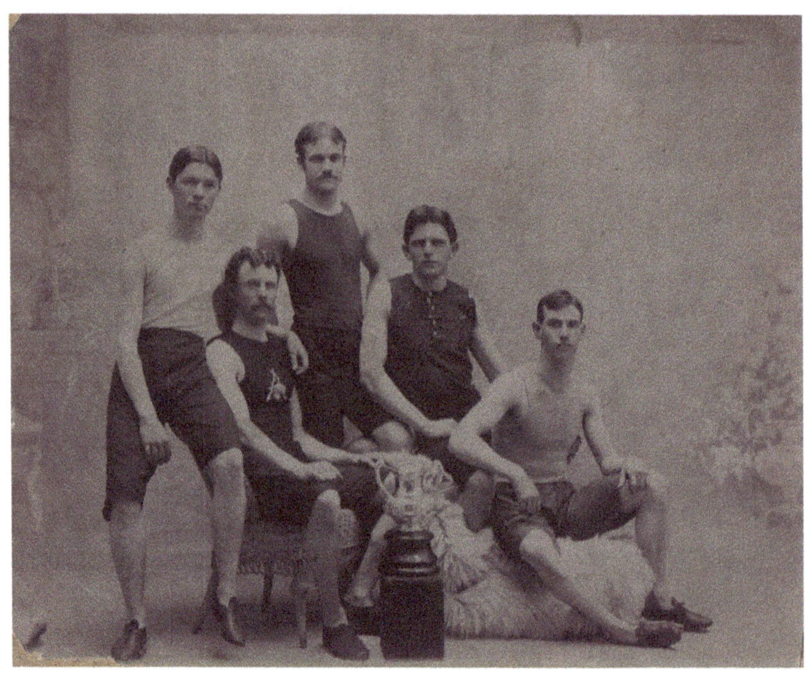
1

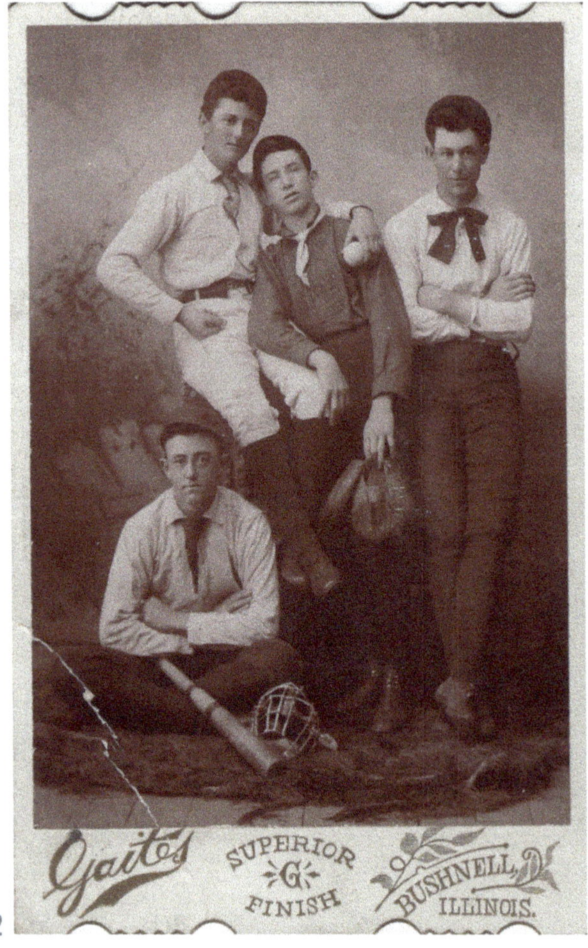

2

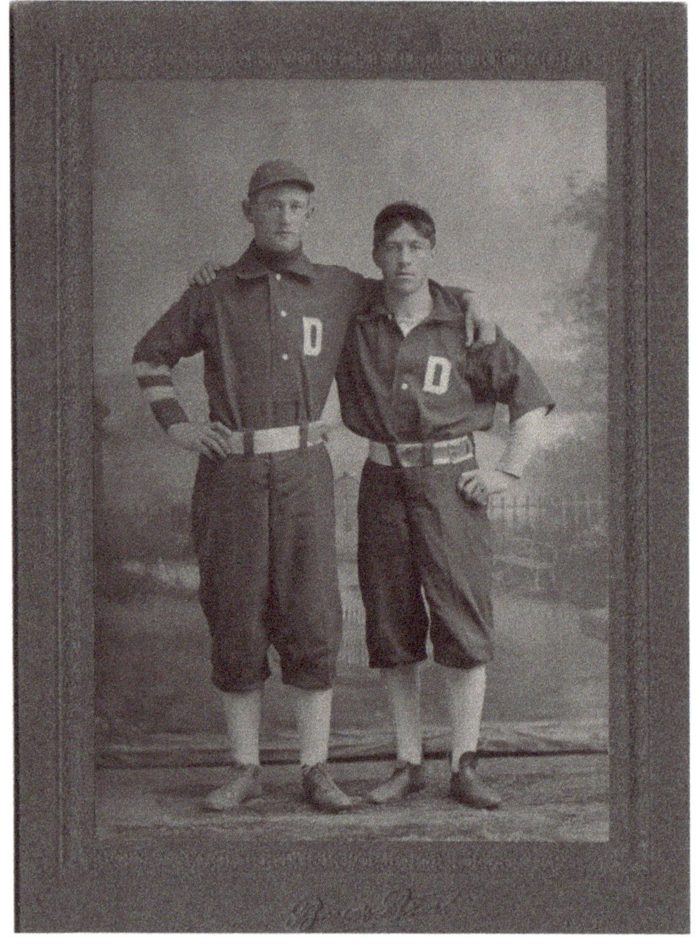
3

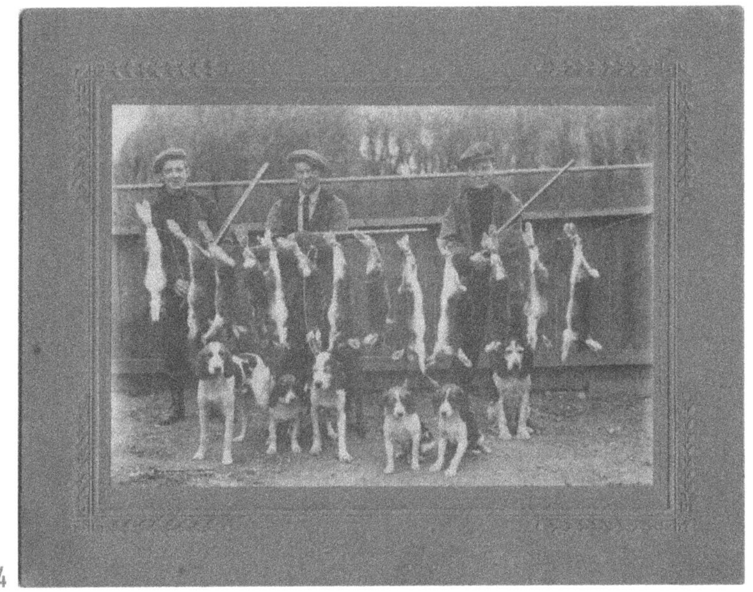
4

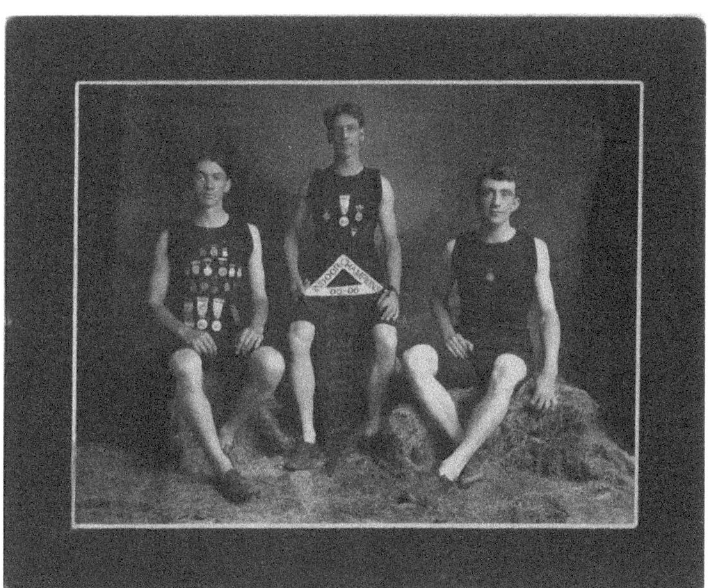
5

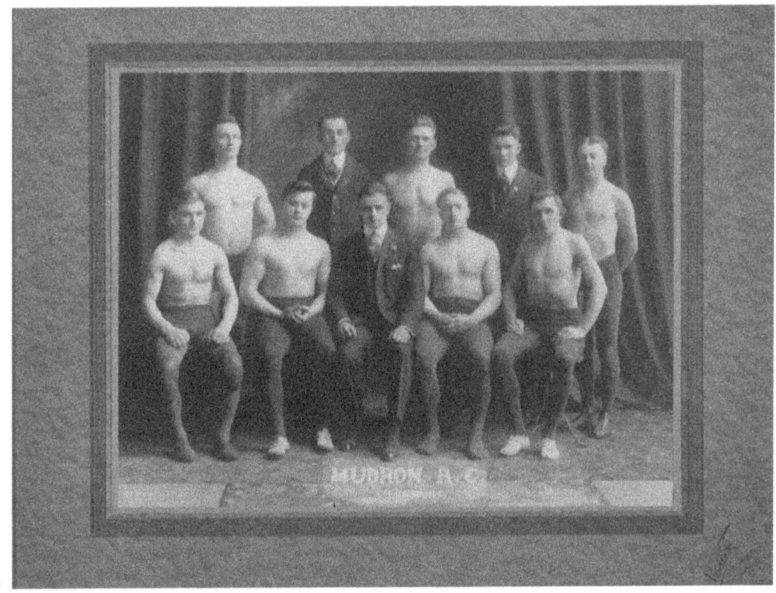

6

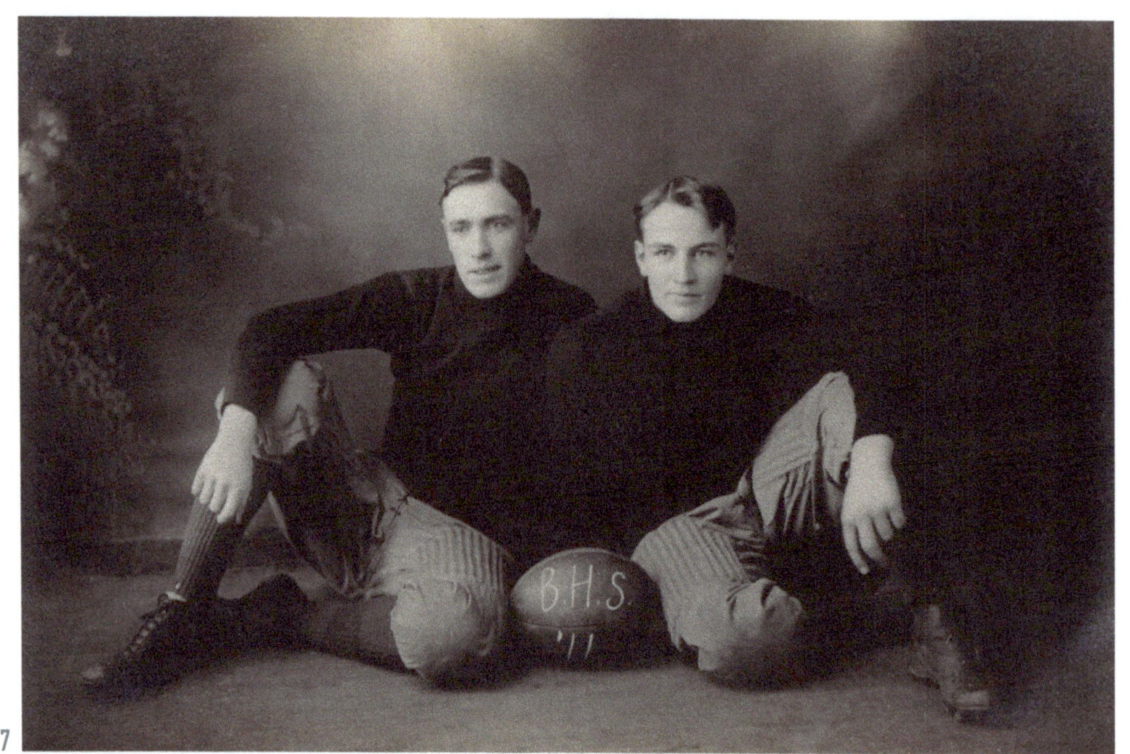

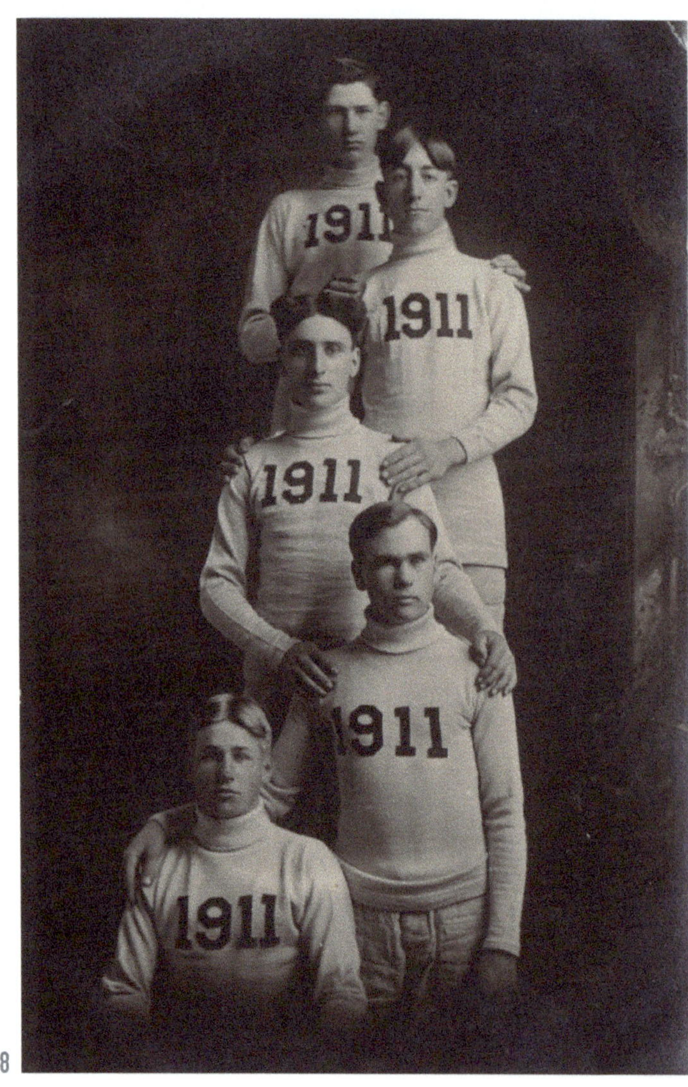

8

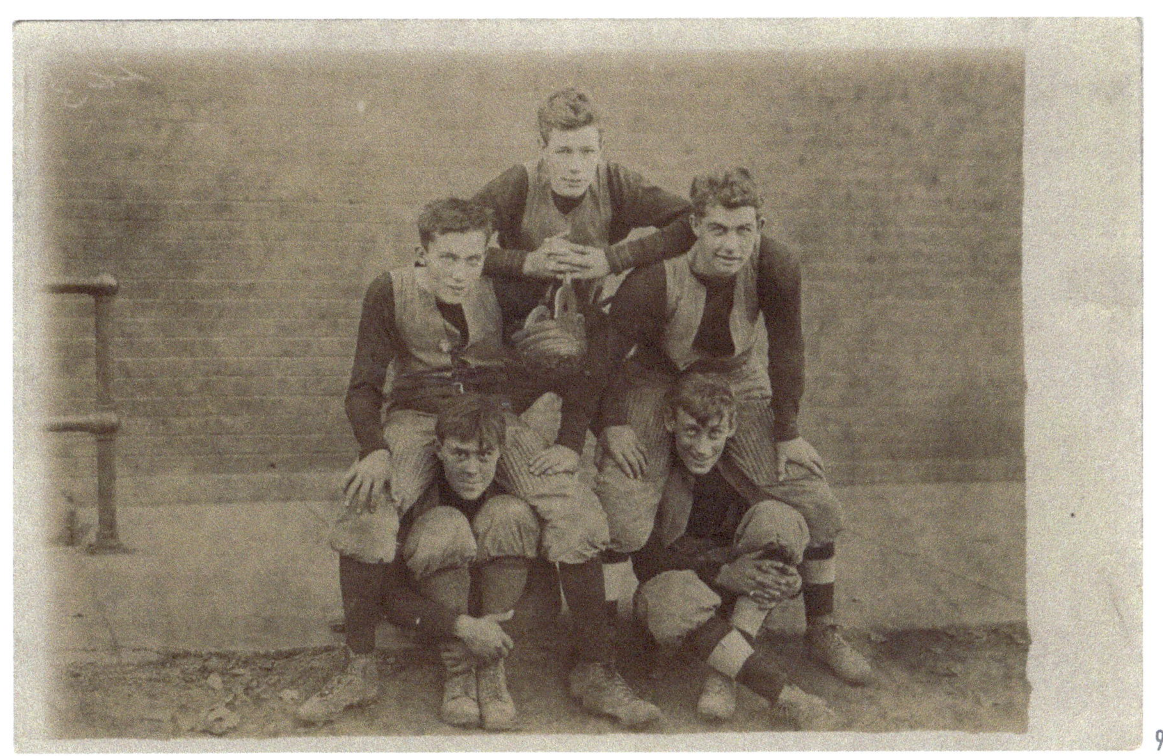

9

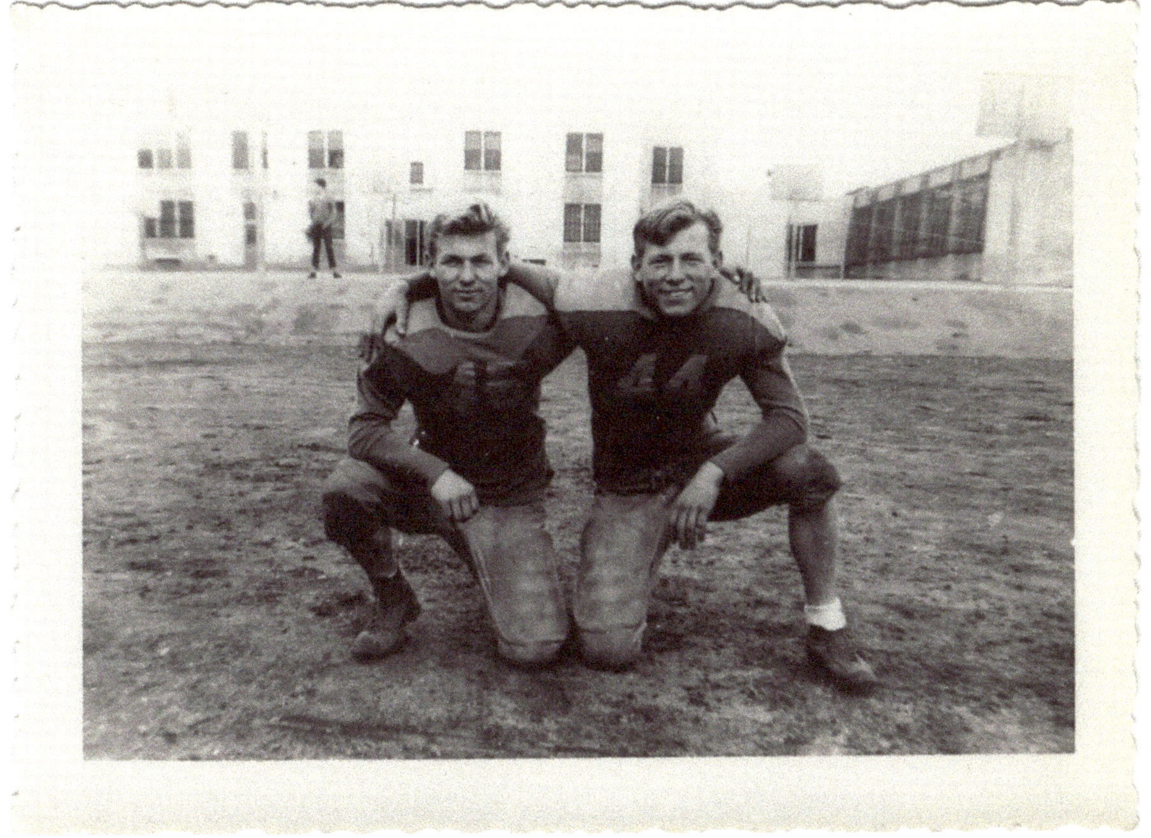

10

CHAPTER 5C

MEN AT WORK: THE OCCUPATIONAL PHOTOGRAPH

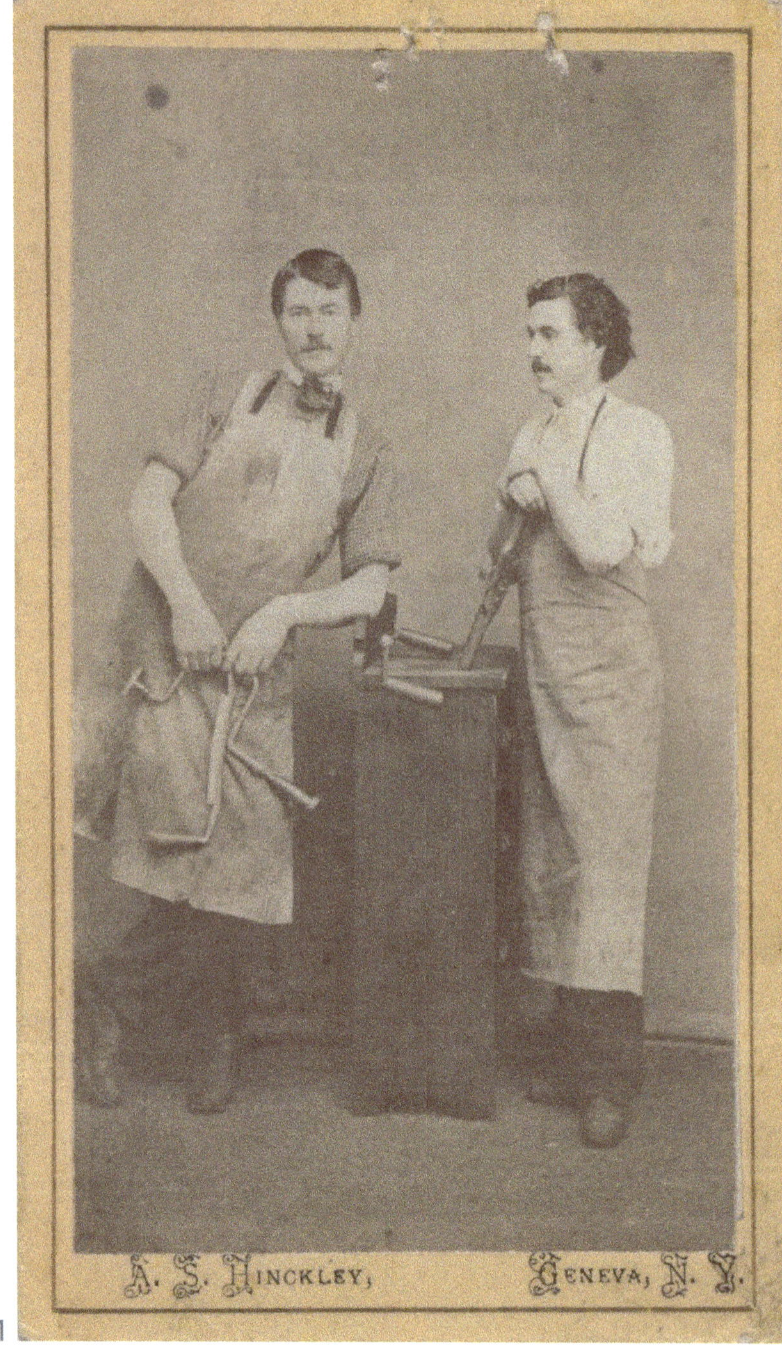

1

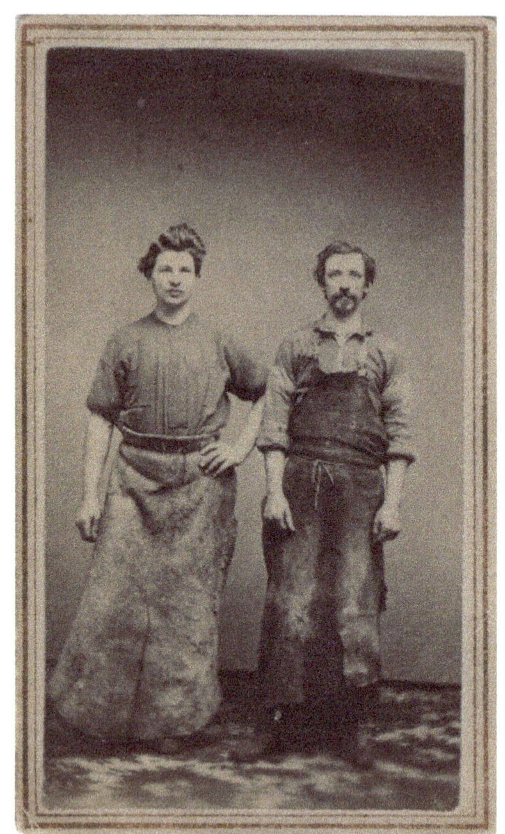
2

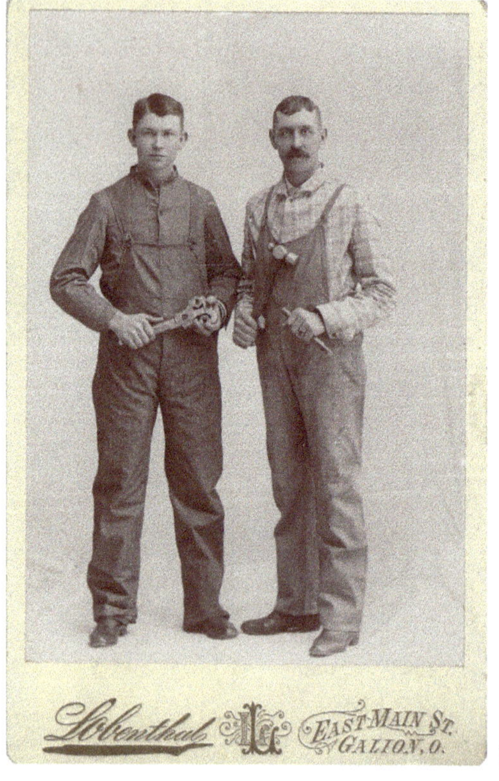

3

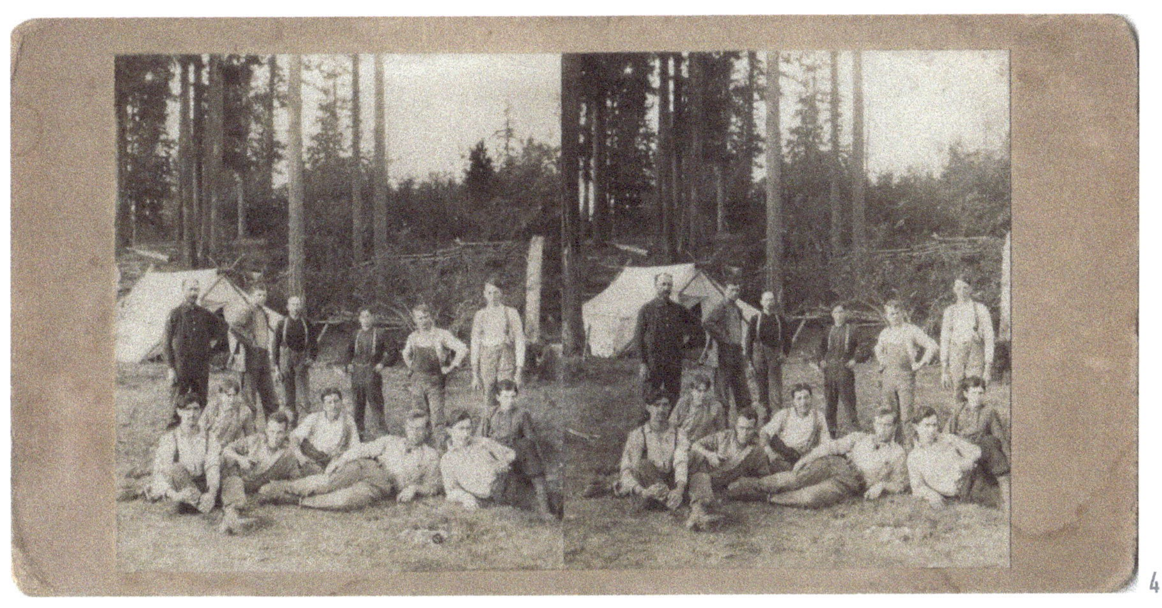
4

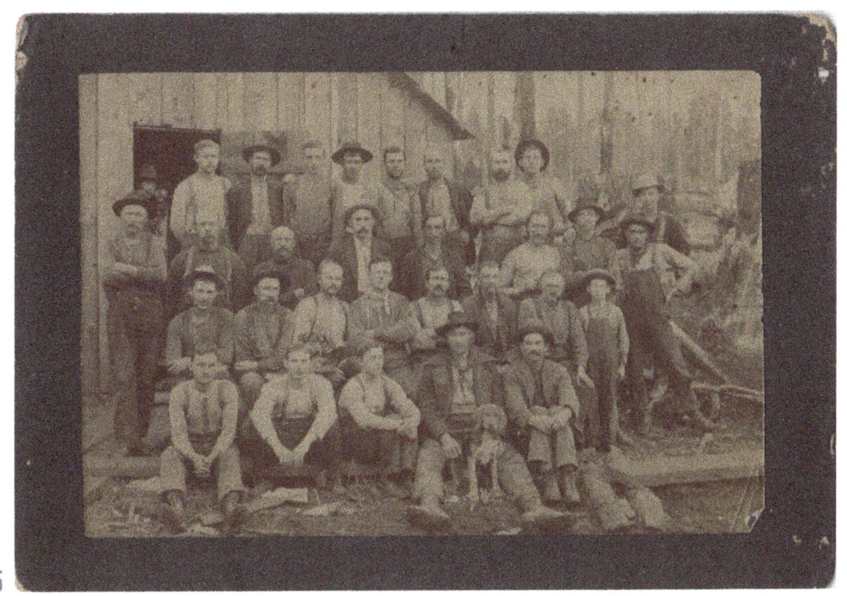
5

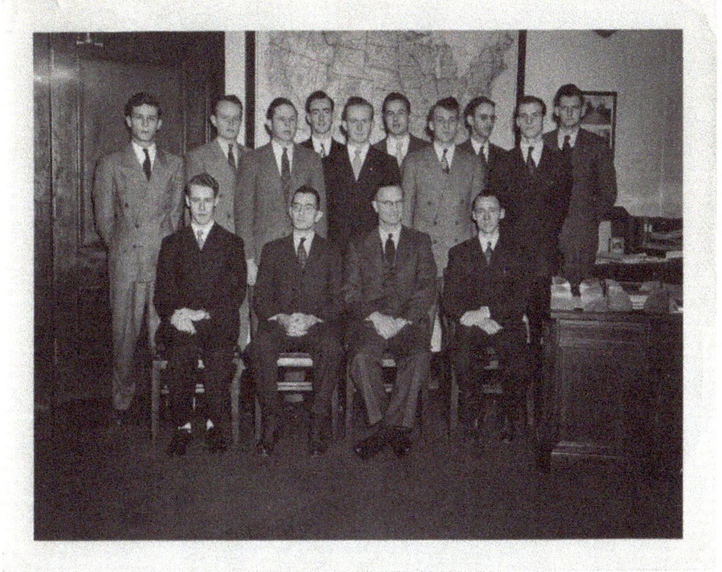
6

MEMBERS ONLY: PHOTOGRAPHS OF MALE ORGANIZATIONS

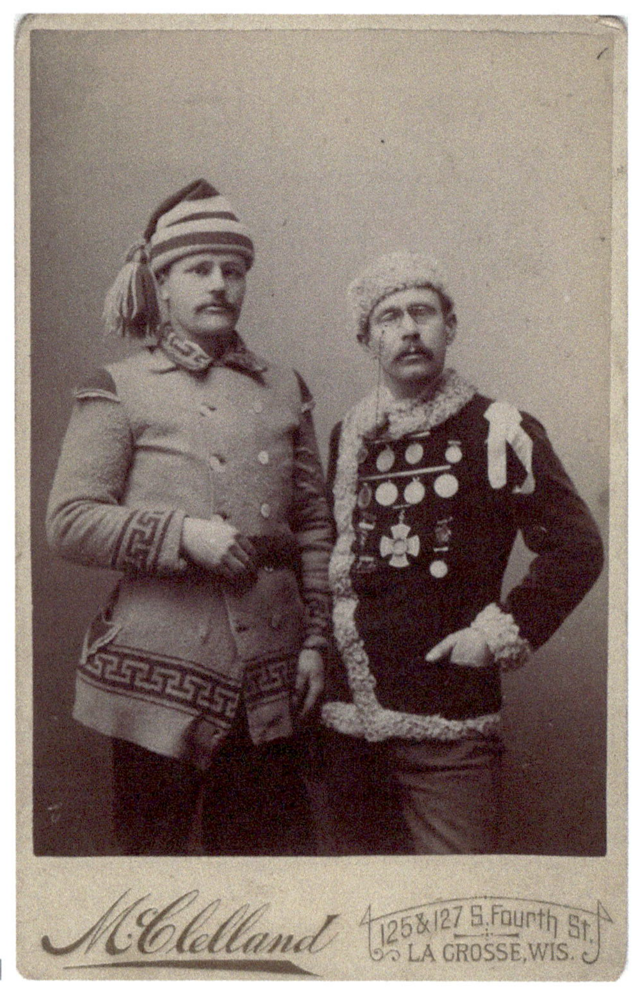

1

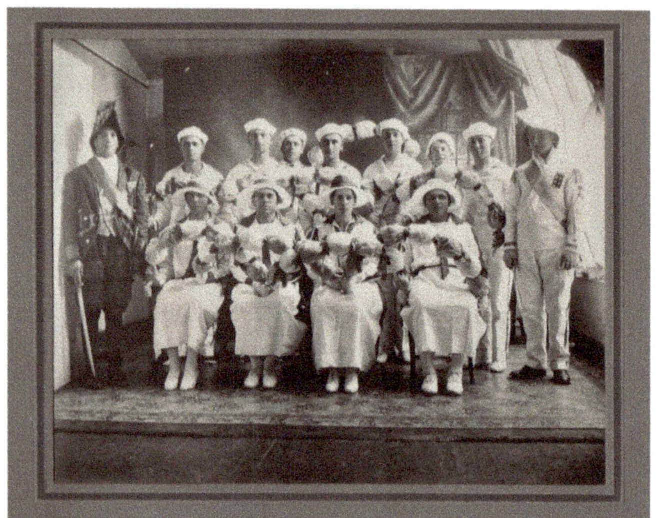
2

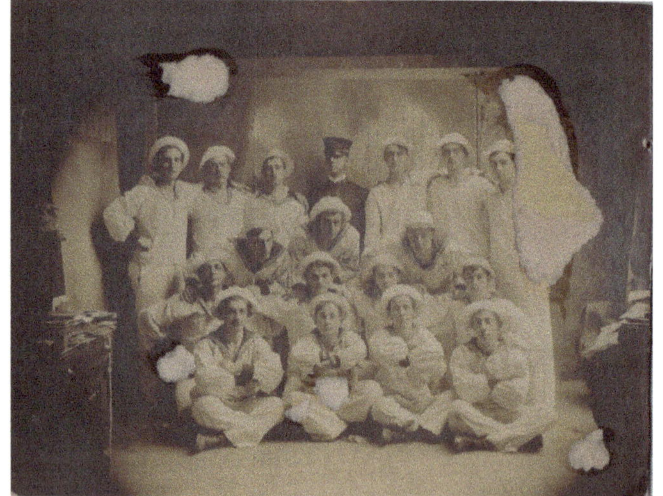
3

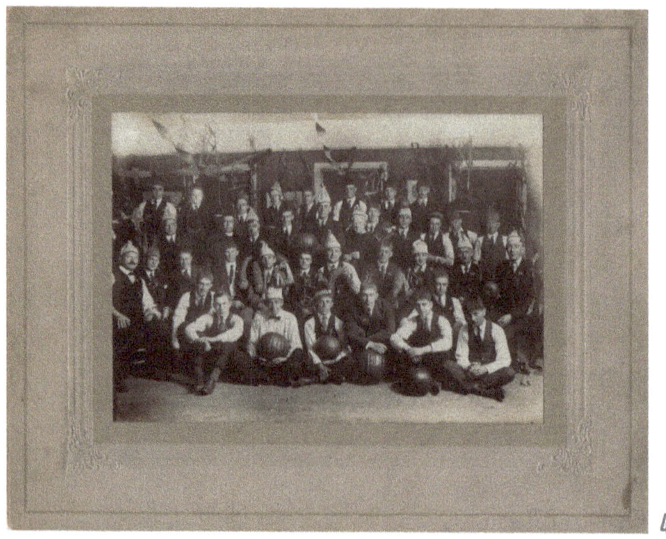
4

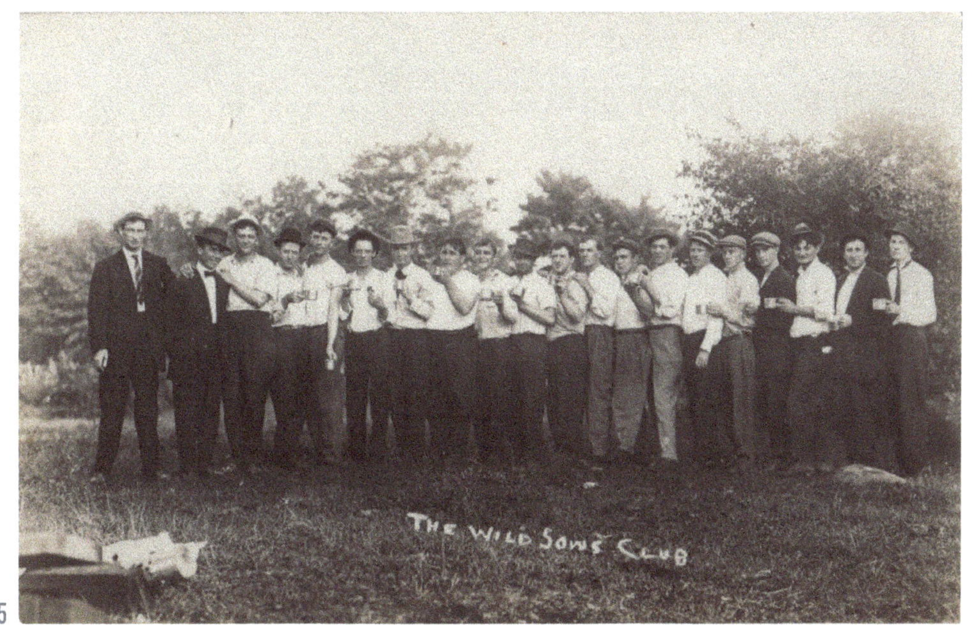

5

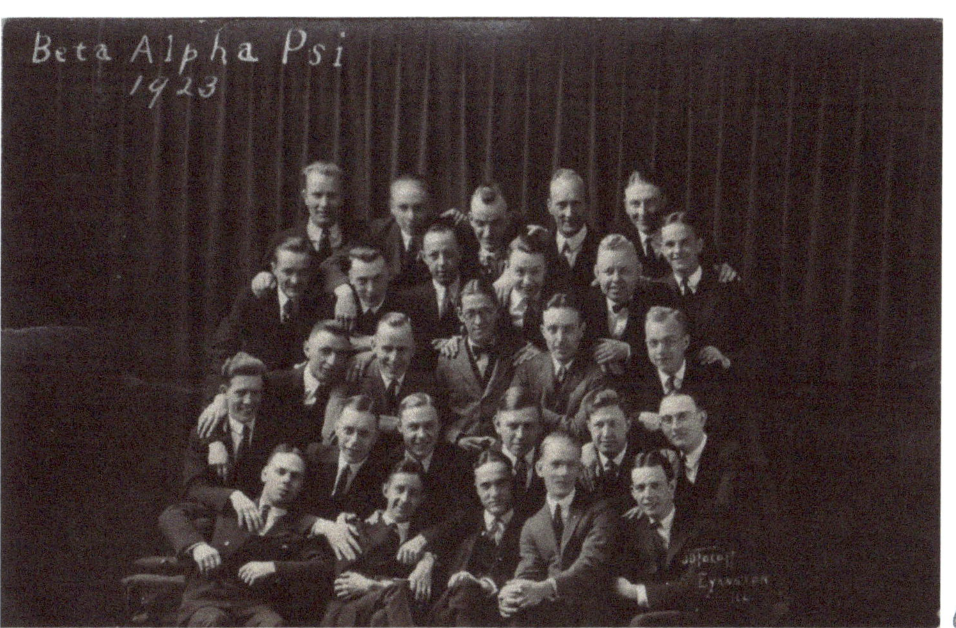

6

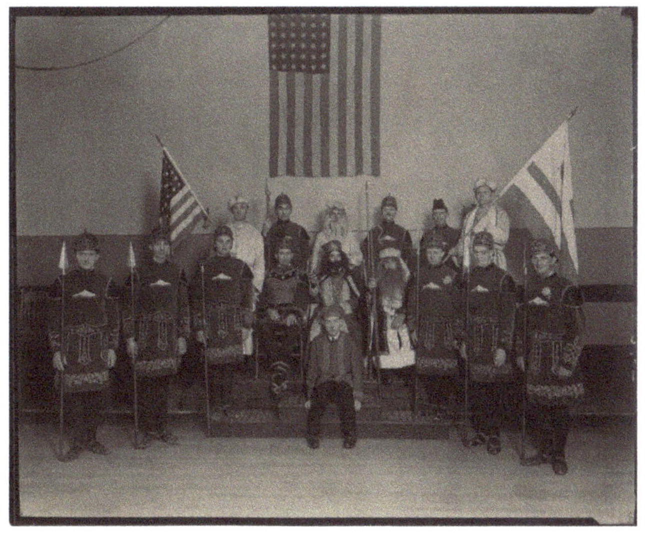
7

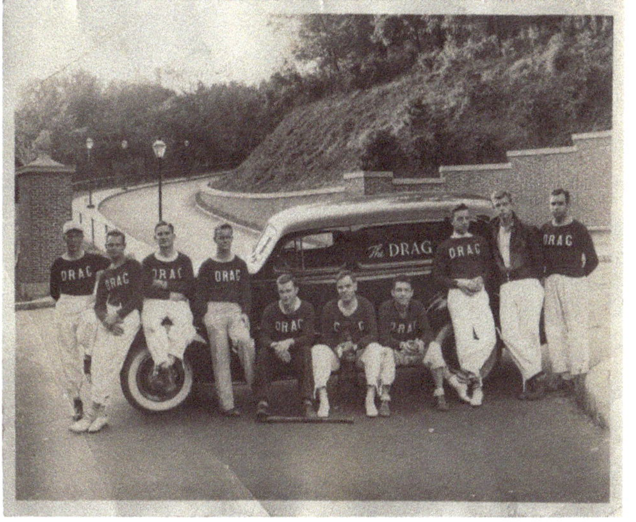

8

MALE SPACE IN THE SAND: BOYS AT THE BEACH

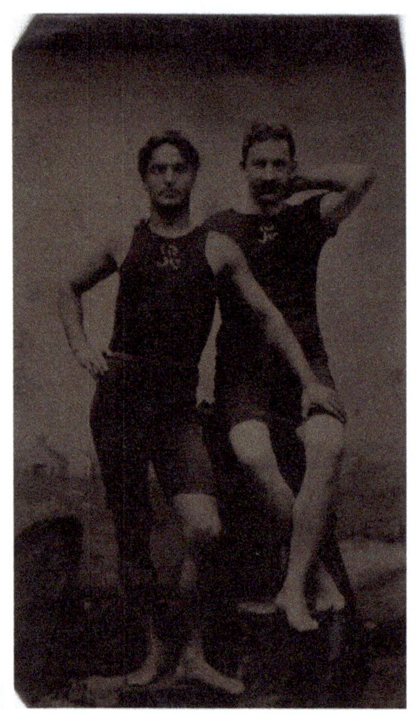
1

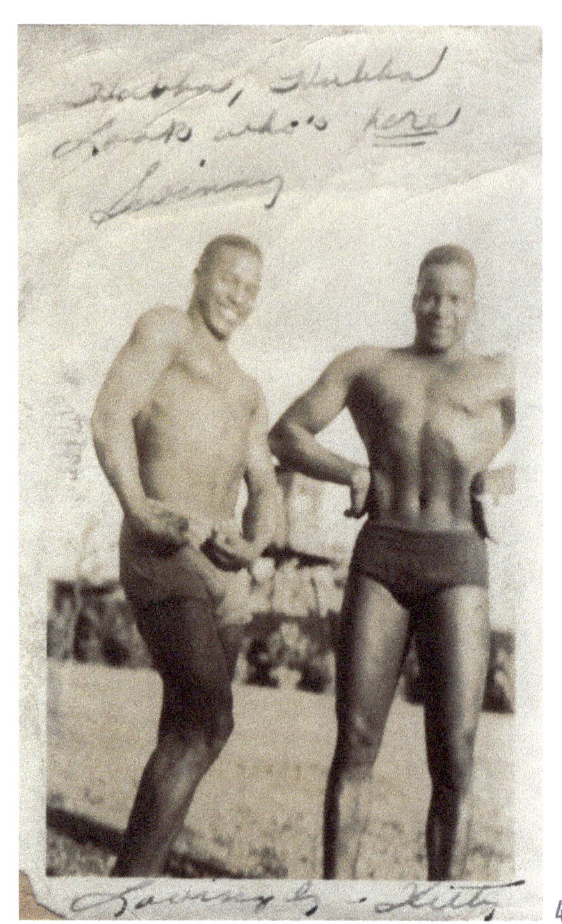

4

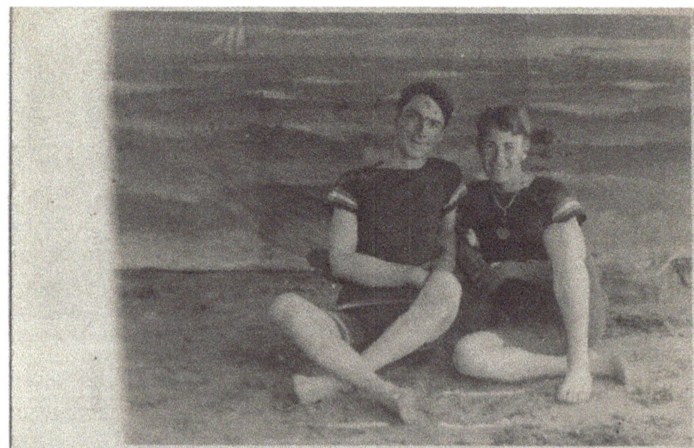
2

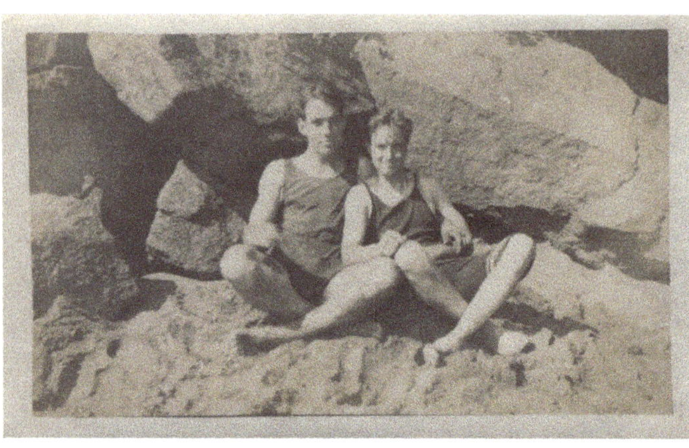
3

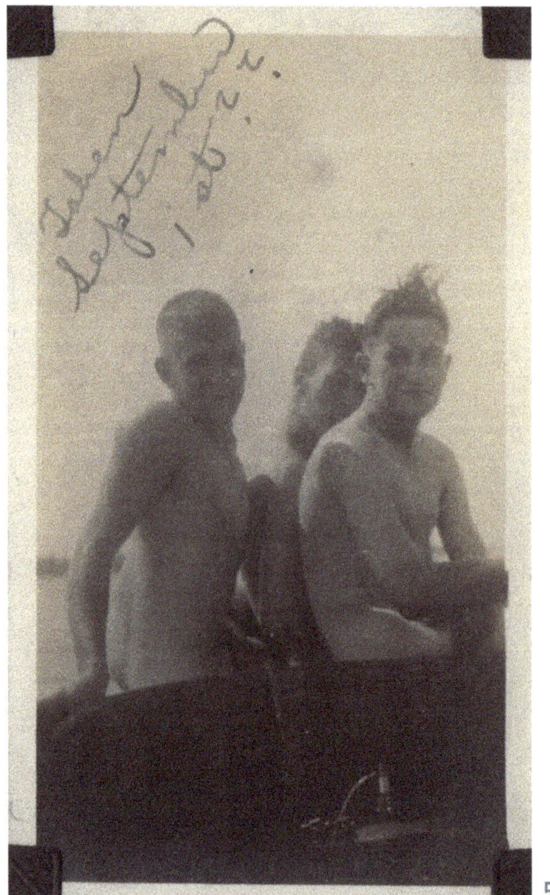

5

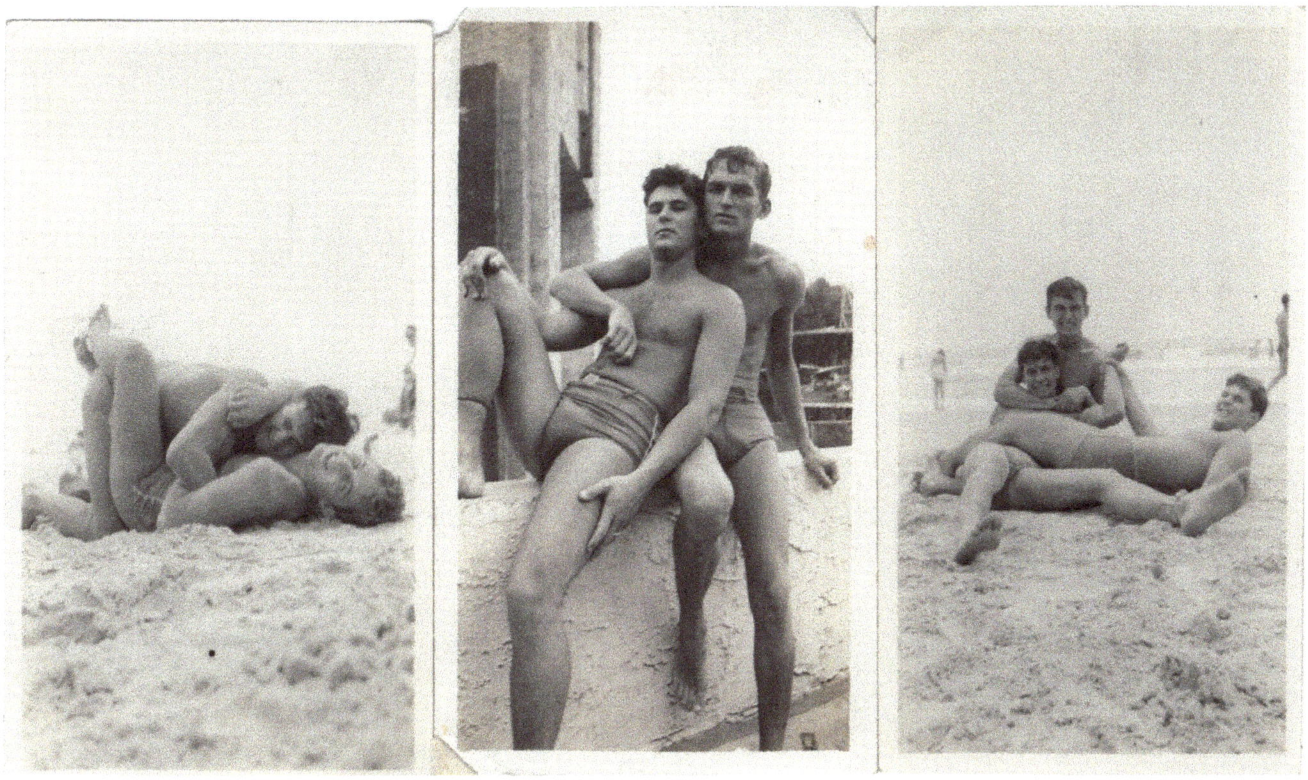

6

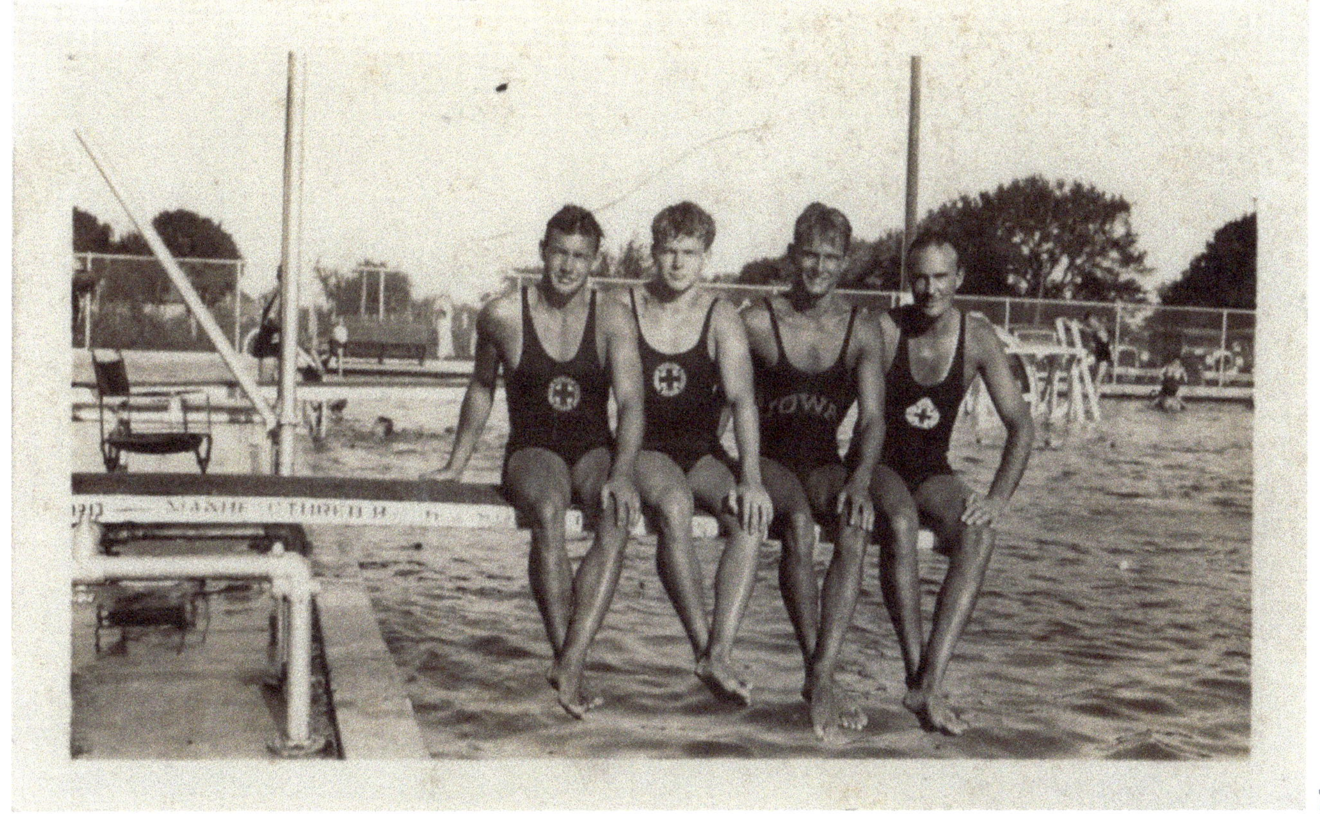

7

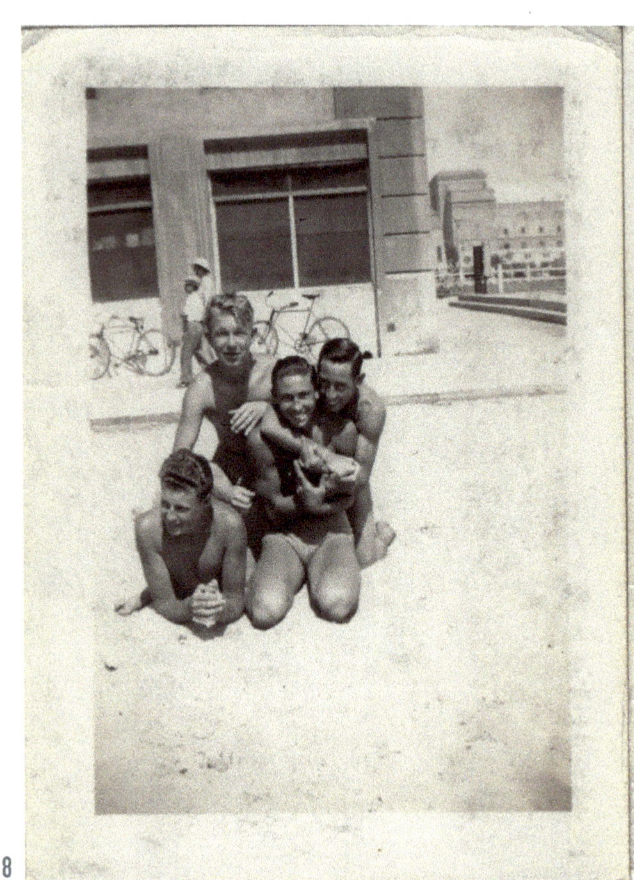

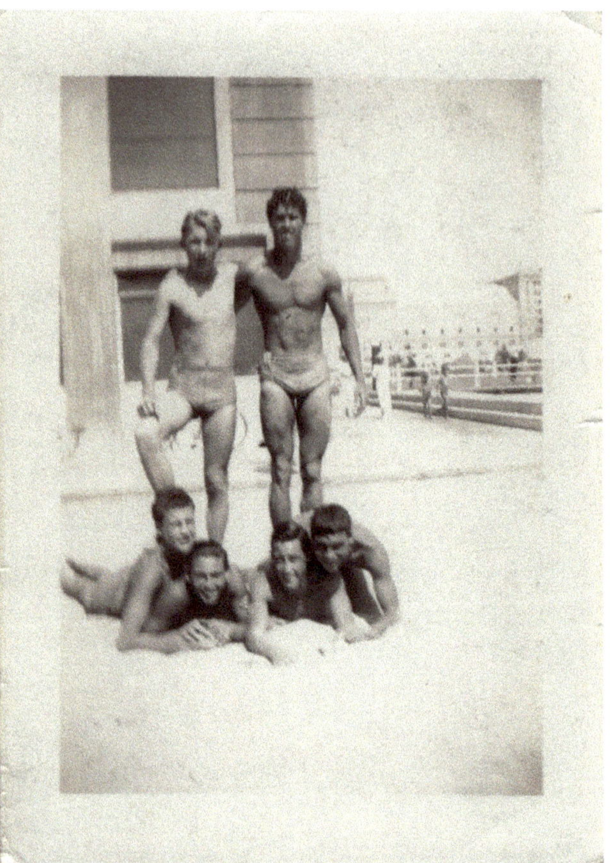

8

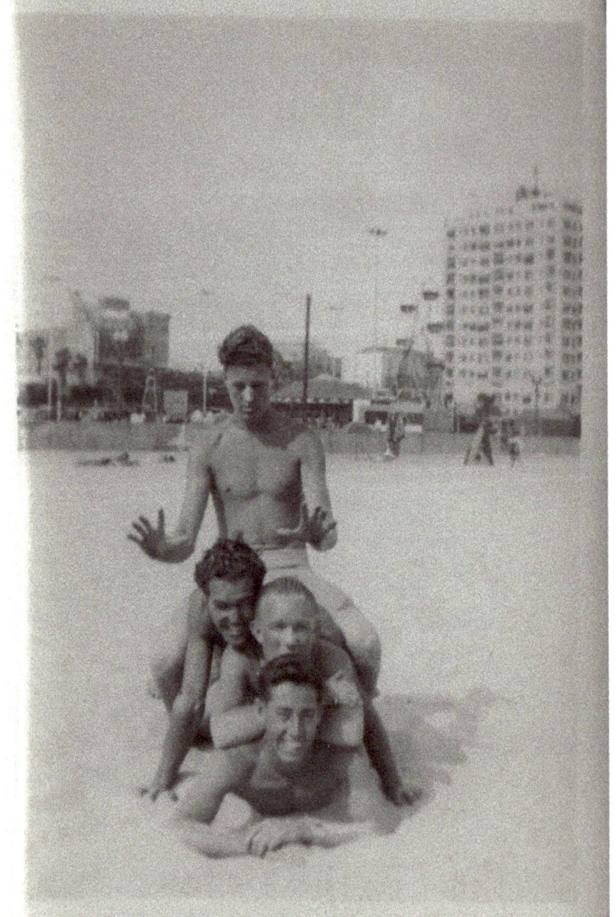

9

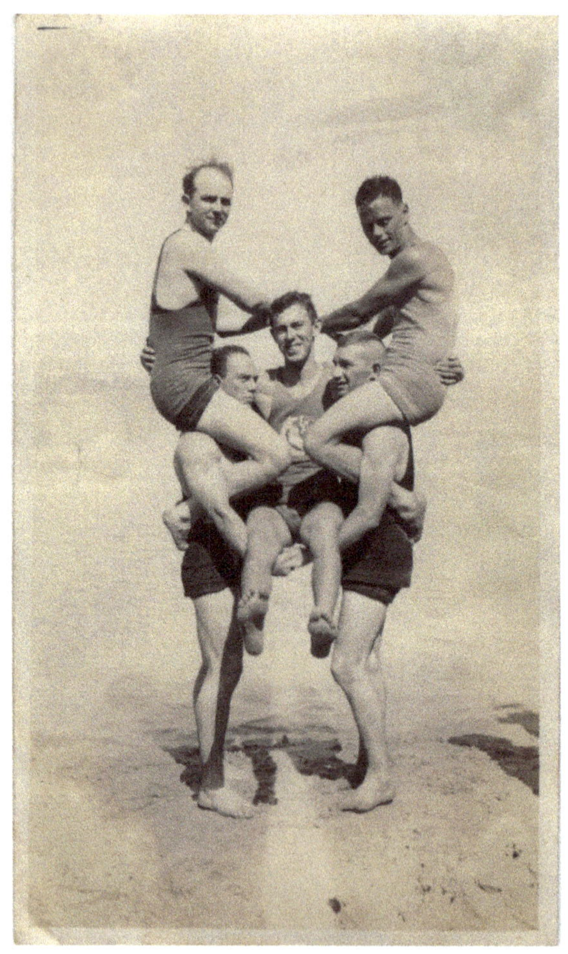

10

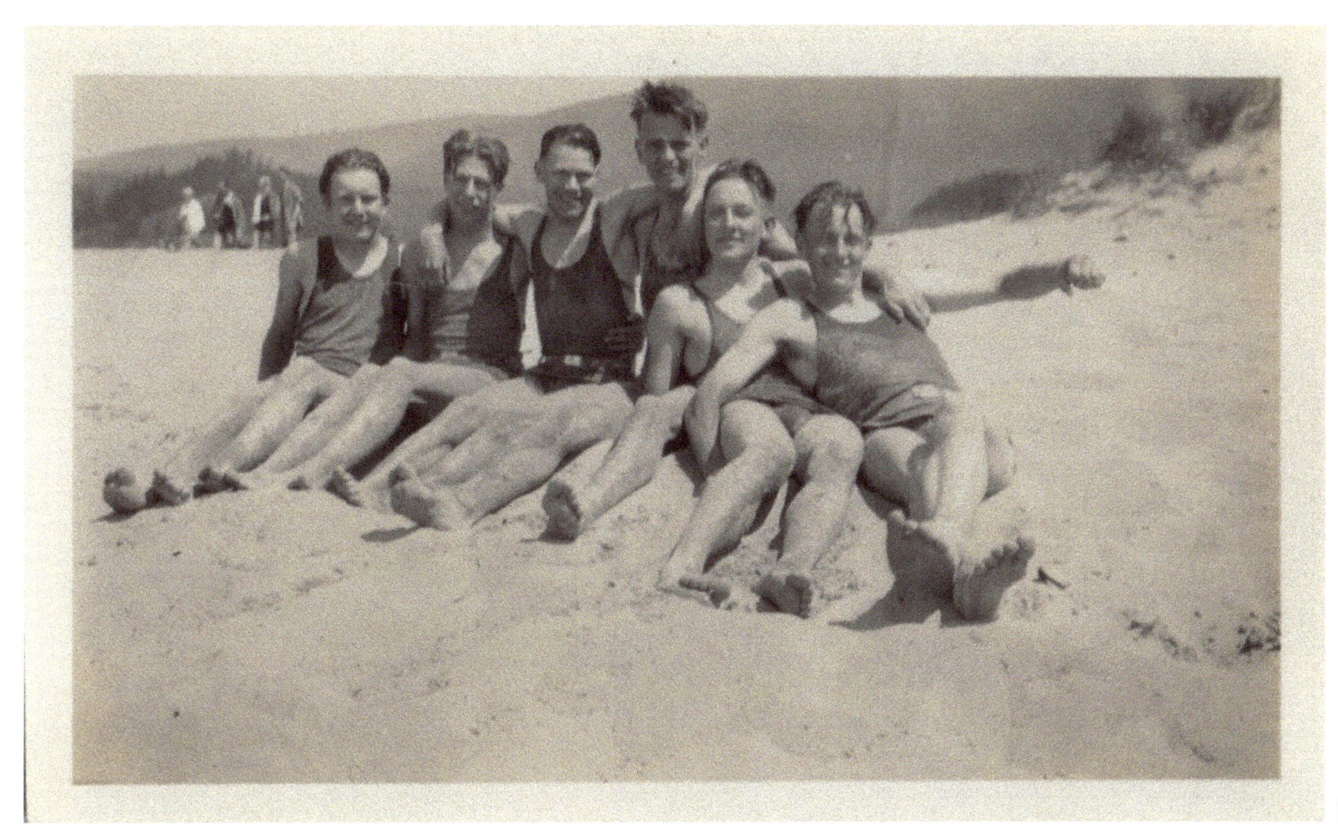

11

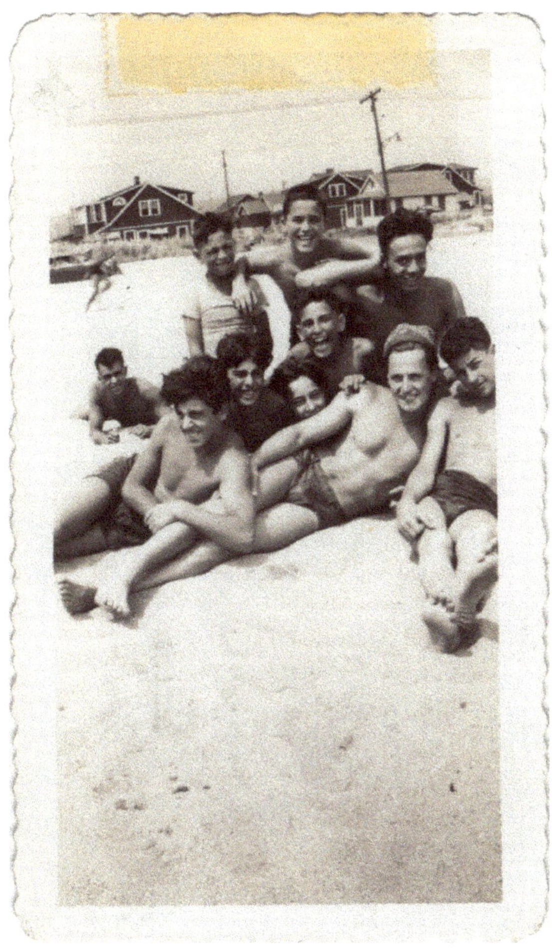

12

EPILOGUE

THE VALUE OF THIS COLLECTION

With the naive arrogance of a young teacher, I once imagined that on the last day of a class I might summon the wisdom and eloquence to leave my students with a summation of our entire semester together that would be so powerful they would be overcome on the spot with gratitude and admiration. After a little experience teaching, however, I realized that if there were any gratitude and respect to be had, it would only come in small increments throughout the semester, if indeed a course had anything substantial to offer. So, too, with a book's epilogue: this is an occasion for a few parting thoughts, not a thorough synthesis of what's come before or a fresh and unexpected insight that I've saved until now.

As I noted earlier, like all historical works, *The Pleasure of His Company* illustrates, literally so in this case, that things can be different than they are at the moment. Perhaps as never before in American history, or nearly so, some of us need the reassurance of that reminder nowadays. This book specifically reminds us that there are many ways, some quite different from each other, of being a male, of manifesting one's masculinity, and, especially, of demonstrating one male's affection for another. The affectionate universe portrayed in these pages—what I've described as a largely lost world in the mainstream cultural encouragement it enjoyed—had its faults, to be sure. But it also had virtues that I believe are at least worth a revisit. That world of unselfconscious male affection is not actually gone; it is instead only lost, a treasure that has been buried but has not vanished. Males, especially younger ones, sometimes find the treasure nowadays, showing a capacity for unembarrassed intimacy that once was much more widespread. It could be so again.

Over three decades, I derived enormous pleasure from acquiring the company of the men in my collection. I hope you can see why. In witnessing their past pleasure, there is hope in these pages. ■

AFTERWORD

WHAT THIS COLLECTION MEANS TO ME

Steve Harrison
(John's Partner, Husband, Challenger, Critic, and Cheerleader)

I've never considered this collection mine. My husband collects men, thankfully in portrait form, sharing with me a latest acquisition or ideas for projects. John's collection includes daguerreotypes, ambrotypes, tintypes, cabinet cards, and modern-day snapshots. All show men together involved in some kind of daily or "manly" ritual, from work to play. I've always thought of these photos as an extension of John's work, his study. Ever the mercenary one in our union, I come up with ideas that might make us money: How about featuring some of the photos on shower curtains, or framed prints, or maybe even t-shirts? We certainly have talked about coffee-table books from time to time, especially after a new one by someone else comes out.

In looking over this latest subset of the collection, thirty years in the making, I can't help but be impressed by John's discipline, his focus, and his eye for detail. I don't think I have ever stuck with any interest as long as he has with this collection—well, except for my interest in him. This grouping of photos in itself is impressive, but knowing that there are around thirty times as many crammed into his study is just mind-blowing. Like many collections that grow over time and aren't always on display, the total can sneak up on you. Collectors frequently cross the line and become hoarders, whether because the collection takes over or the collector's need to fill a void does. John's collection, luckily, can easily be stored in one room, though some photos have broken free, demanding attention on our walls. He frequently, over the years, has joked about my not knowing the size of his collection or the amount of money it represents, but anyone who knows me as well as he does knows I am precisely aware. Most collectors could not afford to buy such a collection "once complete"; it's good they start small and grow gradually. For years I rejected the label of "collector." We have known some great ones, and we never seemed like them. Perhaps it was because we never spent vast amounts on any one item, or maybe it just takes time for an interest to grow. Certainly now, I realize the designation fits.

This time, as I look over these many images, I think of the words, "People Like Us." I think how we have been lucky to live in a time when we have gotten to know people like us. I think of how we have ridden the crest of a wave, with gay people like us being recognized as individuals and as a group, who participate in and create a culture that many besides us enjoy. Think fashion, think movies, think *Will and Grace*. Of course, this movement has brought with it some contempt by those not like us who feel threatened by sharing the stage, the spotlight, the rewards of labor and recognition. Luckily, in our forty-seven years together we haven't often been the target of pointed homophobia, instead participating in the larger culture like many couples: figuring out career paths, establishing a home, and working at balancing all the events that make relationships hard to navigate—all of this happening during a time when LGBTQ people have had more visibility and more respect. It also happened, of course, during a time when many people like us died of AIDS. Seeing all these photos of men, gay or straight, we can see ourselves in these photos, and it's terribly liberating. We've been lucky.

As I've talked with John about someday selling or donating the collection, in parts or as a whole, we talked at length about how his collection is different from the other collectors' photos we have seen. Essentially, his collection's focus is on men together, intimate in proximity and personal space, engaged with one another in work, in play, or in pose. He is quick to point out that it isn't a "gay" book or a collection of gay men, though surely many of these subjects had what we consider in 2025 a homosexual orientation. Some surely were in love. Not the scholar, I wonder to what extent it really matters. I was trained in literary criticism; in that arena, reader response, reader analysis, reader understanding is what matters—what the writer intended, not so much.

As we have talked, I was struck at how lucky younger gays are today to have such photo collections on the internet, in books, and in museums, lovingly elevated to cultural status, recording and providing a past that, until recently, we didn't know existed. As a gay kid growing up isolated, as many of us were initially, how reassuring it could have been to see images of men who may or may not be "in love" or sexually involved, but who are spending time together comfortably, intimately. Photos taken by friends, coworkers, and, occasionally, professional photographers record camping trips, sporting events, and just being together. In these photos, many of these men, gay or straight, have found the fun in camaraderie.

John and I have lived through remarkable times: getting together when California was contemplating passing laws against gays teaching in public schools, witnessing the AIDS massacre of a generation's innocence and the innocent, listening to the discussion about gay marriage, and then recently watching an openly gay man run for president. The collection started halfway through our time together, when we finally had enough money to begin collecting things, feathering a nest, making a home. As John writes about in a previous book, we did this all without the benefit of a cultural map. In 1978, there weren't many works of art that showed men in love, let alone slogging through the navigating of a life together. Today, young same-sex couples have a plethora of examples showing them ways to connect, reassuring them that their love and their attraction isn't taboo; but, still, they have very few representations of how to build a life with someone. Those of us who were lucky enough to have had stable childhoods might be able to look to our parents for some clue about how to make love last. Even today, the number of books, movies, plays, and TV shows conflate coming out with love. And why not? Youth is sexy. We are young, exuding waves of pheromones, our bodies often pumped and trim. Biology leads the way. Beginnings are sexy and easy.

What comes next isn't always so. There is still plenty of work to be done to show gay relationships at work, that work. This collection grew, and all those images have witnessed our changes, our struggles, our celebrations. Thirty-two years into our coupling, we "eloped" to Canada to get married, after same-sex marriage was given to us (at least in California) and then taken away. Most of the people who populate these photos are young, still wondering what life has in store. Now we see the result of all of our work, not only in this collection, but in our other collections, and in the other ways we have feathered our nest. To a degree, this collection becomes a legacy of our life together: a legacy of years of travel, countless outings to antique stores and photo fairs, hours spent, often separately, looking over photos and paintings on eBay. It is a legacy of love and comfort and intimacy shared. My hope is that you who view this collection will savor, relish, and question what John has gathered. I want you to know people like us. Through it all, I'm grateful to have had the pleasure of John's company. ▮

ACKNOWLEDGMENTS

Books don't write themselves, at least not until artificial intelligence arrives on that scene, too. A human working alone, at home in his study, wrote this book, but a lot of other people and certain situations helped out before my writing began or during the time I was writing.

The Department of American Studies at California State University Fullerton was my sole academic home for the forty-seven years of my teaching career, from 1972 until I retired in 2019. And what a comfortable, supportive home it was! I had the tremendous good fortune to have some superb colleagues throughout my time at Fullerton and had the great satisfaction of participating in the hiring and advancement of many of them. Arriving at Fullerton with about thirty minutes of teaching experience myself, I had utterly no idea in 1972 what stimulation, challenges, and pure joy awaited me in the classroom. I simply could not have had a better job. The two retirement parties given to me were among the very best events of my entire life, attended by colleagues as well as students from every stage of my career who have become treasured friends. Mutual affection abounded.

Two sociologists from elsewhere, Mike Messner of University of Southern California (USC) and Tristan Bridges of University of California Santa Barbara (UCSB), have been generous supporters, in print and conversations alike, of my writing on the representation of American masculinity in everyday photographs. Early in 2020, Tristan invited me to UCSB to speak about my research to a group of bright, inquisitive, and receptive students and to be joined in a stimulating public dialogue about gender studies by UCSB's renowned scholar of gender, Leila Rupp. Coming from as eminent a scholar as he is, Mike's enthusiastic support of my work over several recent years has been especially welcome. I've also greatly appreciated the warm and encouraging company—in person, on the phone, and online—of Nick Syrett of the University of Wisconsin-Madison and Bob Young of Quinnipiac University.

It pleases me greatly to have this book published by RIT Press, housed in a city so central to the history of photography in the United States. The outside readers of *The Pleasure of His Company* who were engaged by RIT Press gave me very valuable suggestions as well as effusive encouragement. The same was true of the Press's own editorial board. Alexandra Hoff, the managing editor at RIT Press, has been delightful to work with. My working with Marnie Soom, the talented and good-natured design and marketing specialist at RIT Press, has assuredly made this a better book. This book's copyeditor, Anne Cook, possesses a remarkably keen eye and an abundance of good sense. Laura DiPonzio Heise, director at RIT Press, was warm and wise in her own support for this book.

The isolation brought about by the COVID pandemic gave me plenty of time in 2020 to methodically examine, categorize, and assess my photograph collection in its entirety, a mighty task that I hadn't undertaken for twenty years, when I wrote *Picturing Men* and the collection was much smaller. The more recent inventory was essential for the preparation of this book.

During those tense days of the COVID confinement, wonderfully wide-ranging weekly Zoom sessions with Patrick Heyer, José Zamora, Nick Catt, and me allowed us to share (and thereby lessen) our pandemic anxieties, and they gave the four of us a distinctive, lasting attachment. The Zoom meetings were no substitute for actually being with those guys, but our gatherings met the needs of those bleak moments. We made a very good quartet.

For the nearly fifty years we've been together, my husband, Steve Harrison, has made those years the best of my life. Excitement, encouragement, uncensored candor, and affection that transcends time and space have been his to give. I've hardly had a good idea during those years that I didn't try out first on Steve. And he's saved me from voicing many a bad idea to others. This book belongs to him. ■

INDEX TO PHOTOGRAPHS

CHAPTER 1: COUPLES

1. Daguerreotype in wood and paper case, 1/9 plate, ca. 1850.
2. Daguerreotype in metal frame, 1/6 plate, ca. 1850.
3. Ambrotype in gutta-percha case, 1/6 plate, ca. 1857.
4. Ambrotype in wood and paper case, 1/6 plate, ca. 1857.
5. Tintype in wood and paper case and metal frame, 1/6 plate, ca. 1860.
6. Tintype in wood and paper case and metal frame, 1/6 plate, ca. 1860.
7. Uncased tintype, 1/6 plate, ca. 1875.
8. Uncased tintype, 1/6 plate, ca. 1875.
9. Uncased tintype, 1/6 plate, ca. 1875.
10. Uncased tintype, 1/6 plate, ca. 1875.
11. Carte de visite, ca. 1858. Verso: Saml K. Pennypacker, Boyertown, Pennsylvania.
12. Carte de visite, ca. 1875.
13. Carte de visite, ca. 1880.
14. Carte de visite, ca. 1885, Ritter Brothers, Erie Street, Massillon, Ohio.
15. Cabinet card, ca. 1885, H. H. Peterson, Jr., Hyram, Utah.
16. Cabinet card, ca. 1885, Cooledge, De Smet, S. Dakota.
17. Cabinet card, ca. 1885, Ritter Brothers, Massillon, Ohio.
18. Cabinet card, ca. 1895, Chubbuck, Whitney's Point, New York.
19. Cabinet card, ca. 1895, Cross and Saylor, Dakota, Illinois.
20. Real photo postcard, AZO stamp box, ca. 1910.
21. Photo mounted on cardboard, 4" × 5.5", ca. 1895. Verso: "Chas T. Harris, Melvin E. Crumrinse (?)."
22. Portrait in double cardboard folder, 6" × 2", "Clarence & Lawrence," Bough's Art Studio, Winfield, Kansas, ca. 1915.
23. Portrait in cardboard folder, 5" × 3.5", L.B. Hodges, Covington, Virginia, ca. 1920.
24. Portrait in cardboard folder, 6" × 4", Boutin Studio, Taunton, Massachusetts, ca. 1918.
25. Early snapshot, 3.5" dia., Eastman Kodak Co., ca. 1895.
26. Portrait mounted on cardboard, 2.5" × 2.5", Leffler, Fort Worth, Texas, ca. 1895.
27. Portrait mounted on cardboard, 3.75" × 2.25", Wagner, Depere, Wisconsin, Extra Fine Finish, ca. 1895.
28. Portrait mounted on cardboard, oval, 5" × 2.5", ca. 1895.
29. Three small portraits matted on cardboard, oval, 1.75" × 1.25", Verso: "Jan 14, 1913."
30. Portrait mounted on cardboard, oval, 2" × 2.75", A. J. Horswill, Aberdeen, So. Dak., ca. 1900, Verso: "Mr Letterhoff are you acquainted with this fellow Clarence Miller (The one to the right) [?] Clarence Miller S. Dakota."
31. Real photo postcard, AZO stamp box, ca. 1910.
32. Real photo postcard, AZO stamp box, ca. 1910.
33. Real photo postcard, AZO stamp box, ca. 1920.
34. Real photo postcard, AZO stamp box, ca. 1915.
35. Real photo postcard, AZO stamp box, ca. 1915. Verso: "From Friend Bert."
36. Real photo postcard, AZO stamp box, ca. 1915. Verso: "Jim Edens, Jewel Aldridge."
37. Real photo postcard, Cyko stamp box, embossed borders, ca. 1907.

38. Real photo postcard, stamped, Des Moines, Iowa, September 23, 1912. Verso: "Miss Nellie Cherry, St Joseph Ill RFD, September 23, 1912, Des Moines, Dear Sis: Am very busy boy and yet have time to read a letter if you can find time to write [.] This is my wife Dr Joe Winnett. Write soon. [signed] Edgor E."
39. Real photo postcard, PMC stamp box, ca. 1910.
40. Real photo postcard, DOPS stamp box, ca. 1920.
41. Handmade collage of three photo booth portraits, 1.25" × 1.25" each, ca. 1910.
42. Strip of four photo booth portraits, 1.75" × 1.25", ca. 1915.
43. Arcade photo, 3.25" × 2.25", Verso: "Harry and Ray," ca. 1930.
44. Matted and framed, under glass, photo booth photo, 1.5" × 1", ca. 1925.
45. Pair of matted and framed, under glass, photo booth photos, 2" × 1.5", ca. 1930.
46. Photomatic photo, framed, 2.25" × 1.75", ca. 1940.
47. Arcade photo, 4" × 2.5", ca. 1945.
48. Strip of two photo booth portraits, 2" × 1.5" each, ca. 1948.
49. Strip of two photo booth portraits, 1.75" × 1.5" each, ca. 1948.
50. Photo booth portrait, 1.5" × 1.25", ca. 1948.
51. Photo booth portrait, 1.5" × 1.25", ca. 1948.
52. Photo booth portrait, 1.5" × 1.25", ca. 1948.
53. Arcade portrait, matted, 3" × 2", ca. 1945.
54. Snapshot, trimmed, 3.75" × 2.25", ca. 1950.
55. Snapshot, 3.5" × 2.5", ca. 1935.
56. Snapshot, 4.25" × 3.25", ca. 1940.
57. Uncased tintype, 1/6 plate, ca. 1890.
58. Outdoor portrait mounted on cardboard, 5" × 4", dated [18]95. Verso: "A.J. Bloom, Photographer, Andover, N.J., Instantaneous Pictures, Children's Pictures taken quick as a wink."
59. Snapshot, 3.5" × 2.5", ca. 1925.
60. Snapshot, 4.5" × 2.75", ca. 1930.
61. Snapshot, trimmed, on album paper, 1.5" × 3.25", ca. 1910.
62. Snapshot, 2.25" × 3.25". Verso: "Keep this one not lose it," ca. 1915.
63. Snapshot, 3.5" × 4.5", 1905. Verso: "John—A friend of mine, Herman Heiele, and myself prior to getting up one morning. [signed] Olaf. 8/05"
64. Snapshot, 2.5" × 3.5", 1923.
65. Snapshot, 2.75" × 1.75", mounted on album paper, ca. 1925.
66. Snapshot, trimmed, 3" × 2", ca. 1920.
67. Snapshot, trimmed, 3" × 2", ca. 1915.
68. Snapshot, 4.25" × 2.5", ca. 1925.
69. Arcade photo (?), trimmed, 3.25" × 1.5", ca. 1920.
70. Snapshot, 4.25" × 2.5", ca. 1925.
71. Snapshot, 3.25" × 2.5", ca. 1925.
72. Snapshot, "Earley & Kenneth," 5" × 3.25", ca. 1915.
73. Snapshot, 4.5" × 2.75", "Dick and Cutie," ca.1920.
74. Snapshot, 5" × 3", 1917. Verso: "Ernest Johns [,] Glen Fox [,] 1917."
75. Snapshot, 2.75" × 4.25", ca. 1935.
76. Snapshot, 4" × 3", ca. 1935.
77. Snapshot, 4.25" × 2.5", ca. 1940.
78. Snapshot, 4.25" × 2.5", ca. 1935.
79. Snapshot, 1.5" × 2.5", ca. 1925.
80. Snapshot, 2.5" × 3.5", ca. 1935.
81. Snapshot, 3.5" × 2.5", ca. 1925.
82. Snapshot, 4.5" × 2.75", ca. 1935, "CHARLIE AND SHIRLEY."
83. Snapshot, 3.5" × 5", ca. 1950.
84. Snapshot, 5" × 3.25", 1940. Verso: "July 1940."
85. Snapshot, 4.75" × 3", ca. 1937.
86. Snapshot, 3.5" × 2.5", ca. 1935.
87. Snapshot, 2.5" × 3.5", 1937. Verso: "No. 491 Taken NOV 3 '37"
88. Snapshot, 2.5" × 3.5", ca. 1935.
89. Snapshot, 3.5" × 2.5", ca. 1935. Verso: "Two of my frat brothers[.] This shows a side of my room[.]"
90. Snapshot, trimmed, 2.75" × 2.25", ca. 1935.
91. Snapshot, 3" × 2.25", 1918. Verso: "July 1st/18 [,] Grand Beach [,] "Angels Retreat" Camp[.]"
92. Snapshot, 4.5" × 2.75", ca. 1935.
93. Snapshot, 4.5" × 2.75", 1942. Verso: "Pat & Huffy 7/18/42[.]"
94. Snapshot, 3.25" × 2.25", ca. 1935.
95. Snapshot, 4.5" × 2.75", ca. 1940, "Al & Bob."
96. Snapshot, 4.25" × 2.5", ca. 1930.
97. Snapshot, 2.5" × 2", ca. 1945.
98. Snapshot, trimmed, 4" × 2.25", ca. 1935.
99. Snapshot, 3" × 2.75", ca. 1945.

100. Snapshot, 3" × 2.5", 1945. Verso: "June 1945. SAACC [,] Grizzof, Tony Minneno."
101. Snapshot, 5" × 4", 1941. "1941, "Bob & Gene."
102. Snapshot, 3.5" × 2.5", 1949. Verso: "Dan Conley & Ed Sakcick-1949."
103. Snapshot, 2.5" × 3.5", 1936. Verso: "Tom, Joe and Spike. Sep't. 1, 1936."
104. Snapshot, 4.5" × 3.25", ca. 1935.
105. Snapshot, 4.5" × 3.75", ca. 1940.
106. Snapshot, 3.5" × 2.25", ca. 1935. Verso: "Me & Cooke."
107. Snapshot, pair, 3.5" × 2.5" each, ca. 1940.
108. Snapshot, pair, 4.25" × 3" each, ca. 1945.
109. Snapshot, 4.25" × 3", ca. 1945.
110. Snapshot, 3.5" × 2.5", ca. 1940.
111. Snapshot, 3.5" × 2.5", 1947, "SEPT. 7, 1947 [,] CLEVELAND, OHIO [,] 6009 MEMPHIS AVE. [,] PAUL & LEN."
112. Snapshot, 2.5" × 3.5", ca. 1948. "LOUISE [,] PAT [,] RICHARD [,] Leo."
113. Snapshot, trimmed, 3" × 2", ca. 1947.
114. Snapshot, 2.5" × 3.75", ca. 1947.
115. Snapshot, 3.25" × 4.5", ca. 1950.
116. Snapshot, 2.75" × 4", ca. 1948.
117. Snapshot, 5" × 3.5", ca. 1954.
118. Snapshot, 3.5" × 2.5", ca. 1948.
119. Snapshot, 4.5" × 2.75", ca. 1950.
120. Snapshot, 3.5" × 5", ca. 1952. Verso: "Bobby Pinkleton [,] Randall Little [,] Nashville."
121. Snapshot, 3.5" × 3.5", 1948. Verso: "Gussie & Jim [,] 9 May 48."
122. Snapshot, 4.5" × 3.25", 1950. "1950."

CHAPTER 2: GROUPS

1. Portrait, mounted on heavy board, Pach Bros., 7 1/8" × 9", ca. 1888.
2. Portrait, mounted on heavy board, Howell, Altamont, Ill., 5.5" × 7", ca. 1980.
3. Tintype, 1/6 plate, framed in decorative paper, ca. 1880.
4. Tintype, 1/6 plate, ca. 1880.
5. Tintype, 1/6 plate, ca. 1880.
6. Carte de visite, ca. 1890, H. P. (?) Eggert Studio: Myers Building, Bethlehem, Pa.
7. Carte de visite, 1894. Dunklee, Athol, Mass. Verso: "May 16, 1894."
8. Cabinet card, ca. 1890. Verso: "H. Van Ryan, Portraits [,] Groups & Views, Cor. George & Stryker Ave. West St. Paul."
9. Real photo postcard, AZO stamp box, ca. 1910.
10. Real photo postcard, no stamp box, ca. 1910.
11. Real photo postcard, Cyko stamp box, ca. 1914.
12. Real photo postcard, embossed "Laffler Prineville Oregon," no stamp box, 1915. Verso: "Orville [,] Dude [,] Walt [,] Verl [,] Bub [,] Lee 1915."
13. Real photo postcard, Cyko stamp box, ca. 1914.
14. Real photo postcard, AZO stamp box, ca. 1915. Verso: "The Kregel Photo Parlors, St. Paul, Minneapolis."
15. Real photo postcard, AZO stamp box, ca. 1915.
16. Real photo postcard, AZO stamp box, 1916. Verso: 1916.
17. Real photo postcard, AZO stamp box, 1915. Verso: "Hawaii-1915 [,] Air brakes tested [,] 3-21-15."
18. Real photo postcard, AZO stamp box, 1906. Verso: "Harry Patterson on right and friends. Mt. Blanchard, O. 1906."
19. Real photo postcard, empty stamp box, ca. 1910.
20. Real photo postcard, AZO stamp box, 1908. Verso: "Detroit [,] Mon [.] Oct [.] 12 08 [,] Miss Dorothy. Ionia. Mich."
21. Real photo postcard, Artura stamp box, ca. 1910.
22. Real photo postcard, AZO stamp box, ca. 1915. Verso: "G.G. Grove, Photographer, 119 DeMars Ave., Grand Forks, N.D."
23. Real photo postcard, AZO stamp box, ca. 1915. Verso: "don't know these soaks."
24. Real photo postcard, Artura stamp box, ca. 1910.
25. Snapshot, 3.75" × 4.5", ca. 1915.
26. Snapshot, 3" × 5.25", ca. 1910.
27. Snapshot, 3.25" × 5.5", "4 OF A KIND," ca. 1916. From a Pratt Institute student's album, 1914–1918.
28. Snapshot, 4.25" × 2.5", ca. 1920.
29. Snapshot, 4.5" × 2.75", "AL[,] CHARLES[,] WILLY 7/24/36," 1936.
30. Snapshot, 2.75" × 4.5", "Chopper[,] Nolan[?][,] Buster[,] Jerry[,] Jiggles[,] O'Brien," cut from a photo album, ca. 1935.
31. Snapshot, 3.75" × 5.75", 1932.
32. Real photo postcard, AZO stamp box, ca. 1915.
33. Snapshot, 2.75" × 3.75", ca. 1935.
34. Snapshot, 2.75" × 3.5", "Fred[,] Walt[,] Roger[,] Hammer," ca. 1928.

35. Snapshot, 3.75" × 5.5", ca. 1920.
36. Snapshot, 3.5" × 2.5", ca. 1925.
37. Snapshot, 4.5" × 2.75", ca. 1935.
38. Snapshot, 2.75" × 3.75", ca. 1935.
39. Snapshot, 2.5" × 4.25", ca. 1940.
40. Snapshot, trimmed, 4" × 3.75", ca. 1935. Verso: "C.C. PHOTO, Daytona, Fla."
41. Snapshot, 2.5" × 3.5", ca. 1940.
42. Snapshot, 4.5" × 2.75", ca. 1935.
43. Snapshot, 2.75" × 4.5", ca. 1940. Verso: "Paul H[,] RMB[,] M. Harmon."
44. Photo booth portrait, 3.5" × 2.5", ca. 1950. Verso: "509 15 Ave (illeg) tel 4718[,] 43 41 LW[,] 427½ 2 Ave S[,] Date 34 31 (illeg)."
45. Snapshot, 2.75" × 4.75", "C.C.C. Camps 1939. Verso: "Nov 1 1939."
46. Snapshot, 4.25" × 2.5", ca. 1940.
47. Snapshot, 4.25" × 2.5", ca. 1940.
48. Snapshot, 4" × 5.25", ca. 1945.
49. Snapshot, trimmed, 4" × 2.5", ca. 1950.
50. Snapshot, enlarged, 10" × 8", ca. 1940.
51. Snapshot, enlarged, 8" × 10", 1947. Verso: "1947."
52. Snapshot, enlarged, 8" × 10", ca. 1950.
53. Snapshot, 3.5" × 5", ca. 1950.
54. Snapshot, 3.5" × 3.5", ca. 1955.

CHAPTER 3: MILITARY

1. Tintype in gutta-percha case, embossed brass mat, 1/6 plate, ca. 1863.
2. Tintype in embossed brass mat, 1/9 plate, ca. 1863.
3. Tintype, uncased, two trimmed corners, 1/6 plate, ca. 1863.
4. Carte de visite, ca. 1864. Verso: "E. Jacobs, New Orleans, La."
5. Portrait on embossed board, Follman, Vancouver, Wash., ca. 1880.
6. Portrait on board, 3.75" × 5.5", Illeg., Prescott, Arizona, 1897. Verso: Each man's name in longhand, 1–14.
7. Portrait on board, 3.5" × 4.5", ca. 1896. Verso: "Frank J. Schneller, Neenah, Wis.," ca. 1898.
8. Portrait on board, 4" × 9.75", "The brave boys who responded to their Country's Call," Mason, Marshfield, Wisc., 1898.
9. Real photo postcard, AZO stamp box, ca. 1918.
10. Snapshot, 2.25" × 3.5", 1918. Verso: "Sept 22[,] 1918, Pvt Willis chamberlain & Pvt G.D. Crockett."
11. Snapshot mounted on fragment of album page, 1.75" × 2.75", 1918.
12. Real photo postcard, AZO stamp box, ca. 1918.
13. Real photo postcard, AZO stamp box, 1920. Verso: "M.N. Nelson and friend, # 3 turrett 1920, USS Delaware."
14. Real photo postcard, no stamp box, ca. 1910. Verso: "X-Ray Studio, 200 N. 9th St., 1216 N. 52nd St., Phila, Pa."
15. Real photo postcard, AZO stamp box, ca. 1918.
16. Portrait with olive mat in U.S. Armed Forces gold frame, 5.25" × 3.25", ca. 1910.
17. Real photo postcard, AZO stamp box, in U.S. armed forces silver frame, ca. 1918. Verso: "Farmer's Brown & Bennett, Taken at Ocean View, Va."
18. Real photo postcard, AZO stamp box, ca. 1918. "#1 Turret $5,000 turret of U.SS Arizona" (USS Arizona, subsequently bombed at Pearl Harbor, was commissioned in 1916.)
19. Real photo postcard, AZO stamp box, 1911. Verso: "Ocean View Va 1911."
20. Real photo postcard, Artura stamp box, ca. 1910.
21. Real photo postcard, Cyko stamp box, ca. 1907.
22. Snapshot, 3.5" × 2.75", "Fond Memories," ca. 1915.
23. Real photo postcard, AZO stamp box, ca. 1918.
24. Real photo postcard, no stamp box, "SCRUBBING DECKS," ca. 1918.
25. Snapshot, "Pirates Paying Homage to the Ladies of the Court," 4.5" × 6.75", ca. 1920.
26. Snapshot, "His Royal Highness 'Neptune Rex' & Queen," 5" × 7", 1923. Verso: "Crossing the Line Ceremony Aboard USS Pennsylvania ~1923."
27. Snapshot, USS Minneapolis, 3.5" × 5", "The Captain Welcomes the Royal Party Aboard," ca. 1936.
28. Snapshot, 4" × 6", ca. 1950.
29. Snapshot, 4" × 5", ca. 1950.
30. Snapshot, USS Colorado, 5" × 4", ca. 1950. Verso: "Kissing the Equator Romeo of the South Seas."
31. Arcade (?) portrait, lightly colorized, 7" × 5", ca. 1943.

32. Arcade (?) portrait, 5.75" × 3.25", ca. 1943.
33. Arcade (?) portrait, 7" × 5", ca. 1943.
34. Portrait, 6.25" × 4.25", "Joe & Jersey," ca. 1943.
35. Snapshot with heart-shaped mat, 2" dia., ca. 1943.
36. Snapshot, 4.5" × 2.75", ca. 1944. Verso: "Ipplis, Italy, Lutz & Turner., Peck's Studio, Akron, Ohio."
37. Snapshot, 4.75" × 3", ca. 1942. Verso: "Arrow Photo Service, Box 184, Minneapolis, Minn."
38. Arcade portrait, 3.25" × 2.5", ca. 1944.
39. Two snapshots, 3.5" × 2.5" each, Indian Point Park, New York, July 29, 1944. Verso: Blank, but accompanying snapshots with the locale noted are in my *Mourning After*, 9.
40. Snapshot, 5" × 3.5", "'Red' & 'Jimmie' A swell pal." 1942. Verso: "Just a token of remembrance of the happiest ten days I have had since I started my hitch in the Navy. Taken July 24, 1942, at 1133 South Hope St in Los Angeles, California. Just back from the beach. Edna, Lou, Red and I."
41. Snapshot, trimmed, 3.25" × 2.25", ca. 1943.
42. Snapshot, 1.5" × 1.5", 1943. Verso: "Rusy & Nick 1943, MCC."
43. Snapshot, 4.5" × 2.75", ca. 1944.
44. Snapshot, 3.5" × 2.5", ca. 1944.
45. Snapshot, 3.25" × 5.25", ca. 1943.
46. Real photo postcard, unidentified stamp box, ca. 1944. Verso: "No se olvide de un amigo, [Don't forget about a friend] Martin Nanedo."
47. Snapshot, "Larry Martin Lloyd Emond," 2.5" × 3.5", ca. 1943.
48. Snapshot, 4.5" × 2.75", ca. 1944.
49. Snapshot on portion of album page, Denny and Friend from Detroit Bob Hiltz," 3.25" × 4.5", ca. 1943.
50. Arcade portrait in mat, "Souvenir of the Trianon Ballroom, Chicago, Ill.," 3.25" × 2.5", ca. 1942.
51. Snapshot, 2.25" × 3.25", ca. 1944.
52. Portrait, 3.75" × 2.75", ca. 1944.
53. Snapshot, 2.5" × 4.25", ca. 1944.
54. Snapshot, 3.25" × 2.5", ca. 1942. Verso: "North End Photo Finishing House, Lancaster, Pa."
55. Snapshot, 4" × 3", ca. 1942.
56. Four photo booth portraits, approx. 2" × 1.5" each, ca. 1944. Verso: "Bottom left: 'Lloyd C. (illeg), Co. 'G' 53rd QM (HM) Desent Maneuvers (?) Los Angeles Calif APO 307.'" Others blank or illegible.
57. Photo booth or arcade portrait, 3.75" × 2.5", ca. 1944.
58. Snapshot, 3" × 3", ca. 1942.
59. Portrait, 5.25" × 3.5", ca. 1943.
60. Portrait, 4.75" × 5.75", ca. 1943. Verso: "Duane-Neg (?)-Luke Lancaster, Spartanburg SC."
61. Snapshot, 3.5" × 5", 1951. Verso: "Frendi-Dale Hamilton, Fox-Tone, San Antonio, Texas, January 1951."
62. Snapshot, "Ellis-Barney Cole-Jack Roller," 5" × 4", ca. 1951.
63. Portrait, 5.75" × 4", ca. 1951.
64. Portrait, 8" × 10", ca. 1951. Verso: "Three wintering over personnel, Noonan, Patterson, Bradford."
65. Portrait, 8" × 10", ca. 1945. Verso: "Motion Picture Show in Hospital Ward—Watching Abbott and Costello."
66. Snapshot, enlarged, 8" × 10", ca. 1951.
67. Snapshots, 3.5" × 2.5" and 2.5" × 3.5", 1944. Verso: (l) "Delano, Painter, Sewall, Mandi River, Fiji—1944"; (r) "Delano, Sam, Mandi River, Fiji—1944."
68. Snapshot, 2.25" × 3.25", ca. 1945.
69. Snapshot, 3.5" × 2.5", ca. 1944.
70. Snapshot, 3" × 2", ca. 1944. Verso: "Vern Allen."
71. Snapshot, 3.75" × 2.75", ca. 1943.
72. Four snapshots, 3.5" × 2.5" each, ca. 1943.
73. Snapshot, enlarged, 5" × 7", ca. 1948.
74. Two snapshots, 3.5" × 3.5" each, ca. 1944.
75. Snapshot, 3.75" × 2.5", ca. 1943.
76. Snapshot, 2.25" × 3.25", ca. 1944.
77. Snapshot, 2.25" × 3.25", ca. 1943.
78. Snapshot, 2.75" × 4.75", ca. 1942.
79. Two snapshots, 3.5" × 4.5" each, ca. 1945.
80. Snapshot, "'Free Haircut,'" 4.75" × 3.5", ca. 1945.
81. Snapshot, 4.5" × 3.25", ca. 1945.
82. Snapshot, "V.J. Day at Keesler Field," 3.75 × 2.75", 1945.
83. Snapshot, 4.5" dia., trimmed and placed in homemade frame using spent shell casings and a wood base, ca. 1946.

84. Snapshot, 5" × 3.5", 1952. Verso: "Thursday Feb. 28, 1952, Chas. Miller (Minnesota), Hank Rabinowitz (Chicago), Dick Knepp (Chicago), Arch Patterson (Iowa), Camp Breckinridge, Ky."
85. Snapshot, "Anderson, Akins, Finley, Beecham, Nelams, Chisem, Mahans," 5" × 4", ca. 1952.
86. Snapshot, 4.75" × 3.25", ca. 1952.
87. Snapshot, 2.5" × 3", ca. 1952.
88. Snapshot, trimmed, most names illegible, 3.25" × 3", ca. 1952. Verso: "The Gang (too sunny)."

CHAPTER 4: PERFORMANCE

1. Cabinet card, J.F. Barta's Studio, New Prague, Minnesota, ca. 1890.
2. Cabinet card, R. Alex. Wells, Higginsville, Missouri, ca. 1890.
3. Cabinet card, J.K. Cole, 174 Sixth Ave., New York, ca. 1885.
4. Cabinet card, Joseph Hess Studio, Mifflintown, Pennsylvania, ca. 1885.
5. Cabinet card, Burnett, Le Sueur Center, Minnesota, ca. 1890.
6. Cabinet card, F.A. Beedy, Postville, Iowa, ca. 1895.
7. Cabinet card, Mogensen, Racine, Wisconsin, ca. 1895.
8. Cabinet card, Pratt, Red Oak, Iowa, ca. 1890.
9. Cabinet card, J.M. Newberry's Photo Car, Wyrgonda, Missouri, ca. 1895.
10. Portrait mounted on board, 4.25" × 3", S.(?) Yamanaka, Kobe, Japan, ca. 1900.
11. Portrait mounted on board, 4" × 5.5", Tenyowkwan, Nagasaki, Japan, ca. 1900.
12. Portrait mounted on embossed board, 3.75" × 2.75", Barnes, New Bethlehem, Pennsylvania, ca. 1890.
13. Portrait mounted on board, "THREE MEN (?) AND THE BABY?", 3.75" × 5.5", 1901. Verso: "1. Fred. Yarrington, Lexington, Ky., 2. Frank. R. Janus, Hinton, West Virginia, 3. George Percy Harvey, Jr., Richmond, Va. Taken at Hinton, W. Va., May 3, 1901, just after leaving the C&O R.R. Engr. Corps. To come to Boston, Mass. [signed] G.P.H., Jr. Picture received Jan. 13th, 1902, after many trials, troubles, and tribulations, should have had three but got only one, very thankful to get that. [signed} G.P.H., Jr."
14. Set of two photos mounted on boards, 4" × 6" each, ca. 1890.
15. Portrait mounted on board, M. Gillivray, Forest City Gallery, Ithaca, New York, 5.5" × 4", ca. 1900.
16. Portrait mounted on embossed board, 5.5" × 3.75", ca. 1911. Verso: "This bunch spent the night of Mch 31st 1911 at 'Hals Den' and this was taken next morning, 'All Fools day.'"
17. Portrait mounted on board, 4.5" × 7.5", ca. 1895. Verso: "Geo. G. Hitchcock, Amateur Photographer, Claremont, Cal. [Professor of Chemistry and Physics, Pomona College]."
18. Portrait mounted on embossed board, 4.75" × 6.75", ca. 1910. Verso: "Camp Boyd, Somerville, Mass. New Jersey, Tenn, Texas. This is no place for a minister's son! Tents manufact Detroit Mich."
19. Real photo postcard, trimmed, AZO stamp box, 4.75" × 3.5", ca. 1915.
20. Real photo postcard, NOKO stamp box, ca. 1920.
21. Real photo postcard, AZO stamp box, ca. 1930.
22. Snapshot, "Let's Pretend!" 3" × 5", ca. 1920.
23. Snapshot, "A Mid-night Party," 3.25" × 5.5", Harvard Military School (Los Angeles), ca. 1919.
24. Set of three Real photo postcards, "The Midnight Spread," "a dream," "Afterwards," two with Cyko stamp box, one with AZO stamp box, ca. 1918.
25. Real photo postcard, Velox stamp box, ca. 1910. Verso: "Fraternity Brothers-Dartmouth," from the Robert Bogdan collection.

26. Real photo postcard, with stamp, 1907, "'Camp Setting Sun,'" "10/6/07." Verso: "Miss Frances H. Ohm, Route #3, Cambridge, Ill." Postmarked Moline, Illinois, 1907.
27. Real photo postcard, AZO stamp box, ca. 1915.
28. Set of four snapshots, 3.25" × 2.25" each, ca. 1935.
29. Real photo postcard, AZO stamp box, ca. 1915.
30. Albumen print mounted on board, "That Game," 5.75" × 8", ca. 1880.
31. Carte de visite, ca. 1880. Verso: "D.M. Davidson, G.G. Amos."
32. Cabinet card, ca. 1890.
33. Portrait mounted on embossed board, 2" × 2.75", ca. 1890.
34. Real photo postcard, AZO stamp box, ca. 1918.
35. Portrait mounted on embossed board, 3.25" × 1.25", ca. 1890. Verso: "You can save, from 10 to 50%, by having your Photo Work done at the (illegible) South Minn. Avenue Ground Floor Studio, new light, new and perfect work only (illegible), H. Peter, prop. St. Peter, Minn."
36. Real photo postcard, AZO stamp box, ca. 1918.
37. Snapshot (enlarged), 4.75" × 7.25", ca. 1925.
38. Snapshot (enlarged), 4.75" × 6.75", ca. 1930.
39. Snapshot, 2.75" × 4.5", ca. 1925.
40. Real photo postcard, AZO stamp box, ca. 1918.
41. Carte de visite, ca. 1880. Verso: "Morriece Bros."
42. Portrait mounted on board, 1.25" × 1", ca. 1880. Verso: "Tom West."
43. Snapshot, 4.25" × 2.5", ca. 1890.
44. Snapshot attached to fragment of an album page, "Love knows no crowd," 4.25" × 2.5", ca. 1915.
45. Real photo postcard, AZO stamp box, ca. 1918.
46. Real photo postcard, AZO stamp box, ca. 1918.
47. Real photo postcard, Artura stamp box, 1916. Verso: "American Soldiers, Fort McKinley Carnival, Phillipine [sic] Islands, Jan. 1, 1916."
48. Snapshot, 4.5" × 3.25", 1945. Verso: "Bowe Lake, Luzon 1945."
49. Real photo postcard, Velox stamp box, ca. 1910.
50. Real photo postcard, AZO stamp box, ca. 1918.
51. Snapshot, 3.25" × 3.25", ca. 1950.
52. Cabinet card, 1899. Verso: "Howard Woodhead, age 21½ yrs. old, first row at left and as a girl in the 'Spoon Ballet' in 'The Deceitful Dean,' the first comic opera given at the University of Chicago in Gymnasiums, March 10–11-1899. Howard entered the U of C on Sept 1-1896, just before he was 19 yrs. For many years there was 'open house' at the Girls' Halls, and the young men love to go there to sip tea and talk to the girls. This was a 'take-off' with a clever dance."
53. Snapshot, 4.5" × 2.75", 1919. Verso: "[illegible] 13, 1919."
54. Real photo postcard, AZO stamp box, ca. 1930.
55. Real photo postcard, AZO stamp box, ca. 1918.
56. Snapshot, 3.5" × 2.5", ca. 1925.
57. Snapshot, 3.25" × 4.25", ca. 1930.
58. Snapshot, 2.5" × 4.25", 1938. Verso: "Pilgrim Fellowship Conference, Craterville Park, Okla., August 23 – to Sept 1 – 1938. 'The Beauty Contest' L to R: Jean Rorie-OCO, Coy Lay-Austin, Raymond Pittman-OCO, 'Pop' Burguret-Drummond, 'Frizzy' Hadly, George Shorter-Goltry, Ted Immel-Carrier, Jim Pierce-Goltry, Pat Early-OCO."
59. Snapshot, 5" × 3.5", ca. 1950.
60. Snapshot, 3.25" × 4.25", ca. 1950.
61. Arcade portrait, International Settlement, San Francisco, 3.25" × 2.5", ca. 1943.
62. Snapshot, 2.5" × 3.5", ca. 1950.
63. Real photo postcard, Cyko stamp box, ca. 1907.
64. Snapshot, 5.5" × 3.25", ca. 1925.
65. Real photo postcard, Cyko stamp box, ca 1907.
66. Real photo postcard, AZO stamp box, ca. 1925. Verso: "Merrie: If you can't identify me in this one, (taken a year ago as all these were) let me know and I'll solve the puzzle. This was a Mock Wedding, the nearest I have been to the real thing. [signed] Doug."
67. Real photo postcard, AZO stamp box, ca. 1916.
68. Portrait, 8" × 10", 1925. Verso: "Womanless Wedding, 1925."
69. Portrait, Smoot Studios Milwaukee and Cudahy, 4" × 9.75", ca. 1930.
70. Portrait, 11" × 20", 1932.

CHAPTER 5: BOYS AND MEN AT PLAY AND WORK

5A. BOYHOOD

1. Portrait mounted on board, 4.5" × 6.5", ca. 1900.
2. Set of two portraits mounted on board, oval, 3" dia., The (illegible) Studio, Lewiston, Maine, ca. 1900. Verso: "A.H." (both).
3. Portrait mounted on embossed board, 1.75" × 2.75", ca. 1890. Verso: "Charlie and Wilmer."
4. Three portraits in trimmed oval mats, 1" dia. each, ca. 1895.
5. Enlarged snapshot mounted on embossed board, "Rough House Boys," 5" × 6.5", ca. 1905.
6. Real photo postcard, no stamp box, ca. 1915.
7. Snapshot, 2.75" × 4.5", 1918. Verso: "'Some boys of school '18'"
8. Snapshot, 2.75" × 4.5", ca. 1920.
9. Snapshot, 2.75" × 4.5", ca. 1925.
10. Snapshot, 2.5" × 3.5", ca. 1930.
11. Snapshot, 3.75" × 2.75", ca. 1935.
12. Snapshot, 3.5" × 2.5", ca. 1940.
13. Snapshot, 2.5" × 3.5", ca. 1945.
14. Enlarged snapshot, 4.75" × 6.75", 1940. Verso: "2nd annual outing, Walt Klein, Sid Sichel, Bob Sommer, Lee steiner, Mel Schiff, Lou Aronson, Stan Sommer, June 1940."
15. Portrait, 7.5" × 9.75", ca. 1940.

5B. SPORTS

1. Team portrait mounted on board, 7.5" × 9.5", ca. 1890.
2. Cabinet card, Gaites, Bushnell, Illinois, ca. 1890.
3. Cabinet card, Boyer Bros., Duluth and W. Superior, ca. 1900.
4. Enlarged snapshot mounted on embossed board, 4.5" × 6.75", ca. 1915. Verso: "Lew Soule, John Turner, Leon Thompson."
5. Team portrait mounted on board, 6" × 8", 1906.
6. Team portrait mounted on embossed board, Veelik, Chicago, ca. 1915.
7. Real photo postcard, Cyko stamp box, 1911. Verso: "Burlington, Kansas, 1911."
8. Real photo postcard, mailed, 1911. Verso: "What do you think of this bunch of fellows? We did not all play in one game tho. But we all played in some games. Albert and I were the only ones that played in all the B.B. games. Am going to N.P. [North Platte?] to a musical comedy next week." Addressed to "Miss May Stevenson, Liberal, Kansas." Postmarked Gothenburg, Nebr., April 12, 1911.
9. Real photo postcard, AZOstamp box, ca. 1910.
10. Snapshot, 3.25" × 4.5", ca. 1940.

5C. WORK

1. Carte de visite, A.S. Hinckley, Geneva, New York, ca. 1860.
2. Carte de visite, ca. 1860. Verso: "E.M. Van Aken, Photographer, Lowville, N.Y."
3. Cabinet card, Lobenthal, East Main Street, Galion, Ohio, ca. 1890.
4. Stereo card, outdoor workers' portrait, (lumberjacks?), ca. 1880.
5. Portrait mounted on board, 5.5" × 8.25", ca. 1915.
6. Office workers' portrait, 8" × 10", ca. 1945.

5D. MEMBERS ONLY

1. Cabinet card, ca. 1890. Verso: "Geo. B. McClelland Photographic Art Studio, La Crosse, Wis., Special attention given to all kinds of Portraiture In crayon, ink, oil, and water color."
2. Portrait mounted on embossed board, 8" × 9.5", The Cook Studio, Salinas, California, ca. 1910. (Cropped out.)
3. Portrait mounted on board, 7.25" × 9.5", ca. 1900.
4. Portrait mounted on embossed board, 4.5" × 6.5", ca. 1915. Verso: "3rd row, 2nd from left, Father Cornelius Richards, 2nd row, 1 at left Mr Essel."
5. Real photo postcard, Cyko stamp box, "THE WILD SONS CLUB," ca. 1907. Verso: "Canton, Ohio."
6. Real photo postcard, "Beta Alpha Psi, 1923," AZO stamp box, 1923.
7. Portrait, 8" × 10", ca. 1927. Verso: "Initiatory Team-Portland Tent #1, Knights of Pythian Hall, About 1926–7-when initiated 1928-by this team."
8. Portrait, 8" × 10", ca. 1938. Verso: "Mueller Studio Arcade, Newark, Ohio."

5E. BEACH

1. Tintype, 1/6 plate, ca. 1890.
2. Real photo postcard, 1907. Verso: "Miss Ellen Chenoworth, 115 Houston St., Dallas, Texas. My dub and I out for a time. Were just chatting up. Got drowned three times already. Wish you were here. [signed] HB."
3. Snapshot, 2.75" × 4.5", ca. 1915.
4. Snapshot, "Hubba, Hubba. Look who's here Swimming. Lovingly-Kitty," 5.75" × 3.75", ca. 1940.
5. Snapshot, "Taken September 1st ??," 4.25" × 2.5", ca. 1935.
6. Set of three snapshots, 4.25" × 2.5" each, 1942. Verso: "July 4, 1942 (2), Aug. 1, 1942."
7. Snapshot, 2.5" × 4.25", ca. 1935. Verso: "Colter, Eldridge, Zulia, Voss."
8. Snapshot, 5" × 3.25", 1936. Verso: "Taken July 10, 1936."
9. Set of two snapshots, 3.75" × 2.75", ca. 1935.
10. Snapshot, 5.5" × 3.25", ca. 1925.
11. Snapshot, 2.75" × 4.5", ca. 1930.
12. Snapshot, 4.5" × 2.75", ca. 1940.

INDEX

PAGE NUMBERS IN ITALICS INDICATE ILLUSTRATIONS

www.ingramcontent.com/pod-product-compliance
Lightning Source LLC
LaVergne TN
LVHW060621110826
845147LV00019B/1065
9781956313406